P9-AGM-378
McDonald, Laughlin.
American Indians
and the fight for
equal voting rights
JAN 06 2012

American Indians and the Fight for Equal Voting Rights

American Indians and the Fight for Equal Voting Rights

Laughlin McDonald

University of Oklahoma Press : Norman

Also by Laughlin McDonald

Racial Equality (Skokie, Ill., 1977)

(with E. Richard Larson) *The Rights of Racial Minorities* (New York, 1980)

(with john a. powell) *The Rights of Racial Minorities* (Carbondale, Ill., 1993)

(with john a. powell) *The Rights of Racial Minorities* (New York, 1998)

A Voting Rights Odyssey: Black Enfranchisement in Georgia (Cambridge, N.Y., 2003)

Library of Congress Cataloging-in-Publication Data

McDonald, Laughlin.
American Indians and the fight for equal voting rights / Laughlin McDonald.
p. cm.
Includes bibliographical references and index.
ISBN 978-0-8061-4113-8 (hardcover : alk. paper)
1. Indians of North America—Suffrage—United States—History. 2. Indians of North America—United States—Government relations. I. Title.
KF8210.S84M34 2010
342.73'07208997—dc22

2009025772

The paper in this book meets the guidelines for permanence and durability of the Committee on Production Guidelines for Book Longevity of the Council on Library Resources, Inc. ∞

1 2 3 4 5 6 7 8 9 10

Contents

Preface

I have been the director of the American Civil Liberties Union (ACLU) Voting Rights Project since 1972. The project was established in 1965, with its office in Atlanta, Georgia, and has undertaken hundreds of cases in the South, most of them on behalf of African Americans who have been the special victims of discrimination in voting. The litigation challenged an extraordinary variety of election practices: discriminatory or malapportioned congressional, legislative, county, and local districting plans; at-large elections that diluted minority voting strength; refusals to comply with Section 5 of the Voting Rights Act; efforts to blunt increased minority registration; intimidation of minority voters; and so forth.

The Voting Rights Project's first case in Indian Country[1] was *Windy Boy v. County of Big Horn, Montana*. The suit was filed in 1983 by Jeffrey Renz, an attorney in Billings, on behalf of members of the Crow and Northern Cheyenne tribes challenging at-large elections for the county commission and two school boards. Renz, whose wife was at that time the director of the ACLU of Montana, requested the assistance of the Voting Rights Project. We agreed, and I became co-counsel. The plaintiffs prevailed in the litigation, and at the election held under a new, remedial single-member district plan, an American Indian, for the first time in history, was elected to the county commission.

Since then, and as a direct result of my participation in *Windy Boy*, I have been involved as a lawyer in numerous other lawsuits challenging discriminatory election practices filed on behalf of tribal members. There was more litigation in Montana as well as in Nebraska, Colorado, South Dakota, and Wyoming. These cases, almost all of which were strongly contested, produced voluminous records and documents. Rather than store this valuable trove in an archive where it would gather dust until discovered by some future researcher, I have used it as a major source for this book. It is my hope that this book, which gives voice to both American Indian and non-Indian communities, will shed light on the common humanity of all Americans and help dissipate the misunderstandings, anger, and biases we frequently harbor against those we do not know or regard as different.

Acknowledgments

I am deeply indebted to the ACLU attorneys, cooperating and staff, and other ACLU staff members who assisted in the litigation discussed in this book: Nancy Abudu, Andrew Baldwin, Meredith Bell-Platts, Neil Bradley, Linda Burt, Beth Brenneman, Robert Coulter, Scott Crichton, Berthenia Crocker, Patrick Duffy, Elizabeth Griffing, Andrew Huff, John Keller, Tim LaFrance, Daniel Levitas, Donna Matern, Fred McBride, James Molloy, Brian Morris, Trudy Miller, Katie O'Connor, Jeffrey Renz, Jennifer Ring, James Ruegamer, Bryan Sells, Michael Simpson (Nebraska Legal Aid Society), Brian Sutherland, Jim Tucker, Jim Vogel, Mary Wycoff, and Maha Zaki.

Special thanks also go to the expert witnesses who prepared reports and testified in the litigation: Amanda Bandy, Steven Cole, William Cooper, Richard Ellis, Richard Engstrom, Joe Floyd, Gordon Henderson, Martha Hipp, Garth Massey, and Daniel McCool.

As important, none of the litigation and activities discussed in this book would have been possible without the advice, cooperation, and assistance of countless tribal members and others in the affected jurisdictions.

Finally, and ironically, without the determined opposition of the defendants and their attorneys to the relief sought by the American

Indian plaintiffs, most of the research and discovery that form the basis for this book would have been unnecessary.

Any errors of fact or judgment that this book contains are, of course, of my own making.

Introduction

This book is about the past and ongoing struggle by American Indians for equal voting rights. The Supreme Court has described the right to vote as "fundamental" because it is "preservative of all rights."[1] Indeed, a group denied the effective exercise of the vote is necessarily deprived of the ability to protect its rights. Because elected officials are free to disregard its needs and concerns, a disfranchised group is denied an effective voice in policy-making decisions and is relegated to second-class status.

In recognition of its importance, the right to vote is protected by more constitutional amendments—the First, Fourteenth, Fifteenth, Seventeenth, Nineteenth, Twenty-fourth, and Twenty-sixth—than any other right we possess as Americans. Despite this constitutional protection and the fundamental nature of the right to vote, American Indians have been effectively disfranchised for much of our history.

In this book, I focus on litigation seeking to restore equal voting rights for Indians filed since the early 1980s in five western states: Montana, Colorado, Nebraska, South Dakota, and Wyoming. Although there has been litigation on behalf of Indians in other states, I selected these five states because of the extensive records compiled during the course of the litigation, most of which was brought by the

ACLU Voting Rights Project. Those records include the following: extensive interviews with tribal members and other local residents; depositions; trial transcripts; reports by historians, political scientists, anthropologists, statisticians, and other experts; territorial, state, and federal laws and resolutions; state and federal archives; legislative histories; government reports; local histories; state and local newspaper articles; and minutes of town and county governing bodies. The records in some states were more voluminous than in others, and in some states more jurisdictions were the subject of litigation than in others. The litigation in Nebraska, for example, involved only one county, whereas the litigation in Montana, which I discuss over the course of two chapters, involved numerous counties as well as statewide redistricting.

The litigation challenged, or has exposed, a broad range of discriminatory election practices, including at-large elections, districting plans that diluted Indian voting strength, unfounded allegations of election fraud on Indian reservations, new and onerous identification and registration requirements for voting, efforts to suppress the Indian vote, lack of minority language assistance in voting, and the refusal to comply with the preclearance provisions of the Voting Rights Act.

Special attention is given to the Voting Rights Act of 1965[2] and its subsequent amendments, because a full understanding of the protection the act affords American Indians and other covered minorities is central to realizing the goal of equal political participation. One of the most important of those provisions is Section 2, which prohibits the use of voting practices and procedures that deprive minorities of the equal opportunity to participate in the political process and elect candidates of their choice. Another important provision is Section 5, which requires "covered" jurisdictions to secure federal approval of any proposed changes in voting and demonstrate that they do not have a discriminatory purpose or effect. Section 203 of the act requires that American Indians and other minorities in certain designated jurisdictions be given assistance in voting in their native languages.

In this book, I also give an overview of the volatile and often contradictory federal policy toward American Indians, from treating them as independent nations, to placing them on reservations, to assimilating them and allotting their lands to whites, to giving them rights of U.S. citizenship, to terminating the reservations and tribal governments, and, in more recent times, to protecting the tribal system and giving American Indians maximum opportunities for self-development and self-determination.

In the chapters that follow, I describe how American Indians in the five aforementioned states were confined to their reservations, and I illustrate the discrimination that has been practiced against them, including taking Indian land, destroying the bison herds and the Indian way of life, attempting to assimilate Indians and eradicate Indian language and culture, and trying to remove and in some cases exterminate the tribes. The effects of this discrimination are continuing and include a severely depressed socioeconomic status; voting that is sharply polarized on racial lines; disagreements with non-Indians over issues such as water rights, taxation, and tribal sovereignty; the isolation of the Indian community; and the lack of meaningful social and political interaction between Indians and non-Indians, particularly in the towns and communities that border the reservations. This lack of interaction and access has made it very difficult for Indians to elect candidates of their choice in jurisdictions in which they are a numerical minority.

But despite these obstacles, and in large measure as a result of enforcement of the Voting Rights Act, Indian political participation has advanced significantly in recent years. These advances have had, and will continue to have, a profound and positive impact on the general welfare and vitality of the American Indian community.

American Indians and the Fight for Equal Voting Rights

CHAPTER 1

Evolution of Federal Policy toward American Indians

United States policy toward American Indians has been remarkably volatile and contradictory. At various times in history, Indians have been regarded as independent nations, political communities that should be removed or placed on reservations, dependent wards of the federal government, and a race that should be assimilated, suppressed, or simply allowed to vanish and whose lands should be sold or allotted to whites. In more modern times, and in an equally contradictory manner, Congress has provided that American Indians be given the right to vote, that the tribes be firmly established as viable units of self-government, that the reservation system be maintained, that the reservation system be terminated and tribal governments dissolved, that the states assume jurisdiction over Indians, and, most recently, that the federal/tribal system be maintained, that state jurisdiction over Indians be retroceded (i.e., given back), that traditional Indian religions and culture and family units be protected, and that Indians be given maximum opportunities for self-development and self-determination.

Although the Constitution of the United States does not deal comprehensively with the status of American Indians, two provisions indicate that American Indians were regarded as distinct political communities. Article I, Section 2, provides that in apportioning the House of Representatives, "Indians not taxed" should be excluded from the population count. Article I, Section 8, provides that Congress has the power "To regulate Commerce with foreign Nations, and among the several States, and with the Indian Tribes." Thus, Indians were distinguished both from foreign nations as well as the states composing the Union.

John Marshall, chief justice of the Supreme Court, wrote three important opinions in the 1820s and '30s, often in contradictory terms, addressing the relationship between Indian tribes and the United States. In *Johnson v. McIntosh,*[1] the Court held that grants of land by Indian tribes or nations to private individuals could not be recognized or enforced in the courts of the United States. The Court said that upon discovery of North America,

> the great nations of Europe were eager to appropriate to themselves so much of it as they could respectively acquire. Its vast extent offered an ample field to the ambition and enterprise of all; and the character and religion of its inhabitants afforded an apology for considering them as a people over whom the superior genius of Europe might claim an ascendency. The potentates of the old world found no difficulty in convincing themselves that they made ample compensation to the inhabitants of the new by bestowing on them civilization and Christianity, in exchange for unlimited independence.[2]

In recognition of the "superior genius of Europe," the Court concluded "that the Indian inhabitants are to be considered merely as occupants, to be protected, indeed, while in peace, in the possession of their lands, but to be deemed incapable of transferring the absolute title to others."[3]

In a second opinion, the Court declined to grant an injunction sought by the Cherokee Nation prohibiting the state of Georgia from enforcing its laws on the reservation. The Court concluded "that an Indian tribe or nation within the United States is not a foreign state in the sense of the Constitution, and cannot maintain an action in the courts of the United States."[4] Rather, Indian tribes were "domestic dependent nations . . . in a state of pupilage" whose "relations to the United States resemble that of a ward to his guardian."[5]

Subsequently, however, the Court characterized Indian communities as independent "nations" in striking down Georgia's attempt to enforce its criminal laws on the Cherokee Nation:

> From the commencement of our government Congress has passed acts to regulate trade and intercourse with the Indians; which treat them as nations, respect their rights, and manifest a firm purpose to afford that protection which treaties stipulate. All these acts . . . manifestly consider the several Indian nations as distinct political communities, having territorial boundaries, within which their authority is exclusive, and having a right to all the lands within those boundaries, which is not only acknowledged, but guaranteed by the United States.[6]

Marshall noted that Congress had passed an act in 1819 authorizing the president to intrude upon Indian authority to the extent of introducing among the tribes "the habits and arts of civilization" in an effort to convert them "from hunters to agriculturists" and thus save them from "further decline and final extinction," but he stressed that congressional policy evidenced "a settled purpose to fix the Indians in their country by giving them security at home."[7]

But even as Marshall was writing his opinions, U.S. policy toward American Indians was undergoing profound change. The demand for Indian land by advancing settlers was so great that under the administration of President Andrew Jackson, who had achieved fame as an Indian fighter, Congress passed the Indian Removal Act, authorizing the president to relocate eastern tribes to areas west of the Mississippi River.[8] Jackson justified removal as benefitting the Unites States and the several states, and as "perhaps" allowing Indians under the protection and influence of the national government "to cast off their savage habits and become an interesting, civilized, and Christian community."[9] This process of removing American Indians, rather than giving them security in their acknowledged homes, became a dominant aspect of federal Indian policy during the ensuing decades.[10] By 1850, some 60,000 members of the

Five Tribes in the East (Cherokee, Chickasaw, Choctaw, Creek, and Seminole) were removed to Indian Territory in what is now the state of Oklahoma.[11]

Treaty System

A central feature of early federal Indian policy was entering into treaties with American Indians for the purposes of extinguishing their title to large tracts of land—which would then be opened up for white settlement—and establishing territorial boundaries, or reservations, for the various tribes. In return for Indian land, the United States typically guaranteed federal protection to the tribes and provided for the payment of annuities.[12]

The first treaty with American Indians—the Delaware Tribe—was made in 1778. Over the course of the next century, the U.S. government entered into more than 600 treaties and agreements with Indian tribes in North America.[13]

Some of the treaties provided that Indians could become citizens of the United States, such as the treaty with the Delawares of July 4, 1866, treaties with various tribes in Kansas and with the Pottawatomies in 1867, and a treaty with the Sioux in 1868.[14] The treaty with the Sioux provided that Indians who received an allotment of land, made substantial improvements on it, and continually occupied it for three years could become citizens. But the naturalization process was often so demanding that few Indians could be expected to undertake it. An act providing for naturalization of members of the Winnebago Indians in Minnesota, for example, provided that Indians desiring to become citizens must file an application in the federal district court and in open court make the same proof and take the same oath of allegiance as provided by law for the naturalization of aliens.[15] They were also required to prove to the satisfaction of the court that they were sufficiently intelligent and prudent to control their affairs and interests, that they had adopted the habits of civilized life, and that they had been able for at least the last five years to support themselves and their families. In addition, they were required to renounce their tribal membership. A similar provision was made for the naturalization of adult members of the Miami Tribe in Kansas as well as for their minor children.[16]

The U.S. Peace Commission negotiated several treaties with Indians in 1867 and 1868. Nathaniel G. Taylor, the commissioner of Indian Affairs, was its chair. He was a Methodist minister and was firmly committed to the "civilization" of the Plains Indians and the end of their nomadic way of life. As he explained to Crow Indians at Fort Laramie:

> Upon the reservations you select, we propose to build a house for your agent to live in, to build a mill to saw your timber, and a mill to ground your wheat and corn, when you raise any; a blacksmith shop and a house for your farmer, and such other buildings as may be necessary. We also propose to furnish to you homes and cattle, to enable you to begin to raise a supply of stock with which to support your families when the game has disappeared. We desire also to supply you with clothing to make you comfortable and all necessary farming implements so that you can make your living by farming. We will send you teachers for your children.[17]

The Indians did not agree with this rosy vision of their future life. As Black Foot of the Crows put it, "You speak of putting us on a reservation and teaching us to farm. We were not brought up to that and are not able to do it. The talk does not please us. We want horses to run after the game and guns and ammunition to kill it. I would like to live just as I have been raised."[18] The views of the Indians, however, were ignored.

The treaty system proved to be notoriously unfair and corrupt, and in many cases it amounted to little more than the fraudulent expropriation of tribal lands. The treaties were always written in English and generally had to be explained to the Indians by interpreters, who did not always tell the truth about the treaty provisions. Red Cloud, an Oglala Sioux leader who signed the Treaty of Fort Laramie of 1868,[19] said that "men came out and brought papers. We could not read them, and they did not tell us truly what was in them. . . . When I reached Washington the Great Father explained to me what the treaty was, and showed me that the interpreters had deceived me."[20] The U.S. Senate would also often amend the treaties to change their meaning.[21]

George W. Manypenny, the commissioner of Indian Affairs, lamented in an 1856 report that "[t]he most dishonorable expedients have, in many cases, been made use of to dispossess the Indians; demoralizing means employed to obtain his property; and, for the want of adequate laws, the department is now often perplexed and embarrassed, because of inability to afford prompt relief."[22] Jacob D. Cox, the secretary of the interior, noted in his annual report of 1869 that despite the existence of treaties, "[r]eservations have been surrounded and gradually invaded by the white settlers, and the Indians crowded out of their homes and forced to negotiate for a new settlement, because their presence, their habits, and their manners were distasteful to their new and more powerful neighbors."[23] Some historians have characterized the early white settlers as "inveterate Indian haters."[24]

In 1869, Congress authorized the creation of a Board of Indian Commissioners to study and report to the president on how "to promote civilization among Indians, [and] bring them, where practicable, upon reservations."[25] The same year, the board issued its first report, which contained a strong indictment of past dealings with Indians:

> The history of the government connections with the Indians is a shameful record of broken treaties and unfulfilled promises. The history of the border white man's connection with the Indians is a sickening record of murder, outrage, robbery, and wrongs committed by the former as the rule, and occasional savage outbreaks and unspeakably barbarous deeds of retaliation by the latter as the exception. . . . The testimony of some of the highest military officers of the United States is on record to the effect that, in our Indian wars, almost without exception, the first aggressions have been made by the white man, and the assertion is supported by every civilian of reputation who has studied the subject. . . . Against the inhuman idea that the Indian is only fit to be exterminated,

> and the influence of the men who propagate it, the military arm of the government cannot be too strongly guarded.

The report also found that the soldiers sent for the protection of Indians under the treaties "too often carried demoralization and disease into their midst," while "[t]he agent, appointed to be their friend and counselor, business manager, and the almoner of the government bounties, frequently went among them only to enrich himself in the shortest possible time, at the cost of the Indians."[26]

Rep. Edgar Howard of Nebraska described the Indian reservation/guardianship system as "an almost uninterrupted succession of broken treaties and promises, and a record of the ruthless spoliation of defenseless wards."[27] In recognition of that fact, Congress later created the Indian Claims Commission to hear claims by Indian tribes against the United States involving the revision of treaties or agreements "on the grounds of fraud, duress, unconscionable consideration, mutual or unilateral mistake."[28] According to a 1978 report of the commission, "'it would be difficult, indeed, to find a land cession made by the Indians entirely of their own volition.' The American right to buy always superseded the Indian right not to sell. The white man's superior power allowed this policy, and pro forma use of the treaty conformed to his Anglo-Saxon tradition and concern for the law. For the Indian the legality of it all was of little comfort."[29]

End of the Treaty System and Increased Indian Dependence

In 1871 Congress terminated the treaty-making process by declaring that "[n]o Indian nation or tribe within the territory of the United States shall be acknowledged or recognized as an independent nation, tribe, or power with whom the United States may contract by treaty."[30] Although existing treaties were still enforceable, treaties were replaced by "agreements" with the tribes, executive orders, and congressional legislation.[31] The end of the treaty system further eroded the sovereign, or semi-sovereign, status of Indian nations.

Over the next three decades Indians were transformed by various congressional acts and Supreme Court decisions into complete dependents of the government, with Congress and the Bureau of Indian Affairs (BIA) in almost absolute control of their affairs.[32] As dependents, or "wards of the nation" as they were described by the Supreme Court,[33] Indians were neither citizens nor foreigners but, rather, a special dependent and administratively controlled class.

The commissioner of Indian Affairs said in an 1881 report that "[s]avage and civilized life cannot live and prosper on the same ground. One of the two must die. If the Indians are to be civilized and become a happy and prosperous people, which is certainly the object and intention of our government, they must learn our language and adopt our modes of life."[34] Henry M. Teller, in the 1883 *Annual Report of the U.S. Secretary of the Interior*, characterized Indian culture as "savage and barbarous," denounced the "pernicious influence of these savage rites and heathenish customs," and recommended that Indian ceremonial dances be banned.[35]

The Indian Department issued rules the following year that the "'sun dance,' the 'scalp-dance,' the 'war-dance,' and all other so-called feasts assimilating thereto, shall be considered 'Indian offenses,'" punishable by withholding of rations and imprisonment. The rules also provided that the "usual practices of so-called 'medicine men' shall be considered 'Indian offenses' cognizable by the Court of Indian Offenses" and punished by imprisonment. Indians were also not allowed to leave their reservations without a permit from the agent, and movement within the reservations was restricted.[36] Indians who violated the rules and regulations were often punished by imprisonment and restricted to a diet of bread and water.[37]

For American Indians, a particularly debilitating consequence of whites' westward migration was the extermination of the buffalo herds. There was massive killing for the hide trade, to supply meat for crews building the railroads, and to implement U.S. policy to end the nomadic hunting style of the Indians. According to Joseph K. Dixon, the slaughter "was done, if not with the actual connivance, at least with the knowledge and approval of the Federal Government, for it was realized that the most efficient way of solving the

'Indian problem' was to starve them and their women and children by destroying their means of subsistence."[38] J. J. Saville, the first agent of the Red Cloud Agency in Nebraska, which was established in 1873, asked the people in Wyoming to kill off the buffalo and the game so that Indians would have no incentive or reason to leave the reservation.[39]

An estimated fifteen million buffalo were killed between 1872 and 1883. By 1878, the great herd south of the Oregon Trail had been completely destroyed. Five years later, the northern herd met a similar fate. Indians, as a consequence, were forced more completely into a position of dependency upon the United States. Francis E. Leupp, commissioner of Indian affairs (1905–09), later acknowledged that white settlers united to kill off the game to keep Indians on the reservations.[40]

Old Lady Horse, a member of the Kiowa Tribe, explained what the buffalo, and its loss, meant to her tribe: "Everything the Kiowas had came from the buffalo. Their tipis were made of buffalo hides, so were their clothes and moccasins. They ate buffalo meat. Their containers were made of hide, or of bladders or stomachs. The buffalo were the life of the Kiowas." Old Lady Horse also recounted the folktale of a young woman who witnessed the disappearance of the last buffalo herd that had appeared to her in the dawn mist like a spirit dream:

> Straight to Mount Scott the leader of the herd walked. Behind him came the cows and their calves, and the few young males who had survived. As the woman watched, the face of the mountain opened. Inside Mount Scott the world was green and fresh, as it had been when she was a small girl. The rivers ran clear, not red. The wild plums were in blossom, chasing the red buds up the inside slopes. Into this world of beauty the buffalo walked, never to be seen again.[41]

Tribal independence was further eroded by passage of the Major Crimes Act of 1885.[42] That act made the commission of major crimes by Indians federal offenses and removed them from tribal jurisdiction.

The status of Indians was rendered even more vulnerable by the generally hostile relationships they had with the states in which they resided. Sen. George Vest of Missouri reported to Congress in 1885 that on a recent tour of the West, he heard nothing else but "'Get rid of the Indians; drive them away;' and whenever anything was said about giving them more rations, 'Cut off their rations; let them work or die.'"[43] In a decision affirming the constitutionality of the Major Crimes Act, the Court acknowledged that "[b]ecause of the local ill feeling, the people of the states where [Indians] are found are often their deadliest enemies."[44]

Significantly, Indians who were not citizens had no federally protected right to vote or to direct representation and thus lacked any power to pass or modify laws enacted by Congress to control their affairs. In upholding the state of Nebraska's refusal to allow Indians to vote, the Supreme Court declared in an 1884 opinion that Indians "are not citizens," and in the absence of being naturalized were not entitled to the franchise.[45] This view was said to be confirmed by the second section of the Fourteenth Amendment, which provided that "[r]epresentatives shall be apportioned among the several States according to their respective numbers, counting the whole number of persons in each State, excluding Indians not taxed." The Court reasoned that nontaxed Indians' "absolute exclusion from the basis of representation, in which all other persons are now included, is wholly inconsistent with their being considered citizens."[46]

A later decision of the Supreme Court abrogated Indians' hunting rights, upon which they were largely dependent for their survival and well-being. The Bannock Tribe had been granted a reservation in present-day Idaho by treaty in 1868.[47] The treaty provided that the Indians should have "the right to hunt on the unoccupied lands of the United States, so long as game may be found thereon." A few days later Congress passed an act creating the Territory of Wyoming, which stipulated that "nothing in this act shall be construed to impair the rights of persons or property now pertaining to the Indians in said territory, so long as such rights shall remain unextinguished by treaty between the United States and such Indians."[48] Wyoming was later admitted into the Union as a state in 1890. Five years later, Race Horse, a member of the Bannock Tribe, hunted on unoccupied land owned by the United States in the state of Wyoming, where he killed seven elks. He was arrested by the local sheriff and charged with violating Wyoming law regulating the hunting and killing of game. Race Horse argued that he was merely doing what the treaty of 1868 expressly allowed him to do, but the argument was rejected by the Supreme Court. It held that the language in the treaty and the territorial act notwithstanding, Wyoming had the right to regulate hunting on nonreservation land as "an essential attribute of its governmental existence."[49] Thus, the inherent power of the state was deemed to trump the rights conferred upon Indians by treaty.

Assimilation and Allotment

A major goal of federal policy during the latter part of the nineteenth century was the assimilation of Indians into white society and culture. Special emphasis was placed on "civilizing" Indian youths by taking them from their parents and sending them to federally supervised schools. Boarding schools, such as the Carlisle Indian Training School in Pennsylvania established in 1879, tried both to "detribalize" Indian young people and to prepare them for a life independent of the Indian community.[50] Indian students were forbidden to speak their native languages, their braids were cut, and they were prohibited from practicing Indian traditions. Instruction in reservation schools "in any Indian language" was prohibited.[51] By 1887, more than 200 such schools had been established, with a total enrollment of more than 14,000 students.[52] The government also appropriated funds for Christian missionary efforts, including operating schools, in an effort to suppress Indian religions and educate Indian students in the ways of white civilization.[53]

Attendance at the boarding schools was not voluntary. From 1891 forward it was required, and a 1893 law stipulated that if parents did not send their children to school their rations would be withheld.[54]

One of those who sent his children to a special Indian school was Chief Runs the Enemy, a Teton Sioux. But his children were exposed to more than the learning and culture of the white man; they were also exposed to his diseases. Whatever the government told him to do, "I did," he said. "They told me if I sent the children to school and educated them, they would be all right. Instead of that I sent them to school and they all came home with consumption and died, seven in number. If I had kept them home, some of them might have been living today."[55] Another Indian who sent his children to special Indian schools was Chief White Horse, who was born in the Black Hills. In complying with the white man's wishes, and to set an example for other Indians, he said he sent his children to "a nearby school until they were old enough and then I was one of the first to send my children to Hampton, Virginia, to school. They all came home and died of consumption."[56]

Estelle Reel was appointed by President McKinley in 1898 as superintendent of Indian schools. She believed in the innate superiority of whites, and that Indians were inescapably conditioned by heredity and environment to be less than whites. She said "the Indian child is of lower physical organization than the white child of corresponding age . . . his face seems stolid because it is without free expression, and at the same time his mind remains measurably stolid because of the very absence of mechanism, for its own expression."[57]

Most of the Indian boarding schools located off the reservations were closed by the 1930s, but many boarding schools, run by missionaries or the BIA, remained on the reservations. And although most did not impose the harsh treatment of earlier times, some continued the policy of "civilizing" the Indian students. A report issued by Congress in 1969, known as the Kennedy Report, was sharply critical of U.S. policy on Indian education. It described the boarding schools as "a kind of battleground where the Indian child attempts to protect his integrity and identity as an individual by defeating the purpose of the school." The schools failed "to recognize the importance and validity of the Indian community" and compiled a "dismal record of absenteeism, dropouts, negative self-image, low achievement, and ultimately, academic failure for many Indian children."[58]

According to the *Final Report* of the American Indian Policy Review Commission:

> The effects of boarding school experience upon the Indian students ranged from frustration to psychological destruction. . . . [I]n later years,

> more youngsters emerged from the experience as psychological casualties of American good intentions than as functioning, self-reliant adults. . . . Intervention into the parent–child relationship further undermined Indian family life, already weakened by the transition from older life style to reservation existence. In time, Indian communities came to view education with great suspicion and hostility—seeing it as a threat to the Indian community.[59]

In response to intense state and local pressure, and to speed the assimilation process, Congress passed the General Allotment Act of 1887, known as the Dawes Act, which authorized Congress and the president to survey tribal lands and enter into agreements with tribal nations allotting plots to individual Indians to be held in trust by the federal government for twenty-five years, with the remaining lands to be sold to the public.[60] The act granted citizenship to any allotted Indian following termination of the trust but only on the condition that the Indian resided "separate and apart from any tribe of Indians therein, and has adopted the habits of civilized life." The purpose of the act, as explained by the Supreme Court, was the "eventual assimilation of the Indian population" and the "gradual extinction of Indian reservations and Indian tribes."[61] But the Court made clear that even though land was allotted, Indians did not become citizens until termination of the trust period; thus, they remained "wards of the nation," subject to federal jurisdiction, including federal criminal laws.[62]

The Dawes Act and the subsequent Burke Act of 1906,[63] which allowed the secretary of interior to bypass the trust period restrictions of the Dawes Act, decimated the Indian land base. As a result of allotments, sales by impoverished Indians, and tax foreclosures, the number of acres of land owned collectively by Indian tribes shrank from 138 million in 1887 to 47 million by 1934. The allotment system was described by the American Indian Policy Review Commission as "an efficient device for separating Indians from their land and pauperizing them."[64]

More than half of all Indians became citizens as a result of the Dawes and Burke Acts but only by accepting allotments and leaving the reservations or severing their ties to tribal society. The Indians became citizens, but only by ceasing to be Indians.[65]

Vanishing Red Man

Thomas Jefferson Morgan, commissioner of Indian Affairs, declared in 1889 that the official policy of the government, which came to be known as the Vanishing Red Man Policy, was that

> The reservation system belongs to a "vanishing state of things" and must soon cease to exist. . . . The logic of events demands the absorption of Indians into our national life, not as Indians, but as American citizens. . . . The Indians must conform to "the white man's ways," peaceably if they will, forceably if they must. This civilization may not be the best possible but it is the best the Indians can get. They cannot escape it, and must either conform to it or be crushed by it.[66]

In 1903, the Supreme Court ruled that treaties with the Indians, like federal statutes, could be altered by Congress. Although they remained generally enforceable, Congress had power "to abrogate the provisions of an Indian treaty, though presumably such power will be exercised only when circumstances arise which will not only justify the government in disregarding the stipulations of the treaty, but may demand, in the interest of the country and the Indians themselves, that it should do so."[67] In a decision handed down two years later, the Court ruled that a treaty was "not a grant of rights to the Indians, but a grant of right from them . . . [and] a reservation of those not granted."[68]

In 1917, the commissioner of Indian Affairs announced that "[t]he time has come for discontinuing guardianship of all competent Indians." Reservation land would be distributed to Indians. "It means the ultimate absorption of the Indian race into the body politic of the Nation. It means, in short, the beginning of the end of the Indian problem."[69]

According to the 1977 *Final Report* of the American Indian Policy Review Commission, for most of the period from 1820 to 1920 national and state policy assumed that Indians "lacked biological vigor and would succumb to invading diseases and abusive use of alcohol," and that "the Indian way of life could not compete with the more aggressive, more 'rational' ways of the dominant society and must yield to it."[70] Reginald Horsman, writing for the *American Quarterly* in 1975, noted that "by the middle of the nineteenth century science itself had endorsed the earlier popular feeling that the Indians were not worth saving and envisaged a world bettered as the all-conquering Anglo-Saxon branch of the Caucasian race superseded inferior peoples."[71]

Joseph K. Dixon wrote a popular, and largely sympathetic, book about Indians in 1913 entitled *The Vanishing Race*. It was based on the 1909 meeting of chiefs from various tribes across the nation on the Crow Indian Reservation in Montana near the historic Custer Battlefield. Dixon gloomily predicted that Indians would inevitably cease to exist as a distinct people. "We have come to the day of audit," he wrote. "Annihilation is not a cheerful word, but it is coined from the alphabet of Indian life and heralds the infinite pathos of a vanishing race. We are at the end of historical origins. The impression is profound."[72]

Numerous court decisions adopted and applied the assumptions of the subordinate state of the Indians. In an 1883 opinion, the Supreme Court denigrated the "savage nature" of Indians and described whites as "the superiors of a different race."[73] A decade later the Court continued to describe Indians as "an ignorant and dependent race."[74]

Efforts to suppress Indian culture persisted into the twentieth century. In 1923, Indian Commissioner Charles Burke instructed his field officers to require: "(1) that Indian dances be limited to one each month in the daylight hours, in midweek, and at only one center in each district (except that during planting and harvesting no dances were to be allowed): (2) that no individuals under the age of 50 take part as dancers or as spectators: and (3) that the field employees carry on an education campaign against the dances."[75]

Indian Citizenship Act of 1924

In addition to various treaties and the Dawes Act, Indians were given or offered citizenship by other congressional enactments. In 1890, Congress passed the Indian Territory Naturalization Act, which allowed Indians living in Indian Territory to petition the federal courts for citizenship.[76] Under this statute, Indians did not lose tribal membership or the right to share in distributed tribal assets when they became a U.S. citizen. In 1901, Congress granted citizenship to all Indians in the Indian Territory by an amendment to the Dawes Act.[77] In 1919, Congress declared that all of the approximately 7,000 Indians who had served honorably in the armed forces in World War I were eligible for American citizenship.[78] Two years later, Congress passed a law giving citizenship to members of the Osage Tribe.[79] By the early 1920s, about two-thirds of Indians had become American citizens. Congress subsequently passed the Indian Citizenship Act of 1924, which gave U.S. citizenship to all Indians, regardless of whether they had relinquished tribal membership or continued to live on reservations.[80] The act, at least in theory, also conferred the federally protected equal right to vote.

There was strong support among many Indians for the Indian Citizenship Act. One group that was outspoken in its endorsement was the Society of American Indians. It was formed in 1911 and was composed of full- and mixed-bloods, many of whom had attended industrial or boarding schools and had become prominent leaders in the larger Indian community. The society's agenda included Indian education, Indian citizenship, and the creation of a federal agency to hear Indian court cases.[81]

Not all Indians, though, welcomed being given the right to vote. Some thought it would undermine tribal sovereignty. As explained by Clinton Rickard, a Tuscarora chief, "[w]e wished to remain treaty Indians and preserve our ancient rights. There was no great rush among my people to go out and vote in white man's elections. Anyone who did so was denied the privilege of becoming a chief or a clan mother in our nation."[82] There was opposition to the citizenship act for similar reasons among the Seminole and Creek Nations as well as the Six Nations Iroquois Confederacy.[83] Warren Green, a member of one of the Six Nations, challenged the constitutionality of the citizenship act, as well as the Nationality Act of 1940, after he was drafted into the Army. He contended that he was not a U.S. citizen, and that the conferral of citizenship violated his tribe's treaty rights. The federal court disagreed and held that the 1940 act "unequivocally made Green a citizen" and thus subject to the draft.[84]

After passage of the American Citizenship Act, some commentators, taking a page from the history of black disfranchisement in the South after passage of the Fifteenth Amendment—which prohibited discrimination in voting "on account of race, color, or previous condition of servitude"—suggested that it would still be proper for the states to "discriminate" in voting between tribal Indians on reservations and other citizens. They argued that states could enact literacy tests or poll taxes or deny the franchise absolutely to Indians living on reservations and enjoying immunity from state authority.[85] Charles H. Burke, commissioner of Indian Affairs, wrote a letter to all Indian superintendents on July 10, 1924, in which he stated that the Indian Citizenship Act did not necessarily give all Indians the right to vote, because "as some States require electors to be taxpayers, etc., in order to vote in certain elections, such as those involving the creation of bonded indebtedness, etc., you should endeavor to advise your Indians so as to avoid embarrassment or disappointment."[86] Many states blunted the impact of the Indian Citizenship Act by making registration more difficult, requiring re-registration, or simply denying registration altogether.[87]

South Dakota, despite passage of the act, continued to deny Indians the right to vote and hold office until the 1940s.[88] Five other states (Idaho, Maine, Mississippi, New Mexico, and Washington) prohibited "Indians not taxed" from voting, although there was no similar disqualification from voting by non-taxpaying whites.[89] Arizona denied Indians living on reservations the right to vote on the ground that they were "under guardianship" of the federal government and thus disqualified from voting by the state constitution. The practice was not struck down until 1948, when the state supreme court ruled that the language in the state constitution referred to a judicially established guardianship and had no application to the status of Indians as a class under federal law.[90] Utah denied Indians living on reservations the right to vote on the ground that they were nonresidents under state law. The law was upheld by the state supreme court but was repealed by the legislature after the U.S. Supreme Court, at the request of the state attorney general, agreed to review the case.[91]

The Indian Citizenship Act did not translate into significant Indian participation in the federal and state political processes. It did, however, reflect Congress's increasing awareness of and concern with the conditions of Indians, and it set the stage for passage of additional federal legislation that would constitute another sea change in federal Indian policy.

Indian Reorganization Act of 1934

The position of Indians in American society was so marginal and problematical that in 1926 Congress authorized funding for a special study of Indians to be done by a nongovernment agency, the Brookings Institute. The study was completed in 1928 and was called *The Problem of Indian Administration*, but it became more popularly known as the Meriam Report, named after project director Lewis Meriam. The 872-page report found that the health of Indians was bad, living conditions were conducive to the development and spread of disease, earned income was extremely low, and the economic base of the Indians had been largely destroyed. The report recommended that Indians be allowed freedom both to maintain Indian cultural forms and to continue adapting to the white man's world, either through direct participation or preparation to live in the presence of the white man's civilization.[92]

Some of the findings of the Meriam Report were incorporated into President Franklin Roosevelt's New Deal legislation affecting Indians: the Indian Reorganization Act of 1934.[93] The bill was developed by commissioner of Indian Affairs John Collier and drafted by Felix Cohen, author of the *Handbook of Federal Indian Law*.[94] Sen. Burton Wheeler of Montana and Rep. Edgar Howard of Nebraska sponsored the bill. Howard said that Indian policy of the past fifty years "has not stopped with the mere destruction of the material assets of the Indians. It has destroyed Indian social and political institutions, Indian arts and culture, Indian individuality and point of view."[95]

The reorganization act repudiated the prior policy of allotment and provided that "no land of any Indian reservation, created or set apart by treaty or agreement with the Indians, Act of Congress, Executive order, purchase or otherwise, shall be allotted to any Indian."[96] The act also extended existing periods of trust until otherwise directed by Congress, restored surplus land to tribal ownership, provided for the creation of new reservations for landless tribes, gave Indians preference in BIA hiring, and—after a long period of attempted suppression and assimilation—in general established the tribal unit as a viable self-determining authority. The various tribes were extended the power of local self-government as federal corporations with the right to organize for the common welfare and authority to negotiate with federal, state, and local governments. The overall effect of the act was to emphasize modernization of tribal government, make them more equivalent to other local governmental units, and initiate more contacts between Indians and other governments and units of the private sector. The purpose of the Indian Reorganization Act, according to the legislative history, was "to rehabilitate the Indian's economic life and to give him a chance to develop the initiative destroyed by a century of oppression and paternalism."[97] The true significance of the act, said Collier, was that it emphasized responsible democracy, "of all experiences, the most therapeutic."[98]

The federal government, however, retained significant control or supervision of Indian affairs under the reorganization act. The secretary of the interior retained the following powers (among others): to purchase land, water rights, or surface right to land; to proclaim new Indian reservations; to sell or transfer tribal lands; to defray the costs of establishing new Indian corporations; to make loans to Indian corporations; to make rules and regulations for the operation and management of Indian forestry units; to restrict the number of livestock on Indian reservations; to establish standards for employment by the Indian Office; to supervise elections for the adoption of Indian constitutions and bylaws; and to call elections for voting on acceptance of the Indian Reorganization Act.

Before the reorganization act could be implemented, tribal members had to vote within a two-year period to accept it. Within that time frame 181 tribes out of 263 voted to accept it, and 77 voted to reject it.[99] Many Indians, suspicious of the government's track record of broken promises and treaties, objected to the reorganization act as imposing a white form of government on the tribes. As one member of the Sioux Tribe put it, the act retained too much federal control over Indian affairs and established "a paternalistic type of government."[100] Other Indians argued that the reorganization act was a form of communism, that it would return Indians to a primitive condition, or was a program "to colonialize the Indian tribes."[101]

Termination of the Reservations

The period following World War II saw yet another dramatic change in federal Indian policy. In 1953 the House of Representatives adopted a resolution establishing a policy of terminating the federal–tribal relationship and declaring that federal benefits and services to various Indian tribes should be ended "at the earliest possible time."[102] The tribes would cease to exercise governmental power, and all reservation land would be dispersed to tribal members. The states would thereafter exercise jurisdiction over the land and its residents.

Indians in general, and some legislators, opposed the termination policy. Congressman Lee Metcalf of Montana, in a speech at the Thirteenth Convention of the National Congress of American Indians in Salt Lake City in 1956, described the new termination policy as a "most persistent and serious attack" on Indians and their property.[103] Despite such opposition, over the next decade Congress terminated its assistance to over 100 tribes and required them to distribute their land and property to their members and dissolve their tribal governments.[104] According to the U.S. Commission on Civil Rights, the termination policy "was aggressively carried out by Dillon Myer, former director of detention camps for Japanese Americans, who became the commissioner of Indian Affairs in 1950."[105] As a result of termination, Indians lost some 3.3 million acres of land between 1948 and 1957.[106]

In a further effort to displace federal authority, Congress enacted statutes in 1953 giving five states complete criminal, and some civil, jurisdiction over Indian reservations located within their states and authorized all other states at their option to assume similar jurisdiction.[107] The relocation of Indians was the subject of other legislation during the 1950s involving job training and education of tribal members in urban areas.[108] The legislation was designed to support the integration of Indians into the regional and national economies and weaken their ties to the reservations.

The U.S. Commission on Civil Rights issued a report in 1981 that summarized the conflicting, though essentially racist, views that underlay the divergent shifts in federal policy toward Indians:

> Since colonial times Indians have been viewed as an "inferior race"; sometimes this view is condescendingly positive—the romanticized noble savage—at other times this view is hostile—the vicious savage—at all times the view is racist. . . . At one extreme the concept of inferior status of Indians was used to justify genocide; at the other, apparently benevolent side, the attempt was to assimilate them into the dominant society. Whatever the rationale or motive, whether rooted in voluntary efforts or coercion, the common denominator has been the belief that Indian society is an inferior lifestyle.[109]

New Era of Self-Determination

In the wake of the Great Society, the civil rights movement, and the War on Poverty, federal Indian policy changed abruptly once again in 1968 under the administration of Lyndon Johnson, which repudiated the policy of terminating the federal–tribal relationship. Congress amended the 1953 act that had authorized the states to assume civil and criminal jurisdiction over Indian reservations; as amended, the consent of the affected tribes was required and the United States had authority to accept a retrocession—or return—by any state of criminal or civil jurisdiction over Indian reservations.[110] Johnson also articulated a national policy of "maximum choice for the American Indian: a policy expressed in programs of self-help, self-development, self-determination."[111]

Numerous congressional and Civil Rights Commission reports of the 1960s and 70s documented the extent and continuing effects of discrimination against Indians, supporting and setting the stage for further remedial action by Congress. A 1969 Senate report, for example, concluded that the prior policy of "coercive assimilation" had resulted in the "destruction and disorganization of Indian communities and individuals," and it catalogued some of the present-day effects:

> A desperately severe and self-perpetuating cycle of poverty for most Indians. . . . Prejudice, racial intolerance, and discrimination towards Indians . . . [with] the classroom and the school becoming a kind of battleground where the Indian child attempts to protect his integrity and identity. . . . Schools which fail to understand or adopt to, and in fact often denigrate, cultural differences. . . . Schools which fail to recognize the importance and validity of the Indian community. . . . A continuous desire to exploit, and expropriate, Indian land and physical resources. . . . A self-righteous intolerance of tribal communities and cultural differences. . . . An anti-Indian attitude . . . in white communities in which Indians receive public school education.[112]

Other congressional reports were to the same effect. A 1974 report concluded that "[a]ll the traditional indicators of economic levels place Indians and Indian reservations at the bottom of the scale. On every reservation today, there is almost a total lack of an economic community."[113] Another report from 1976 found that "[t]he prevalence of disease among Indians cannot but have a significant adverse impact on the social and cultural fiber of their communities, contributing to general societal disintegration, and the attendant problems of mental illness, alcoholism, accidents, homicide and suicide."[114] A 1978 report noted non-Indian officials' "[l]ack of knowledge, unawareness, insensitivity, and neglect" of traditional Indian religions and culture.[115] Still another report from the same year found that "[t]he wholesale separation of Indian children from their families is perhaps the most tragic and destructive aspect of American Indian life today."[116]

In a message to Congress in 1970, President Richard Nixon summed up the plight of American Indians in terms similar to those used by Johnson:

> The First Americans—the Indians—are the most deprived and most isolated minority group in our nation. On virtually every scale of measurement—employment, income, education, health—the condition of the Indian people ranks at the bottom. This condition is the heritage of centuries of injustice. From the time of their first contact with European settlers, the American Indians have been oppressed and brutalized, deprived of their ancestral lands and denied the opportunity to control their own destiny.

Nixon proposed to "break decisively" with past policies of termination and excessive dependence on the federal government and "create the conditions for a new era in which the Indian future is determined by Indian acts and Indian decisions."[117]

During the decade of the 1970s, Congress enacted a number of laws to implement the policies outlined by Johnson and Nixon. In 1974 it passed the Indian Financing Act "to provide Indian tribes and individuals capital in the form of loans and grants to promote economic and other development."[118] The following year it passed the Indian Self-Determination and Education Assistance Act "to provide the quantity and quality of educational services and opportunities which will permit Indian children to compete and excel in the life areas of their choice, and to achieve the measure of self-determination essential to their racial and economic well-being."[119]

One of the most critical enactments by Congress was the extension of the Voting Rights Act in 1975 to "language minorities," including American Indians, after finding that voting discrimination against citizens of language minorities was "pervasive and national in scope."[120] The 1975 amendment was designed to give Indians a more active voice in the adoption of national, state, and local laws that directly affected their lives and well-being. And for that reason, it would help advance the goals of self-help, self-development, and self-determination set by Congress.

In 1976 Congress enacted the Indian Health Care Improvement Act "to provide the quantity and quality of health services which will permit the health status of Indians to be raised to the highest possible level and to encourage the maximum participation of Indians in the planning and management of those services."[121] Two years later it enacted the American Indian Religious Freedom Act "to protect and preserve for American Indians their inherent right of freedom to believe, express, and exercise the traditional religions of the American Indian . . . including but not limited to access to sites, use and possession of sacred objects, and the freedom to worship through ceremonials and traditional rites."[122] Also in 1978 Congress enacted the Indian Child Welfare Act to establish "minimum Federal standards for the removal of Indian children from their families and the placement of such children in foster or adoptive homes which will reflect the unique values of Indian culture," and to provide "assistance to Indian tribes in the operation of child and family service programs."[123]

More recent congressional enactments positively affecting tribal economies include the Indian Mineral Development Act of 1982,[124] which authorizes any Indian tribe, subject to the approval of the secretary of the interior, to enter into joint agreements for the development of mineral resources owned by the tribe. The Indian Tribal Government Tax Status Act of 1982,[125] which treats tribal governments as states for certain tax purposes, allows tribes, among other things, to issue tax-exempt bonds to finance tribal projects. The Indian Gaming Regulatory Act of 1988[126] allows tribes to conduct gaming on Indian lands (unless prohibited by state law) to promote tribal economic development, self-sufficiency, and strong tribal government. The Native American Business Development, Trade Promotion, and Tourism Act of 2000 promotes the growth of Indian economies through a variety of means, and it reaffirms "the special government-to-government relationship between Indian tribes and the United States."[127]

Table 1 provides a chronological list (from 1830 to 2000) of federal enactments, discussed in this chapter, that affect American Indians.

The Supreme Court has also affirmed that Indian tribes retain those aspects of sovereignty that have not been withdrawn by treaty or statute. According to the Court, "[t]he sovereignty that the Indian tribes retain is of a unique and limited character. It exists only at the sufferance of Congress and is subject to complete defeasance. But until Congress acts, the tribes retain their existing sovereign powers. In sum, Indian tribes still posses those aspects of sovereignty not withdrawn by treaty or statute, or by implication as a necessary result of their dependent status."[128]

Aside from acts of Congress and Supreme Court decisions, recent presidents have also affirmed the need to respect and support tribal sovereignty. President Clinton issued an executive order in 1994 requiring federal agencies to deal with tribes on a "government-to-government" basis.[129] He issued another executive order in 2000 recognizing "the right of Indian tribes to self-government" and requiring federal agencies to protect "tribal trust resources, and Indian tribal treaty and other rights."[130] In 2004, President Bush issued a memorandum to the heads of executive departments and agencies reaffirming the U.S. policy of working with tribes on a government-to-government basis and strongly supporting "tribal sovereignty and self-determination for tribal governments."[131] In his campaign for the presidency in 2008, Barack Obama similarly pledged to honor the government-to-government relationship tribes have with the United States.[132]

Federal Indian policy has undergone enormous and contradictory changes over the last two centuries. It is ironic that current policy is now similar to what Justice Marshall described more than 175 years

Table 1

General Federal Enactments Affecting American Indians

Year	Enactment
1830	Indian Removal Act: authorized the president to remove the Cherokee, Chickasaw, Choctaw, Creek, and Seminole tribes to Oklahoma
1871	Indian Appropriation Act: terminated the practice of making treaties with Indian nations or tribes
1885	Major Crimes Act: removed tribal jurisdiction over the commission of major crimes by tribal members
1887	General Allotment Act, or Dawes Act: authorized the allotment of reservation land to individual Indians
1906	Burke Act: authorized the secretary of interior to bypass the trust period restrictions of the Dawes Act
1919	World War I Veterans' Citizenship Act: granted citizenship to all Indians who had served honorably in WW I
1924	Indian Citizenship Act: granted U.S. citizenship to all Indians
1934	Indian Reorganization Act: ended the policy of allotment and authorized the formation of tribal governments
1953	House Concurrent Resolution No. 108: established a policy of terminating the federal–tribal relationship and allocating all reservation land to individual Indians
1953	Public Law 280: authorized states to assume criminal and civil jurisdiction over Indian reservations
1956	Relocation Act: authorized job training and relocation of tribal members to non-reservation, urban areas
1968	Public Law 90-284: required the consent of tribes to state assumption of criminal and civil jurisdiction over Indian reservations and authorized the United States to accept a retrocession of such jurisdiction
1974	Indian Financing Act: authorized loans and grants to tribes to promote economic development
1975	Indian Self-Determination and Education Assistance Act: provided educational services to Indian children
1975	Extension of the Voting Rights Act: extended protection of the act to "language minorities," including American Indians
1976	Indian Health Care Improvement Act: provided health services to Indians
1978	American Indian Religious Freedom Act: protected Indian religions
1978	Indian Child Welfare Act: set standards for removal and adoption of Indian children and provided assistance to child and family service programs
1982	Indian Mineral Development Act: authorized tribes to enter into agreements for the development of mineral resources

TABLE 1 *(continued)*
General Federal Enactments Affecting American Indians

1982	Indian Tribal Government Tax Status Act: treated tribes as states for certain tax purposes and authorized tribes to issue tax-exempt bonds
1988	Indian Gaming Regulatory Act: allowed tribes to conduct gaming on Indian lands, unless prohibited by state law
2000	Native American Business Development, Trade Promotion, and Tourism Act: promoted growth of Indian economies and reaffirmed the "government-to-government" relationship between tribes and the United States

ago. As various congressional enactments and declarations of executive policy demonstrate, Indian nations are once again regarded and dealt with as "distinct political communities" whose rights and authority are acknowledged and protected by the United States.[133]

CHAPTER 2

Voting Rights Act: How It Works

Following the Civil War the Southern states adopted a variety of measures to deny the franchise to recently freed blacks. These measures included literacy and understanding tests for voting, poll taxes, felony disfranchisement laws, onerous residency requirements, cumbersome registration procedures, voter challenges and purges, the abolition of elected offices, discriminatory redistricting and apportionment schemes, the expulsion of elected blacks from office, and the adoption of primary elections in which only whites were allowed to vote. And when these technically legal measures failed to work or were thought to be insufficient, the states were more than willing to resort to fraud and violence in order to smother black political participation and safeguard white supremacy.[1] The Voting Rights Act of 1965 was, in the words of the Supreme Court in upholding its constitutionality, "designed by Congress to banish the blight of racial discrimination in voting, which has infected the electoral process in parts of our country for nearly a century."[2]

The Voting Rights Act as first enacted was a complex, interlocking set of both permanent provisions that applied nationwide and special five-year provisions that applied only in jurisdictions that had used a "test or device" for voting and in which registration and voting were depressed. One of the most important permanent provisions, Section 2, prohibited the use of voting practices or procedures that denied or abridged the right to vote "on account of race or color."[3] Other permanent provisions (1) authorized civil and criminal sanctions against persons who interfered with the right to vote, (2) facilitated challenges to the imposition of poll taxes for state and local elections, and (3) excluded citizens educated in American schools conducted in a foreign language from having to pass English-language literacy tests in order to vote.[4]

The special provisions, described by the Supreme Court as the "heart of the Act," were aimed at states or places, known as "covered" jurisdictions, where discrimination in voting had been most persistent and flagrant.[5] Coverage was determined by the U.S. attorney general and the director of the census on the basis of whether a jurisdiction used a literacy or other test for voting on November 1, 1964, and whether less than 50 percent of voting-age persons were registered for or voted in the presidential election of November 1964.[6] The covered jurisdictions were the states of Alabama, Alaska, Georgia, Louisiana, Mississippi, South Carolina, and Virginia as well as forty counties in North Carolina and a handful of counties in Arizona, Hawaii, and Idaho.[7] A court could also subject a jurisdiction to coverage if it found a violation of voting rights protected by the Fourteenth or Fifteenth Amendments.[8]

There was no appeal from a coverage decision, but a jurisdiction could "bail out" by bringing a lawsuit in the Federal District Court for the District of Columbia and showing that it had not used a test or device within the preceding five years with the purpose or effect of discriminating.[9] Several jurisdictions successfully bailed out under this provision: Alaska; Wake County, North Carolina; Elmore County, Idaho; and Apache, Navaho, and Coconino counties, Arizona.[10]

The special provisions did several things. In the covered jurisdictions, the special provisions suspended the use of tests, such as literacy and good character and understanding tests, that had been used to deny minorities the right to vote.[11] Under Section 5 of the act, covered jurisdictions were required to get federal approval, or "preclearance," of their new voting laws or practices before they could be implemented.[12] Other special provisions authorized the attorney general to appoint federal examiners to register qualified voters and poll watchers to observe the conduct of elections.[13]

Section 5 was designed to prohibit states from replacing their registration tests with other equally discriminatory voting practices. The courts have interpreted Section 5 broadly to cover practices that alter the election laws of a covered jurisdiction in even a minor way.[14] Covered changes have run the gamut from redistricting plans, to annexations, to setting the date for a special election, to moving a polling place.[15]

Section 5 contains two unique features that have been essential to its operation. First, preclearance can be granted only by the Federal District Court for the District of Columbia in a lawsuit or by the U.S. attorney general in an administrative submission. Local federal courts have the power, and duty, to enjoin the use of "unprecleared" voting practices (i.e., those voting practices that have not been precleared), but they have no jurisdiction to determine whether a change should be approved.[16] Second, Section 5 places the burden of proof on the jurisdiction to show that a proposed voting change does not have a discriminatory purpose or effect. A voting change has a discriminatory effect under Section 5 if it leads to a "retrogression" in minority voting rights, that is, makes them worse off.[17] The statute was designed "to shift the advantage of time and inertia from the perpetrators of the evil [of discrimination in voting] to its victims."[18]

Congress placed the initial burden of "voluntary" compliance with the statute on the covered jurisdictions,[19] but it also authorized the U.S. attorney general and private citizens to bring suit in local federal court to block the use of unprecleared voting practices.[20] It also made it a crime to fail to comply with the act.[21]

The preclearance requirement was undoubtedly the most controversial feature of the Voting Rights Act. Justice Hugo Black, an Alabamian, expressed the resentment of many white southerners over Section 5 in a dissenting opinion in *South Carolina v. Katzenbach*, the 1966 Supreme Court decision that held the basic provisions of the act constitutional. He characterized Section 5 as "a radical degradation of state power" and said that forcing "any one of the States to entreat federal authorities in far-away places for approval of local laws before they can become effective is to create the impression that the State or States treated in this way are little more than conquered provinces."[22] Returning to the subject in a later case, he complained that preclearance was "reminiscent of old Reconstruction days when soldiers controlled the South and when those States were compelled to make reports to military commanders of what they did."[23] The majority of the Court acknowledged that Section 5 was an uncommon exercise of congressional power but found it was justified by the "insidious and pervasive evil which had been perpetuated in certain parts of our country through unremitting and ingenious defiance of the Constitution."[24]

Congress defended the requirement that covered jurisdictions seek judicial preclearance in the District of Columbia, rather than a local federal court, as necessary to provide a uniform interpretation and application of Section 5 standards.[25] But there is little doubt that Congress also acted out of distrust of some federal judges in the South, fearing that they would not enforce Section 5 effectively or would be swayed by the hostile anti-civil-rights sentiment that pervaded the region. In the words of the Senate report that accompanied subsequent amendments of the act, placing venue in the District of Columbia over actions involving Section 5 would "ensure judicial decision making free from local pressures."[26]

Congress assumed, or at least hoped, that once the formal barriers to registration were dismantled in the states that had erected them, and once those states were prohibited from enacting new discriminatory voting laws, blacks would participate in politics on a basis of equality with whites. Congress also thought, in retrospect unrealistically, that the five-year "cooling-off" period prescribed by Section 5 was sufficient "to permit dissipation of the long-established political atmosphere and tradition of discrimination in voting because of color" that existed in the covered jurisdictions.[27] But experience proved otherwise.

1970 Amendments

Congress began considering legislation in 1969 to extend the special provisions of the Voting Rights Act. Citing the continued depressed levels of black voter registration and the significant noncompliance with Section 5 by the covered jurisdiction, it voted to extend the special coverage provisions for another five years. In doing so it concluded that extension "is essential . . . in order to safeguard the gains in Negro voter registration thus far achieved, and to prevent future infringements of voting rights based on race or color."[28] Congress also made the suspension of tests or devices for voting effective nationwide and revised the coverage formula to include the 1968 presidential election. As a result of the revision, four election districts in Alaska; Elmore County, Idaho; and the three counties in Arizona were recaptured.[29] Other jurisdictions that became covered by Section 5 were additional counties in Arizona (Cochise, Mohave, Pima, Pinal, and Santa Cruz), California (Monterey and Yuba), New York (Kings, New York, and Bronx), and Wyoming (Campbell), and several towns in Connecticut, New Hampshire, Maine, and Massachusetts.[30] The election districts in Alaska and the three counties in New York bailed out from Section 5 in 1972. Two years later, however, the three counties in New York were recovered.[31]

The U.S. attorney general sued the state of Georgia in 1972 for failing to implement a new legislative reapportionment to replace a plan that had been objected to under Section 5. The state argued that Section 5 was not applicable to its plan, but if so, the statute as extended was unconstitutional. The Supreme Court disagreed and held that "for the reasons stated at length in *South Carolina v. Katzenbach* . . . we reaffirm that the Act is a permissible exercise of congressional power under § 2 of the Fifteenth Amendement."[32]

1975 Amendments

Against a backdrop of continuing opposition to Section 5 and the adoption of new discriminatory voting practices, Congress in 1975 once again considered legislation to extend and expand the coverage of the Voting Rights Act. It concluded that progress under the act "has been modest and spotty in so far as the continuing and significant deficiencies yet existing in minority registration and political participation." The Senate report noted that "[t]his past experience [of evading Section 5] ought not be ignored in terms of assessing the future need for the Act." It was "imperative," it said, that the protections of Section 5 apply to the redistricting that would take place after the 1980 census.[33]

Congress passed legislation in 1975 that made the nationwide ban on tests for voting permanent, extended Section 5 for an additional seven years, and broadened the reach of the statute by including the 1972 presidential elections in the coverage formula. It also extended coverage to language minorities, defined as American Indians, Asian Americans, Alaskan natives, and those of Spanish heritage.[34] The term "test or device" was amended to include English language registration procedures or elections where a single linguistic minority comprised more than 5 percent of the voting-age population of the jurisdiction.[35] As a result of the 1975 amendments, the states of Alaska, Arizona, and Texas; counties in California (Kings and Merced), Florida (Collier, Hardee, Hendry, Hillsborough, and Monroe), and South Dakota (Todd and Shannon); and two townships in Michigan (Clyde and Buena Vista) were added to the list of jurisdictions covered by Section 5.[36]

Another important special provision, Section 203, required certain states and political subdivisions to conduct bilingual elections and registration campaigns.[37] The requirement was imposed upon both covered jurisdictions in which a single language minority was more than 5 percent of the eligible voters as well as noncovered jurisdictions in which a language minority was more than 5 percent of the eligible voters and where the illiteracy rate within the language minority was higher than the national average.[38]

After the 1975 extension, the City of Rome, Georgia, filed an action to bail out from Section 5 coverage and argued that the statute violated principles of federalism, or states' rights, and that even if the preclearance requirements were constitutional when enacted in

1965, "they had outlived their usefulness by 1975."[39] The Court rejected the federalism argument, noting that the Fourteenth and Fifteenth Amendments "were specifically designed as an expansion of federal power and an intrusion on state sovereignty." As for the argument that Section 5 had outlived its usefulness, the Court concluded that "Congress' considered determination that at least another 7 years of statutory remedies were necessary to counter the perpetuation of 95 years of pervasive voting discrimination is both unsurprising and unassailable."[40]

Reasons for Language-Minority Coverage

When it extended Section 5 and the other special provisions to cover language minorities, Congress concluded that they had been the victims of pervasive discrimination in voting. Indians, as a "cognizable racial group," were undoubtedly already covered by the permanent provisions of the original Voting Rights Act of 1965, which prohibited discrimination on the basis of "race or color."[41] Although Indians were held to be a political, not a racial, group for purposes of determining the constitutionality of granting members of federally recognized tribes preference in hiring by the BIA,[42] the courts have also held that Indians were entitled to claim the protection of the Fourteenth Amendment. The Supreme Court has held that Indians would be entitled to the protection of a state law prohibiting discrimination on the basis of "race or color,"[43] whereas other courts in a variety of contexts have held that Indians, in their capacity as a racial group, were entitled to the protection of the Constitution and federal civil rights laws, for example, in legislative redistricting, jury selection, and public education.[44] In addition, a number of jurisdictions that had substantial American Indian populations were covered by Section 5 of the Voting Rights Act of 1965, including the state of Alaska and four counties in Arizona. The 1975 amendments made the coverage of Indians explicit.

During the 1975 hearings on the amendments, Rep. Peter Rodino, chair of the House Judiciary Committee, said that members of language-minority groups, including American Indians, related "instances of discriminatory plans, discriminatory annexations, and acts of physical and economic intimidation." According to Rodino, "[t]he entire situation of these uncovered jurisdictions is tragically reminiscent of the earlier and, in some respects, current problems experienced by blacks in currently covered areas."[45] Rep. Robert Drinan noted similarly during the floor debate that there was "evidence that American Indians do suffer from extensive infringement of their voting rights," and that the Department of Justice "has been involved in 33 cases involving discrimination against Indians since 1970."[46] House members also took note of various court decisions documenting voting discrimination against American Indians, including *Klahr v. Williams* (finding that legislative redistricting in Arizona had been adopted for the purpose of diluting Indian voting strength),[47] *Oregon v. Mitchell* (noting that literacy "tests have been used at times as a discriminatory weapon against . . . American Indians"),[48] and *Goodluck v. Apache County* (finding that a county redistricting plan had been adopted to diminish Indian voting strength).[49]

The House report that accompanied the 1975 amendments found there was "a close and direct correlation between high illiteracy among [language-minority] groups and low voter participation." The illiteracy rate among American Indians was 15.5 percent, compared with a nationwide illiteracy rate of only 4.5 percent for Anglos. The report concluded that these disparities were "the product of the failure of state and local officials to afford equal educational opportunities to members of language minority groups."[50]

During debate in the Senate, Sen. William Scott read into the record a report prepared by the Library of Congress entitled "Prejudice and Discrimination in American History," which concluded that "[d]iscrimination of the most basic kind has been directed against the American Indian from the day that settlers from Europe set foot upon American shores. . . . [A]s late as 1948 certain Indians were still refused the right to vote. The resulting distress of Indians is as severe as that of any group discriminated against in American society."[51] The Senate report made similar findings of discrimination against language minorities, including Indians, in access to voter registration, public education, housing, administration of justice, and employment.[52]

1982 Amendments

Congress again amended and extended the Voting Rights Act in 1982. It extended Section 5 for twenty-five years, the longest extension in the act's history. In doing so it recited an array of ongoing voting rights abuses, including the maintenance of discriminatory election procedures, the adoption of new and more sophisticated devices that diluted minority voting strength, intimidation and harassment, discouragement of registration and voting, and widespread noncompliance with Section 5. It acknowledged that progress had been made in minority political participation but concluded that "racial and language minority discrimination affecting the right to vote persists throughout the jurisdictions covered by the Section 5 preclearance requirement," and that "[w]ithout the preclearance of new laws, many of the advances of the past decade could be wiped out overnight with new schemes and devices."[53] The minority-language provisions were also extended for ten years.

The act also provides that any voter who requires assistance because of a disability or an inability to read or write is entitled to assistance by a person of the voter's choice, except for an employer or agent of the employer or an officer or agent of the voter's union.[54] The exception was designed to protect a voter from possible undue influence.

Congress altered the bailout formula so that for the first-time jurisdictions down to the county level could bail out independently. One of the main purposes of the new bailout was to provide local jurisdictions with an incentive to change their voting practices by eliminating structural and other barriers to minority political participation. To bail out, a jurisdiction must show that it has not used a discriminatory test or device within the preceding ten years, has fully complied with the Voting Rights Act, and has engaged in constructive efforts to facilitate equal access to the electoral process.[55]

Congress also amended Section 2 of the act to include a discriminatory "results" standard. The amendment was in response to the Supreme Court's decision in *City of Mobile v. Bolden*, which held that to establish a violation of Section 2 minority plaintiffs had to prove that a challenged practice was adopted or was being maintained with a racially discriminatory purpose.[56] Congress concluded that requiring proof of a discriminatory purpose was "unnecessarily divisive," placed an "'inordinately difficult' burden of proof on plaintiffs, and it 'asks the wrong question.'"[57] The "right" question, according to the legislative history and the Court, is whether a challenged practice results in the denial of a minority group's "equal opportunity to participate in the political process and to elect candidates of their choice."[58]

The legislative history provides that "a variety of factors, depending upon the kind of rule, practice, or procedure called into question," is relevant in determining a violation of the results standard.[59] These factors (the "Senate factors") include the following:

- the extent of any history of official discrimination in the state or political subdivision that touched the right of the members of the minority group to register, to vote, or otherwise to participate in the democratic process;
- the extent to which voting in the elections of the state or political subdivision is racially polarized;
- the extent to which the state or political subdivision has used unusually large election districts, majority vote requirements, anti-single-shot provisions, or other voting practices or procedures that may enhance the opportunity for discrimination against the minority group;
- if there is a candidate slating process, whether the members of the minority group have been denied access to that process;
- the extent to which members of the minority group in the state or political subdivision bear the effects of discrimination in such areas as education, employment, and health, which hinder their ability to participate effectively in the political process;
- whether political campaigns have been characterized by overt or subtle racial appeals; and
- the extent to which members of the minority group have been elected to public office in the jurisdiction.

Whether the policy underlying the use of a challenged practice is "tenuous" and the unresponsiveness of elected official to the particularized needs of the minority group may also have probative value in establishing minority vote dilution.

In *Thornburg v. Gingles*, which first applied amended Section 2, the Court held that to establish a violation of the "results" standard in a challenge to at-large elections, plaintiffs had to show initially that (1) the minority group is sufficiently large and geographically compact to constitute a majority in one or more single-member districts; (2) the minority is politically cohesive that is, tends to vote as a bloc; and, (3) the majority also votes as a bloc "usually to defeat the minority's preferred candidate." The other Senate factors "are supportive of, but *not essential to*, a minority voter's claim."[60] The ultimate determination of a Section 2 violation is to "be assessed 'based on the totality of circumstances,'" but the Court has held that "lack of equal electoral opportunity may be readily imagined and unsurprising when demonstrated under circumstances that include the three essential *Gingles* factors." It would be "the rare case for minority plaintiffs to satisfy *Gingles'* preconditions" but still fail to establish a violation of Section 2 under the totality of the circumstances.[61]

Both minority political cohesion and legally significant white bloc voting are usually established by statistical evidence of racially polarized voting. According to *Gingles*, "[t]he purpose of inquiring into the existence of racially polarized voting is twofold: to ascertain whether minority group members constitute a politically cohesive unit and to determine whether whites vote sufficiently as a bloc usually to defeat the minority's preferred candidates."[62] Racially polarized voting "exists where there is a consistent relationship between the race of the voter and the way in which the voter votes . . . or to put it differently, where black voters and white voters vote differently."[63] Political cohesion can be established by "showing that a significant number of minority group members usually vote for the same candidates." Legally significant white bloc voting occurs when "whites vote sufficiently as a bloc usually to defeat the minority's preferred candidates."[64]

The most important factors in the totality-of-circumstances inquiry are (1) the "extent to which minority group members have been elected to public office in the jurisdiction" and (2) "the extent to which voting in the elections of the state or political subdivision is racially polarized."[65]

The amendment of Section 2 and its interpretation by the Supreme Court represented strong congressional and judicial commitment to equal voting rights. They also brought greater clarity and predictability to challenges to discriminatory voting practices.

After the 1982 extension of Section 5, Sumter County, South Carolina, filed yet another challenge to the constitutionality of the statute. It contended the 1982 extension was unconstitutional because the coverage formula was outdated. The county pointed out that as of May 28, 1982, more than half of the age-eligible population in South Carolina and in Sumter County was registered, facts that it said "distinguish the 1982 extension as applied to them from the circumstances relied upon in *South Carolina v. Katzenbach, supra,* to uphold the 1965 Act."[66] The three-judge court rejected the argument, noting that Section 5 "had a much larger purpose than to increase voter registration in a county like Sumter to more than 50 percent."[67] In support of its conclusion, the court noted "Congress held hearings, produced extensive reports, and held lengthy debates before deciding to extend the Act in 1982."[68]

1992 Amendments

In 1992 Congress extended the minority-language provisions for an additional fifteen years. It concluded that "the type of discrimination previously encountered by these language minority populations still exists," and that the need for the minority-language provisions continues.[69] Congress further noted that without bilingual assistance in voting, the guarantees of the Fourteenth and Fifteenth Amendments "may disappear. In several States, English-only laws may prevent the use of any type of official bilingual ballot if § 203 were not reauthorized."[70]

Seven states (Georgia, Illinois, Indiana, Kentucky, Mississippi, North Carolina, and North Dakota) have "official English" laws. Four states (Alabama, California, Colorado, and Florida) have declared English their official language and empowered the state legislature to act to preserve English as the "common language" of the state. Six states (Arizona, Arkansas, Nebraska, South Carolina, Tennessee, and Virginia) have declared English the language of the ballot and have enacted or imposed restrictions on the use of languages other than English in the exercise of official governmental functions. The minority-language provisions of the act were designed to protect limited-English-proficient citizens from the effect of these laws.[71]

The coverage formula was also augmented to include jurisdictions with 10,000 or more limited-English-proficient voting-age citizens of a single-language minority as well as reservations with 5 percent or more American Indian or Alaska Native limited-English-proficient voting-age citizens.[72] Under the preexisting formula, many such jurisdictions had escaped coverage.

More Constitutional Challenges

In 1999 the Supreme Court rejected yet another challenge to the constitutionality of Section 5 by the State of California. The state argued "§ 5 could not withstand constitutional scrutiny if it were interpreted to apply to voting measures enacted by States that have not been designated as historical wrongdoers in the voting rights sphere."[73] The Court disagreed: "Legislation which deters or remedies constitutional violations can fall within the sweep of Congress' enforcement power even if in the process it prohibits conduct which is not itself unconstitutional and intrudes into legislative spheres of autonomy previously reserved to the States."[74] The Court, reaffirming its ruling in *South Carolina v. Katzenbach,* further held "once a jurisdiction has been designated, the Act may guard against both discriminatory animus and the potentially harmful *effect* of neutral laws in that jurisdiction."[75]

The courts have also rejected challenges to Section 2. In a suit by the United States challenging at-large elections in Blaine County,

Montana, the county argued that Section 2 was unconstitutional as applied in Indian Country. In rejecting the county's argument, and in affirming the finding of vote dilution by the district court, the court of appeals held that "the VRA [Voting Rights Act] stands out as the prime example of a congruent and proportionate [congressional] response to well documented violations of the Fourteenth and Fifteenth Amendments."[76] Blaine County filed a petition for a writ of certiorari asking the Supreme Court to review its claim that Section 2 was unconstitutional, but the petition was denied.[77]

2006 Amendments and Extension

Congress last amended and extended the Voting Rights Act in 2006.[78] In doing so, it made extensive findings that

> Present day discrimination experienced by racial and language minority voters is contained in evidence, including the objections interposed by the Department of Justice in covered jurisdictions; the section 2 litigation filed to prevent dilutive techniques from adversely affecting minorities; the enforcement actions filed to protect language minorities; and the tens of thousands of Federal observers dispatched to monitor polls in jurisdictions covered by the Voting Rights Act of 1965.

Congress concluded that "without the continuation of the Voting Rights Act of 1965 protections, racial and language minority citizens will be deprived of the opportunity to exercise their right to vote, or will have their votes diluted, undermining the significant gains made by minorities in the last 40 years."[79]

In addition to extending Section 5 for an additional twenty-five years to 2032, Congress also redressed two decisions of the Supreme Court that had restricted the application of Section 5. In the first decision, the Court held that a voting change enacted with a discriminatory, but nonretrogressive, purpose was not objectionable under the statute.[80] Thus, a voting change enacted with a purpose to discriminate against minorities, but which would not make them worse off than under the preexisting practice, could be implemented free and clear of Section 5. Congress remedied that by providing that the term "purpose" as used in Section 5 "shall include any discriminatory purpose."[81] In the second decision, the Court held that a redistricting plan that diminished the ability of minorities to elect candidates of their choice was not necessarily objectionable if it provided them the ability to "influence" the election of candidates "sympathetic to the interests of minority voters."[82] Congress remedied the decision by amending Section 5 to provide that the statute's purpose "is to protect the ability of such citizens to elect their preferred candidates of choice."[83]

Predictably, shortly after passage of the 2006 extension, a lawsuit was filed challenging the constitutionality of renewed Section 5. The plaintiff was a municipal utility district in Austin, Texas, with an elected board of directors. It argued that it was entitled to bailout from coverage, but if not that Section 5 was now unconstitutional. In rejecting these arguments, the three-judge court in the District of Columbia held that the utility district was not a political subdivision entitled to bailout, and that given the extensive legislative record documenting contemporary racial discrimination in voting in the covered jurisdictions, Congress's decision to extend Section 5 for another twenty-five years was constitutional.[84] The district has appealed the decision to the Supreme Court, which held in an eight-to-one opinion that the district was eligible to bail out from Section 5 coverage and therefore it was not necessary to reach or decide the issue of the statute's continuing constitutionality.[85] Many observers believe the decision shows that a majority of the Supreme Court was not prepared to strike down Section 5, one of the most successful and iconic civil rights laws in American history.

Covered Jurisdictions

Jurisdictions now covered by Section 5 are as follows: Alabama, Alaska, Arizona, California (five counties), Florida (five counties),

Georgia, Louisiana, Michigan (two towns), Mississippi, New Hampshire (ten towns), New York (three counties), North Carolina (forty counties), South Carolina, South Dakota (two counties), Texas, and Virginia.[86]

Jurisdictions covered by the bilingual election requirement include the entire states of California, New Mexico, and Texas and several hundred counties and townships in Alaska, Arizona, Colorado, Connecticut, Florida, Hawaii, Idaho, Illinois, Kansas, Louisiana, Maryland, Massachusetts, Michigan, Mississippi, Montana, Nebraska, Nevada, New Jersey, New Mexico, New York, North Dakota, Oklahoma, Oregon, Pennsylvania, Rhode Island, South Dakota, Utah, and Washington.[87] Eighty counties in seventeen states were covered because of their Indian populations.

Table 2 contains a list of jurisdictions required to provide minority-language assistance in voting because of their American Indian populations. In addition, it indicates which jurisdictions are also covered by Section 5.

The Voting Rights Act of 1965 has been described as creating a "Quiet Revolution" in African American voting rights and office holding in the South.[88] The act precipitated a similar revolution in the West on behalf of American Indians, but for a variety of reasons it was later in coming. American Indians were not covered by the minority-language provisions of the act until the amendments in 1975. Other factors that contributed to lack of the act's enforcement were the debilitating legacy of years of discrimination by federal and state governments, the limited resources of the Indian community and its access to legal assistance, inaction by the Department of Justice in implementing the act, the isolation of the Indian community and its alienation from nontribal elections, and the anti-Indian sentiments of many whites. There were also some Indians who were concerned that participation in local, state, and national elections would undermine tribal sovereignty. Matthew Fletcher, the director of the Indigenous Law & Policy Center at Michigan State University College of Law, however, says such opposition was "not very widespread—a small minority."[89]

TABLE 2
Jurisdictions Required to Provide Minority-Language Voting Assistance Because of Their American Indian Populations

State	Jurisdiction covered by Sec. 203	Also covered by Sec. 5
Alaska	6 census areas or boroughs: Bethel, Dillingham, Kenai, North Slope, Wade Hampton, and Yukon-Koyukuk	All (6)
Arizona	9 counties: Apache, Coconino, Gila, Graham, Maricopa, Navajo, Pima, Pinal, and Yuma	All (9)
California	2 counties: Imperial and Riverside	None (0)
Colorado	2 counties: La Plata and Montezuma	None (0)
Florida	3 counties: Broward, Collier, and Glades	Collier (1)
Idaho	5 counties: Bannock, Bingham, Caribou, Owyhee, and Power	None (0)
Louisiana	1 parish: Allen	All (1)
Mississippi	9 counties: Attala, Jackson, Jones, Kemper, Leake, Neshoba, Newton, Scott, and Winston	All (9)
Montana	2 counties: Big Horn and Rosebud	None (0)
Nebraska	1 county: Sheridan	None (0)
Nevada	5 counties: Elko, Humbolt, Lyon, Nye, and White Pine	None (0)
New Mexico	11 counties: Bernalillo, Catron, Cibola, McKinley, Rio Arriba, San Juan, Sandoval, Santa Fe, Socorro, Taos, and Valencia	None (0)
North Dakota	2 counties: Richland and Sargent	None (0)
Oregon	1 county: Malheur	None (0)
South Dakota	18 counties: Bennett, Codington, Day, Dewey, Grant, Gregory, Haakon, Jackson, Lyman, Marshall, Meade, Mellette, Roberts, Shannon, Stanley, Todd, Tripp, and Ziebach	Shannon and Todd (2)
Texas	2 counties: El Paso and Maverick	All (2)
Utah	1 county: San Juan	None (0)
Total	80	30

Note: The requirement to provide minority-language voting assistance is covered under Section 203 of the 2006 extension of the Voting Rights Act.

But change in Indian political participation was inevitable, and one of the places where it began was in Big Horn County, Montana, site of the historic battle in 1876 between a combined force of Sioux and other Indian nations and the 7th U.S. Cavalry under the command of Gen. George Armstrong Custer. A successful challenge brought in 1983 to at-large elections that diluted the voting strength of Crow and Northern Cheyenne Indians would prove to be a catalyst for other, similar litigation in Montana as well as in other states in Indian Country.

CHAPTER 3

MONTANA I

The first suit brought in Indian Country after Section 2 of the Voting Rights Act was amended in 1982 was *Windy Boy v. County of Big Horn*,[1] a challenge to at-large elections for the three-member county commission of Big Horn County, Montana, and two smaller school districts in the county that shared a common board of education. The plaintiffs were members, or their spouses, of the Crow and Northern Cheyenne tribes and were represented by the ACLU. Approximately 90 percent of the Indian residents of the county lived on the reservations: 3,893 on the Crow and 872 on the Northern Cheyenne.[2] The plaintiffs contended that the at-large system of elections allowed the white majority to control the outcome of elections and prevented Indian voters from electing representatives of their choice. At the time the complaint was filed in 1983, no Indian, despite the fact that Indians were 41 percent of the voting-age population, had ever been elected to the county commission or the school board.

According to the Supreme Court, "[t]he essence of a § 2 claim is that a certain electoral law, practice, or structure interacts with social and historical conditions to cause an inequality in the opportunities enjoyed by [minority] voters to elect their preferred representatives."[3] Big Horn County was a classic example of a place where historical and present-day conditions had left the Indian community isolated and powerless to participate on a basis of equality in the local political process.

Crow and Northern Cheyenne Tribes: The Early Years

The Crow Tribe moved south from the Lake Winnipeg area in Canada to the Northern Plains in about the year 1550, living first on the Missouri River and then along the Yellowstone, Big Horn, Powder, and Wind rivers in present-day southeastern Montana and northern Wyoming. During the time they lived on the Missouri, the Crow hunted and raised corn. While living on the plains, they became equestrian, and their economy was based almost exclusively on hunting buffalo and other game as well as on trade with other tribes and white men.[4] In terms of horses, the Crow Tribe was one of the richest Indian nations of any residing on the plains. One trader estimated that in 1853 the Crow owned an average of twenty horses per lodge.[5]

The Northern Cheyenne originated in the Valley of the Minnesota, where they were horticulturalist and lived in villages. Under pressure from neighboring tribes, they migrated southwest to the Missouri River, acquired horses sometime after 1750, and moved out onto the Northern Plains. Although they continued farming into the nineteenth century, their economy, like that of the Crow, relied primarily on hunting buffalo and other game as well as on trading with other tribes and white men.[6]

There has been a long history of official and private discrimination against the Crow and Northern Cheyenne since their first contact with whites. The first so-called friendship treaties with the Crow and Cheyenne tribes were negotiated in 1825. Both established trading rights with the United States and acknowledged the "supremacy" of the U.S. government, although it is doubtful that the tribes intended to relinquish their sovereignty to the Unites States.[7] As Felix Cohen has noted, "[t]he practical inequality of the parties must be borne in mind in reading Indian treaties."[8]

The first major treaty with the tribes delineating tribal boundaries was the First Treaty of Fort Laramie of 1851.[9] Its purposes were to ensure safe passage for settlers across Indian lands; to compensate the tribes for loss of buffalo, other game animals, timber, and forage; to promote intertribal peace; and to establish a way of identifying Indians who committed depredations against whites. The treaty identified approximately 38.5 million acres as Crow territory, whereas the Cheyenne and Arapahoe were recognized as owning an interest in approximately 51.2 million acres in what is now Wyoming, Nebraska, Western Kansas, and Colorado.[10]

The Territory of Montana was organized in 1864, and the authorizing legislation expressly limited the franchise "to citizens of the United States, and those who have declared their intentions to become such."[11] Because Indians were not citizens, they were not entitled to vote in territorial elections. The legislation further provided that the treaties and laws of the United States with the Indian tribes inhabiting the Montana territory "shall be faithfully and rigidly observed." One of the first acts of the Montana territorial legislative assembly, however, was to petition the secretary of the interior to "[extinguish] the Indian title to the country now claimed and occupied by the Snake and Crow Indians" so that it could be opened up to white settlement.[12] Congress acceded to this request by adopting legislation to finance and facilitate negotiations with American Indians in Montana for the purpose of acquiring treaty land.[13] Territorial legislation also made it explicit that voting in all elections—congressional, territorial, county, and precinct—was limited to "white male citizens of the United States."[14]

The hostility of many whites toward American Indians and the desire for their removal, or extinction, was bluntly expressed by the editor of the *Montana Post*. Writing in 1865, he said a grizzly bear was superior to an Indian because he had a good, usable hide, and "because we of the mountains know what an Indian is and feel what he does, that we hate him and desire his death."[15]

Subsequent federal legislation enacted in 1867 continued the exclusion of noncitizen Indians from voting, and the territory passed laws the same year limiting service on grand and trial juries to "white male citizens."[16] The territory also resolved that the creation of permanent Indian reservations "would be most prejudicial to the interest of the great west, and a staggering blow to the progress of civilization," that the western lands were "valueless to the [Indian] barbarian," and that Congress should "transfer the Indian Bureau to the war department, and abolish the whole system of Indian agencies."[17]

Conflict and war between the various tribes and between the tribes and whites led to the Second Treaty of Fort Laramie of 1868.[18] The treaty established a Crow Reservation of roughly 8 million acres—a vast reduction in size from the 38.5 million acres recognized as Crow territory in the First Treaty of Fort Laramie—"set apart for the absolute and undisturbed use and occupation of the Indians."[19] The Montana territorial legislature promptly memorialized Congress that, in order "to save bloodshed," the treaty should be revised to allow white settlers who "have acquired rights . . . as pioneers of this mountain region" to remain and that their "rights and privileges" be recognized.[20]

In an effort to assimilate American Indians into the white community, the treaty provided that members of the tribe who commenced farming would be allotted land and given agricultural supplies; in addition, it required the mandatory education of children "to insure the civilization of the tribe." It established a "trust relationship" in which the United States pledged to protect the tribe and the tribe pledged friendship to the United States. Indians were not at that time confined to the reservation but, rather, were free to leave to travel, hunt, and visit. In exchange for the immense tract of land that was ceded, the United States agreed to make payments to the tribe that involved annuities of food, clothing, and other assistance.

Almost a hundred years later, in 1960, the Indian Claims Commission held that the Crow were entitled to recover additional compensation for the land ceded by the Second Treaty of Fort Laramie. The land had a market value in 1868 of $.40 per acre, but the tribe had been paid less than $.054 per acre, a consideration the court of claims found was "unconscionable."[21]

The Second Treaty of Fort Laramie also assigned a permanent home for the Northern Cheyenne on reservations of the Southern

Cheyenne and Arapahoe or Brule and other bands of Sioux. As it did with the Crow Tribe, the treaty similarly provided that members of the Northern Cheyenne Tribe who took up farming would be allotted land and given agricultural supplies, and it provided for mandatory education of children. In 1963, the Indian Claims Commission awarded $4.4 million to the Northern Cheyenne as additional compensation for lands reserved to them under the First Treaty of Fort Laramie of 1851 and later ceded to the United States.[22]

The territorial legislature continued to deny Indians the right to vote or serve on juries. It also made it a misdemeanor to establish a voting precinct "at any Indian agency, or at any trading post in the Indian country, or on any Indian reservation whatever."[23] Other laws made it a felony to give or sell intoxicating liquor "to any Indian or half-breed" and a misdemeanor to sell or give firearms to "any hostile Indians within this territory."[24]

The increasing westward migration of whites, including into the regions occupied by the Crow and Northern Cheyenne, prompted the territorial legislature to memorialize Congress in 1875 to rescind the Second Treaty of Fort Laramie and open up for white settlement "that portion of the country on the north bank of the Yellowstone."[25] Recision would simply acknowledge the facts that "numerous settlements already exist there," that "many more are desirous of settling there," that the land was "utterly valueless to the Indians," and "[t]hat the great national enterprise must of necessity push its way westward with all possible rapidity." Two year later the territorial legislature again memorialized Congress to open up land on the Crow reservation for further white settlement, this time the "gold-bearing quartz" and "rich mineral country" of the upper Yellowstone River.[26] The request was repeated in 1879, that the "rich mineral country . . . be restored to the public domain, and declared open to settlement."[27] And the legislature again urged Congress to transfer the BIA to the U.S. War Department because of the exposure of white settlers in the territory "to Indian wars, depredations, and incursions . . . of large tribes of semi-hostile Indians."[28]

Tensions between whites and Indians increased as a consequence of westward expansion, and armed conflicts between the tribes and whites intensified. Among the Northern Plains tribes, the Sioux and Cheyenne did the most to prevent the intrusion of non-Indians into their territory through the use of force. The Crow, who were fewer in number and more accommodating, chose to become allies of the whites rather than to fight them. Crow scouted for and fought with the U.S. Army against the Sioux and Cheyenne. The intense Indian warfare reached an apogee at the June 1876 Battle of the Little Big Horn in Big Horn County, in which Gen. George A. Custer and his troops were killed in a fight with a massed Indian village of Sioux and other tribes along the Little Big Horn River.

In 1880 and 1882, the Crow were induced into selling the western third of their reservation, including the gold-rich lands of the upper Yellowstone, and into allowing the building of the Northern Pacific Railroad through the Yellowstone Valley.[29] However, the pressure to open reservation land further to white settlement continued unabated. In an 1885 memorial to Congress, the territorial legislature condemned the practice of Crows leasing grazing land to white ranchers and urged that the land in question be restored "to the public domain, for the benefit of actual settlers only."[30]

The BIA issued rules and regulations in 1884 designed to further control Indian movement. Joe Medicine Crow, a modern-day Crow tribal historian and anthropologist, explained how the travel restrictions worked:

> In each district the government would station an Indian boss foreman, as he's called, and whenever a member, let's say of Lodge Grass District, wants to go see his mother or relative at Reno District, or St. Xavier District, he has to get a pass, four, five-day pass, and go there, no place else, just to that place, and when the time is up, he's supposed to bring it and show that pass to the boss foreman. That's the way it worked.[31]

Violations of the rules were enforced by the Indian agent or superintendent at Crow Agency. "He had a police force there composed of Indians themselves," explained Medicine Crow, "and they would go out and bring the violator, or alleged violator, and put him in a jail with the help of his Indian police, and give him bread and water if his crime or his violation was serious enough."[32] The U.S. Army was also assigned to confine the Indians to their various reservations.

The Tongue River Reservation was established for the Northern Cheyenne by executive order in 1884 to confine members of the tribe to a designated territory and to fulfill earlier promises to the Cheyenne. Cheyenne who had already settled outside the reservation area were forced to relocate within it. The territorial legislature predictably memorialized the president to revoke his executive order. The creation of the reservation would "discourage good men from coming into our territory" and would deprive those already living there "of the benefits of schools and other advantages of a civilized community," the memorial said. "[T]he Indian reservations now in Montana should be diminished, and not increased."[33]

Most of the local cattlemen protested the establishment of reservations, and tension ran high. Area newspapers during this period depicted both the Crow and Cheyenne as primitive and uncivilized and the Cheyenne as hostile and dangerous. The Cheyenne were referred to as "marauders," "truant Indians," and "a lot of half savage Indians," and likened to a "nest of rattlesnakes planted in the midst of a public park." The Crow were "professional cutthroats" and "a filthy, lazy tribe."[34] The papers continued to stress removal of "backward" Indians, including relocation of the Cheyenne and opening of the Crow Reservation to non-Indian homesteaders so that progressive whites could develop the territory.

During the period of time beginning in 1864 when Montana was organized as a territory until it achieved statehood in 1889, the American Indian population in the area was substantially reduced, their territory was greatly diminished, and their economic and social base as a separate and sovereign people was destroyed. The Crow and Northern Cheyenne were still semi-sovereign, but they became de facto and legal wards of the United States who were in almost complete cultural and territorial isolation from the American mainstream. Their affairs were regulated almost entirely by Congress and the BIA, upon whom they were dependent for their survival. In an 1883 report, the commissioner of Indian Affairs described the condition of Indians in Montana as "deplorable."[35] The commissioner reported in 1886 that 63 percent of the Crow and 75 percent of the Northern Cheyenne were subsisting on government rations.[36]

Montana Statehood

The federal legislation admitting Montana to statehood in 1889 continued the existing restrictions on voting and directed that the state constitution make no distinction in civil or political rights based on race, "except as to Indians not taxed."[37] The legislation also provided that the state disclaim all right and title to unappropriated Indian lands, which were to remain under the absolute jurisdiction and control of the U.S. Congress.

State law expressly provided that voters must be resident freeholders, and the Montana Constitution restricted the franchise to male citizens of the United States who were twenty-one years of age or older.[38] These provisions excluded noncitizen, non-property-owning Indians from voting. Voter registrars were required to be resident freeholders, qualified voters, and citizens, which excluded Indians from any role in the registration process.[39] At the time of statehood, most Montanans assumed, as did the commissioner of Indian Affairs Thomas Morgan, that the federal–tribal tie would soon be broken, Indian lands would be opened up to non-Indians, and the Indians themselves were part of "a vanishing state of things." As Morgan explained, "[t]he Indians must conform to 'the white man's ways,' peaceably if they will, forcibly if they must. . . . This civilization may not be the best possible, but is the best the Indians can get. They cannot escape it, and must either conform to it or be crushed by it."[40] As one Montana military officer put it in 1889, "[l]ittle can be done with the old Indian, but the young ones are easily educated and if we get to work in earnest in two or at most three generations *savages* will have disappeared from the American Continent."[41]

The Crow Reservation was further reduced in size by Congress in 1891 when the tribe ceded a substantial portion of the western part of the reservation.[42] The state legislature predicted in a memorial to the House and Senate that the opening of the new lands "will bring to Montana a large immigration of industrious and enterprising persons seeking homes on the public domain."[43] Congress appointed a commission in 1896 to negotiate with the Northern Cheyenne for their removal and with the Flathead for a cession of reservation lands.[44] The legislature later complained that Indians were wandering off the reservation "to the terror and annoyance of the people" and asked Congress "to make it unlawful for Indians resident upon reservations in the State of Montana to ever at any time or for any purpose leave or be found off their reservation and to enact such measures as will stringently enforce such legislation."[45]

Pressure to open up even more Indian lands to white settlement continued to be exerted by the state, which in 1901 and 1903 memorialized Congress to "speedily open . . . up for the settlement of our citizens" non-allotted lands on the Crow Indian Reservation.[46] In response, Congress again reduced the size of the reservation by ceding more Indian land in 1904.[47]

The call for further reductions in Indian land continued to be sounded in the press. The *Hardin Tribune* described the Crow as "a vanishing race," and said it was hopeless "to stay the relentless tide of civilization that was to drive them from the land."[48] Another article predicted confidently that "[i]n a few rapidly passing years the white man will own practically all of the Crow country."[49] In a 1909 memorial to Congress, the state legislature urged that "the Crow Reservation should be speedily opened for settlement and all Indian rights adjusted."[50] Two years later, and again in 1915, the legislature enacted similar petitions.[51]

The exclusion of American Indians from public life and their treatment as an inferior class were mandated by various state statutes and constitutional provisions: the Montana Constitution of 1889 provided that no person could be a representative, senator, governor, lieutenant governor, superintendent of public instructions, a justice of the supreme court, or a member of the militia who was not a "citizen of the United States"; an 1891 law limited voting in school elections to citizen taxpayers; an 1897 law limited the right to vote on municipal bond issue to "tax payers"; a 1901 law limited voting in road district elections to property taxpayers and provided for voter challenges on the basis of noncitizenship; a 1903 statute made it a misdemeanor for an Indian off the reservation to carry a firearm; a 1915 law made it a crime to sell or give liquor to an Indian; a 1919 law prohibited the establishment of voting precincts "within or at the premises of any Indian agency or trading post"; and a 1923 law made it criminal to possess peyote, a substance used in Indian religious ceremonies.[52]

Theoretically, American Indians could become citizens and voters through service in the armed forces or operation of the Dawes Act of 1887 and the Burke Act of 1906, that is, by accepting allotments of land and severing all tribal ties. The state, however, effectively nullified these provisions of federal law by enacting a statute in 1911 providing that no person living upon an Indian reservation could be deemed a resident of Montana for purposes of voting unless the person had acquired a residence in some county in Montana prior to taking up residence upon the reservation.[53]

The attorney general of Montana issued several opinions that Indian reservations should not be included in a voting precinct, that "wards" of the federal government could not vote, and that even those Indians who owned land in fee patent could not vote if they took part in the transactions of the tribe.[54] *The Hardin Tribune* reported in 1913 that the attorney general, in response to a request from Big Horn County, confirmed that an Indian who owns his land in fee but still participated in tribal activities could not vote.[55] According to the paper, as of October 16, 1914, there was only one Indian registered to vote in all of Big Horn County.[56]

The Crow opposed the federal allotment policy and rejected the notion that they were a vanishing race. In a special tribal resolution to the president and Congress in 1915, the tribe "earnestly and vigorously" protested against further opening of the reservation. "We intend to increase our farming and agricultural pursuits," the resolution said, "and want our lands and reservation to remain undisturbed." The push to open up tribal lands was a "diabolical" scheme of "designing politicians and land sharks and stockmen" and was fueled by "racial feeling, the white man feeling much superior to the Indian, therefore unfit for his association, as evidenced by the fact that 'Jim Crow' tables are in existence in both Hardin, Montana, and Crow Agency," and that "the public schools of Wyola and Lodge Grass have refused to admit Indian children who were eligible by reasons of their legal status, and were shown the greatest of racial hatred."[57]

Public schools in Montana were traditionally segregated on the basis of race, and no Indian child was allowed to attend public school unless under white guardianship or unless the child had severed tribal relations.[58] Official racial segregation in public schools in Big Horn County continued until after passage of the Crow Allotment Act of 1920, which provided for still further allotment of unreserved land on the Crow Reservation and ceded to the state of Montana land for common school purposes on the condition that Crow Indian children "shall be permitted to attend the public schools of said State on the same condition as the children of white citizens of the State."[59] The *Hardin Tribune* surmised that "[t]hese allotments will practically wipe out the Crow reservation."[60]

Although the purpose of government policies and the various allotment laws was the assimilation of the Indian population and the gradual extinction of Indian reservations and Indian tribes,[61] Indians did not vanish as official policy dictated or assumed. The Crow and Northern Cheyenne continued to speak their tribal languages, to practice traditional religious ceremonies (sometimes in secret), and to maintain their traditional social ties. In 1900, about 44 percent of Montana Indians over the age of ten did not speak English. Anthropologist Robert H. Lowie, who studied the Crow from 1907 to 1931, found their culture "was spiritually very much alive," especially in speech, belief, and social custom.[62] Indian culture had been considerably weakened by its contact with white society, but it had not been destroyed. According to Adrian Heidenreich, a professor of American Indian Studies at the University of Montana in Billings, the various attempts at cultural destruction had led to the phenomenon of "ethnic resistance" and "defensive structuring," in which the Indian community placed increased emphasis on its unique Indian identity.[63]

The Crow Reservation was systematically diminished over the years by the various allotment acts so that at the present time only 2.3 million acres of reservation land remain. Approximately 52 percent is allotted to members of the tribe and held in trust by the United States, 17 percent is held in trust for the tribe itself, and 28 percent is held in fee by non-Indians. The state of Montana owns 2 percent of the reservation in fee simple, and the United States owns less than 1 percent.[64]

The Northern Cheyenne Reservation at the present time contains only about 433,000 acres. Some 262,000 acres are owned by the tribe, with more than 171,000 acres allotted to individuals.[65]

The Northern Cheyenne incorporated under the Indian Reorganization Act and established a tribal council form of government in 1936. The Crow approved an alternate constitution that formalized their general council form of government in 1948.[66] Subsequently, both tribes established three-branch governments consisting of executive, legislative, and judicial branches.

Impact of the Indian Citizenship Act

All Indians born within the United States were granted citizenship by the Indian Citizenship Act of 1924.[67] Local Montana officials, however, opposed the granting of equal voting rights to American Indians. C. H. Asbury, superintendent of Crow Agency, wrote a letter to the commissioner of Indian affairs on June 9, 1924, after passage of the act; in the letter, he declared that the state legislature would be justified in making an educational requirement for new voters, "as there are certainly many Indians that are absolutely incapable of voting intelligently."[68] Others, taking a cue from southern states, which had disfranchised blacks after passage of the Fourteenth and Fifteenth Amendments,[69] suggested it would be proper for the states to discriminate against Indians by enacting literacy tests or poll taxes or by denying the franchise outright to Indians living on reservations and enjoying immunity from state authority.[70]

After passage of the 1924 act, there was a surge of political activity in the Indian community in Big Horn County. The *Hardin Tribune* noted that between 1,000 and 1,100 Big Horn County Indians were eligible to vote, and "if they all register they will cut a considerable figure in the result this fall."[71] On July 25, 1924, the newspaper reported that approximately 600 Indians had registered, with more likely to register by November.[72] The paper also reported that 200 Indians had attended a recent candidate forum, and that "you should have seen the energy and political capacity they have exerted in getting more than 500 Crow and Cheyenne Indian men and women registered."[73]

Three American Indians ran for office in 1924: Robert Yellowtail for Congress, who styled himself in his political ads as "A Real American for Congressman," and Russell White Bear and Anson Pease for sheriff. All the Indian candidates were defeated.[74] Frank Yarlott and Harry Whiteman, both Indians, ran for state representative in 1928 but were also defeated.[75] Robert Yellowtail ran for state senator in 1932 and lost.[76] Russell White Bear ran for public office again in 1934, this time for county assessor, and was again defeated.[77]

Stories of the day from local and regional newspapers reporting on Indians were remarkably condescending and made frequent use of racial stereotypes, suggesting that Indian candidates could expect to get little support from white voters. The *Billings Gazette* noted that spring weather "and a government allotment" had brought Crows from the reservation who "paraded the city in leisurely fashion, stopping to try all the slot machines and other marvels of civilization."[78] An Indian jailed for drinking was dubbed "the worthy ward of Uncle Sam," whereas his wife, who was referred to as his "squaw" and who had been brought in on a similar charge, was booked as "Susie Alcohol, drunk."[79] The newspaper speculated in another story that an American Indian girl who had been named Carrie Crow Feathers by a medicine man may have been named differently if "the medicine man had happened to make his official visit last year" when the girl was riding a Rock Mountain goat her father had recently caught.[80] Still another story reported that a number of Indian families had established homes on the west side of town "to the discomfiture of the residents and members of the city council," and that the Indians were to be removed to the Rocky Boy's Reservation in northern Montana.[81]

Despite passage of the Indian Citizenship Act, Montana continued to restrict access by Indians to voter registration. It enacted a statute in 1937 requiring all deputy voter registrars to be "qualified, tax-paying" residents of their precincts.[82] Because Indians living on the reservations were exempt from some local taxes, the requirement excluded virtually all Indians from serving as deputy registrars and denied Indians access to voter registration in their own precincts on the reservation. This provision of state law remained in effect until it was repealed in 1975.[83] Also in 1937, the state enacted a statute cancelling all voter registration as of June 1, 1937, and requiring the re-registration of all voters. It also adopted a requirement that county clerks cancel any registration when three qualified electors presented an affidavit challenging a voter's qualifications.[84] Indian voter registration in Big Horn County remained depressed after the purge and did not return to pre-purge levels until the 1980s.[85]

State and local governments continued to regard American Indians as wards of the federal government whose welfare was of little or no concern to the state and its political subdivisions. A 1938 Montana Supreme Court decision, for example, prohibited Big Horn County officials from paying out money from the county's poor fund or other funds for direct relief to "ward" Indians of the United States.[86] The Montana Relief Commission was similarly prohibited from furnishing assistance to indigent Indians, even though they were citizens.[87] Indians were barred from receiving pensions under the Montana Old Age Pension Act, even though they had received a patent in fee.[88] Counties were prohibited by state law from making payments for general relief to Indians. Counties were also barred from contracting with the federal government to provide relief to Indians, even if they would be reimbursed by the federal government.[89]

The state also continued to restrict the service of American Indians on juries. A 1939 statute limited jury service to those who had property assessed "on the last assessment role of the county."[90] The effect of the requirement was to exclude from jury duty Indians who did not own assessed land.

The Years after World War II

During World War II, many American Indians were drafted or volunteered for service in the U.S. armed forces. After the war, there was another surge of political participation in the Indian community in Montana. An important manifestation of this participation was the establishment in 1944 of the National Congress of American Indians. Montana also participated in the Governor's Interstate Council on Indian Affairs, which began in 1949 and encouraged Indians to participate more in the larger political process. Several Crow and Northern Cheyenne representatives were involved in the annual meetings of the governor's council.[91]

Indians also occasionally ran for office but without success. Robert Yellowtail ran for the state senate in 1954 and was defeated.[92] William Wall, the Crow Tribal Chair, ran unsuccessfully for Congress in 1956.[93] Fourteen years passed before another Indian in Big Horn County, Ivan Small, would run for public office. He ran for sheriff in 1970 and was defeated.[94]

The obstacles facing Indian candidates were numerous and formidable and included not only the racial polarization that existed in the county and the isolation of the Indian community, but also a profoundly depressed socioeconomic status that made it difficult for Indian candidates to finance and conduct political campaigns. During the 1980s, unemployment on the Crow Reservation was as high as 74 percent and was approximately 60 percent on the Northern Cheyenne Reservation.[95] Per capita income of Indians was less than half that of whites.[96] On the Crow Reservation, 70 percent of Indian housing was substandard, and more than 500 Indian families were without any housing.[97]

There were also significant differences between Indian and non-Indian religions that divided the two communities. Indians have many ceremonies or religious observances that have no counterpart in non-Indian places of worship, such as peyote rituals, the Sun Dance, tobacco ceremonies, and sacred bundle rituals.

Language traditions also separated Indians and whites. English was a second language for 78 percent of Crows and 37 percent of

Northern Cheyennes.[98] Many children did not learn English until after they began grammar school. Most Crows over the age of forty-five were not fluent in English. Today, Crow is the official language of the Crow Tribe and is spoken at public functions. Crow Indians generally speak Crow among themselves and in their homes.

In 1980, nearly three-fourths of whites in Big Horn County age twenty-five or older were high school graduates, compared with a little more than half of Indians.[99] Crow Indian students in the Hardin public schools achieved at a level approximately one and a half years below that of whites. Their achievement was lowest in the language skills part of achievement tests.[100] One study from the mid-1960s found that over 40 percent of Indian elementary pupils at Lame Deer had a reading deficiency of two years or more, and that the deficiency at the high school level was even more serious.[101] Indian students also began to fall behind after the third and fourth grades, when the social awareness of discrimination began to adversely affect educational attainment.

American Indians were caught in a vicious cycle of self-perpetuating causation. Their depressed socioeconomic status, their lack of access to decent-paying jobs (or any jobs at all), their isolation from the majority community, the stereotyping inflicted on them by some whites, and their lower levels of educational attainment all coalesced to perpetuate the disadvantages that plagued them in most areas of life. Their poverty bred poverty. Their isolation bred isolation. Their lack of advantages bred disadvantages. The Montana legislature has similarly recognized that "Native American learners are caught in a network of mutually reinforcing handicaps ranging from material poverty to racism, illness, geographical and social isolation, language and cultural barriers, and simple hunger."[102]

Geography also worked against Indian candidates. Big Horn County is larger in size than the State of Connecticut. It also contains two mountain ranges—the Pryor and Big Horn—and two major rivers—the Big Horn and Little Big Horn. As a result, distances between various places in the county are extreme, and the number of primary roads is limited. The round trip from Wyola to Pryor, for example, is 230 miles.

Not only are distances great, but in November the weather in Big Horn County can be severe. Many of the roads in the county are impassable during the fall and winter months except by four-wheel-drive vehicles.

The extreme distances between communities in Big Horn County placed a particular burden on poorly financed Indian candidates. Whites, by contrast, at least those living in Hardin, had an enormous advantage in campaigning. Up to the 1980s, nearly a third of the county's residents lived in Hardin and about half the county's whites. As a result, a white candidate who had ready access to these voters had an obvious advantage over an Indian candidate living in one of the rural areas.

Growing Up Indian

Indians living in Big Horn County all have stories to tell of the discrimination they experienced growing up in the county. Joe Medicine Crow said that during the 1940s, "discrimination was still very positive and quite intense in the Indian community. In those days there were signs on restaurant doors, 'No Indians Allowed.' Or sometimes, 'No Dogs or Indians Allowed.' It was harsh, very harsh, crude." After World War II things improved somewhat, but discrimination was still there. "When you would go into a restaurant the proprietor would shake his head. That means get out of here. And after being given that treatment for a while, you know where to go or where not to go."[103]

Janine Windy Boy is a member of the Crow Tribe and lived in Lodge Grass. A relative of White Mans Run Him, one of Custer's Indian scouts at the Battle of the Little Big Horn, she is a striking looking women—tall, graceful, with intense dark eyes. Seeing Windy Boy camped with her family in late summer in a lodge on the banks of the Little Big Horn during the annual Crow Fair, dressed in a ceremonial buckskin dress adorned with Elk's teeth, and with the low afternoon sun sending brilliant shafts of light through a grove of cottonwoods, she seems part of another time, as if suspended in a magic, golden moment. But Windy Boy is very much of the modern world. She has served on the staff of the governor of Washington State, been president of Little Big Horn College, and garnered a MacArthur Foundation "genius award." And she, like virtually every American Indian who has grown up in Big Horn County, has experienced discrimination at the hands of whites. As late as the 1960s she was denied service at a local restaurant. "My aunt, uncle, and cousin went into a restaurant in Hardin," she said, "and we waited and waited, and finally I went to the cash register and asked the waitress if she had any intention of serving us, and she ignored me. We never did get waited on and finally left."[104]

Jim Kindness, a tribal member, tells of his encounter with whites in Hardin when he was a young teenager in the 1960s. "I was working with a crew on a building in Hardin, and I got to feeling sick from the sun and the heat. The other guys took me over to a park that was nearby and told me to rest in the shade. But I started getting worse, and I stopped some white people walking through the park and asked them if they would take me to a doctor, but they refused to do it. They said—maybe it was because of my work clothes—but they called me a 'dirty Indian' and walked away."[105]

Dan Half, another tribal member who lives at Crow Agency and works as a ranch hand, had a similar experience at the county fairgrounds during the Little Britches Rodeo in the 1990s. "I started having chest pains, a heart attack, so I went behind the bucking chutes and saw that there was some shade behind a semi-truck. I laid there for a while, and I must have blacked out, and when I came to I went over to the arena where a county ambulance was parked and asked the drivers if they would take me to the hospital. But they refused, said if I had any friends around they could take me."[106]

Clo Small is not an American Indian, but she is married to a tribal member. Since coming to Big Horn County in 1979, she has experienced discrimination. When she is by herself, she is waited on in restaurants, and the service is prompt and courteous. But when she is in the company of Indians, the treatment is different. "It is just a feeling you get of being a second class person. They would not wait on you, not make any effort to put a place for you."

In stores, she has seen clerks follow Indian people around. "One time I was in the meat department and one of the checkout clerks came up the aisle and told the man behind the meat department, 'watch that Indian right there and make sure he doesn't put any meat in his coat.' It's been a very shocking experience for me."[107]

Leo Hudetz is another non-Indian who is married to a tribal member. He moved to Crow Agency in 1978 as a Volunteers in Service to America (VISTA) volunteer. After that, he taught business courses at Little Big Horn College and worked as a certified public accountant. When he first got to Big Horn County, "it was obvious to me that there was heavy prejudice in Hardin against the Indian people. I remember going to buy a car in Hardin, and the salesman there told me 'we hate to deal with Indians, we sell them some of our junk cars.' I heard that and I walked out. I had a State of Montana auditor who audits tax returns tell me 'you can't trust Indians, they are goddamn liars.' I had a minister in Hardin ask me, 'how can you stand to live with those animals down there for so long?'" After his daughter was born, Hudetz and his family moved to Illinois in 1984 because he didn't want his little girl, who is a tribal member, to go to the schools in Hardin.[108]

One place where the effects of discrimination were particularly apparent was the public schools. Many Indian students dropped out of school, and for a variety of reasons, including language and cultural differences, a sense of isolation and lack of academic achievement, the relative lack of Indian teachers, academic tracking, and real and perceived discrimination by white students and the school administration. According to data from the 1980 census, this dropout rate was reflected in the disproportionately lower percentage of American Indians than whites who graduated from high school in Big Horn County: 56 percent as opposed to 71 percent, respectively.[109]

Elementary School District 17H adopted a written policy creating zones for attendance at its elementary schools prior to the 1970s. The Fort Smith zone encompassed the area around Fort Smith Elementary School. The Crow Agency zone—with one exception—encompassed the area around the Crow Agency school. The exception was an area around the Custer battlefield, which included a small community of white National Park Service employees. It was designated as part of the Hardin zone, which allowed the white park service employees to send their children to the more distant, but predominantly white, schools in Hardin.

In the 1970s, School Districts 17H and 1 adopted an unwritten "administrative procedure" allowing freedom of choice in school attendance, which resulted in the total re-segregation of the Crow Elementary School. Although white families lived in the Crow Agency area, the school district permitted them to bus their elementary-age children past Crow Agency Elementary School to predominantly white schools in Hardin.

Harvey Pitsch, a non-Indian and a member of the school board, had elementary-age children and lived near Crow Agency. He bused his children to Hardin after the adoption of the new policy, however, so that they would not have to attend school with Indian children at Crow. As Pitsch explained, "We thought outside of the class room, that the Indian children speak Crow and my children do not and we thought it was socially for my kid's benefit, [if] we sent them to Hardin."[110]

Windy Boy says that many Indian parents would not send their children to Hardin because "they felt it was a harsh environment. The school was primarily white. The teachers were 99 percent white. The Indian children were isolated and were put at the very bottom of their classes, and there was a high drop out rate for Indian Children."[111]

Tyrone Ten Bear, a liaison officer between the BIA and the Crow Tribe, attended school in Hardin and says that Indians were discouraged from taking courses in science, math, and literature. "In 1958, when I entered high school, they automatically shoved a schedule in front of me saying I should be taking woodwork, workshop, and welding. And when I said I wanted to take courses that would prepare me for college, the school counselor said, 'well, you're an Indian, you shouldn't be trying to pursue anything higher than high school.'" The policy of steering Indians into vocational courses still existed, he said, when his two sons graduated in 1983 and 1984.[112]

When Dan Brown, a member of the Crow Tribe, went to high school in Hardin in 1959,

> A white counselor took one look at me and said, "you got broad shoulders, you look like you would make a good auto mechanic." That's how all the Indians were treated. They steered us into vocational studies. They put me in a carpentry class. There are two roads. Whites go on one because of their academic superiority and Indians take another road because of their academic inferiority. There were about 40 Indians in my freshman class at Hardin. By the end of the school year there were only six Indians left. Some dropped out, some went to Indian schools. Mr. Dyke, the principal, told me that I didn't have the mental capacity to do high school work. Those kind of things get you riled up. They made you feel inferior, so I withdrew and went to an Indian boarding school in Oklahoma.[113]

But Brown didn't stop there. He went on to earn a bachelor's degree from a college in Wyoming and then a master's in education from the University of South Dakota in 1976.

Dale Old Horn is a Crow tribal member, has a master's degree in linguistics from Massachusetts Institute of Technology, and is head of the Social Science and Crow Studies Department at Little Big Horn College. He finished seventh grade at Crow Agency, where he first learned English, and then went to high school at Hardin. "We were dealt with in a very different way there because of our race," he says. "All of the Crow Agency students were placed in an all Indian classroom. We didn't know that this was something that we could protest, and this was just something that was shoved down our throats. The segregation continued in the ninth grade. Our section was 9-D, and we were told that the achievers in Hardin High School were 9-A. So it was generally implied that we the Crow students were nonachievers." There were frequent fights between the white and Indian students over "name calling, insulting our heritage because of our color, about our ambition. I don't know if I want to repeat some of them." There was positive interaction between whites and Indians in athletics, but that did not spill over into social interaction off the playing field. "Right after the basketball season we became nonentities once again."[114]

Old Horn has a daughter in school at Hardin who is on the basketball team. Her friendships with whites are basically limited to fellow team members. But even those were subject to disruption. "At one time she was a real good friend with this young white student, and she came home one day and told us that her friend was asked by her father to terminate their friendship, not to be friends anymore."[115]

The daughter of Eloise Pease, who is Indian, had a similar experience. "In 1960," said Pease, "my daughter was asked by a white boy to go the school prom. I called the boy's home to discuss the arrangements and his mother answered. Later, the boy called my daughter and said that he was not allowed to take her to the prom. She ended up going with a boy who was part Indian." Some years later Eloise was a den mother for a group of Cub Scouts. "We were supposed to put on an Indian dance as part of the monthly pack meeting, but one of the white scouts refused to participate because his mother told him he couldn't dress up and dance like an Indian." And then there was the time she went to a professional woman's club, but they never asked her back. "They said 'I don't think Mrs. Pease would be interested in our club,' but the truth is they weren't interested in me."[116]

Sharon Peregoy is another Crow tribal member who went to school in Hardin in the 1970s. She has a bachelor's degree in elementary education and is the director of the Crow Headstart program, but the journey through high school was not an easy one for her. "The Crow Indian children from the Crow public school," she said, "were segregated into different academic levels, most going into the lower two levels, C and D. There were few Indian teachers, no Indian role models, and in high school they recommended that you go into a vocational track more so than the pre-college track." High school for her "was not a very good time. I felt if I had to go back through the system again, I would not. If I had a choice, I would not. We were labeled as 'squaws,' you did not know much. When I went to college it took a while to rid some of the fears that were imbedded in me going through the school system."[117]

After she graduated from Winthrop College in South Carolina in 1965, Carlene Old Elk, who is not an Indian, came to Big Horn County as a VISTA volunteer. She married a member of the Crow Tribe, and they have five children, all of whom are tribal members. When her oldest daughter entered the ninth grade at Hardin, she was reading at the eleventh-grade level. Despite that, she was placed in a remedial reading class.[118]

Katie Pretty Weasel, who was one of the first Indians to graduate from Hardin High in 1946, had a similar experience. "There was a lot of discrimination," she said, "but I would not retaliate. I left everybody alone. Some of the white students would call us names. A lot of them didn't care for Indians." She did not participate in the social life of the school or extracurricular activities "because I was not very happy there. I kept away as much as I could. I just wanted to finish school." Growing up, she saw the "No Dogs or Indians Allowed" signs. One that she particularly remembers was hanging above a garbage dump in an alley in Hardin.[119]

Dessie Bad Bear was a teacher's aide in a primary school in Hardin in the 1970s. She worked in special education and was the only Crow teacher at the school. "Some of the white teachers were very nice and friendly," she recalled, "but some weren't." When she went in the teachers' lounge during recess for coffee, some of the white teachers would "just get up and leave. I know them teachers didn't like Indians, so I didn't go there for coffee any more all the rest of the time I worked there."[120]

Not all whites in Hardin shunned Indians. Henry Ruegamer, who owned the Ford–Mercury dealership in town, recalled selling a car to a Crow Indian friend in 1964. The man was accompanied by his wife, who wore a traditional Indian blanket, and Ruegamer wanted to treat them to lunch. He gave his friend some money and directed the couple to a local café. They soon returned, however, and said they had been denied service. Ruegamer attended the same church as the café owner and called him on the phone. "I said to him, 'I just sent two of my good friends down there to have lunch. Don't you serve the Crows?' And he says, 'Not the blanket ones.' Well, I slammed the receiver down, I was really burned up about it, and in two minutes he was down to my place to apologize. I said, 'I don't want your apology. Just get the hell out of here.'"[121]

Continuing Polarization

Churches have traditionally been segregated in Big Horn County. Morley Langdon, a Baptist minister with two churches at Lodge Grass—one that is basically Indian and the other white—says that Indians and whites prefer to be with their own kind. "Church membership is based more on social compatibility than anything else," he says. "The churches now are made up of people who have been there for 40, 50 years and they are just comfortable with one another and prefer to be there." A third church, the conservative Faith Baptist Church, has also been organized in Lodge Grass. The congregation is exclusively white, Langdon says, and "tends to be very prejudicial in that they prefer not to see Indian people in a positive light. Any discussion that I have with them has been negative toward Indian people. They have the idea that Indians are just totally incompetent and can't do anything right."[122]

Civic and social organizations, such as the Kiwanis and Masons, are segregated as a matter of practice. Although American Indians would be allowed to join some of these organizations, they would not always be welcomed. Tribal members almost without exception say there is very little significant social interaction between the white and Indian communities in Big Horn County.

Hardin banks required whites to cosign promissory notes before they would lend money to American Indians, according to testimony given in 1985. During one period in the 1970s, a Hardin bank advertised for new auto loans but advised Indians not to apply. One Indian said he was refused a loan, although 90 percent of his loan was guaranteed by the federal government, because bank officials said, "Indians cannot even balance a check book."[123]

During the 1980s, Indians in Big Horn County experienced discrimination in housing. Indians who called to rent apartments or houses were often told they were taken and later learned they were still available. Indians were quoted rental rates higher than those advertised, were required to pay higher security deposits than advertised, or were required to pay advance rentals.

The tribes and the non-Indian community have also been polarized over resource and environmental issues. A major conflict involved ownership of the Big Horn River and fishing and access rights. The dispute was ultimately resolved by the Supreme Court in 1981.[124] Environmental concerns raised by the Northern Cheyenne over the building of Coalstrip Power Plants 3 and 4 prompted a Montana Power Company spokesman to say that Indians, along with non-Indian ranchers in southeastern Montana, were trying to retard progress. The Crow and Northern Cheyenne were described in the local and national press as "the Arabs of the Plains."[125] Many whites harbor resentment that Indians do not pay certain county and state taxes.

Montana's state legislature adopted legislation in 1972 requiring local county governments to adopt one of six alternate forms of government. Each county was required to elect a local government study commission to undertake a study of local government, conduct hearings, and make a recommendation as to which form of government to adopt and the method of elections.

In 1976, the Big Horn County Local Government Study Commission, after conducting a series of hearings throughout the county, proposed the adoption of the commission–manager form, with five commissioners, three of whom would be elected from single-member districts and two at-large. According to the final report issued by the study commission, an advantage of the district method of elections was that it "assures the Commission view points from all sections of the county."[126] The chairman of the study commission elaborated that one of the reasons for proposing district elections was to provide a better opportunity for Indian representation on the county government.

A referendum was held on the issue, and the precincts on the Indian reservations voted in favor of adopting the form of government recommended by the study commission. The predominantly white precincts in Hardin, however, strongly opposed it, and the referendum was defeated.

The division between the tribes and non-Indian communities is further evident from the number of so-called states' rights groups with a distinctly anti-Indian agenda organized in Montana and Big Horn County in the 1970s. The U.S. Commission on Civil Rights reported in 1981 that

> During the second half of the seventies a backlash arose against Indians and Indian interests. Anti-Indian editorials and articles appeared in both the local and the national media. Non-Indians, and even a few Indians as well, living on or near Indian reservations organized to oppose tribal interests. Senator Mark Hatfield (R-Ore.) said during Senate hearings in 1977 said that "[w]e have found a very significant backlash [against Indians] that by any other name comes out as racism in all its ugly manifestations."[127]

These groups have included Montanans Opposed to Discrimination (MOD), organized in 1974; the Citizens Rights Organization (CRO), which was formed in Big Horn County; and the Interstate Congress for Equal Rights and Responsibilities (ICERR), formed in 1976. The Indian Affairs Committee of the National Association of Counties (NACO) was also formed in 1977. The Montana Association of Counties (MACO) is affiliated with NACO. The Big Horn County MACO representative was Commissioner Alvin Torske, a non-Indian.

In general, these organizations advocate that the states should have exclusive jurisdiction over all non-Indians and non-Indian lands, wherever located. The organizations are also interested in eliminating or terminating the Indian reservations and have clashed with the tribes over specific issues such as taxation, tribal sovereignty, hunting and fishing rights, water rights, and appropriation and development of tribal resources. Joe Medicine Crow says the mentality of MOD is "do not give the Indians the opportunity to enjoy those rights that have been traditionally the white man's rights, don't let them have it."[128]

The U.S. Commission on Civil Rights also concluded that taxation was a "frequent arena of dispute between the States and local government and Indians. States, pressed for funding sources, aggressively sought to tap Indian assets on reservations that under Federal law were to be protected from State incursions. The State of Montana was particularly aggressive in this arena, frequently asserting that tribes were not governmental entities but rather something akin to property owners associations. This argument was rejected by the Supreme Court."[129]

Indian Political Participation in the 1980s

The first modern-day success Indians had at the polls in Big Horn County was in 1982 when Romona Howe, an Indian, was elected to the state legislature, and Bill Joy, who was married to a tribal member and was regarded as "pro Indian," was elected sheriff. One of those who played a central role in these victories was Jim Ruegamer, a non-Indian whose father owned the Ford–Mercury dealership in Hardin.

Ruegamer had spent most of his life in Big Horn County, except for time in California getting a degree in political science from the University of Santa Clara and in Nepal pursuing a personal interest in Buddhism. Ruegamer has a well-developed sense of the absurd in human life and a lively appreciation of the discriminatory treatment that had been inflicted on Indians and the acquiescence in it by many in the white community. And he has an infectious sense of humor, the kind of person who chooses to laugh, rather than despair, at the calamities and absurdities life frequently hands out. It was only a question of time before Ruegamer, a man who was restless to make life a little more rational and equitable, would turn to politics, which he did in 1980 when he won the chair of the Big Horn County Democratic party. And almost the first thing he did drew flack from the white community.

"The party was just flat on its back," he said, "and I wanted to bring some life into it, get some activity going."[130] At his urging, the party undertook two projects: to increase Indian voter registration—because Indians tended to vote Democratic—and to send out mailings urging newly registered voters to support Democratic candidates.

Indian voter registration was significantly depressed in Big Horn County at that time. There were almost no Indian deputy registrars, and some 1,500 to 2,000 eligible Indian voters were unregistered.

One of the Democratic candidates running for county commission in 1980 was Dick Gregory. Ruegamer, Leo Hudetz, and a couple of others registered approximately 1,000 Indian voters and prepared a campaign letter addressed to Indian people. The letter urged Indians to support Democratic candidates, including Gregory, whom the letter pointed out was married to an enrolled member of the Crow Tribe. Gregory reviewed the letter in its final form, and his wife helped stuff envelopes for the mailing.

Gregory won the election, but afterwards he paid a visit to Ruegamer and was decidedly unhappy. "He said he was taking a lot of heat from the ranching people because of the statement in the letter that his wife was Indian," Ruegamer said. "He asked me to put an ad in the Hardin paper saying that the letter was all my responsibility and none of his. He obviously wanted to get some of the white people off his back because he felt he was trapped and tied to the Indians." But Ruegamer refused to take out an ad as requested by Gregory. "Hell no," he said, breaking out in one of his trademark grins. "He had approved the letter himself."[131]

In 1981, Ruegamer became involved in state legislative redistricting and proposed a plan that would keep the Crow and Northern Cheyenne Reservations together. Under the existing plan the Crow Reservation was divided among three districts and the Northern Cheyenne Reservation among two. As a result of the fragmentation of the Indian population, each house district was majority white, ensuring white control of the elections. Ruegamer's proposed plan, however, created two house districts and one senate district with Indian majorities. The boundaries of one of the house districts encompassed most of the Crow Reservation but only two of three Hardin precincts. The other house district encompassed all of the Northern Cheyenne Reservation and a few precincts on the Crow Reservation. The senate district encompassed the entirety of both the Crow and Northern Cheyenne Reservations. "I made the suggestion that the party would be stronger if these discreet minorities, meaning the Cheyenne and the Crow, were allowed to vote in a district, or were allowed to vote together," Ruegamer said.[132]

Local Big Horn County officials, including Commissioner Seader, Representative Conroy, Senator Graham, and Clyde Rader, the chairman of the Democratic Party, supported a reapportionment plan that perpetuated the fragmentation of the Indian community and maintained white majorities in all the house districts. Public hearings were held by the Montana Districting and Apportionment Commission on the various plans in Billings and Helena in August and November of 1982. Ruegamer's plan was adopted by the commission, for implementation in 1984, for the reason that the Voting Rights Act prohibited the unnecessary fragmentation of concentrations of Indian population.

Not only was his plan rejected by other county party officials, but Ruegamer was not reelected as party chairman. "I think it was mostly because I favored my plan," he said, "or a plan that gave Indians a chance to elect someone of their choice. I remember when we had a special meeting to discuss the plans that the man who had been elected to replace me as chair, he was an elderly man and was sitting behind me, reached over and struck me, physically struck me."[133]

The Democratic Party of Big Horn County was traditionally controlled by whites. Some Indians, however, were able to win positions as Democratic precinct committee persons because members were elected from individual precincts and not at-large. Pius Real Bird was one of the first Indians elected as a precinct committeeman in 1975 from the predominantly Indian precinct of Wyola. But he was never given notice of committee meetings and thus never participated in the election of members of the executive committee. "Indians had no real input," he said, "the whites ran the show. They wouldn't listen to our ideas at all."[134]

Before the election in 1982, Ruegamer, his brother Robert, and Leo Hudetz led another registration campaign and succeeded in registering 1,000 to 1,500 new Indian voters. Ruegamer also decided to run for the county commission after four others entered the primary for one open seat. "I figured they would split the white vote and I could win with the Indian vote in view of the increased registration," he reasoned. Crow tribal elections were also being held three weeks before the primary, so he piggy backed on campaigns by tribal members. "I would go to the tribal rallies, be introduced, give a short speech, and have a town crier or Indian politician speak for me in Indian. Then I would leave there and go to the next one. So I took advantage of the situation, and I was surprised that I was the only candidate down there."[135]

His strategy worked. The Hardin vote split four ways between the other four white candidates, and Ruegamer squeaked by with a plurality, getting 37 percent of the votes. Ramona Howe, who was opposed by two whites who split the white vote, won the primary with 42 percent of the vote. Joy, who had four white opponents, also won the primary with about half of the votes.

Many in the white community in Big Horn County were stunned by the results of the 1982 primary elections. The night of the primary Leo Hudetz went to the county courthouse to observe the precinct counts as they came in and were tallied. After the Hardin precincts had been counted, "There was a jubilant feeling among the Hardin people because all of the Hardin candidates were winning," he said. "The place was packed. As soon as the Crow precincts came in, 90 to 99 percent supporting our candidates, immediately the mood dropped. There was cussing. There was complaining we did it illegally, we were campaigning illegally, we were buying people off with dinners, we were paying them off.[136]"

A traditional form of campaigning on the Crow Reservation is to hold a "feast," which is a kind of barbecue or picnic where voters and candidates congregate. This same technique is used to get out the vote on election day and was used at the 1982 primary. Carroll Graham, a non-Indian and a state senator from Big Horn County, charged that election fraud had been committed during the 1982 primary and requested an investigation by the state commissioner of political practices. He complained, among other things, that Indian voters had been bribed with sandwiches and potato chips by the successful primary candidates or their supporters. Jack Lowe, an attorney with the commission, conducted a four-day investigation of the allegations and concluded that no fraud had occurred. According to Lowe, the practices complained of "would raise no eyebrows in some other parts of the state." Lowe concluded that "the most striking feature of Big Horn County politics is this: there is a very unfortunate racial polarization taking place. This election is seen by some as a sort of latter-day Indian uprising."[137]

Ruegamer described the response of whites to the primary election as "collective shock that so many Indians could vote and that those votes would count and elect people."[138] The chairman of the Democratic Party was quoted in the local paper as saying, "We kind of got caught with our pants down."[139] White voters quickly formed a Bipartisan Campaign Committee (BCC) to counter the results of the election. The committee advertised extensively and stressed that Democrats and Republicans should come together for the "election of qualified candidates for office."[140]

Hudetz said, "The white Democrats jumped ship. They said 'we don't like these candidates, the vote doesn't really reflect the true feelings of the voters in Big Horn County, we are leaving the party.' The newspapers referred to us as a splinter group of radicals, but I don't know how 50 percent of the county can be a splinter group. It was a difficult time. They were shocked at what happened, and then it turned everything bitter, and you just had the feeling wherever you went in Hardin, you felt that bitterness."[141]

The BCC recruited white candidates to run a write-in campaign to oppose the Indian or pro-Indian candidates and received widespread support in the white community. The BCC had no Indian members, it supported no Indian candidates, and it opposed only Indians or pro-Indian candidates in contested races. The campaign literature of the BCC raised no substantive issues. Instead, it stated that the candidates chosen at the Democratic Primary were not "qualified" and "did not reflect the majority opinion of the voters in this County."[142]

Pius Real Bird said he began to get calls urging him not to support Ruegamer. "I got about a dozen calls during that time saying, 'Jim Ruegamer is just using you. He's really against the Indian.' The accents of the callers sounded white. You know," he added, "a lot of people don't want to see the Crows prosper. They want to put us in a bag and just keep us there."[143]

At the 1982 general election, the Democratic Party's nominees were strongly challenged by their write-in opponents. Voter turnout was high, but the challengers could not overcome the inherent difficulties of mounting a write-in campaign, and the Democratic candidates managed to win. Howe got about 54 percent of the vote, Ruegamer 52 percent, and Joy 53 percent.

Robert Ruegamer was elected to the Hardin City Council the same year. However, when he ran for reelection in 1985, he was defeated. "I don't imagine that my registering Indian voters for the Democratic Party enhanced my position in the city of Hardin at all," he said.[144]

In the state legislative session following the 1982 elections, Senator Graham introduced a bill making it a crime to give anything "of value" to a voter on election day. Anything costing more than a dollar was deemed to be something of value within the meaning of the statute. The bill, which was derided by some as the "baloney sandwich bill," failed passage in the legislature.

Ruegamer became increasingly ostracized by the Democratic Party. "There was always, I suppose, an undercurrent of resistance to registering so many Indians to vote," he said, "but suggesting that they be allowed to vote in one legislative district was, I guess, well, too much to swallow." And after he won the election in 1982, "that is when I was perceived as being pro-Indian, not so much because of anything I did, but because of where my votes came from." According to Ruegamer, "it is not possible to be responsive to the Indian community and still enjoy the support of whites. As an elected official, you have a duty to provide services equally, but when you do that, you are targeted by whites as being pro-Indian."[145]

In 1983, as a result of increased Indian voter registration, Indians were also able to elect Janine Windy Boy, a member of the Crow Tribe, as chairman of the Democratic Party. She was the first Indian ever to hold the position. "I was elected at the party's semi-annual convention by a secret ballot," she said, "and after they announced my name as the winner, almost all of the white people in the room, down to the last person, got up and walked out of the meeting."[146] The woman who had opposed her for the chairman's position later quit the Democratic Party and became a Republican.

"There was a lot of hatred at that time," said Pius Real Bird. "All those years when we got defeated we stayed with the party. But when they lost, they left. The whites removed themselves from the Democratic Party."[147]

Prior to the *Windy Boy* litigation brought in 1983, no Indian had ever been elected to either the county commission or to the city council of Hardin, the county seat. Not surprisingly, few Indians were employed by the county. As late as 1974, only one Indian was a full-time county employee. A decade later, the number had climbed to six, still only 2 percent of the total full-time workforce.

Few American Indians were appointed to local boards and commissions. From 1924 to 1983, some 455 people were appointed to various boards (health board, planning board, and so forth) by the county commission, but only fourteen (3 percent) of them were Indian. In 1983 Joe Medicine Crow, who had extensive experience in museum work and served on the boards of nationally known historical societies and museums, was nominated by one of the commissioners to the Big Horn County Historical Museum's board. The nomination died for want of a second. Two Indians, Urban Red Fox and Leonard Bends, were nominated by one of the county commissioners in 1985 to fill a vacancy on the Local Government Study Commission. The nominations died for want of a second.

Indians were also excluded from service on juries as a matter of local custom and practice. Coroner's juries in Big Horn County were chosen by the coroner from friends and acquaintances he found on the streets on an as-needed basis. Between 1966 and 1983, of 331 persons selected to serve on coroner's juries, only three (1 percent) were Indians.

District court and justice court jurors were chosen from the list of registered voters, which underrepresented Indians. In addition, no effort was made to enforce subpoenas against Indians who were actually summoned for jury duty. The tribal police offered to help serve the subpoenas, but the offer was refused; as a result, Indians were significantly underrepresented on district and justice court juries.

In 1982, the city council of Hardin proposed that a Law Enforcement Commission be created to consider complaints by citizens about abuses by county police officers. The initial proposal called for a member to be appointed from the city of Hardin, from the county, from the Northern Cheyenne Tribe, and from the Crow Tribe, with a fifth member to be elected by the four. The Crow and Northern Cheyenne seats, however, were rejected by the city and county in the final proposal. As late as 1985, the commission had never had an Indian member.

After the 1982 elections, Indians were generally unsuccessful in their efforts to win public office. In 1984, Patrick Doss, a member of the Crow Tribe, ran for the Big Horn County Board of Commissioners. He was born and raised in Billings and attended school there. He has a degree from the University of Montana and is manager of the Division of Environmental Quality for the Crow Tribe. Doss is well-spoken and, he says, does not "look" like an American Indian in appearance.

Doss ran for county commissioner as a Democrat and tried to conduct an issues campaign involving fiscal responsibility and county–tribal relations. He also campaigned extensively, attended public functions, and made several mailings to every registered voter in the county. But after about two months on the campaign trail, he became convinced that it was futile to try to get white votes. "I heard many times during the campaign that . . . non-Indians were not allowed to participate in tribal government, therefore, there should be no Indian involvement in county government. I found that as I talked to the constituency throughout Big Horn County, that Indians were not looked upon as competent human beings able to become involved in the process. I found there is very little opportunity for Indian individuals to participate in county government." He lost the primary to his white opponent, with most of his support coming from Crow Agency and very little from Hardin. "I believe," he said, "that issues were not important to the public at large, it had turned into an Indian versus a non-Indian campaign, and it was very obvious. My defeat was based on the fact that I'm a Crow Indian."[148]

The Hardin Chamber of Commerce conducted a candidate forum prior to the general election in 1984. As chairman of the Democratic Party, Windy Boy was present and assisted. One of the ground rules set by the chamber was that no written questions from the audience would be allowed concerning the issue of race or Indians. She asked why and was told by a lady from the chamber that "she didn't want any trouble here." Some 250 people attended, only about half a dozen of whom were Indian. Questions were also allowed from the audience, and some of those audience members peppered the two Indian candidates who were present with questions like, "What right do you have to run for county office?" "What right do you have to vote on policies that affect taxes when you don't pay taxes?" and "You're advocating taxation without representation, aren't you?"[149]

English is a second language for a substantial number of Crow and Northern Cheyenne, and many of them needed assistance in voting. Election materials were not bilingual but were printed only in English. As Dessie Bad Bear, who became an election judge at a Crow Agency precinct in 1976, explained, "Some of the Crow, they can't hardly read, and they need assistance in reading and where to write their names." Prior to the 1984 election, the bilingual Indian judges routinely spoke in Crow or Northern Cheyenne to those whom they were assisting. At the 1984 election, however, poll watchers who were associated with the BCC objected to bilingual election judges speaking with any voters in Indian languages. Bad Bear recalled that "an older Crow couple came in and asked me in Crow where to write their name, and this white lady said, 'Don't talk Indian in here, talk English.' I was scared and I didn't say anymore."[150] The aggressive conduct of the poll watchers intimidated some of the Indians, who left without voting. The Indian judges stopped giving assistance in Crow until Leo Hudetz, the treasurer of the Democratic Party, told them that it was all right to give assistance in Indian languages.

On election day, Tim Bernardis, a librarian and part-time instructor at Little Big Horn College, was handing out stickers at the polling place at Crow Agency for a write-in candidate for the county commission. Senator Graham approached him and said, "Do you realize you are to be 200 feet from the polling place? You people wouldn't want this election thrown out, would you?" Bernardis said the senator's "entire language was spiced by a lot of foul language, a lot of damns, a lot of hells. I got the feeling he was attempting to intimidate me to get me out of there."[151] Bernadis refused to move, and Graham left. Shortly after that, Bernardis was relieved by Tyrone Ten Bear.

Ten Bear continued to pass out stickers but kept approximately 300 yards from the polling place. Soon, he was approached by four or five police officers from Big Horn County and the BIA federal force. They said, "Based on the complaint at the county courthouse of Mr. Graham you are supposed to leave your area because you are in violation of a voting law." And then they left, saying, "We just want to put it on record that we informed you that you are in violation of the law."[152]

In the 1984 general election, white poll watchers from Hardin came to observe the counting of ballots at the Crow Agency precinct. This was the first time this had ever happened, and Indians found it intimidating.

Clarence Belue, a non-Indian, ran successfully for county attorney in the 1984 general election. Although he had substantial Indian support, he ran a low-key campaign and avoided the appearance of being "pro-Indian." After his election he tried to administer the law fairly and made complaints about the exclusion of Indians from local juries and selective enforcement of the law. As a result, he received crank calls from people calling him an "Indian lover" and telling him to move to the reservation. "I used to be, I think, a respected leader," he says. "I was president of the Kiwanis Club, for example, but now I feel unwelcome there, and that is something that has occurred in the last two or three years since I began publically to support fair treatment for Indians. You can't be fair towards Indians and not be accused by whites of being pro-Indian."[153] Following the expiration of his four-year term, he did not seek reelection as county attorney.

Following implementation of the new legislative districting plan in 1984, Ramona Howe was elected to the state house and Bill Yellowtail, a Crow, was elected to the state senate. Both were elected from the majority-Indian districts.

The first Indian to win a school board election was Wayne Moccasin in 1984. Two seats were open, and all voters were thus entitled to vote for two positions. There were three non-Indian candidates. Moccasin instructed his supporters to vote only for him, in what is called a single-shot vote. This strategy was adopted so that Moccasin's supporters would not have to vote for his opponents and would thereby maximize Moccasin's chances of election. The strategy worked, and Moccasin was elected. His supporters, however, had to forfeit half of their voting strength. Even with this strategy, Moccasin came in second, beating the third-place candidate by only thirty-four votes.

A number of former Indian candidates have said they did not go door to door in the City of Hardin because of the prejudice they encountered there. Gail Small is a member of the Northern Cheyenne Tribe and a graduate of the University of Oregon law school, where she studied natural resource and water law. In 1984, she ran for state representative in a district that comprised parts of Big Horn, Rosebud, and Powder River counties, including two precincts in Hardin. She attempted to raise issues of natural resources and water in her campaign, because the district encompassed a coal-rich, water-lean area. But she was unable to do so. The only issue in her campaign was race, she said. "I just wasn't received favorably in Hardin. I couldn't even begin discussing issues with these people. Some of the ranchers were also very racist, and I was totally unprepared for it. I was humiliated many times, and because of that I'm not going to run for any type of political office in that area."[154]

Whites have regarded increased Indian political participation as a threat to the status quo and have resisted it. According to a government report, "Significant change in the composition of the county government would constitute an important alteration of the existing stratification system and would almost certainly, in the short run at least, create additional tensions and conflict between the anglos, the Crow, and potentially, the Northern Cheyenne."[155] After the 1984 election, more than a quarter of Indian voters were purged from the county rolls for failure to vote in the presidential election.

Indians have also experienced significant problems in voter registration. In the 1982 and 1984 elections, Indians who had registered to vote were often not on the list of registered voters. Even though they brought proof of registration with them, county election officials refused to allow election judges to permit them to vote. Morley Langdon said he had registered both Indian and white voters at his churches but later found that only Indian voters were not on the registration lists. Whites whom he had registered had no problems in voting. Leo Hudetz said Indians he had registered prior to the 1982 and 1984 elections were not on the voter list and were not allowed to vote.

Clo Small said Indians she had registered were not permitted to vote, and that she was herself dropped from the registration list even though she had voted in the previous election. On one occasion, she and her husband were required to vote at different precincts over twenty miles apart.

In 1984, the clerk of court began to number voter registration cards and write down the name of the person to whom cards were given in order to keep a record of who was doing voter registration. Gail Small said when she was a candidate for the state legislature in 1984, she attempted to obtain blank registration forms from the courthouse to hand out at political breakfasts she was attending at Busby and Kirby in Big Horn County. She made a special trip to Hardin, approximately fifty miles from her home, but was turned away by the county registrar. "She told me she had a few days earlier given some cards to another Cheyenne woman in Busby, and that if I wanted to have any cards I would have to get them from her, but she wasn't going to give out any more cards to Northern Cheyenne until those she had given out were returned."[156] Small was forced to go to the state commissioner on campaign practices to get registration cards.

That same year, Mark Small and his wife, Clo, went to Hardin to do some shopping. Before leaving Mark stopped at the courthouse to get some registration cards. He went inside while his wife waited in the car. He returned with about a dozen cards and asked his wife, who is non-Indian, if she would go in and get some more cards. She did and returned with around 100 cards, "a whole stack of them," said Small, "without any questions asked."[157]

In the 1985 school election, Theresa Plenty Hoops, a Shoshone, and Frank Back Bone, a Crow, ran for two vacant seats. They were opposed by whites, and both lost. White turnout in school board elections was typically in the 20 percent to 30 percent range. In the 1985 election, which followed the election of Moccasin and in which there were two Indian candidates, white turnout jumped to more than 50 percent.

Back Bone says he tried to campaign in downtown Hardin, but of the five people he first approached, "just one shook hands with me. The other four just walked on, ignored me." After that, he had a "feeling of rejection because I'm an Indian candidate,"[158] and he limited his campaigning in Hardin to those people he personally knew. When he filed for office, Back Bone thought he would receive support from Hardin residents, because he had attended high school and coached softball there and had a number of acquaintances. He now believes that it is impossible for him, as an Indian, to run successfully for the school board.

An estimated forty-eight Indians cast votes in Hardin in the 1985 school board election. Back Bone received forty-nine votes in Hardin. Theresa Plenty Hoops received almost the same number of votes as Back Bone. She assumed their vote totals would be different because she was not born in the county, had not grown up there, and was a Shoshone and a woman. However, what they had in common, and what was apparently important to white voters, was that they were both Indians.

Campaigns for public office in Big Horn County are not generally important for the issues they raise. Instead, people tend to run on their status—that is, who they are in the community—and draw on the contacts they have built up over the course of their lives. Where whites are in the majority and where de facto segregation in churches, clubs, and so forth is a fact of life, minority candidates who are excluded from or do not belong to these organizations are significantly disadvantaged in establishing meaningful contact with white voters.

Convinced that the at-large systems discriminated against Indian voters, Mark Small and several tribal members met with members of the county commission and school board to see if they would be open to having a system of district elections where Indians could elect candidates of their choice. But the answer was, "'the system is working.' Obviously it was working for them," Small said. "They didn't want Indian people involved. And they would say, 'Do you have competent people? Do you have people educated enough to run a county, or be involved in the school board?'"[159] It was after the failure of these meeting that Small, Windy Boy, and the others went forward with the lawsuit challenging the at-large method of elections.

Windy Boy v. County of Big Horn

The plaintiffs' analysis of election returns showed that voting in Big Horn County was significantly polarized along racial lines. A simple comparison of election results from the predominantly Indian Crow Agency precinct and the predominantly white Hardin precincts between 1924 and 1985 showed that in elections in which Indian or "pro-Indian" candidates had run, the candidates did well in the Indian precinct and very poorly in the Hardin precincts. Over this sixty-year period Indians ran as Republicans and as Democrats and were of different ages, genders, backgrounds, and religions. Nevertheless, the election results from these precincts were consistent.

Joe Floyd, a political science professor at Eastern Montana College in Billings (now Montana State University Billings), did an analysis of voting behavior and elections in Big Horn County. He examined the 1974, 1982, and 1984 general elections; the 1982 and 1984 primary elections; and the 1983, 1984, and 1985 school board elections in which Indian or pro-Indian and non-Indian candidates opposed each other. He determined that in the general elections, approximately 87 percent of non-Indians voted for non-Indian candidates, whereas about 90 percent of Indians voted for Indian candidates. In the primary elections, about 95 percent of non-Indians voted for non-Indian candidates, whereas about 84 percent of Indians voted for Indian candidates. In the school elections, about 93 percent of non-Indian voters voted for non-Indian candidates, whereas about 80 percent of Indians voted for Indian candidates. According to Dr. Floyd, "I believe it is without question that there is racially polarized voting in Big Horn County in the elections I analyzed."[160]

The county defended its at-large system on a number of grounds: that partisanship, not race, explained voting patterns in Big Horn County; that plaintiffs had not demonstrated that voters in the county were motivated by racial animus; that past discrimination against Indians was the fault of the federal government, not the county government; and that the county government was increasingly responsive to Indian concerns.[161] Following a lengthy trial, the federal court rejected the county's arguments and held that at-large elections for the county commission and school board diluted Indian voting strength in violation of Section 2 of the Voting Rights Act. In doing so, the court made extensive findings of past and continuing discrimination:

- There was "substantial probative evidence that the rights of Indians to vote has been interfered with, and in some cases denied, by the county."
- The evidence "tends to show an intent to discriminate against Indians."
- The county had failed "to appoint Indians to county boards and commissions."
- "[T]here has been discrimination in the appointment of deputy registrars of voters and election judges limiting Indian involvement in the mechanics of registration and voting."
- "[I]n the past there were laws prohibiting voting precincts on Indian reservations."
- Politics in Big Horn County was "race conscious" and "racially polarized."

- "[T]here is racial bloc voting in Big Horn County and . . . there is evidence that race is a factor in the minds of voters in making voting decisions."
- "Indians have lost land, had their economies disrupted, and been denigrated by the policies of the government at all levels."
- "[D]iscrimination in hiring has hindered Indian involvement in government, making it more difficult for Indians to participate in the political process."
- "[R]ace is an issue and subtle racial appeals, by both Indians and whites, affect county politics."
- There was "a strong desire on the part of some white citizens to keep Indians out of Big Horn County government."
- "Indians who had registered to vote did not appear on voting lists."
- "Indians who had voted in primary elections had their names removed from voting lists and were not allowed to vote in the subsequent general elections."
- Indians were "refused voter registration cards by the county."
- "When an Indian was elected Chairman of the Democratic Party, white members of the party walked out of the meeting."
- "Unfounded charges of voter fraud have been alleged against Indians and the state investigator who investigated the charges commented on the racial polarization in the county."
- There was "[i]ndifference to the concerns of Indian parents" by school board members.
- "English is a second language for many Indians, further hampering participation."
- A depressed socioeconomic status makes it "more difficult for Indians to participate in the political process and there is evidence linking these figures to past discrimination."[162]

The county filed a notice of appeal of the district court's decision but later withdrew it. As a remedy, the court adopted single-member districts for the county commission and the school board. At the next election held under the new plan, an Indian was elected to the county commission, the first in Big Horn County's history.

Dramatic Change in Big Horn County Demographics

The American Indian population in Big Horn County has increased significantly since the *Windy Boy* decision. On the basis of 1980 census data, Indians were 46.2 percent of the population of the county. By 1990, Indians were 56 percent of the population, and as of 2000 the Indian population had increased to 61.4 percent. Given that they are now the largest demographic group in the county, Indians have regularly been able to elect candidates of their choice to county offices. Today, two members of the county commission (John Pretty on Top and John T. Doyle, Jr.) are American Indians, as is the sheriff (Lawrence Big Hair), the county attorney (Georgette Hogan), the clerk of court (Karen Yarlott-Molina), and the justice of the peace (Leroy Not Afraid). Ironically, the single-member district plan adopted by the court for the county commission to provide Indians with an equal opportunity to elect candidates of their choice now provides the white minority the comparable opportunity in the majority-white district that encompasses the city of Hardin.

Ongoing Allegations of Indian Election Fraud

Despite the gains Indians have made in achieving public office in Big Horn County, racial polarization remains a fact of life there. One manifestation of that polarization is the ongoing allegations by white residents and members of states' rights organizations of election fraud on the Crow Reservation. Members of two such organizations, Citizens Equal Rights Alliance (CERA) and Montana Citizens Rights Alliance (MCRA), filed suit in June 2007 alleging various forms of voter fraud—double voting, insecure ballot boxes, and the endorsement of candidates by the tribal government.[163] As an alternative remedy, and taking a page out of the state's long history of discrimination against Indians, the plaintiffs sought the removal of all polling places from the reservation, which would have effectively disfranchised large numbers of Indians and facilitated control of county elections by whites.

Tribal and county election officials insisted the charges were baseless and noted that one of the plaintiffs, Christopher Kortlander, had made similar allegations in the past. When the charges were proven to be groundless, he apologized and sent the clerk and recorder a bunch of roses.

Nellie Little Light, a member of the Crow Tribe, works for the Big Horn county clerk and recorder, where she has been employed for sixteen years. "No double voting took place," she said. "That is just not true. I am personally familiar with about everybody at Crow, and there was no double voting." "This is a very prejudiced place," she added. "We have grown up with it. When it comes to the elections, the whites are sore losers. That's why they brought this suit."[164]

On November 5, 2007, the federal court granted a motion to dismiss filed by county and state election officials and held the plaintiffs failed to state a violation of federal law. The court also held the plaintiffs failed to show the defendants acted with any discriminatory intent or racial animus toward the plaintiffs or white voters. Tribal members sought to intervene in opposition to the complaint, but their motion was rendered moot by the dismissal of the plaintiffs' case. The CERA plaintiffs, however, were later allowed to file an amended complaint joining Department of Interior and BIA officials as parties. But in March 2008, and without explanation, they dismissed their complaint, bringing the litigation to a close.

Jim Ruegamer says: "A few diehards still exist in Big Horn County, and there is still a lot of polarization in the vote. But things have changed. It's not like it used to be. Plenty of Indians are now at the courthouse, and a lot more Indians know more whites and vice versa. Having Indians involved in the political process and in office has helped bring about the change, but it has been slow—really, really slow."[165]

Blaine County

The *Windy Boy* decision led to other voting rights litigation on behalf of American Indians in Montana. Blaine County, located in north central Montana, is 45 percent Indian and home to the Fort Belknap Reservation (Gros Ventre and Assiniboine).[166] The county commission consisted of three members elected at-large. Despite the county's large Indian population, no Indian had ever been elected to the commission. In 1999, the United States sued the county alleging that its at-large elections diluted Indian voting strength in violation of Section 2 of the Voting Rights Act.[167] Both the district court and court of appeals agreed that the challenged system violated the statute. Indians were geographically compact and politically cohesive, whereas whites voted sufficiently as a bloc usually to defeat the candidates preferred by Indian voters.[168]

Turning to the totality of circumstances, the courts concluded the following:

- There was a history of official discrimination against Indians, including "extensive evidence of official discrimination by federal, state, and local governments against Montana's American Indian population."
- There was racially polarized voting that "made it impossible for an American Indian to succeed in an at-large election."
- Voting procedures, including staggered terms of office and "the County's enormous size [which] makes it extremely difficult for American Indian candidates to campaign county-wide," enhanced the opportunities for discrimination against Indians.
- Depressed socioeconomic conditions existed for Indians.
- There was a tenuous justification for the at-large system, in that at-large elections were not required by state law while "the county government depends largely on residency districts for purposes of road maintenance and appointments to County Boards, Authorities and Commissions."[169]

Tribal members, represented by the ACLU, were permitted to intervene at the remedy stage of the case and supported a single-member districting plan containing a majority-Indian district. The court adopted such a plan, and at the next election an Indian (Delores Plumage) was elected from the majority-Indian district.[170]

Rosebud and Roosevelt Counties and Ronan School District 30

Two other counties, Rosebud and Roosevelt, and a local school district, Ronan School District 30, were also sued for their use of at-large elections as diluting Indian voting strength. Rosebud County is home to the Northern Cheyenne Reservation. Roosevelt County is home to the Fort Peck Reservation (Assiniboine and Sioux). Ronan School District 30 is in Lake County on the Flathead Indian Reservation (Confederated Salish and Kootenai).[171] Rather than face protracted litigation, as Big Horn and Blaine counties had elected to do, the three jurisdictions entered into settlement agreements adopting district elections.[172]

The difficulty American Indians have experienced in getting elected to public office was particularly evident in the Ronan school district. From 1972 to 1999, seventeen Indians had run for the school board, and only one, Ronald Bick, had been elected. Bick, who had no formal or announced tribal affiliation at the time, was elected to the board in 1990. However, when he ran for reelection in 1993, and after it became known that he had joined the Flathead Nation, he was defeated. The settlement plan agreed to by the parties called for an increase in the size of the school board from five to seven members and the creation of a majority-Indian district that would elect two members to the school board. At the ensuing election held under the new plan, two Indians were elected from the majority-Indian district.

American Indians have made undeniable progress in political participation and office holding in Montana, and much of it has been as the result of litigation under the Voting Rights Act. White resistance is still prevalent, as evidenced by a pervasive pattern of racial bloc voting and ongoing antagonism between the Indian and non-Indian communities. A growing Indian population and an increased percentage of Indian voters, however, should continue to advance the goal of equal political participation envisioned by the U.S. Constitution and the Voting Rights Act.

CHAPTER 4

Montana II

There are a total of seven Indian reservations in Montana: Crow, Northern Cheyenne, Flathead (Confederated Salish and Kootenai), Blackfeet, Fort Peck (Assiniboine and Sioux), Fort Belknap (Assiniboine and Gros Ventre), and Rocky Boy's (Chippewa-Cree). The Little Shell, a band of the Chippewa Tribe, is recognized by the state but has no designated reservation.

Like the Crow and Northern Cheyenne, the other American Indian tribes in Montana were subjected to systematic discrimination that has isolated them and diminished their ability to participate in local, state, and federal elections. The tribes were forced to cede large portions of their traditional homelands and were confined to reservations. The Treaty of Fort Laramie of 1851 established territorial boundaries for the Sioux, Crow, Assiniboine, and Gros Ventre tribes and guaranteed federal protection for those tribes against "depredations" by U.S. citizens.[1] Four years later, in 1855, the United States entered into the Treaty of Hell Gate with the confederated tribes of the Flathead, Kootenai, and Upper Pend d'Oreille. The treaty reserved 1.25 million acres in the Jocko Valley for the tribes, closed the Bitter Root Valley to white settlements, and ceded 16.4 million acres to the United States.[2] That same year, the United States entered into the Lame Bull's Treaty with, among others, the Blackfeet, Gros Ventre, Flathead, Upper Pend d'Oreille, and Kootenai tribes. That treaty reserved 13.3 million acres for the Blackfeet in north-central Montana, established for the collective tribes "a common hunting-ground for ninety-nine years" consisting of 19,000 square miles, and guaranteed federal protection against "depredations and other unlawful acts [by] white men."[3]

From the time of its organization as a territory in 1864, Montana constantly pressured the federal government to terminate the reservations and extinguish Indian title to land. As one early resolution put it, Montana's interests "would be greatly promoted, and its early settlement hastened" by extinguishing Indian title or revising treaty terms so that settlers and others could mine for gold and other minerals, undertake agricultural pursuits, raise stock, and drive beef cattle over Indian property.[4]

The land that had been set aside for the Blackfeet and Flatheads was a special target of the territorial legislature. It adopted a resolution in 1867 seeking to have Indian title in the northern territory, "known as the Blackfeet country," extinguished so that the "industrious white population" could look for gold. The alternative, it said, was "a general Indian war, with all its horrors."[5] It requested Congress to appoint a commission to supervise the removal of the Indians. Another resolution said that the establishment of Indian reservations would be "a staggering blow to the progress of civilization" and "would be valueless to the barbarian."[6]

The legislature also requested Congress to open up the Bitter Root Valley and passed a resolution that it was "impossible for the two races to live on amicable terms" because the Flathead tribe's "habits and customs are so different from those of the whites."[7] It asked that a commissioner be appointed to remove the Flatheads from the valley.

In response to the pressure to open Indian lands to white settlement, the United States entered into a number of treaties that further reduced the land base of the Blackfeet, the Assiniboines, and the Gros Ventre but again promised that "[n]o white person" would be "permitted to reside or make settlement" on the much-reduced reservations.[8] Despite these representations, tribal lands were reduced through a series of congressional enactments and executive orders. An 1872 act removed the Flatheads from the Bitter Root Valley to the Joco reservation and opened the valley for white settlement and the railroad.[9] By executive order, a new reservation for Indians in northern Montana was established in 1873, with more land opened for white settlement.[10] The following year, Congress removed the Teton Valley from the land reserved for the Indians.[11] Some 4.6 million acres of reservation land was transferred to the public domain in 1880.[12] Congress appropriated money in 1886 "to enable the Secretary of the Interior to negotiate with the various bands or tribes of Indians in Northern Montana . . . for a reduction of the respective reservations, or for a removal therefrom to other reservations."[13] Then, in 1888, Congress ratified an agreement with the tribes ceding all their rights to the reserved lands in northern Montana—17.5 million acres—for $4.3 million and accepting three much smaller parcels surrounding the Blackfeet Agency, the Fort Belknap Agency, and the Fort Peck Agency.[14] Thereafter, Indian lands transferred to the public domain were opened to both white settlement and the railroad and were available for purchase under the provision of the mineral land laws. The tribes opposed these reductions but were told by government officials they had no choice: "The white men will come after mineral in spite of all that you and the government can do."[15]

Following passage of the Dawes Act in 1887, pressure from Montana to reduce tribal lands proceeded apace. The state legislature adopted a number of resolutions seeking to have the Flathead Reservation "thrown open to actual settlers and miners." It described the reservation as possessing "magnificent agricultural land" and being "practically uninhabited by any one."[16] Although the land was in fact occupied by Indians, they apparently did not qualify as inhabitants.

The state legislature similarly adopted resolutions seeking to have the Fort Peck Reservation opened for white settlement, representing that it contained "many thousand acres of desirable agricultural land . . . which is now of no material benefit to the said Indians."[17] The legislature requested that this "most fertile and productive valleys in the State of Montana [would] make homes for thousands of families" for "farming and stock raising" and should be opened "under conditions similar to the opening of the Crow and Flathead Indian Reservations."[18]

In response to the continuing pressure from the state, and the entire assimilation and allotment movement of the latter part of the nineteenth century and early part of the twentieth century, Congress continued to allot the land of Montana Indians. In 1904, it passed the Flathead Allotment Act, which provided for the survey, break-up, and allotment of all lands on the Flathead Reservation and, after allotment to Indians, for the sale and disposal of all surplus lands.[19] Congress opened the Fort Peck Reservation for allotment in 1908.[20] In 1921, Congress passed the Fort Belknap Allotment Act, allowing for the allotment of all unreserved land, granting land to the state of Montana for common-school purposes, and providing that Fort Belknap Indian children "shall be permitted to attend the public schools . . . on the same condition as the children of white citizens."[21]

Congress originally proposed to relocate or deport to Canada the Cree Indians residing in Montana, who were characterized as homeless or landless.[22] Later, it appropriated money to settle the band of Chippewa and Cree Indians led by Chief Rocky Boy (the correct translation of his name is Stone Child) on public lands or on some other Indian reservation in Montana.[23] In 1916, Congress reserved 56,035 acres on the abandoned Fort Assiniboine Military Reservation for the "Rocky Boys Band."[24] The reservation was expanded by 45,523 acres in 1947, bringing it to its current size.

The land ceded from the Greater Blackfeet Reservation between 1855 and 1874 was in excess of fifteen million acres.[25] The ceded land transferred by the 1886 and 1887 agreements was in excess of seventeen million acres.[26] There is virtual unanimity that not one of the cessions or allotments of land was done with the consent of the affected tribes, and frequently such cessions and allotments were in open violation of treaties or agreements. Although the 1895 agreement with the Blackfeet provided that the break-up and allotments of the reservation would be made only at the written request of "a majority of the adult males of the tribe," Congress ordered the survey, break-up, and sale of "surplus" land in 1907 without tribal consent.[27]

In a similar manner, the Flathead Indians did not consent to the opening of their reservation and the allotment of surplus land. As one court has held, "[i]t is clear that [the tribes] did not consent to the opening of the [Flathead] Reservation and the sale of surplus land in [the Hell Gate Treaty of] 1855, nor, for that matter, at any time thereafter."[28] Grants of land to railroads and the reservation of a site for the town of Poplar were also made without the consent of Fort Peck Indians.[29]

The U.S. Court of Claims subsequently held in 1935 that the United States deprived the Blackfeet and Fort Belknap reservation Indians, through various treaties, agreements, and orders between 1855 and 1910, of 12,261,749 acres without compensation, and that they were entitled to be paid $6,130,874.[30] In the late 1960s, the claims commission found that the consideration of twenty-nine cents an acre paid by the United States to the Blackfeet, Gros Ventre, Assiniboine, and Sioux tribes of the Blackfeet and Fort Peck reservation Indians in exchange for 14,969,156 acres was "unconscionable on its face."[31] The U.S. Indian Claims Commission also found that the consideration of $593,377 paid by the United States to the Flathead, Upper Pend d'Oreille, and Kootenai Indians in exchange for 12,005,000 acres was so inadequate as to be "unconscionable." A proper valuation was set at $5,300,000.[32] In another opinion, the court held the Flathead Tribe was entitled to recover $6,066.668.78 plus interest for lands taken without the Indian's consent by Congress and allotted pursuant to the 1904 Flathead Allotment Act.[33]

Although Indians were assigned to reservations, many remained landless and essentially homeless. The state legislature noted in the 1940s and 1950s that 1,500 to 2,000 Indians were living on the outskirts of various Montana cities "in makeshift dwellings"; for the most part, they were "ill-fed, ill-clothed" and their living conditions "are deplorable, in that said Indians do not receive the common necessaries of life."[34] One of the most notorious examples of landless Indian poverty was "Hill 57" outside of Great Falls, where Chippewa-Cree lived in cardboard houses, tents, and converted car bodies.[35]

Today, the Flathead Reservation consists of 1.3 million acres, the Blackfeet Reservation of 1.5 million acres, the Fort Peck Reservation of 2 million acres, and the Fort Belknap Reservation of 675,147 acres.

1990 Redistricting

Earl Old Person, the chair of the Blackfeet Indian Tribe, and other tribal members in Montana brought suit in 1996 (*Old Person v. Cooney*) challenging the 1992 redistricting plans for the state house and senate. They contended that the plans diluted Indian voting strength in the area encompassed by the Blackfeet and Flathead reservations (including portions of Flathead, Lake, Glacier, and Pondera Counties), where an additional majority-Indian house district and a majority-Indian senate district could be drawn.[36]

Since 1972, the Montana constitution has granted the exclusive power to conduct legislative redistricting to a Districting and Apportionment Commission. The commission is reconstituted every ten years in advance of the release of the federal census and consists of five members, four of whom are chosen by the majority and minority leaders of each house. The fifth member is selected by the four commissioners, and if they cannot agree, by the state supreme court. The commission must hold at least one public hearing on its proposed plan at the state capitol. The legislature is given an opportunity to comment on the plan, but the commission is not bound by any recommendations it may make. Upon the filing of the plan by the commission with the secretary of state, the plan becomes law and the commission is dissolved.[37]

On the basis of 1990 census data, Indians comprised 6 percent of the total population and 4.8 percent of the voting-age population (VAP) of Montana. Although the state population increased by 1.6 percent between 1980 and 1990, the Indian population had not only not vanished—as some had predicted—but it increased 27.9 percent. Approximately 63 percent of the Indian population lived on the state's seven Indian reservations.[38]

The preexisting 1982 plan contained only one majority-Indian house district for the Montana State Legislature: House District 9 on the Blackfeet Reservation in Glacier County.[39] The 1982 plan also effectively fragmented the Indian population in other parts of the state by dividing the Fort Belknap Reservation between two senate districts, the Fort Peck Reservation among three senate districts, the Rocky Boy Reservation between two house districts, and the Blackfeet Reservation among four house districts. The Flathead Reservation was divided among eight house districts.

As a result of the growth in Indian population reflected in the 1990 census, three majority-white districts under the 1982 plan had become majority Indian: House District 20 (portions of Fort Peck), House District 99 (portions of Crow), and Senate District 50 (portions of Crow and Northern Cheyenne).[40] Another district, House District 100 (portions of Crow and Northern Cheyenne), was approximately 50 percent Indian in light of the new census.

The election of two Indians to the state legislature—Ramona Howe to the house in 1982 and Bill Yellowtail to the senate in 1984—had a strong catalytic effect and intensified Indian interest in the 1990 redistricting and the possibility of creating additional majority-Indian house and senate districts. In anticipation of the upcoming hearings before the redistricting commission, the tribes prepared a number of plans that would keep the reservations intact and combine them to create majority-Indian districts.

The Flathead Tribe proposed a plan creating an additional house district encompassing the reservation, which could be combined with the existing majority-Indian house district at Blackfeet to create an additional majority-Indian senate district. The plan was endorsed by the Blackfeet Nation and the Montana–Wyoming Tribal Chairmen Association, and the 1992 redistricting proposal of the Flathead Nation and Blackfeet Nation said that "all of Montana's Indian citizens are a 'community of interest' and have similar needs, concerns, and identity—as Indian people." The plan was also endorsed, and for similar reasons, by the Missoula Women for Peace, the Missoula Indian Alcohol and Drug Service, the ACLU of Montana, and the Missoula County Democratic Central Committee. The tribal proposal complied with the mandatory and discretionary criteria later adopted by the redistricting commission in that it was composed of compact and contiguous territory, contained minimum population deviations, avoided diluting minority voting strength, considered local governmental units, preserved communities of interest, and ignored the residences of incumbents.

The tribes also prepared a plan that combined the Rocky Boy's and Fort Belknap reservations into a majority-Indian house district. That district could be linked with the majority-Indian house district in the area of Fort Peck to create a majority-Indian senate district. And again, the tribal proposals complied with the mandatory and discretionary criteria adopted by the redistricting commission and were endorsed by the tribal councils from both reservations.

The Districting and Apportionment Commission appointed in 1990 consisted of five non-Indians. They held twelve hearings on redistricting around the state, each of which was usually preceded by an afternoon work or planning session. All the sessions were recorded on audiotapes, which were later transcribed for use at trial. The statements made by the commissioners during their planning sessions, as opposed to during the public meetings when they were more circumspect, can only be described as overtly racial and showed an intent to limit Indian political participation.

The Flathead–Blackfeet proposal was first considered by the commission at its meeting at Kalispell on April 3, 1992. In their discussion of the Voting Rights Act at the afternoon session, the commissioners joked about the racial fairness provisions of Section 2. Commissioner Pinsoneault wanted to know if the French were protected. "How about the French, I'm French?" he asked. Commissioner Rehberg replied, "How about Republicans?" According to Commissioner Frisbee, "We're a minority, right?" "[A]nd men?" asked Commissioner Rehberg, amid general laughter, "How about men?"[41] There was, of course, no evidence that men, Republicans, or the French had ever been discriminated against in voting as had Indians.

At the evening session, a number of tribal members and non-Indians spoke in favor of the Flathead–Blackfeet proposal, including Rep. Ben Cohen from House District 3, Rep. Bruce Measure from House District 6, and Rep. Bob Gervais from House District 9. Plaintiff Old Person stressed the need for Indians both to retain their identity and to participate in the state system: "The Indian people are striving to find ways to help themselves, protect what needs protection, and still be part of the system. They have a right to exist, be a part of this system, and be represented. . . . The mountains are not barriers. The Salish-Kootenai and the Blackfeet work together. Indian people learned that the way to survive is to help one another."[42] At the conclusion of the hearing, Commissioner Frisbee said that although there is some community of interest among the Flatheads and Blackfeet, "it is not the type of community of interest that the voting [rights act] is talking about."[43]

At a conference call on April 14, 1992, the commission rejected the Blackfeet–Flathead proposal. Commissioner Rehberg said the proposal "does not fit any of the criteria." Commissioner Pasma agreed that "[t]he Tribal Proposal violates all the criteria except the racial criteria."[44]

The commission held its next meeting at Anaconda on May 15, 1992. When an upcoming meeting at Hardin was discussed at the afternoon session, Commissioner Pasma groaned, "God, the Ruegamer brothers will be there. You'll only let that happen once. Just once, never do it again." Commissioners Frisbee and Rehberg added that "[o]ne of the Reugamers is . . . part of that lawsuit. Lawsuit, right, yea, with the Crows."[45] Jim Ruegamer, the object of Commissioner Pasma's scorn, was a member of the Big Horn County Commission who joined the Indian plaintiffs in their successful lawsuit challenging at-large election for the county commission.

The state's demographer, Susan Fox, gave the commissioners copies of the plan proposed by Rocky Boy's and Fort Belknap, which combined the two reservations and Blaine County into one legislative district. However, she inadvertently gave some of the commissioners blank pieces of paper. Commissioner Pinsoneault said, "I got a blank one too. . . . This is typical of them Indians the way they come." Ms. Fox, however, told the commissioners "[w]ell no, I made the copies. Something we messed up, so this wasn't their fault."[46]

The plan had been prepared for the tribes by a demographer who lived in Virginia and was associated with the ACLU. After Commissioner Pasma looked at the plan, he exploded, "The very first line of this absolutely infuriates me. The American Civil Liberties Union, what the hell do they have to say about what we do at

Rocky Boy or Fort Belknap or anything else." Commissioner Pinsoneault gave encouragement to Commissioner Pasma. "Give 'em hell," he said. "Give 'em hell there, Jim," added Commissioner Rehberg, "[w]e're all applauding under the table."[47] As for the tribe's demographer, he was, according to Commissioner Pasma,

> some jackass from Virginia [who] comes out and tells me, "That's a good idea." Well, I can tell you one person he's going to have a hell of an argument from. I've been out there messing around and working with those people at Rocky Boy while that S.O.B. was still messing in his knickers and it just irritates me to have him come out from God-Knows-Where and put this on us. . . . If I go out there and speak to that Tribal Council, that bugger better not even show up for the meeting. I'll toss him in the trees someplace.[48]

Commissioner Frisbee said he had "a better idea" about how to deal with the tribes, which was to pack all the Indians in the state in one district, an idea which Commissioners Pasma and Rehberg readily endorsed.

> Frisbee: . . . we'd start down here in the Crow going down . . .
> Pasma: Well, they did it in North Carolina? Remember that map we had?
> Rehberg: . . . give them one District and we go from there.[49]

The commissioners then started laughing and making jokes about Indians.

> Pasma: How are you doing, Seldin?
> Frisbee: Well, I'm a member of the Tribe. Yeah, I'm a member of the Tribe.
> Pasma: Yeah, you're kidding about . . .
> Frisbee: And I'm not Indian, you know.
> Pasma: Oh, I see.
> Frisbee: My name is Raising Wolf, Maquiapons.
> Pasma: Is that right?
> Frisbee: Any time you run for office up there, you've got to be a member of the Tribes.

Pasma: Oh!

Frisbee: Hugo Aronson, for example, was Awakemau, All Wise.[50]

Another hearing was held at Shelby on June 24, 1992. At its afternoon session, the commission discussed a proposal that would have put majority-white East Glacier in a majority-Indian house district. According to Commissioner Frisbee, putting whites in a majority-Indian district would "emasculate" white voters.[51]

The redistricting proposals submitted by tribal members that would create majority-Indian districts were ridiculed by commission members as "idiotic" and "a bunch of crap." As Commissioner Pasma put it when he looked at a plan that would have created a majority-Indian district in the area of the Rocky Boy's and Ft. Belknap reservations, "I can feel anger coming on and I might as well spew it here tonight . . . before tonight, I mean. Now, just to be really blunt, this is a bunch of crap."[52] Creating majority-Indian districts was nothing more than gerrymandering. "We're being gerrymandered," he said. "I guess gerrymandering is okay if you're Red; if you're White, it's a terrible sin." Moreover, according to Pasma, the Indians didn't know what was going on: "[Y]ou get somebody that's getting in there and stirring them up, yeah, they'll get to thinking hell's an icebox."[53]

At the evening meeting a number of people spoke in favor of both the Blackfeet–Flathead and Rocky Boy's–Fort Belknap plans, including representatives of the tribal councils. Jim Morsette, a member of the tribal council from Rocky Boy's, said he supported the tribal proposal and that "this is a time to look at the moral obligations of this issue and to consider the equal treatment of the Indian people."[54] But following a heated exchange with another supporter of the tribal plans, Commissioner Rehberg declared that "[i]f the federal government wants to redistrict Montana according to the Indian Tribes and the Reservations, they are going to have to do it. I am not going to do it."[55]

At its July 22, 1992, meeting at Wolf Point, the commission rejected the tribes' proposal and adopted a plan that put Rocky Boy's and Fort Belknap in different house districts. And Commissioner Frisbee renewed his suggestion that the commission pack all the Indians in the state in one or two districts.

Frisbee: You know, I think what we should do—turn off the recorder—I thought what we should do is alert a long district, two districts, representative districts, one up in the north, a very narrow corridor, going down to the Salishes.
Barrett: We'd better turn off the recorder.
Voice: Alright, Mr. Frisbee, that's enough of that.
Frisbee: That would keep Yellowtail in, but . . .
Pasma: That's right.[56]

Commissioner Frisbee's views about redistricting were similar to those he expressed when he appeared before the commission in 1982 and argued against a plan that would have divided Cut Bank and placed a part of the town in a majority-Indian district. Dismissing the suggestion by a commission member that Cut Bank would have two representatives under such a plan, he said,

> "they wouldn't be representing us." He argued "there's a complete diversity and philosophy regarding water, payment of taxes, sovereignty versus state government. . . ." He went on to assert, "So don't come from outside Cut Bank and tell us, when we have lived with these sorts of things, that a representative from one portion, of a different race is going to be a representative of a completely different philosophy. . . . The City of Cut Bank is entitled to somebody representing them who has the philosophy of the majority of those people."[57]

Commissioner Frisbee also believed that "one of the big, big mistakes that was made at the very early outset was the creation of Indian reservations." If he "had it to do," he said, he would terminate the reservations.[58]

At its meeting in Glendive on July 23, 1992, the commission agreed to reconsider its decision to put Rocky Boy's and Fort Belknap in different house districts. Commissioner Pasma concluded "if the Commission goes to court over this matter, it will lose." "We're being had here, ladies and gentlemen," he said, and the Indians "don't even know what the hell is going on and don't care." Commissioner Rehburg added, "[a]nd we can't do anything about it."[59]

The commission met again in Great Falls on August 26, 1992, and adopted a plan creating a majority-Indian district containing Rocky Boy's and Fort Belknap.[60] Commissioner Pasma voted "no." The plan, he said, "violates 100% of the criteria." The commission also adopted a plan maintaining a majority-Indian district in the Fort Peck area, but it declined to adopt a configuration that would have allowed for the creation of a majority-Indian senate district by combining the Fort Peck and Rocky Boy's–Fort Belknap house districts. The commission also maintained a majority-Indian district in the area of the Northern Cheyenne reservation.[61]

Under the plan finally adopted by the commission, the house consisted of one hundred single-member districts and the senate fifty single-member districts formed by combining two adjoining house districts. Five of the house districts were majority Indian: House District 85 (66 percent Indian VAP) on the Blackfeet Reservation within Glacier County; House District 92 (52 percent Indian VAP), which included the Rocky Boy's and Fort Belknap reservations in Hill and Blaine counties; House District 98 (55 percent Indian VAP) on the Fort Peck Reservation within Roosevelt County; House District 5 (50 percent Indian VAP), which contained the Northern Cheyenne Reservation and a portion of the Crow Reservation between Rosebud and Big Horn counties; and House District 6 (53 percent Indian VAP), which was composed mainly of the Crow Reservation and Big Horn County and which included the Crow Reservation portion of Yellowstone County.[62] As a practical matter, the 1992 plan increased the number of majority-Indian house districts contained in the 1982 plan—which was based on the 1990 census—by only one: the Rocky Boy's–Fort Belknap district. There was one majority-Indian senate district in the 1982 plan and only one in the 1992 plan, Senate District 3, which consisted of House Districts 5 and 6.[63]

Indians were disproportionately underrepresented in the 1990 plan. Indians were 6 percent of the total population and 4.8 percent of the VAP of the state. Were they proportionally represented on the basis of total population, they would have been a majority in nine, rather than six, of the house and senate districts. Indians therefore had only about two-thirds (67 percent) of the representation based on total population that they would have had under a proportional plan. Were they proportionally represented on the basis of VAP, they would have been a majority in 7.2 percent of the house and senate districts. Indians therefore had only 83 percent of the representation based on VAP they would have had under a proportional plan.

The lack of proportionality was more extreme in the senate. Indians were a majority in only one of the fifty senate districts and thus had only a third of the representation they would have had under a proportional plan based on total population. On the basis of VAP, they had less than half the representation in the state senate they would have had under a proportional plan.

The lack of proportionality was greater still when one looked not at the state as a whole, but at the areas of the state where the vote dilution was alleged to occur. There were no majority-Indian senate districts in the northern part of the state where the Blackfeet, Flathead, Rocky Boy's, Fort Belknap, and Fort Peck reservations were located. Far from being roughly proportional, Indians had 0 percent representation in the senate in those areas.

The *Old Person* Trial

At the trial, which was held in Great Falls, plaintiffs showed that American Indians were sufficiently large and geographically compact to constitute a majority in additional single-member legislative districts. An additional reasonably compact and regular house district could be created that included portions of Flathead, Lake, Glacier, and Pondera counties and major portions of the Blackfeet and Flathead Indian reservations.[64] In addition, the district could be combined with the majority-Indian district at Blackfeet to create an additional majority-Indian senate district. Plaintiffs also showed that the two majority-Indian house districts in the northeast part of the state (Rocky Boy's–Fort Belknap and Fort Peck) could be reconfigured to retain their Indian majorities and combined to create an additional majority-Indian senate district.[65]

The districts proposed by the tribes complied with the commission's mandatory criteria in that they were composed of contiguous territory, they achieved minimum population deviations of less than 5 percent, they were based on the 1990 census, they avoided diluting the voting strength of racial or language minorities, and they were compact. The tribal proposals also complied with the commission's discretionary criteria of considering local government units; preserving communities that had similar social, cultural, and economic interests; and being politically "fair."

Plaintiffs also showed that Indians were politically cohesive in that they have consistently been recognized as "distinct political communities."[66] Political cohesion was also apparent from the fact that Indians tended to vote as a bloc.

Plaintiffs introduced substantial evidence of both Indian and white bloc voting through statistical analysis (bivariate ecological regression analysis, or BERA) and homogeneous precinct analysis, which looks at voting results in precincts predominantly of one race. In state and county primary elections from 1990–1996 involving Indian candidates, BERA showed that on average 79 percent of Indians voted for the Indian candidates. An analysis of the homogeneous Indian precincts showed that on average 92 percent of Indians voted for the Indian candidates. BERA also showed that on average 79 percent of whites voted for white candidates. An analysis of the homogeneous non-Indian precincts showed that on average 95 percent of whites voted for white candidates.[67] Both BERA and homogeneous precinct analysis thus showed that voting in all of the primary elections was racially polarized, in that a majority of Indian voters favored the Indian candidates and a majority of white voters favored the white candidates.

In the general elections from 1990 to 1996, BERA showed that, on average, 87 percent of Indians voted for the Indian candidates, whereas 73 percent of whites voted for white candidates. Homogeneous precinct analysis showed that, on average, 93 percent of Indians voted for the Indian candidates, whereas 73 percent of whites voted for white candidates.[68] Both BERA and homogeneous precinct analysis showed that voting in all but one of the general elections was racially polarized. The sole exception was the 1992 election for district court clerk in which the Indian candidate got a minority of both Indian (31 percent) and white (1 percent) votes.

The testimony of lay witness was also to the effect that voting was racially polarized. According to Commissioner Frisbee, there was electoral "polarization. . . . There is polarization in almost everything we do."[69]

The evidence also showed that the white majority voted sufficiently as a bloc to enable it usually to defeat the candidates preferred by American Indian voters. To the extent that Indians had been elected, it was primarily in jurisdictions such as Glacier County and House District 98 that were majority Indian.

Because of the polarization that exists, white politicians were often reluctant to openly campaign or solicit votes on the reservations for fear of alienating white voters. According to Joe MacDonald, who was one of the plaintiffs in the *Old Person* case and was the president of the Salish–Kootenai College at Flathead, when U.S. Rep. Pat Williams, who was chair of a House education committee, visited the tribal college he didn't want any publicity or even to attend a reception to meet members of the faculty. According to MacDonald, "[h]e slid in the side door, he and I went around the campus, [he] went to his car and he was gone."[70] Another plaintiff, Margaret Campbell, echoed MacDonald's comments:

> Non-Indians come to the Native Americans for their support, but they would prefer that . . . we do not support them publicly among the non-Indian community. For example, they don't bring us bumper stickers and huge yard signs, that sort of thing. . . . If a non-Indian candidate were to make it known that they had the broad support of the Native American community, it would be the kiss of death to their campaign.[71]

In addition to the white backlash against Indians that began in the 1970s, the Constitution Party, which has a controversial, distinctly anti-Indian platform, is gaining a foothold in Montana. As appears from its website,[72] its 2000 national platform included the following: repeal of the Voting Rights Act; opposition to bilingual ballots; an end to all federal aid, except to military veterans; repeal of welfare; and abolition of the U.S. Department of Education.

In the 2000 general election for the Montana legislature, there were eleven Constitution Party candidates on the ballot. Where they faced candidates from both major parties, they did poorly. Where they faced only one major party candidate, they did better, with one candidate getting 25 percent of the vote. A notable exception was House District 73 in Lake County, the home of the Flathead Reservation and where the only major party candidate was an Indian. There, the Constitution Party candidate got 49 percent of the total vote, 62 percent of the white vote, and came within fifty-four votes of being elected.[73]

Campaigns have been characterized by overt or subtle racial appeals. When Joe MacDonald, a Flathead tribal member, ran for the state house in 1982, his opponent ran radio adds that MacDonald was a relative of Bear Head Swaney, a person known in the community to be an outspoken advocate for Indian interests. In another contest in Lake County, a non-Indian candidate whose last name was White put up signs saying, "Vote Right, Vote White."

In addition to showing racially polarized voting, the plaintiffs produced substantial evidence that Indians had a depressed socioeconomic status compared with whites that hindered their ability to participate effectively in the political process. Those disparities existed in all areas—income, employment, years of schooling, home ownership, and car ownership. There was also statewide discrimination in housing. According to a 1989 report by the Montana Human Rights Commission, which conducted a fair housing study in Great Falls, Missoula, and Billings, "Negative stereotypical assumptions about Indians were evident in the terms and conditions offered to some of the Indian testers. Landlords gave Indians lease terms which limited the number of occupants, warned about parties, or warned about drinking. Landlords asked Indians for higher deposits, more rent per month, and more references than white applicants."[74] The report also found "an extremely high incidence of discrimination against Indians seeking housing. Although sixty tests is a fairly small sample, the results of the tests are dramatic evidence that race discrimination in housing is a serious problem in Montana."[75]

The Montana legislature has acknowledged both the long history of discrimination against Indians and its continuing effects. In the 1950s and 1960s, it adopted resolutions describing the "suffering, great hardship and poverty" of Montana Indians as an "embarrassment and disgrace."[76] The reservations were economically depressed with "serious unemployment and welfare problems" requiring "special attention."[77] There was a critical need for economic expansion through loan programs on the reservations because "unemployment is a most severe problem on Montana Indian reservations, resulting in a low standard of living for Indian people" who are unable to "secure a place in the commercial stream of American life."[78]

The state legislature has also encouraged the adoption of a Native American Indian Day because the state contains the fourth largest Indian population in the country, and the "distinct and unique cultural heritage of the American Indian . . . is gradually being lost to citizens of the state of Montana." It found "there is a general lack of understanding of the unique psychological background of native American Indians which can be understood only by sharing the views and beliefs of native American Indians."[79]

The state defendants agreed that Indians were politically cohesive, that there was a history of discrimination by federal and state governments against Indians, and that Indians had a depressed socioeconomic status that hindered their ability to participate fully in the political process. However, the state argued that the districts proposed by plaintiffs did not contain large enough majorities to provide Indian voters an opportunity to elect candidates of their choice, and that white crossover voting for Indian candidates that ranged from 22 percent to 38 percent precluded a Section 2 vote dilution claim. The state also argued that voting was drive by partisan politics and not race, thereby foreclosing a Section 2 challenge.[80]

Following trial, the district court dismissed the complaint on the grounds that the 1990 redistricting plan did not dilute Indian voting strength. It was of the view that white bloc voting was not legally significant, and that the number of legislative districts in which Indians constituted an effective majority was proportional to the Indian share of the VAP of the state. It did note, however, "[t]he history of official discrimination against American Indians during the 19th century and early 20th century by both the state and federal government."[81]

The district court also found that "Indians continue to bear the effects of past discrimination in such areas as education, employment and health, which, in turn, impacts upon their ability to participate effectively in the political process." The effects of discrimination included low Indian voter participation and turnout and few Indian candidates.[82]

As for plaintiffs' claim of purposeful discrimination, the court held that the challenged plan had not been adopted with a discriminatory purpose. The derisive and condescending comments made by the commissioners about Indians were dismissed as "moment[s] of levity."[83] Plaintiffs appealed, and the court of appeals reversed and remanded for further proceedings.[84]

The court of appeals held that plaintiffs established the three primary factors identified in *Thornburg v. Gingles* as probative of vote dilution under Section 2 (geographic compactness and political cohesion of the minority group and legally significant white bloc voting), and that "in at least two recent elections in Lake County . . . there had been overt or subtle racial appeals." The court directed the district court to reconsider its ruling in light of its "clearly erroneous finding that white bloc voting was not legally significant" and its erroneous finding of "proportionality between the number of legislative districts in which American Indians constituted an effective majority and the American Indian share of the voting age population of Montana."[85]

As for the anti-Indian comments made by the commissioners, the appellate court acknowledged they were "inflammatory" but declined to reverse the ruling of the district court that there was no discriminatory purpose in the adoption of the commission's plan.[86] An unwillingness of many local federal judges, who are, after all, political appointees, to find that members of their state or community committed acts of *purposeful* discrimination, and the unwillingness of appellate judges to reverse those decisions, underscores the wisdom of Congress in dispensing with any requirement of proving racial purpose to establish a violation of Section 2.

2000 Districting and Apportionment Commission

Prior to the decision of the court of appeals, a new commission was appointed by the legislature in 1999 to redistrict the state in anticipation of the 2000 census. The four appointed members could not agree on the fifth member, who would serve as chair, and accordingly the state supreme court did the appointing. It chose Janine Windy Boy, a Crow Indian who had been the lead plaintiff in the Big Horn County voting rights lawsuit. Having an Indian for the first time on the commission would ensure that the language of the commissioners would not be as "inflammatory" as it had been in the past. It would also help to ensure that Indians would be treated fairly in the redistricting process. The subsequent adoption of a redistricting plan creating a new majority-Indian house district and a new majority-Indian senate district in the area of the Flathead and Blackfeet Reservations would also render the *Old Person v. Cooney* lawsuit moot.

Attorney General Mike McGrath, who as state attorney general was also counsel for the defendants, appeared before the commission at its meeting in April 2001 to discuss the *Old Person* case. He publicly acknowledged that the existing redistricting plan violated Section 2. According to General McGrath: "I think ultimately that we will not prevail in this litigation; that the Plaintiffs will indeed prevail in the litigation . . . I think the Ninth Circuit opinion is fairly clear and I think it's ultimately the state of Montana is going to have to draw a Senate district that is at least somewhat similar to that that the Plaintiffs have requested."[87]

Joe Lamson, another member of the commission, shared the views of General McGrath. He was of the opinion that the 1993 plan "did result in voter dilution of our Native American population in Montana. And that when you look at proportionality, they're certainly entitled to another Senate district." A third commissioner, Sheila Rice, who was a member of the state legislature when the existing plan was enacted, said that "I actually sat on that House Committee that reviewed this exact plan that was taken to Court—it must have been the 1993 session, and argued pretty strenuously that we were diluting the Native American population, and that we should redraw that district."[88]

The commission conceded the 1992 plan diluted Indian voting strength and adopted a resolution to create "an additional majority Indian House District and an additional majority Indian Senate District in the region of Montana that is dealt with in *Old Person*, in recognition of the rights of Indians on the Blackfeet and Flathead Reservations under Section 2 of the Federal Voting Rights Act of 1965."[89]

A second trial was held in *Old Person* after the remand from the court of appeals, and the district court again dismissed the complaint. It held that the three *Gingles* factors continued to be met taking into account intervening elections in 1998 and 2000, and that the gap between the number of majority–minority districts to minority members' share of the relevant population had increased based on the 2000 census. It reaffirmed the prior findings that American Indians suffered from a history of discrimination, that Indians have a lower socioeconomic status than whites, that these social and economic factors hinder the ability of Indians in Montana to participate fully in the political process, and that in at least two recent elections in Lake County there had been overt or subtle racial appeals.

Despite these findings, the court ruled that three Indian-preferred candidates (one white, one Indian who had no major party opposition in the general election, and another Indian from a majority-Indian district) had been elected to the legislature from the Blackfeet–Flathead area. The court also emphasized the difficulty of redistricting only part of the state using the 2000 census and "the very real prospect that comprehensive and long-term relief designed to address vote dilution throughout the State of Montana is in the offing within a year under the auspices of the Montana Districting and Apportionment Commission."[90]

Plaintiffs appealed once again, but this time the court of appeals affirmed—it affirmed all the prior findings showing vote dilution. In addition, and setting aside the finding of the district court once again, the panel held that Indians' share of majority–minority districts "is not proportional under either a four-county or a statewide frame of reference, [and that] the proportionality factor weighs in favor of a finding of vote dilution." But despite proof of the *Gingles* and other factors showing vote dilution, including the lack of proportionality, the panel concluded that Indian voting strength was not diluted because of "the absence of discriminatory voting practices, the viable policy underlying the existing district boundaries, the success of Indians in elections, and official responsiveness to Native American needs."[91] The court ignored the evidence presented by the plaintiffs of the 2000 Districting and Apportionment Commission's resolution and its individual members' statements that the 1993 plan diluted Indian voting strength. But in any event, the 2000 redistricting would shortly render the case moot.

After holding a series of hearings around the state, the new commission submitted its redistricting plan to the state legislature for comments on January 6, 2003. The plan provided for one hundred house districts, six of which were majority Indian, and fifty senate districts, three of which were majority Indian. An additional majority-Indian house district (House District 1) was created that included parts of the Flathead and Blackfeet Indian Reservations. That district, when combined with the preexisting majority-Indian house district on the Blackfeet Reservation (House District 85), created an additional majority-Indian senate district (Senate District 1).[92] The districts for the house contained a total deviation of 9.85 percent.[93]

Both the house and senate immediately condemned the proposed plans and demanded that the commission adopt new ones. The house, in a resolution passed on February 4, 2003, charged that "the 5% population deviation allowance contained in the plan was used for partisan gain," that the plan was "mean-spirited," "unacceptable," and that "the legislative redistricting plan must be redone." It also condemned the creation of majority-Indian districts as being "in blatant violation of the mandatory criterion that race may not be the predominant factor to which the traditional discretionary criteria are subordinated."[94] The senate leveled virtually identical charges and concluded that "the legislative redistricting plan must be redone."[95]

The legislature then enacted HB 309, which the governor signed into law on February 4, 2003, which sought to invalidate the commission's plan and alter or amend the provisions of the state constitution. Although Article V, Section 14(1), of the Constitution of Montana provides that "[a]ll districts shall be as nearly equal in population as is practicable," HB 309 provided that the districts must be "within a plus or minus 1% relative deviation from the ideal population of a district." HB 309 further provided that "[t]he secretary of state may not accept any plan that does not comply with the [1% deviation] criteria."[96]

On February 5, 2003, the commission formally adopted its plan for legislative redistricting and filed it with the secretary of state. The secretary of state, however, refused to accept it and on the same day filed a complaint against the commission in state court for declaratory judgment that the plan was unconstitutional and unenforceable for failure to comply with the population equality standard of HB 309.[97] Following a hearing, the state court ruled on July 2, 2003, that HB 309 was unconstitutional and that the secretary of state was required to accept the commission's plan. The secretary of state did not appeal but accepted the commission's plan for filing. It thus became the state's redistricting plan, superseding the 1993 plan and rendering the plaintiffs' challenge to the prior plan moot. The Supreme Court, however, denied without comment a petition for a writ of certiorari seeking to vacate the final decision of the lower court on mootness grounds.[98]

The *Old Person* litigation spanned eight years, and the federal court's findings of the factors probative of Indian vote dilution were relied on by the Districting and Apportionment Commission in adopting its plan in 2003. That plan provided Indian voters for the first time with an equal opportunity to elect candidates of their choice to the state legislature. As of 2007, ten Indians served in the Montana house and senate, the largest number in the state's history.[98] The Native American success at the polls was testimony to the application of the standards of the Voting Rights Act by the Districting and Apportionment Commission, the adoption of a racially fair redistricting plan, and the increased interest and power of the Native vote.

CHAPTER 5

South Dakota

By the end of the eighteenth century, the Sioux Indians, composed of seven groups known as the Seven Council Fires, dominated the Northern Plains. Their territory extended from the Mississippi Valley in Minnesota and Iowa across the Missouri River to beyond the Black Hills in present-day South Dakota. The Sioux Tribe had three main divisions—the Dakota in the east, the Lakota in the west, and the Yankton-Yanktonai in the center—each with numerous subdivisions.[1]

Lt. Zebulon Pike negotiated the first treaty with the Sioux in 1805, in which they ceded land near present-day St. Paul for the establishment of U.S. military posts.[2] Fort Snelling was subsequently built at the junction of the Mississippi and Minnesota rivers in 1819 to keep British fur traders out of American territory and to keep peace between the Sioux and other tribes. Following the close of the War of 1812, various Sioux bands entered into "peace and friendship" treaties with the United States at Portage des Sioux.[3] Then, in 1825, the Teton, Yancton, Yanctonies, Sioune, Oglala, and Hunkpapa signed treaties acknowledging the "supremacy" of the United States and admitting "the right of the United States to regulate all trade and intercourse" with the tribes.[4] Most commentators agree that the tribes did not understand the treaties to be admissions of U.S. sovereignty but, rather, trade agreements among equals.[5]

Succumbing to increasing encroachment by white settlers from the east and mounting pressure from the federal government, the Dakota entered into a treaty in 1837 ceding all their territory east of the Mississippi to the United States in return for various payments and annuities.[6] White settlers poured into the newly opened area. The Sioux also experienced increased migration in the 1840s by settlers traveling up the Platte and North Platte rivers to Oregon, by Mormons on their way to Utah, and later by those pursuing the gold rush in California. In 1849, 25,000 emigrants crossed the plains, more than five times the number in the preceding year.[7] Not only did they have an adverse impact on the environment and the buffalo herds, but they also spread cholera, measles, and smallpox.

In 1851 the Sioux, along with other Indian tribes, signed the Treaty of Fort Laramie, which for the first time assigned the tribes to designated areas. The Sioux territory included all of present-day South Dakota and land in what is now Nebraska, Wyoming, North Dakota, and Montana.[8] In other treaties, Sioux tribes relinquished all their land in Iowa and Minnesota Territory and agreed to be removed to other country.[9]

The Dakota Territory was created by an act of Congress in 1861, which restricted suffrage in the first legislative election, as well as office holding, to free white men who were citizens of the United States.[10] The initial territorial assembly meeting in 1862 placed similar limitations on the right to vote and hold office.[11] Indians were prohibited from entering ceded lands without a permit.[12] Jury service was restricted to "free white males."[13] The territory immediately asked Congress to extinguish title "to the country now claimed and occupied by the Brule Sioux Indians"[14] and to extinguish title to land occupied by the Chippewa Indians.[15] It praised the "indomitable spirit of the Anglo-Saxon" and described Indians as "red children" and the "poor child" of the prairie.[16]

As American expansion into Indian Country intensified, there were numerous conflicts between the Sioux tribes and emigrants, white settlers, and the U.S. military. One of the most divisive was the Great Sioux Uprising of 1862. The Dakota, driven by hunger and angered by unfair treatment by and distrust of whites, attacked the town of New Ulm, occupied two Indian agencies, and drove many settlers from their farms, resulting in the death of some 500 non-Indians.[17] In response, the military launched an attack and forced the Dakota to surrender on September 26, 1862. Thirty-eight Indians were hanged on December 26, 1862, in Mankato, Minnesota, for their part in the uprising, still the largest mass execution in American history. The military conducted subsequent attacks in 1863 and 1864 against Indians who had fled westward after the uprising. The government also abrogated all Dakota treaty rights by the Forfeiture Act of 1863 and removed the Lower Sioux from Minnesota.[18] But rather than subduing the Indians, the military attacks fueled further resentment and hostilities.

The territory asked the secretary of war in 1863 to establish a military post on the Big Sioux River near Sioux Falls to protect against "hostile Indians."[19] Three years later it requested the secretary to establish a series of military posts, one on the Niobrara River to promote settlement and to protect mineral prospectors, another on the Vermillion River to fend off "hostile bands of savages," and another to protect "the colonization of the Black Hills."[20] Now the territorial legislature no longer described the American Indian as the "poor child" but, rather, as the "revengeful and murderous savage."[21] It further passed a law making it a crime to harbor or keep on one's premises or within any village settlement of white people any reservation Indians "who have not adopted the manners and habits of civilized life."[22]

Several treaties were negotiated with "friendly" tribes in 1865, in which the tribes acknowledged themselves "to be subject to the exclusive jurisdiction and authority of the United States."[23] However, none of the warrior chiefs signed the treaties, and as a result such treaties were largely ignored and were ineffective.[24]

Hostilities between whites and Indians were further fueled by miners' use of a new route to Montana, the Bozeman Trail, which went through the heart of Sioux territory. Open warfare ensued in what became known as Red Cloud's War (1866–1868), and in

December 1866 the Sioux killed Col. William J. Fetterman and eighty men under his command.[25]

In 1867, the South Dakota assembly asked that additional federal troops be sent to the territory and declared Indians were "our implacable enemies," "Hell Hounds," and "a wild, turbulent and hostile people." It requested that the Santee Sioux be removed and that the Black Hills be opened to "armed bands of immigrants and miners."[26]

In a mutual effort to end the hostilities, the Sioux entered into the Fort Laramie Treaty of 1868, which closed the Bozeman Trail and created the Great Sioux Reservation, composed of approximately 60 million acres and extending from the Missouri River to the Wyoming–Dakota border.[27] The United States agreed that the land would be "set apart for the absolute and undisturbed use and occupation of the Indians." Red Cloud insisted that government forts built along the Bozeman Trail be removed before he agreed to sign the treaty.[28] The signing of the treaty did not, however, bring an end to war with the Sioux.

The Dakota legislature sent a stream of resolutions and memorials to Congress urging it to extinguish Indian title to land and remove the Indians to make way for more white settlement. In 1868, it proposed removing Dakota Indians and excluding from "habitation of the Indians that portion of Dakota known as the Black Hills."[29] It further asked for a military post in the Red River Valley to protect against "continued jeopardy by the Indians."[30] In 1871 and 1873 it renewed its request for the removal of Chippewa Indians from ceded lands[31] and again asked Congress to open the Black Hills to white settlement.[32]

Despite the 1868 treaty, whites continued to encroach upon Indian land, including the Black Hills, where gold had been discovered during an expedition led by Gen. George Armstrong Custer in 1874. In 1875 the territory again urged Congress to open the Black Hills to white settlement.[33] The United States negotiated with the Sioux in an effort to buy the Black Hills, but the negotiations failed. The following year, the military launched a major offensive to subdue what it described as the "hostile Sioux."[34]

Sitting Bull, Crazy Horse, and other Sioux leaders who had not signed the treaty of 1868 engaged in numerous battles with the military, including the Battle of the Little Big Horn in 1876, in which Custer and 210 of his men were killed by a massed Indian force of 1,800 warriors.[35] As a result of intense pressure from the territorial government, white miners, and settlers, and despite the Fort Laramie Treaty of 1868, the United States took the Black Hills from the Indians by congressional enactment in 1877. It added to the reservation some 900,000 acres of land to the north but took out an area of over 7 million acres.[36] The Court of Claims later awarded the Sioux $17.1 million for the taking of their land, plus interest at the annual rate of 5 percent dating from 1877. In affirming the decision in 1980, the Supreme Court said the government was obligated "to make just compensation to the Sioux Nation, and that obligation, including an award of interest, must now, at last, be paid."[37]

Gen. William T. Sherman was authorized to assume military control of all Sioux reservations and to treat Indians as prisoners of war.[38] In 1877, the United States undertook a campaign against the Sioux that resulted in the surrender of Crazy Horse.[39] Sitting Bull later surrendered in 1881 at Fort Buford, located at the confluence of the Yellowstone and Missouri Rivers.[40]

The South Dakota Territory was unceasing in its demands that Indian land be opened for white settlement. It requested Congress to open the Devil's Lake Indian Reservation and a portion of the Sioux Indian Reservation to settlement by whites.[41] In response to local pressure, the Sioux reservation was again diminished in size by congressional enactment in 1889.[42] About one-half was "restored to the public domain," and separate reservations were carved out from the remainder for the Indians.[43] Still, the demand for more Indian land continued. After South Dakota became a state in 1889, it requested Congress to open both the Yankton and Crow Creek reservations to settlement.[44]

The last major confrontation between the United States and the Sioux took place at Wounded Knee in December 1890. A Paiute holy man named Wovoka told the tribes that by practicing a "Ghost Dance" they could make the white man go away, that the buffalo would return, and the tribes would be restored to their former traditional way of life.[45] The Lakota Sioux, out of desperation over the quality of their life on the reservation and hope for a better future, took up the Ghost Dance. A band of Minneconjou Ghost Dancers led by Chief Big Foot was making its way to the Pine Ridge Reservation when they were intercepted by U.S. soldiers and taken to Wounded Knee for the night. In the morning, during an effort to disarm the Indians, a shot was fired, which triggered a massacre by the U.S. troops. More than 120 Indian men and 230 Indian women and children were killed. The war period, known as the Sioux Wars, is considered to have ended after the massacre at Wounded Knee.[46]

Congress further diminished the size of the Rosebud Sioux Reservation by acts passed in 1904, 1907, and 1910.[47] Today, there are nine Sioux reservations located in whole or in part in South Dakota: Lake Traverse, Flandreau, Yankton, Crow Creek, Lower Brule, Rosebud, Pine Ridge, Cheyenne River, and Standing Rock. Approximately 59,000 American Indians live in the state.

Continued Denial of Indian Voting Rights

The state of South Dakota has continued to discriminate against Indians in voting. The legislature approved a constitutional amendment in 1890 restricting voting and office holding to free white males and citizens of the United States.[48] Indians who sustained tribal relations, who received support from the government, or who held untaxable land were prohibited from voting in any state election.[49] The state also forbade the establishment of precincts on Indian reservations.[50] Another law provided for the selection of jurors from tax lists, which excluded non-taxpaying Indians from participation in the judicial process.[51] In an effort to eradicate Indian languages, the state passed laws that instruction could be given only in English in public and private schools.[52]

The state also asked Congress to open portions of the Rosebud Reservation to white settlement.[53] Congress agreed to do so, and by a series of acts took from the Indians three-quarters of their reservation land.[54]

Despite passage of the Indian Citizenship Act of 1924,[55] which granted full rights of citizenship to all Indians, South Dakota officially excluded Indians from voting and holding office until the 1940s.[56] Even after the repeal of state law denying Indians the right to vote, as late as 1975 the state prohibited voters in "unorganized" counties from voting in elections in the counties to which they were attached.[57] The three unorganized counties were Todd, Shannon, and Washabaugh, whose residents were overwhelmingly Indian. The state also prohibited residents of the unorganized counties from holding county office until as late as 1980.[58]

For most of the twentieth century, voters in South Dakota were required to register in person at the office of the county auditor.[59] Getting to the county seat was a hardship for Indians who lacked transportation, particularly for those in unorganized counties who were required to travel to another county to register. Moreover, state law did not allow the auditor to appoint a tribal official as a deputy to register Indian voters in their own communities. There was one exception, however. State law required the tax assessor to register property owners in the course of assessing the value of their land. Thus, taxpayers were automatically registered to vote, whereas nontaxpayers, many of whom were Indian, were required to make the trip to the courthouse to register in person.[60] Mail-in registration was not fully implemented in South Dakota until 1973.[61]

Refusal to Comply with Section 5

The disdain of some state officials for Indian voting rights was apparent from the state's refusal to comply with Section 5 of the Voting Rights Act. Ten years after the act's 1965 enactment, Congress amended the Voting Rights Act to cover American Indians, to expand the geographic reach of the special preclearance provisions of Section 5, and to require certain jurisdictions to provide bilingual election materials to language minorities. As a result of the amendments, two counties in South Dakota, Shannon and Todd, which are home to the Pine Ridge and Rosebud Indian Reservations, respectively, became subject to preclearance.[62] Eight counties in the state, because of their significant Indian populations, were also required to conduct bilingual elections: Todd, Shannon, Bennett, Charles Mix, Corson, Lyman, Mellette, and Washabaugh.[63]

William Janklow, at that time the attorney general of South Dakota, was outraged over the extension of Section 5 and the bilingual election requirement to his state. In a formal opinion addressed to the secretary of state, he derided the 1975 law as a "facial absurdity." Borrowing the states' rights rhetoric of southern politicians who opposed the modern civil right movement, he condemned the Voting Rights Act as an unconstitutional federal encroachment that rendered state power "almost meaningless." He quoted with approval Justice Hugo Black's dissent in *South Carolina v. Katzenbach* (which held the basic provisions of the Voting Rights Act constitutional) that Section 5 treated covered jurisdictions as "little more than conquered provinces."[64] Janklow expressed the hope that Congress would soon repeal "the Voting Rights Act currently plaguing South Dakota." In the meantime, he advised the secretary of state not to comply with the preclearance requirement. "I see no need," he said, "to proceed with undue speed to subject our State's laws to a 'one-man veto' by the United States Attorney General."[65]

Although the 1975 amendments to the Voting Rights Act were never in fact repealed, state officials followed Janklow's advice and essentially ignored the preclearance requirement. From the date of its official coverage in 1976 until 2002, South Dakota enacted more than 600 statutes and regulations having an effect on elections or voting in Shannon and Todd Counties but submitted fewer than ten for preclearance.

The Department of Justice, which has primary responsibility for enforcing Section 5, was surely aware of the failure of the state to comply with the preclearance requirement. It had, for example, sued the state in 1978 and 1979 for its failure to submit for preclearance reapportionment and county reorganization laws affecting the covered counties.[66] But after that, the department turned a blind eye to the state's failure to comply with Section 5.

Depressed Socioeconomic Status

Aside from formal barriers, Indian political participation was significantly reduced by a depressed socioeconomic status, one of the many legacies of past discrimination. On the basis of 2000 census data, the unemployment rate for Indians in South Dakota was 23.6 percent, compared with 3.2 percent for whites.[67] The unemployment rates on the reservations were even higher. In 1997 the unemployment rate on the Cheyenne River Sioux Reservation was 80 percent. At the Standing Rock Indian Reservation it was 74 percent.[68] Life expectancy for Indians is shorter than for other Americans. According to a 2000 report by the South Dakota Advisory Committee to the U.S. Commission on Civil Rights, "Indian men in South Dakota . . . usually live only into their mid-50s." Infant mortality in Indian Country "is double the national average."[69]

American Indians experience a poverty rate that is five times the poverty rate for whites. The 2000 census reported that 48.1 percent of Indians in South Dakota were living below the poverty line, compared with 9.7 percent of whites. Sixty-one percent of American Indian households received incomes below $20,000, compared with 24.4 percent of white households. The per capita income of Indians was $6,799, compared with $28,837 for whites.[70]

Eighteen percent of American Indian households are without access to vehicles versus 5.4 percent of white households. Of American Indians twenty-five years of age and over, 29 percent have not finished high school, whereas 14 percent of whites are without a high school diploma. The dropout rate among Indians aged sixteen to nineteen is 24 percent, four times the dropout rate for whites.[71]

The link between a depressed socioeconomic status and reduced political participation is direct. As the Supreme Court has recognized, "political participation tends to be depressed where minority group members suffer effects of prior discrimination such as inferior education, poor employment opportunities, and low incomes."[72]

Given the socioeconomic status of American Indians in South Dakota, it is not surprising that their voter registration and political participation have been severely depressed. As late as 1985, only

9.9 percent of Indians in the state were registered to vote.[73] The South Dakota Advisory Committee to the U.S. Commission on Civil Rights concluded in a 2000 report that "[f]or the most part, Native Americans are very much separate and unequal members of society. . . . [who] do not fully participate in local, State, and Federal elections. This absence from the electoral process results in a lack of political representation at all levels of government and helps to ensure the continued neglect and inattention to issues of disparity and inequality."[74]

Beginning in the 1980s, numerous jurisdictions in South Dakota have been sued for violating Indian voting rights: Roberts, Marshall, Shannon, Ziebach, Dewey, Day, Charles Mix, and Buffalo counties; the Wagner Community School District; and the city of Martin. The state has also been sued for its long-time failure to comply with the preclearance provisions of Section 5 of the Voting Rights Act, for adopting a discriminatory mid-decade redistricting plan in 1996 in violation of the state constitution, and for adopting another redistricting plan in 2002 that packed Indians into a district and diluted their voting strength.

Roberts and Marshall Counties

The first challenge in South Dakota under amended Section 2 of the Voting Rights Act was brought in 1984 by members of the Sisseton-Wahpeton Sioux Tribe in Roberts and Marshall counties. Represented by the Native American Rights Fund, they claimed that the at-large method of electing members of the board of education of the Sisseton Independent School District diluted Indian voting strength. The trial court dismissed the complaint, but the court of appeals reversed. It held that the trial court failed to consider "substantial evidence . . . that voting in the District was polarized along racial lines." The trial court had also failed to discuss the "substantial" evidence of discrimination against Indians in voting and office holding; the "substantial evidence regarding the present social and economic disparities between Indians and whites"; the discriminatory impact of staggered terms of office and apportioning seats between rural and urban members on the basis of registered voters, which under-represented Indians; and the presence of only two polling places.[75] On remand, the parties reached a settlement using cumulative voting for the election of school board members.[76]

Shannon County

Joe American Horse, a tribal member and resident of the Pine Ridge Indian Reservation in Shannon County, attempted to register to vote prior to the November 1984 general election. His application was rejected, however, on the grounds that it was received after the deadline for registration, despite the fact it was received by the auditor prior to the deadline that had been agreed upon by various county officials and publicly announced. In a lawsuit filed by American Horse on his own behalf, and on behalf of others whose applications had been similarly rejected, the court ordered the rejected applications be accepted and that the applicants be allowed to vote in the upcoming elections.[77]

Ziebach County

In 1986, Alberta Black Bull and other Indian residents of the Cheyenne River Sioux Reservation brought a successful Section 2 suit against Ziebach County because of its failure to provide sufficient polling places for school district elections. Prior to the lawsuit, Indians had to travel up to 150 miles round trip to vote, significantly depressing Indian political participation. The district court ordered the school district to establish four new polling places on the reservation.[78]

Dewey County

In 1986 Indian residents of the Cheyenne River Sioux Reservation in South Dakota launched a campaign to register Indian voters.

However, Dewey County's auditor limited the number of application forms given to voter registrars—who had to travel approximately eighty miles round trip to the auditor's office in the courthouse—to ten to fifteen apiece. The Indians filed suit under the Voting Rights Act, and the court concluded the county auditor had discriminated against Indians by limiting the number of application forms, ordered that more forms be provided, and extended the deadline for voter registration for an additional week.[79]

Legislative Redistricting, 1970–1996

In the 1970s, a special task force consisting of the nine tribal chairs, four members of the legislature, and five lay people undertook a study of Indian–state government relations. One of the staff reports of the commission concluded that "[w]ith the present arrangement of legislative districts, Indian people have had their voting potential in South Dakota diluted." The report recommended the creation of a majority-Indian district in the area of Shannon, Washabaugh, Todd, and Bennett counties.[80] Under the existing plan, there were twenty-eight legislative districts, all of which were majority white and none of which had ever elected an Indian. Thomas Short Bull, a member of the Oglala Sioux Tribe and the executive director of the task force, said the plan gerrymandered the Rosebud and Pine Ridge reservations by "divid[ing them] into three legislative districts, effectively neutralizing the Indian vote in that area." The legislature, however, ignored the task force's recommendation. According to Short Bull, "the state representatives and senators felt it was a political hot potato. . . . [T]his was just too pro-Indian to take as an item of action."[81]

After the release of the 1980 census, the South Dakota Advisory Committee to the U.S. Commission on Civil Rights made a similar recommendation that the legislature create a majority-Indian district in the area of the Pine Ridge and Rosebud reservations. The committee issued a report in which it said the existing districts "inherently discriminate against Native Americans in South Dakota who might be able to elect one legislator in a single-member district."[82] The Department of Justice, pursuant to its oversight under Section 5, advised the state it would not preclear any legislative redistricting plan that did not contain a majority-Indian district in the Rosebud/ Pine Ridge area. The state bowed to the inevitable and in 1981 drew a redistricting plan creating for the first time in the state's history a majority-Indian district, District 28, which included Shannon and Todd counties and half of Bennett County.[83] Thomas Short Bull ran for the senate the following year from District 28 and was elected, becoming the first Indian ever to serve in the state's upper chamber.

Following the 1990 census, the South Dakota legislature adopted a new redistricting plan in 1991.[84] The plan divided the state into thirty-five districts and provided, with one exception, that each district would be entitled to one senate member and two house members elected at-large from within the district. The exception was House District 28. The 1991 legislation provided that "in order to protect minority voting rights, District No. 28 shall consist of two single-member house districts."[85] District 28A consisted of Dewey and Ziebach counties and portions of Corson County, and it also included the Cheyenne River Sioux Reservation and portions of the Standing Rock Sioux Reservation. District 28B consisted of Harding and Perkins counties and portions of Corson and Butte counties. According to 1990 census data, Indians were 60 percent of the VAP of House District 28A and less than 4 percent of the VAP of House district 28B.[86]

Five years later, despite its pledge to protect minority voting rights, the legislature abolished House Districts 28A and 28B and required candidates for the house to run in District 28 at-large.[87] Tellingly, the repeal took place after an Indian candidate, Mark Van Norman, won the Democratic primary in District 28A in 1994. A chief sponsor of the repealing legislation was Eric Bogue, the Republican candidate who defeated Van Norman in the general election.[88] The reconstituted House District 28 contained an Indian VAP of 29 percent.[89] Given the prevailing patterns of racially polarized voting, of which members of the legislature were surely aware, Indian voters could not realistically expect to elect a candidate of their choice in the new district.

Emery v. Hunt: Challenge to the 1996 Legislative Plan

Steven Emery, Rocky Le Compte, and James Picotte, residents of the Cheyenne River Sioux Reservation, and represented by the ACLU, filed suit in 2000 challenging the state's 1996 interim legislative redistricting plan. They claimed that the changes in District 28 violated Section 2 of the Voting Rights Act as well as Article III, Section 5, of the South Dakota Constitution. The state constitution provided that:

> An apportionment shall be made by the Legislature in 1983 and in 1991, and every ten years after 1991. Such apportionment shall be accomplished by December first of the year in which the apportionment is required. If any Legislature whose duty it is to make an apportionment shall fail to make the same as herein provided, it shall be the duty of the Supreme Court within ninety days to make such apportionment.[90]

The constitution thus contained both an affirmative mandate and an implied prohibition. It mandated reapportionment in 1983, 1991, and in every tenth year thereafter, and it also prohibited all interstitial reapportionment. The South Dakota Supreme Court had expressly held that "when a Legislature once makes an apportionment following an enumeration no Legislature can make another until after the next enumeration."[91] Any reapportionment that occurred outside of the authority granted by the state constitution was therefore invalid as a matter of state law.[92]

Pronouncements by the South Dakota Legislative Research Council were to the same effect. According to a 1995 memorandum prepared by the council, "[i]n the absence of a successful legal challenge, Article III, section 5 of the South Dakota Constitution precludes any redistricting before 2001."[93] In another memorandum prepared in 1998, the council reiterated that "[u]nder the provisions of Article III, section 5, the Legislature is, however, restricted to redistricting only once every ten years."[94] Despite the prohibitions of the state constitution and the views of the research council, the legislature adopted the mid-census plan abolishing majority-Indian District 28A.

Dr. Steven Cole, an expert witness for the *Emery* plaintiffs, analyzed the six legislative contests involving Indian and non-Indian candidates in District 28 held under the 1991 plan between 1992 and 1994 to determine the existence, and extent, of any racial bloc voting. Indian voters favored the Indian candidates at an average rate of 81 percent, whereas whites voted for the white candidates at an average rate of 93 percent. In all six of the contests, the candidate preferred by Indians was defeated.[95]

Dr. Cole also analyzed one countywide contest involving an Indian candidate: the 1992 general election for treasurer of Dewey County. Indian cohesion was 100 percent, white cohesion was 95 percent, and again the Indian-preferred candidate was defeated.[96]

There were five legislative contests from 1992 to 1998 in which all of the candidates were white, four of which were head-to-head contests and one of which was a vote-for-two contest. All of the contests showed significant levels of polarized voting. For the six seats filled in the five contests, the candidates preferred by Indians lost four times. The Indian-preferred white candidates won only in majority-Indian District 28A. The white candidate (Schrempp) preferred by Indian voters in District 28A in the 1992 and 1996 general elections won both times. In the 1998 general election, however, he ran for state senate in District 28. Although he was again preferred by Indian voters, when he ran in a district in which Indians composed 29 percent of the VAP he lost. This sequence of elections demonstrated in an obvious way the manner in which at-large elections in District 28 diluted or submerged the voting strength of Indian voters.[97]

White cohesion also fluctuated widely depending on whether or not an Indian was a candidate. In the four head-to-head white–white legislative contests, where there was no possibility of electing an Indian candidate, the average level of white cohesion was 68 percent. In the Indian–white legislative contests, the average level of white cohesion jumped to 94 percent.[98] This phenomenon of increased white cohesion to defeat minority candidates has been called "targeting," and it illustrates the way in which majority-white districts operate to dilute minority voting strength.[99]

The vote-for-two election for the house in 1998, the first such election held after the repeal of District 28A, also showed a remarkable divergence between Indian and white voters. The candidate with the least amount of Indian support (Wetz, with 8 percent of the Indian vote) got the highest amount of support from white voters (70 percent). The candidate with the next lowest support from Indian voters (Klaudt) received the second highest white support.[100]

The plaintiffs' Section 2 claim was strong. They met the basic requirements set out in *Gingles* for proof of vote dilution: they were sufficiently geographically compact to constitute a majority in a single-member district; they were politically cohesive; and whites voted as a bloc usually to defeat the candidates of their choice. In addition, other factors probative of vote dilution identified in the Senate report that accompanied the 1982 amendments were present. Indians had a depressed socioeconomic status. There was an extensive history of discrimination in the state, including discrimination that impeded the ability of Indians to register and otherwise participate in the political process. The history of Indian and white relations in South Dakota was, in the words of the South Dakota Advisory Committee, one of "broken treaties, and policies aimed at assimilation and acculturation that severed Indians of their language, customs, and beliefs."[101] Voting was polarized. District 28 was also large, twice the size of District 28A, making it much more difficult for poorly financed Indian candidates to campaign.

The state, in defending its plan, argued that the complaint should be dismissed on a number of grounds: plaintiffs were guilty of laches, or delay in filing suit; the complaint failed to state a claim; District 28A was drawn based on race in violation of the Fourteenth Amendment; and Section 2 of the Voting Rights Act was unconstitutional.

But before the Section 2 vote dilution claim could be heard, the district court certified the state law question to the South Dakota Supreme Court. That court accepted certification and held that in enacting the 1996 redistricting plan, "the Legislature acted beyond its constitutional limits."[102] It declared the plan null and void and reinstated the preexisting 1991 plan. At the ensuing special election ordered by the district court, Tom Van Norman was elected from

District 28A, the first Indian in history to be elected to the state house from the Cheyenne River Sioux Indian Reservation.[103]

Bone Shirt v. Hazeltine: A Challenge to the 2001 Legislative Redistricting

The South Dakota legislature adopted a redistricting plan in 2001 based on the 2000 census that divided the state into thirty-five legislative districts, each of which elected one senator and two members of the house. No doubt because of the litigation involving the 1996 plan, the legislature continued the exception of using two subdistricts in District 28, one of which included the Cheyenne River Sioux Reservation and a portion of the Standing Rock Indian Reservation. The boundaries of the district that included Shannon and Todd counties, District 27, were altered only slightly under the 2001 plan, but the demographic composition of the district was substantially changed. Indians were 87 percent of the population of District 27 under the 1991 plan, and the district was one of the most underpopulated in the state. Under the 2001 plan, Indians were 90 percent of the population, and the district was one of the most overpopulated in the state. As was apparent, Indians were more "packed," or overconcentrated, in the new District 27 than under the 1991 plan. Had Indians been "unpacked," they could have been a majority in adjacent District 26.[104]

Indeed, James Bradford, an Indian representative from District 27, proposed an amendment reconfiguring Districts 26 and 27 that would have retained District 27 as majority Indian and divided District 26 into two house districts, one of which, District 26A, would have had an Indian majority. Bradford's amendment was voted down fifty-one to sixteen.[105] Thomas Short Bull criticized the way in which District 27 had been drawn because there were "just too many Indians in that legislative district," which he said diluted the Indian vote.[106] Elsie Meeks, a tribal member at Pine Ridge and the first Indian to serve on the U.S. Commission on Civil Rights, said the plan "segregates Indians" and denied them equal voting power.[107]

Despite enacting a new legislative plan affecting Todd and Shannon counties, which were covered by Section 5, the state refused to submit the 2001 plan for preclearance. Alfred Bone Shirt and three other Indian residents from Districts 26 and 27, represented by the ACLU, sued the state in December 2001 for its failure to submit its redistricting plan for preclearance. The plaintiffs also claimed the plan unnecessarily packed Indian voters in violation of Section 2 and deprived them of an equal opportunity to elect candidates of their choice.

A three-judge court was convened to hear the plaintiffs' Section 5 claim. The state argued that because district lines had not been significantly changed insofar as they affected Shannon and Todd counties, there was no need to comply with Section 5. The three-judge court disagreed. It held "demographic shifts render the new District 27 a change 'in voting' for the voters of Shannon and Todd counties that must be precleared under §5."[108] The state submitted the plan to the U.S. attorney general, who precleared it, apparently having concluded the additional packing of Indians in District 27 did not have a retrogressive effect.

The district court, sitting as a single-judge court, subsequently heard plaintiffs' Section 2 claim. The state argued that plaintiffs failed to establish the three factors required by *Thornburg v. Gingles*, that is, that Indians were geographically compact, that they were politically cohesive, and that whites voted as a bloc usually to defeat the Indians preferred candidates. The court, however, in a detailed 144-page opinion invalidated the state's 2001 legislative plan as diluting Indian voting strength.

The court initially found the plaintiffs had established the three *Gingles* factors. Then, turning to the totality of circumstances analysis, it found there was "substantial evidence that South Dakota officially excluded Indians from voting and holding office." Indians in recent times have encountered numerous difficulties in obtaining registration cards from their county auditors, whose behavior "ranged from unhelpful to hostile." Indians involved in voter registration drives have regularly been accused of engaging in voter fraud by local officials, and although the accusations have proved to be unfounded they have "intimidated Indian voters."[109]

One example of unfounded allegations of Indian voter fraud occurred in 1978 when a coalition of Indian and civic organizations sponsored a voter registration drive focused on members of the state's American Indian tribes. Just before the election, allegations surfaced that some Indians who might be convicted felons were registering voters and that federal dollars were being used illegally by the tribes to finance the registration effort. Both the South Dakota Division of Criminal Investigation and the Federal Bureau of Investigation sent agents to investigate the allegations of fraud on the Pine Ridge and Rosebud reservations. The investigations, however, ended without any charges being brought.[110]

Charlene Black Horse, who worked on the registration drive, believes the allegations of fraud were racially motivated. "We felt that," she said. "We always feel that because we're always being intimidated by somebody. And when you grow up there, that's just how you live with things."[111]

History repeated itself in 2002. Indians launched another major voter registration drive, and just before the 2002 election it, too, was hit with allegations of voter fraud. Susan Williams, the auditor of Bennet County, announced publically that Indians doing voter registration were committing fraud. Once again investigators fanned out on the Pine Ridge and Rosebud reservations, but again no one was ever charged with registering or attempting to register anyone illegally. After the investigation, South Dakota attorney general Mark Barnett announced there was "no basis" for the claimed widespread Indian voter fraud.[112]

According to Dr. Dan McCool, the director of the American West Center at the University of Utah and an expert witness for the plaintiffs, the accusations of voter fraud were "part of an effort to create a racially hostile and polarized atmosphere. It's based on negative stereotypes, and I think it's a symbol of just how polarized politics are in the state in regard to Indians and non-Indians."[113]

Following the 2002 elections, which saw a surge in Indian political participation, the legislature passed laws that added additional requirements for voting, including a law requiring photo identification at the polls. Rep. Van Norman said that in passing the burdensome new photo requirement "the legislature was retaliating because the Indian vote was a big factor in new registrants and a close senatorial race."[114] During the legislative debate on a bill that would have made it easier for Indians to vote, representatives made comments that were openly hostile to Indian political participation. According to one opponent of the bill, "I, in my heart, feel that this bill . . . will encourage those who we don't particularly want to have in the system." Alluding to Indian voters, he said "I'm not sure we want that sort of person in the polling place."[115] Bennett County did not comply with the provisions of the Voting Rights Act requiring it to provide minority-language assistance in voting until prior to the 2002 elections, and it only did so then because it was directed to by the Department of Justice.[116]

The county auditor admitted there had been "an Indian versus white mentality" in recent elections in Bennett County.[117] A prime example of that was the 2002 election for the county commission. After three Indians won the Democratic primary, Gary Nelson, the chair of the county Democratic Party, got the county auditor to file a complaint with the Department of Justice that two of three Indian candidates, Gerald Bettelyoun and Francis Rough, were federal employees and were thus barred by the Hatch Act from seeking public office. As a result of the complaint, Rough withdrew from the election. Bettelyoun took early retirement, which cost him a significant cut in pay. The county Democratic Party, in a further attempt to avoid having Indians on the county commission, recruited a slate of three whites to run as Independents in the general election against its own duly nominated candidates.

The district court also found that "[n]umerous reports and volumes of public testimony document the perception of Indian people that they have been discriminated against in various ways in the administration of justice." Thomas Hennies, chief of police in Rapid City, has said, "I personally know that there is racism and there is discrimination and there are prejudices among all people and that they're apparent in law enforcement." Don Holloway, the sheriff of Pennington County, concurred that prejudice and the perception of prejudice in the community were "true or accurate descriptions."[118]

Belva Black Lance, who works for the Rosebud tribal housing authority, said she has frequently been stopped by the police when she has left the reservation. "I got stopped twice in one day," she said. "I don't leave the reservation very much because of that." When she bought a new car, she had it registered in Mellette County, which is off the reservation. "I haven't been stopped since," she said.[119]

Rep. Bradford said he has been the victim of racial profiling and has been stopped by the police off the reservation because of his Shannon County license plates. Rep. Van Norman said he has also been stopped numerous times by law enforcement officers. "Many Indians," he said, "fear going off the reservation to the store at certain places because they think they're going to get harassed by police unfairly."[120]

The court concluded that "Indians in South Dakota bear the effects of discrimination in such areas as education, employment and health, which hinders their ability to participate effectively in the political process." There was also "a significant lack of responsiveness on the part of elected officials to Indian concerns."[121] Rep. Van Norman said in the legislature any bill that has "[a]nything to do with Indians instantly is, in my experience treated in a different way unless acceptable to all." "[W]hen it comes to issues of race or discrimination," he said, "people don't want to hear that." One member of the legislature even accused Van Norman of "being racist" for introducing a bill requiring law enforcement officials to keep records of people they pulled over for traffic stops.[122]

Some of the most compelling testimony in the *Bone Shirt* case, and which was credited by the district court, came from tribal members who recounted numerous incidents of being mistreated, embarrassed, or humiliated by whites. Elsie Meeks, for example, told about her first exposure to the non-Indian world and the fact "that there might be some people who didn't think well of people from the reservation." When she and her sister enrolled in a predominantly white school in Fall River County in the 1960s and were riding the bus, "somebody behind us said . . . the Indians should go back to the reservation. And I mean I was fairly hurt by it . . . it was just sort of a shock to me." Meeks said that there is a "disconnect between Indians and non-Indians" in the state. "[W]hat most people don't realize is that many Indians, they experience this racism in some form from non-Indians nearly every time they go into a border town community. . . . [T]hen their . . . reciprocal feelings are based on that, that they know, or at least feel that the non-Indians don't like them and don't trust them."[123]

Meeks was a candidate for lieutenant governor in 1998. She said she felt welcomed "in Sioux Falls and a lot of the East River communities." But in the towns bordering the reservations, the reception "was more hostile." There, she ran into "this whole notion that . . . Indians shouldn't be allowed to run on the statewide ticket and this perception by non-Indians that . . . we don't pay property tax . . . that we shouldn't be allowed [to run for office.]" Such views were expressed by a member of the state legislature, who said he would be "leading the charge . . . to support Native American voting rights when Indians decide to be citizens of the State by giving up tribal sovereignty and paying their fair share of the tax burden."[124] Gary Nelson, the chair of the Democratic Party in Bennett County, called officials at the courthouse to see if Meeks paid any property taxes. Others called her campaign headquarters and complained that "we don't understand why Bernie [the non-Indian candidate for governor] has her on the ticket when we can't go to her reservation and vote."[125]

Craig Dillon, a tribal member living in Bennett County, told of his experience playing on the varsity football team of the county high school in the 1970s. After practice, members of the team would go to the home of the mayor's son for "fun and games." The mayor, however, "interviewed" Dillon in his office to see if he was "good enough" to be a friend of his son. Dillon says that he flunked the interview. "I guess I didn't measure up because . . . I was the only one that wasn't invited back to the house after football practice after that." He found the experience to be "pretty demoralizing."[126]

Monica Drapeaux said one of the reasons she did not want to attend the public school in Winner during the 1970s was because of the racial tension that existed there. White students "often called Indians 'prairie niggers' and made other derogatory comments."[127]

Lyla Young, who grew up in Parmalee, said the first contact she had with whites was when she went to high school in Todd County in the late 1950s. The Indian students lived in a segregated dorm at the Rosebud boarding school and were bused to the high school, then bused back to the dorm for lunch, then bused again to the high school for the afternoon session. The white students referred to the Indians as "GI's," which stood for "government issue." Young said "I just withdrew. I had no friends at school. Most of the girls that I dormed with didn't finish high school. . . . I didn't associate with anybody. The only contacts that I had, the only time I actually spoke was when I was at boarding school with my peers." Even today, Young has little contact with the white community. "I don't want to. I have no desire to open up my life or my children's life to any kind of discrimination or harsh treatment. Things are tough enough without inviting more." Testifying in court was particularly difficult for her. "This was a big job for me to come here today. . . . I'm the only Indian woman in here, and I'm nervous. I'm very uncomfortable."[128]

Belva Black Lance first came into contact with whites in 1964 when she was six and went to public school in Todd County. "We were treated very mean," she said. "One of the teachers normally had a ruler and would hit your hands if you said something wrong, or we couldn't talk our language. If they didn't understand, we would be in trouble. We wouldn't be able to go out and play." Today, she doesn't like to leave the reservation because "I'm kind of like afraid. Because when we leave the reservation, it seems like we left a safe area and we have to go into an area where it's prejudice. It's normal for us to experience that in the State of South Dakota."[129]

Arlene Brandis, a Rosebud tribal member, remembers walking to and from school in Tripp County in the 1960s. "Cars would drive by and they would holler at us and call us names, like dirty Indian, drunken Indian, and say 'why don't you go back to the reservation.'"[130] Although that was many years ago, Brandis doesn't see much difference between then and now.

The testimony of Young, Meeks, and the others illustrates the polarization that continues to exist between the Indian and white communities in South Dakota, which manifests itself in many ways, including in patterns of racially polarized voting.

Quick Bear Quiver v. Hazeltine: The Other Unsubmitted Voting Changes

Aside from its 2001 legislative redistricting, a number of other voting changes that South Dakota enacted after it became covered by Section 5, but which it refused to submit for preclearance, had the potential for diluting Indian voting strength. One was authorization for municipalities to adopt numbered seat requirements. A numbered seat provision, as the Supreme Court has noted, disadvantages minorities because it creates head-to-head contests and prevents a cohesive political group from single-shot voting, or "concentrating on a single candidate."[131] Another unsubmitted change was the requirement of a majority vote for nomination in primary elections for the U.S. Senate, the U.S. House, and governor.[132] A majority vote requirement can "significantly" decrease the electoral opportunities of a racial minority by allowing the numerical majority to prevail in all elections.[133]

Elaine Quick Bear Quiver and several other members of the Oglala and Rosebud Sioux Tribes in Shannon and Todd counties, and again represented by the ACLU's Voting Rights Project, brought suit against the state in August 2002 to force it to submit for preclearance the 600-plus voting changes it had enacted since its coverage under Section 5.[134] Following negotiations among the parties, the court entered a consent order in December 2002, in which it immediately enjoined implementation of the numbered seat and majority vote requirements absent preclearance and directed the state to develop a comprehensive plan "that will promptly bring the State into full compliance with its obligations under Section 5."[135] The state made its first submission in April 2003 and began a process that took approximately three years to complete.

Many jurisdictions in the South also failed to comply with Section 5 in the years following their coverage. But in none was the failure as deliberate and prolonged as in South Dakota.[136]

Day County

The United States sued officials in Day County in 1999 for denying Indians the right to vote in elections for a sanitary district in the area of Enemy Swim Lake and Campbell Slough. Under the challenged scheme, only residents of several noncontiguous pieces of land owned by whites could vote, whereas residents of the remaining 87 percent of the land around the two lakes, which was owned by the Sisseton-Wahpeton Sioux Tribe and about 200 tribal members, were excluded from the electorate. In an agreement settling the litigation, local officials admitted Indians had been unlawfully denied the right to vote and agreed on a new sanitation district that included the Indian-owned land around the two lakes.[137]

Wagner Community School District

A Section 2 case was filed in March 2002 by Indian plaintiffs against the at-large method of electing the board of education of the Wagner Community School District in Charles Mix County. The parties eventually agreed on a method of elections using cumulative voting to replace the at-large system, and a consent decree was entered by the court on March 18, 2003.[138] At the next election John Sully, an Indian, was elected to the board of education.

City of Martin

Martin, the county seat of Bennett County, has a population of just over 1,000 people, nearly 45 percent of whom are Native American. The city is near the Pine Ridge and Rosebud reservations, and like many border towns it has had its share of racial conflict. In the mid-1990s, there were deep racial divisions over the homecoming ceremony at the local high school, in which male students designated as the "Big Chief" and "Little Chief" selected a "Princess" in a mock Indian ceremony while wearing traditional Indian regalia. Also in the mid-1990s, the federal government successfully sued the local bank for systematic lending discrimination against American Indians.[139] And in early 2002, Indians organized two peaceful marches in Martin to protest what they viewed as racial discrimination and police brutality by the non-Indian sheriff and his deputies.

Just weeks after the 2002 march, the ACLU sued the city on behalf of two Indian voters, alleging that the city's recently adopted redistricting plan violated the constitutional principle of one person, one vote.[140] The city responded by changing its plan to correct the malapportionment, but it did so in a way that fragmented the Indian community and gave white voters an overwhelming supermajority in all three council wards. The city also refused to reopen the candidate qualification period so that prospective candidates could decide whether to run under the new plan.

After a hearing in May 2002, the district court held that the plaintiffs could not challenge the city's decision not to reopen the candidate qualification period because none of the plaintiffs had expressed an intention to run for office under the new plan. The court did, however, allow the plaintiffs to amend their complaint to allege the new plan violated Section 2 and the U.S. Constitution.

After more than two years of discovery, the case went to trial in June 2004. The plaintiffs demonstrated, among other things, that no Indian-preferred candidate had ever been elected to the city council under the challenged plan. The court nonetheless ruled against the plaintiffs in March 2005, finding on the basis of *county* elections that the plaintiffs had not satisfied the third *Gingles* factor.[141] Although Indians are a minority in Martin, they are the majority in Bennett County.

The plaintiffs appealed, and on May 5, 2006, the Eighth Circuit reversed the decision of the district court. It held that "plaintiffs proved by a preponderance of the evidence that the white majority usually defeated the Indian-preferred candidate in Martin aldermanic elections."[142] The court also noted the history of ongoing intentional discrimination against Indians in Martin:

> For more than a decade Martin has been the focus of racial tension between Native-Americas and whites. In the mid-1990s, protests were held to end a racially offensive homecoming tradition that depicted Native-Americans in a demeaning, stereotypical fashion. Concurrently, the United States Department sued and later entered into a consent decree with the local bank requiring an end to 'redlining' loan practices and policies that adversely affected Native-Americans, and censuring

> the bank because it did not employ any Native-Americans. Most recently, resolution specialists from the Justice Department attempted to mediate an end to claims of racial discrimination by the local sheriff against Native-Americans.[143]

On remand, the district court ruled that the at-large system diluted Indian voting strength. Among the findings of the court were the following:

> There is a long, elaborate history of discrimination against Indians in South Dakota in matters relating to voting in South Dakota. . . . Indians in Martin continue to suffer the effects of past discrimination, including lower levels of income, education, home ownership, automobile ownership, and standard of living. . . . Martin city officials have taken intentional steps to thwart Indian voters from exercising political influence. . . . [T]here is a persistent and unacceptable level of racially polarized voting in the City of Martin.[144]

The city was given an opportunity to propose a remedial plan but refused to do so. The court then implemented a system of cumulative voting,[145] and at the elections held in June 2007, three candidates regarded as Indian-friendly were elected. The city has filed a notice of appeal.

Buffalo County

One of the most blatant schemes to disfranchise Indian voters was used in Buffalo County. Based on the 2000 census, the population of the county was approximately 2,000 people, 83 percent of whom were Indian, primarily members of the Crow Creek Sioux Tribe. Under the plan for electing the three-member county commission, which had been in effect for decades, nearly all of the Indian population—some 1,500 people—were packed in one district. Whites, though only 17 percent of the population, controlled the remaining two districts and thus the county government. The system, with its total deviation among districts of 218 percent, was not only in violation of "one person, one vote," but had clearly been implemented and maintained to dilute the Indian vote and ensure white control of county government.

Tribal members, represented by the ACLU, brought suit in 2003 alleging that the districting plan was malapportioned and had been drawn purposefully to discriminate against Indian voters. The case was settled by a consent decree in which the county admitted its plan violated the "one person, one vote" standard of the Fourteenth Amendment and agreed to submit to federal supervision of its future plans under Section 5 of the Voting Rights Act through January 2013.[146]

Charles Mix County

In 2005, members of the Yankton Sioux Tribe, represented by the ACLU, filed suit against Charles Mix County alleging that the three districts for the county commission were malapportioned and had been drawn to dilute Indian voting strength.[147] The total deviation among the districts was 19 percent and almost certainly unconstitutional. Moreover, each district was majority white, despite the fact that Indians were 30 percent of the population of the county and a compact majority-Indian district could easily be drawn. No American Indian had ever been elected under the challenged plan.

South Dakota law prohibited the county from redistricting until 2012.[148] In an effort to avoid court-supervised redistricting following a finding of a "one person, one vote" or Voting Rights Act violation, the county requested the state legislature to pass special legislation establishing a process for emergency redistricting. The legislature complied and passed a bill, which the governor promptly signed, allowing a county to redistrict, with the permission of the governor and secretary of state, at any time it became "aware" of facts that called into question whether its districts complied with federal or state law.[149] Despite the fact that the new law applied to every county in the state, including Shannon and Todd, and was thus required to be precleared under Section 5 as well as the consent decree in the

Quick Bear Quiver case, Charles Mix County immediately sought permission from the governor to draw a new plan. The plaintiffs in *Quick Bear Quiver* then filed a motion for a preliminary injunction before the three-judge court to prohibit the county from proceeding with redistricting absent compliance with Section 5. The court granted the motion.

In a strongly worded opinion, the court noted that state officials in South Dakota "for over 25 years . . . have intended to violate and have violated the preclearance requirements," and that the new bill "gives the appearance of a rushed attempt to circumvent the VRA."[150] Implementation of the new emergency redistricting bill was enjoined until the state complied with Section 5. The state submitted the bill, and the U.S. Department of Justice precleared it.

The county, for its part, argued that the deviation in the challenged plan was constitutional because it was necessary to avoid splitting townships. The court rejected the contention, pointing to redistricting maps prepared by the plaintiffs that achieved almost perfect population equality among districts without splitting any townships. The court ruled that the challenged plan violated "one person, one vote" and gave the county an opportunity to propose a remedial plan.[151]

The county ultimately adopted a plan proposed by the plaintiffs, which created one majority-Indian district out of three with an Indian VAP of just over 60 percent. The first election under the plan was held in 2006, and Sharon Drapeau, a tribal member and a plaintiff in the lawsuit, defeated a non-Indian challenger in the Democratic primary. She went on to win unopposed in the general election and took office in 2007. But the fight over redistricting in Charles Mix County was far from over.

Voters in the county who opposed Indian representation on the county commission began circulating a petition to increase the number of commissioners from three to five. The petition garnered enough signatures to put the issue on the ballot, and it was approved in the November 2006 election. The county redrew the districts in early 2007, creating one majority-Indian district out of five, thus diluting Indian voting strength as well as minimizing the presence of an Indian on the commission.

Even though the court ruled in favor of plaintiffs on the malapportionment issue, their claim that the challenged plan had been adopted and implemented for racially discriminatory reasons remained pending. The parties were subsequently able to agree that the county would be subject to Section 5 until 2024, and that it would submit its five-member plan for preclearance.[152] The plan was submitted, and on February 11, 2008, the U.S. Department of Justice objected to the increase in size of the county commission, concluding "that the county has not sustained its burden of showing that the proposed change does not have a discriminatory purpose."[153]

In reaching its decision the department relied on a variety of factors:

- "[T]he voting changes appear to have a greater impact on Native Americans because, under the proposed plan, Native Americans voters can elect their candidate of choice in only one of five districts, as opposed to one in three under the current plan."
- "Charles Mix County and the State of South Dakota have a history of voting discrimination against Native Americans. Native Americans could not vote in the county until 1951. Even when Native Americans received the right to vote, they were discriminated against in registration and other parts of the voting process."
- Following the 2000 census, "the County Commissioners decided not to redistrict despite the fact that commissioners knew that the districts did not provide Native Americans the voting strength to elect a candidate of choice."
- "[T]he first remedial plan suggested by the county [following the finding of a "one person, one vote" violation] again failed to provide Native Americans with an opportunity to elect a candidate of their choice."
- Following Drapeau's nomination in the 2006 Democratic primary election, "an article about changing the number of county commissioners appeared in *The Lake Andes Wave*. Momentum for the petition then built, and one thousand signatures were obtained to put the referendum on the ballot."

- "Elected officials supported the increase in the number of county commissioners. In particular, the Sheriff and his deputies, actively circulated the petition."
- Members of the community, Indian and non-Indian, "have informed the Section that county commissioners have made comments that evidence a racially discriminatory intent."[154]

The county has the option of seeking judicial preclearance of the proposed change, but has not elected to do so. As a result, the three-member plan remains in effect.

A variety of common factors have coalesced to isolate American Indian voters from the political mainstream in South Dakota and throughout the West—past discrimination, polarized voting, overt hostility of white public officials, cultural and language barriers, a depressed socioeconomic status, inability to finance campaigns, difficulties in establishing coalitions with white voters, a lack of faith in nontribal political systems, and conflicts with non-Indians over issues such as water rights, taxation, and tribal jurisdiction. But as the American Indian population increases in the west, and despite continued resistance from the non-Indian population, American Indians will play an increasingly important role in local, state, and national politics.

The willingness of American Indians in South Dakota to turn to the federal courts to protect and vindicate their voting rights is evidence of the importance American Indians place on participating in nontribal elections. And the success they have had in electing candidates of their choice at every level of government will ensure the continuing and important role of Indian voters and Indian elected officials.

CHAPTER 6

Colorado

Arthur Cuthair and other members of the Ute Mountain Ute Tribe in Montezuma County, Colorado, filed suit in 1989 challenging at-large elections for the board of directors of Montezuma-Cortez School District RE-1.[1] No American Indian had ever been elected to the school board or any other nontribal office in the county. Indeed, Indians living on reservations in Colorado were not allowed to vote until 1970, and they were allowed to vote then only because the Supreme Court held that residents of federal "enclaves" could not be denied the right to vote in state elections.[2] Because the majority of Indians in Montezuma County lived on the Ute Mountain Ute Reservation, Indians had been effectively disfranchised by the state law.

Colorado's history of disfranchising Indians goes back to its early days as a territory, when voting was limited to "white male citizens."[3] "[P]ersons of Indian blood" could vote only if they had been declared by treaty to be citizens of the United States.[4]

On the eve of passage of the Indian Citizenship Act of 1924, the attorney general of Colorado issued an opinion that residence on land under the exclusive jurisdiction of the United States could not satisfy the residency requirement for voting in state elections.[5] And even after passage of the Indian Citizenship Act, Colorado continued to deny reservation Indians the right to vote. In a 1936 letter to the attorney general of Colorado, the superintendent of the Consolidated Ute Agency wrote, "[t]he Indians of my jurisdiction have never, so far as I can determine, tried to exercise the right to elective franchise." In a response to the letter, the Colorado attorney general confirmed that "until Congress enfranchises the Indian, he will not have the right to vote. He could not qualify either under the 14th Amendment to the Constitution of the United States or Article VII, Section 1, Constitution of Colorado or under our statutory qualification of a voter."[6]

In 1960, the attorney general of Colorado reaffirmed that inhabitants of lands over which the federal government has exclusive jurisdiction could not vote in Colorado.[7] As late as 1966, the Colorado legislature enacted a memorial acknowledging that "[u]nder the constitution and laws of the State of Colorado," residents of Indian reservations within the exclusive jurisdiction of the federal government "are not deemed to be 'residents' of the State of Colorado for the purposes of elections."[8]

Even after Indians residing on reservations were allowed to vote, Utes were not allowed to register at the tribal headquarters at Towaoc until the late 1980s or early 1990s, despite the fact the non-Indian population was allowed satellite registration at several communities in the county. A permanent polling place was not established on the reservation until 1991. It is not surprising, given these restrictions on their political participation, that Indians have had significantly lower rates of voter registration and turnout than whites.

The Utes Must Go!

The denial of voting rights to Indians throughout most of the twentieth century is consistent with the long and egregious history of discrimination against Indians in Colorado. Traditionally, the Ute Indians, composed of several subdivisions or bands, occupied some 150,000 square miles in what is now Colorado, part of Utah, and part of northern New Mexico. The first treaty between the Utes and the United States was negotiated at Abiquiu, New Mexico, in 1849.[9] It provided for Ute recognition of U.S. sovereignty, subjected the Utes to federal law, permitted the federal government to establish military posts and agencies in Ute country, and confined the tribe to their accustomed territory.

Soon thereafter settlers began moving from New Mexico into Ute territory in the San Luis Valley of Colorado, which caused conflict between the settlers and Indians. Confrontations in the vicinity of present-day Pueblo, Colorado, resulted in a military campaign against the Utes in 1855. The Utes were defeated in several engagements and agreed to a treaty in 1855, but it was never ratified by the United States.

The gold rush in Colorado in 1858 and 1859 brought increased contact between Utes and whites and increased white demand for access to Ute lands. During and after this period, local newspapers incited fear and hatred of Indians by describing them as "savages, inferiors, lazy, dirty, half-naked."[10] The *Weekly Rocky Mountain News* described the "natural dispositions [of Indians] to beg and steal" and predicted that if trouble occurred "[t]he people will rise in their might and sweep the redskins before them without distinction of nation or tribe."[11] Of twenty-seven stories in the *Rocky Mountain News* in 1863 dealing with American Indians, ten overtly favored extermination. One of the stories was unabashedly titled, "Exterminate Them." In describing American Indians, the paper said, "[t]hey are a dissolute, vagabondish, brutal and ungrateful race and ought to be wiped from the face of the earth."[12]

The territorial legislature sent a memorial to Congress in 1862 asking the secretary of the interior to negotiate treaties with the Utes "by which all their lands (a large part of which are mineral) . . . may be ceded to the general government."[13] In 1863, a Ute delegation was taken to Washington, D.C., and on their return treaty negotiations were held. Only Chief Ouray and other Tabeguache Utes signed the treaty, which was ratified in 1864. The treaty reduced the Ute land base by about one-quarter and included the cession to the United States of the San Luis Valley and the mining areas between the Arkansas River and North Park.[14]

When Indians, believed to be Arapahos, murdered the Hungate family near Denver in the early summer of 1864, white animosity toward Indians grew.[15] On August 10, 1864, Gov. John Evans issued an appeal to the people of Colorado to defend themselves and kill Indians. "Any man who kills a hostile Indian is a patriot," he proclaimed.[16] The *Rocky Mountain News* had asked, "Shall we not go for them, their lodges, squaws and all?" A spokesman for impatient whites answered, "They need killing."[17] According to the paper, "[a] few months of active extermination against the red devils will bring quiet and nothing else will."[18]

In November 1864 a group of Colorado volunteers led by Col. John Chivington, who was also a Methodist minister, made a surprise attack on a Cheyenne and Arapahoe village at Sand Creek in eastern Colorado and massacred several hundred Indians. Most were women, children, and elderly men, and many were scalped and sexually mutilated.[19] Chivington had ordered his men to "kill and scalp all, big and little; nits make lice."[20] Newspapers in the state greeted reports of the Sand Creek Massacre with universal approval.[21] According to a *Rocky Mountain (Colo.) News* editorial published in 1864, the massacre was "[a]mong the brilliant feats of arms in Indian warfare," and the Colorado soldiers "have again covered themselves with glory."

A federal commission, the Joint Committee on the Conduct of the War, conducted an investigation of the massacre and strongly condemned it and recommended that the perpetrators be punished. However, no action was taken to implement the recommendation. Later, in 1909, a civil war memorial was installed at the Colorado Capitol listing the Sand Creek Massacre as one of the Union's great victories.

Shortly after the massacre, Sen. James R. Doolittle of Wisconsin visited Colorado and met with Governor Evans on the stage of the Denver Opera House. In describing the meeting Doolittle wrote, "The question has arisen whether we should place the Indians on reservations and teach them to raise cattle and corn and to support themselves, or whether we should exterminate them, there suddenly arose such a shout as is never heard unless upon some battlefield—a shout almost loud enough to raise the roof of the Opera House—'EXTERMINATE THEM'! 'EXTERMINATE THEM'!"[22]

A Colorado Territorial memorial in 1865 advised Congress that "immediate and efficient action in subduing these hostile Indians is essential to the safety and preservation of the people of this Territory."[23] A memorial in 1866 informed Congress that "our present safety and future security demand a rigorous prosecution of war, until the indians sue for peace."[24] A memorial the following year noted "the growth and prosperity of those sections of country within the range of [the Ute] tribe are greatly retarded by the insecurity to life and property, which results from their being permitted to roam at will through the country."[25]

Indians retaliated against whites for the Sand Creek Massacre, which brought forth even more hatred of Indians. The *Central City Register* described Indians as "a treacherous relentless villainous people, with scarcely a noble trait of character, except such as are manufactured for them by writers of romance." The paper suggested the use of poison on Indians and urged the legislature to authorize a $100 bounty for Indian scalps.[26]

The *Transcript* of Golden, Colorado, opposed efforts to make peace with the Indians. "The day has passed for sympathetic treatment," it said. "We must apply the knife."[27] Four months later, the *Rocky Mountain News* announced, "[w]e are in favor of supplying every indian between the Missouri river and the Pacific coast with powder and ball, but it is from the muzzle of Springfield rifles at short range."[28] The Pueblo *Chieftain* was equally to the point. The Indian "is treacherous, thieving, lying, drunken, sneaking, blood thirsty, brutal, ungrateful, and he has all these and every other bad quality in the superlative degree, unredeemed by a single spark of humanity, generosity, chivalry, or decency."[29]

As a result of increased pressure from whites, a treaty was negotiated in 1868 that further reduced the Ute land base and established for all Ute bands a single reservation composed of roughly the western one-third of Colorado, with an agency at Los Pinos and another on the White River. The treaty stipulated that the United States would supply education, clothing, and food until the Utes were self-sufficient, and it provided that no unauthorized white men would "ever be permitted to pass over, settle upon, or reside in" the territory assigned to the Utes.[30]

Almost immediately after the Ute Treaty of 1868 was approved, miners, in direct violation of its explicit terms, came in increasing numbers to mine the rich minerals of the region.[31] As a result of increased mining activity by whites in 1870, pressure began to mount to force the Utes to cede all the mining area or to remove them completely from the state.[32] In 1872, Congress granted the Denver and Rio Grande Railway Company a right of way over the Ute Reservation without compensation to the Utes.[33] That same year, the territory asked the president to renegotiate the Ute Treaty of 1868 because "[r]ecently most valuable discoveries of gold and silver mines have been made in the southern portion of the reservation. . . . [T]he country referred to will eventually prove one of the most valuable portions of the domain of the United States; and the interest of civilization will be served."[34]

Responding to ever-increasing white demands, a federal commission was appointed and began negotiations with the Utes in August 1872. However, Ouray, a leading spokesman for the Utes, said, "[w]e do not want to sell a foot of our land—that is the opinion of all. . . . We have come here so that you may see that we are not satisfied with this trespassing on our lands; but we do not want to sell any of them."[35]

The negotiations failed, but the pressure to remove the Utes continued to mount. The *Denver Tribune* expressed a prevailing view that "American pioneers should be prodded out of the country by American bayonets, in order that a small band of dirty nomads can idly roam over 20 million acres of hunting ground is an atrocity that no other Government on the face of the earth but our own would be guilty of committing."[36]

The federal government initially ordered the expulsion of miners from the Ute Reservation, but following loud protests across the territory, the order was rescinded. Miners rushed in to the mining areas, and Felix Brunot was sent in 1873 to negotiate with the Utes. Over the continuing objections of Indians, the treaty of 1868 was renegotiated by Brunot. The Brunot agreement, approved by Congress in 1874, ceded the mineral-rich San Juan mountain area—a rectangular tract in the middle section of the 1868 reservation comprising approximately one-fourth of the Ute Reservation—to the United States.[37]

According to historian Robert Delaney, "[t]here seems no doubt that [the negotiators of the Brunot agreement] lied to the Utes to secure this cession of land. The Utes believed that they were ceding only the mines of the area and that the rest of the land was theirs. The government also failed to pay the Utes the amount of money promised."[38] The territorial legislature itself acknowledged that "not one dollar has been appropriated" to fulfill the terms of the Brunot agreement and warned that "the Utes have become exceedingly irritated" at the apparent lack of good faith.[39]

In February 1876, the year of its statehood, the Colorado legislature memorialized Congress for the removal of the Utes to Indian Territory.[40] Congress enacted legislation in 1878 directing the president to negotiate with the Utes for the consolidation of all Ute bands, including those in New Mexico, onto one reservation in northern Colorado.[41] Whites renewed their call for the removal of all Utes and took up the mantra, "The Utes Must Go!"[42]

Pressure to remove the Utes escalated sharply in 1879, when Utes at the White River Agency in northern Colorado killed Agent Nathan Meeker and then engaged in combat with troops that approached the agency from the north. After the Meeker incident, Gov. Frederick W. Pitkin declared, "unless removed by the government, [the Utes] must necessarily be exterminated. . . . The advantages that would accrue from throwing open 12,000,000 acres of land to miners and settlers would more than compensate all the expenses incurred."[43] In subsequent testimony before Congress, Pitkin, in something of an understatement, said "I do not think the people of the State like an Indian."[44]

Both major political parties, and virtually the entire state, continued to demand that the Utes must go. According to the *Denver Daily Times*, "Either they go or we go and we are not going. Humanitarianism is an idea. The western Empire is an inexorable fact. He who gets in its way will be crushed."[45] The *Dolores News* wrote, "if the Utes don't go out. . .they ought to go down—in the ground."[46] Governor Pitkin declared, "when the snow melts if the government has not removed the Indians, the people of Colorado will do it."[47]

In response to demands from the state of Colorado, Congress enacted a law in 1880 relinquishing to the United States a large portion of the previous Ute Reservation. The northern Ute bands were removed to the Uintah Reservation in Utah, and the other Ute bands were removed to smaller tracts in southwestern Colorado.[48]

But there was no end to demands that Indians be expelled from Colorado. An 1882 resolution by a committee of citizens from Gunnison urged that Ute land ceded to the United States in 1880 be opened to settlers wishing to exploit its "great natural resources."[49] Local cattlemen in 1885 massacred a Ute family group of eleven people at Beaver Creek near Dolores, giving further evidence of the degenerate relationship between whites and Indians in Colorado.[50] The Colorado legislature petitioned Congress in 1885 and again in 1887 for the removal of the remaining Ute bands from the state.[51] In 1886, a group of cowboys surrounded a teepee and killed an Indian family of six, including men, women, and children.[52]

Creation of the Ute Mountain Ute Reservation

In 1888 Congress authorized the appointment of a commission to negotiate for the removal of the remaining Utes from Colorado.[53] In 1895, Congress allotted, or deeded, the remaining Ute lands in Colorado to individual members of the southern Ute bands and provided a small reservation "on the west forty miles of the present reservation" for those who chose not to take allotments.[54] Those choosing against allotment included almost the entire Weeminuche band. This was the beginning of the separation of the three bands of the Southern Utes into two groups: (1) the Mouache and the Capote bands, located on the eastern portion of the reservation; and (2) the Weeminuche band, located on the western end of the reservation. After the turn of the century, the two sections became known as the Southern Ute

Reservation, home of the Mouache and Capote bands, and the Ute Mountain Reservation, home of the Weeminuche band.[55]

One of the most imposing geological features on the Ute Mountain Reservation is the Sleeping Ute Mountain, a self-contained range of mountains five by twelve miles with one peak as high as 4,250 feet. Legend has it that it is the resting place of a Great Warrior God, who lay down after a fight with the Evil Ones and fell into a deep sleep. The Sleeping Ute Mountain, visible for miles around, resembles a warrior lying on his back with his arms folded across his chest.

Frederick Chapin described the Ute Mountain Utes in the 1890s as leading "a roaming, pastoral life." In the summer, they lived in "wickyups" made of poles and covered with brush. In the winter, the wickyups were covered with skins or tent cloth but still provided poor protection from the icy cold and snows of winter.[56]

The Weeminuche were promised a system of irrigation with which to reclaim the desert they were confined to. But according to the 1900 *Annual Report of the Department of the Interior*, "[f]ive years have passed and the desert is still there as it was, the Indians barely existing, being wholly dependent upon what is issued them for a livelihood."[57]

Communities surrounding the Ute Mountain Ute Reservation treated Indians as second-class citizens and attempted to keep them out of public schools. The secretary of the school system at Breen wrote the Indian agent at Ignacio in November 1917, advising him that the school district was no longer going to permit four Ute Indian children to attend the district's schools. According to the secretary, "[t]he habits and unsanitary conditions of their homes and the way they associate with other Indians for miles around them are intirely [*sic*] unsatisfactory to the school board and the taxpayers of this district."[58] Fifteen years later, a nurse for the BIA visited Blanding and Towaoc and reported that parents vigorously protested against Indian children attending the public schools. In the 1950s, the bureau reported discrimination against Ute Mountain Ute children in the Blanding area, where Indian children were placed in an old barracks whereas white children were placed in a new and well-equipped building.[59]

Conditions on the reservation did not improve after the turn of the century. The Board of Indian Commissioners reported in 1922 that "[n]one of the Indians live in permanent houses; they move their tepees from place to place in summer and live in shelters built of brush and mud in the winter under physical living conditions which are miserable." The report recommended the Indian "should be provided at once with sheep and induced to house himself and family in a sanitary way."[60] In testimony before a congressional committee in 1931, the Indian agent said the Ute Mountain Utes "do not have any homes or do not have any farms or gardens" and lived off a $50 a year per capita payment. After they were placed on the reservation in the 1890s, the Utes received rations from the U.S. government, consisting mainly of beans and salt. In 1931, however, the rations stopped.[61]

Following passage of the Indian Reorganization Act, some former Ute lands were restored to tribal ownership in 1937.[62] Later, in 1950, the Court of Claims awarded $31,761,207.62 to the Utes as additional and just compensation for lands ceded by them to the United States in 1880. Some $6 million of the award went to the Ute Mountain Utes.[63] Of the $6 million the Ute Mountain Utes got, some was allotted under "family plans" and was used to build homes and purchase furniture, vehicles, and livestock. Some money was put in trust and allocated to children when they became eighteen. This money was known as "eighteen money."

In the 1950s, the Ute Tribal Council decided that Ute children would be less isolated and better served if they attended school in Cortez, rather than the Indian school on the reservation or nearby boarding schools. Accordingly, every year another grade was transported in buses owned by the tribe from Towaoc to the schools in Cortez.[64]

But the condition of the Ute Mountain Utes remained dire. The infant mortality rate was high, and the adult survival rate was low. In the 1960s, there were only 600 tribal members, and many still lived in tepees and hogans, which lacked electricity and running water.[65] Most spoke only Ute and were unable to converse in, or read, English. Only five tribal members had a high school education.[66]

Continuing Discrimination and Polarization

Anti-Indian attitudes remained fixed in the minds of many Coloradans, particularly in the southwestern corner of the state. The *Montezuma Valley Journal*, the most important local newspaper in Montezuma County, throughout the first half of the twentieth century generally ignored the Ute Indian community in its reporting, indicating that the Indian and white communities were distinct and apart, with very little interaction between them. When the *Journal* did report on Indian affairs, the tone was usually quite hostile or condescending. Indians were referred to as "redskins," "papoose," and "squaw." A front-page headline on March 30, 1944, announced a story about a "Peyote-Crazed Indian."[67]

Reflecting the general attitudes of the white community, which was its readership, the *Journal* consistently opposed Indian voting rights, Indian hunting rights, the tribe's choice for the route of new roads across the reservation, and tribal charges of discrimination.[68] There was no appreciable change in the *Journal*'s coverage of Indians until the community of Cortez began to recognize economic benefits from the neighboring Ute Mountain Ute Reservation in the late 1940s and 1950s.

Ute Mountain Ute income increased in the 1950s through the sale of oil and gas leases on the reservation and the receipt of monetary judgments from the cases before the U.S. Court of Claims. The per capita payment to Indians has varied, but since the 1980s it has, on average, amounted to only several hundred dollars a year.

The city of Cortez and Montezuma County also stood to benefit from the expenditure of federal funds for Indian rehabilitation projects such as road building.[69] Hence, many whites for the first time saw Utes as a source of income to be cultivated by the white community. According to Richard Ellis, a professor of Southwest studies at Ft. Lewis College in Durango, "the economic power of the Ute Mountain Utes is the thing that does the most to bring about a moderation of attitude in Montezuma County."[70]

Whatever thaw there was in the economic ties between Utes and whites in Montezuma County, the two communities remained distinct and separate and sharply divided over many issues. The two communities clashed in 1955 over the sale of liquor by Cortez merchants to minors and intoxicated Indians. Indians were not allowed to serve on juries in the county until 1956. Indians and whites were divided in 1959 over a system of Indian peonage operated by the city jail and local farmers and labor contractors, in 1970 over charges of discrimination against Indians in law enforcement (over 83 percent of persons arrested in Cortez were Indians, although Indians were 14 percent of the population in the county), in 1972 over discrimination in the Southwest Memorial Hospital, in 1977 over "double pricing" by merchants in Cortez (charging one price for whites and another, higher price for Indians), in 1978 over Indian hunting rights, in 1980 over discrimination in employment in Cortez, and in 1986 over the beating of a seventy-eight-year-old Ute Indian by two local whites.[71]

The *Journal*, a barometer of community sentiment, continued to reflect an attitude that was negative toward Indians. It opposed bilingual and bicultural education, complained about the bingo operations on the Ute Mountain Ute Reservation, complained about the continuation of Indian land claims, complained about Indian advantages over area farmers because of cheaper water through the Navajo Irrigation Project, opposed concepts of tribal sovereignty, and complained about nonpayment of taxes by Indians.[72]

Robert Delaney, writing in the late 1980s, said "[t]he Ute Mountain Utes have an uncertain future. They are still very isolated. They, like many other Native Americans, have problems identifying with the dominant culture around them. . . . There is a great deal of antagonism between the Utes and the non-Indian community, which generally views the Indians as being social and sexual delinquents, shiftless, and alcoholic, in spite of evidence to the contrary."[73]

Jim Carrier, a journalist who spent three months with the Ute Mountain Utes in 1989 and wrote a book about his experiences, reported a great deal of antagonism between whites and Indians. Merchants, for example, "still harbor attitudes that Utes are lazy and not to be trusted," he said. Both Indians and whites reported stories of how Indians were "ripped off" by businesses when oil and gas royalties enabled tribal members to buy trucks, refrigerators, and other big-ticket items.[74]

Carrier found that few county residents knew Utes on an individual basis or had even visited Towaoc, even though it was just eleven miles down the road from Cortez. The physical separation between the white and Indian communities perpetuated their cultural isolation and also made it extremely difficult for Indians to establish alliances with whites in the political arena.

One example of the disconnect that exists between American Indians and whites occurred in 1992 when the Indian Parent Advisory Committee of School District No. RE-1 asked the board of directors to develop a mission statement for bilingual education and Indian education programs in addition to the existing district mission statement. The board refused, giving as its reason its belief that "District mission statements must be 'ethnically clean.'"[75] Indians interpreted the action of the school board as meaning that the curriculum would be "WASP-based." Clyde Benally, a Navajo who lives in Cortez and works as a seasonal employee at nearby Mesa Verde, was a member of the parent advisory committee. He said the board's decision "was driven by prejudice. There is quite a bit of old style prejudice here."[76] Benally has a son who attends school in Cortez, but he was afraid to do a report on Indians in his history class because he believed the teacher was biased against tribal members.

Historically, the Ute Mountain Ute Reservation had no source of water to irrigate crops. It also had no potable drinking water, which had to be hauled in on trucks from Cortez. It was not until 1992, and after extensive litigation and passage of the Colorado Ute Water Settlement Act of 1988, that the tribe finally got piped drinking water and irrigation water to its farm and ranch project.

There were also occasional violent confrontations between Utes and whites. In 1995, two white youths who said they "wanted to have some fun with a drunk Indian" rousted a sleeping Indian in an alley in Cortez and beat him into insensibility. The same month, two white youths from adjoining LaPlata County murdered two young Ute women for their "eighteen money."[77]

Indians in Montezuma County continue to have a depressed socioeconomic status compared with whites. According to the 1990 census, 47.77 percent of Indians and 16.59 percent of whites had incomes below the poverty level. The per capita income of Indians was $5,555 versus $10,914 for whites. Of Indian households, 28.82 percent had incomes of less than $5,000, compared with 8.49 percent of white households.[78]

Cuthair v. Montezuma-Cortez

The board of directors of School District RE-1 consisted of seven members elected at-large from residential, or director, districts. On the basis of the 1990 census, the total population of the school district was 13,936, of whom 1,969 (14.1 percent) were Indian. One of the director districts, District D, was located on the Ute Mountain Ute Reservation and was majority-Indian (55.3 percent), with an Indian VAP of 53 percent.

The first Indian to run for the board of directors was Mary Coyote in 1969, and she was defeated. Other Indian candidates ran for the board in 1973, 1985, and 1989 and were also defeated. An analysis of the elections showed that voting was sharply polarized, with Indians voting for Indian candidates at an average rate of 76 percent and whites voting for white candidates at an average rate of 80 percent.

After the complaint was filed, and after extensive negotiations, the parties entered into a consent decree on April 9, 1990, establishing District D as a single-member district. The other six members of the board were to be elected from their respective residency districts at-large.

Four years later, however, the board filed a motion to allow it to resume at-large voting for all seven seats. The plaintiffs opposed the motion, but the case was assigned to a different judge, who granted it on the grounds that the consent decree was unenforceable because the defendants had not admitted liability nor had the court made a finding that the at-large system violated either Section 2 of the Voting Rights Act or the Constitution. The court further ordered the case be set for trial on plaintiffs' vote-dilution claim.[79]

Each of the plaintiffs told similar stories of the problems he or she had encountered growing up in the public schools and with the white community in general. Arthur Cuthair, who was a member of the Ute Tribal Council, was born in 1947 at Ignacio. As did his parents, he spoke only Ute. He first began learning English when he was seven or eight and was attending boarding school on the reservation. He then transferred to Cortez for the ninth grade but dropped out because "we've always felt different and isolated. We couldn't speak Ute in the public school. You had to cut your hair. No braids or pony tails were allowed." After he left high school, Cuthair went into the Army. Upon his discharge, he came back to the reservation and helped establish and supervise the Ute Tribal Park, which contains an impressive collection of cliff dwellings, geological formations, ancestral Pueblo petroglyphs, pictographs, and artifacts. He has also worked as an interpretive ranger at Mesa Verde National Park, which borders the reservation.[80]

Cuthair's children have also had problems in the public schools. His three daughters attended school in Cortez, but he took them out after they were accused of scratching a mirror in the restroom. Although the girls denied the accusation, the vice-principal of the school called the police, who arrested the girls and took them to a detention facility in Grand Junction. After they were released, Cuthair sent the girls to a boarding school in Anadarko, Oklahoma. "They were much happier there," he said.

"The at-large system for the school board discourages people from registering and voting," Cuthair said. "The Ute people feel defeated to start with. We think we will lose anyway, because we are so outnumbered. We also feel there is a lot of prejudice against us. Whites say all the time, 'Utes aren't educated enough to run their own programs.' They say we don't need a polling place on the reservation because we can't get it together. They say, 'they'll never advance, they're nothing but drunkards, they're just good for holding a parking meter up or sleeping or laying in the gutter.'"

Cuthair is soft spoken and a dedicated idealist. He ran for the school board in 1989 from District D, the residency district that included the reservation and was majority Indian. He decided to run because he felt Indians wanted and needed a representative on the board. As he put it, "We have to be involved with the public schools. I truly believe that we can all sit down and work together and live together, and get our education in the process. There's a word that goes around saying 'Not I, we.' That's what I believe in, 'we.' All of us together go down the road. If we're going to the top of the ladder, hey, let's all go up to the top of the ladder together, not 'I.'"

Cuthair and other tribal members had appeared before the school board in the past. "We would ask for legitimate things," he said, "fair treatment for tribal children by teachers, principals, whoever. But the school board would argue with us. They didn't want anyone voicing their opinion or asking for legitimate things. I've lived that. I was there. I came with good faith in my heart, thinking that I can deal with people, that they would be fair. But it didn't happen."

Cuthair participated in a major Indian voter registration drive and conducted a word-of-mouth campaign, speaking at forums in Cortez and Towoac. But he campaigned mainly in the Ute areas. "It was the old feeling from the past," he explained, "that it would have been a waste of time and money, that whites had made up their minds to vote for whites. Utes will vote for Utes, and whites will vote for whites." The election proved Cuthair correct. He received 57 percent of the votes in District D and would have won had the election been held only in that district. But the election was held at-large, and he lost to his white opponent, who received 62 percent of the total vote. Significantly, the election involved a hotly contested issue over the makeup of the school board, which resulted in the defeat of all the incumbents who sought reelection—with the exception of Whitmer, who was the only incumbent who faced an American Indian opponent.[81]

Cuthair acknowledged there are still some Indians, known as "Reservation Indians," who "don't really want to have outside contact with the white world. It's part of our history. The Indians who went to World War I and II had outside contact, but others simply wanted to live their own life in a corner of Colorado here. Not to hate anybody. Just want to be left alone. I guess that's where the phrase 'Reservation Indian' comes from."

Jocelyn Dutchie, another of the Ute plaintiffs, was born in 1954. She went to school in Cortez for a year but left because she was not comfortable with what she described as "the racial situation. I felt Indians were always being put down. So many Indian kids leave the schools because they were not being treated fairly." She is married and has three children, two of whom are in the public schools. One of her sons dropped out in the ninth grade "because Anglos picked on him," she said. "The Indians were isolated, and there was a hostile environment racially. I hope my other kids make it through, but I don't know. They put Indians in special ed and don't really give them a chance."[82]

Dutchie and her husband organized the first Indian girls' softball team in Montezuma County in 1986. "We got hassled so badly," she said. "We got put down by people in the bleachers, who called us 'stupid Indians' and said 'you're no good.' We also got hassled by the umpires. The Anglos just don't like to get beat by Indians. The kids took it as best they could, and we had a winning season. Not all Anglos are bad, but the good ones are not that many."

"When you go into stores in town," Dutchie said, "you get rude treatment, and you feel people are watching you for stealing. Anglos think Indians are just no good. There are two societies. Except for the softball team, I don't have any real ties with Anglos off the reservation."

Dutchie's comments were echoed by Angela Badback, another of the Ute plaintiffs. She attended school in Cortez but left after the sixth grade to attend boarding schools in Arizona and New Mexico. She left public school because of fighting among the students and harsh treatment from teachers. "I wasn't being treated fairly," she said. "The Anglos were always right and the Indians were always wrong." She has no significant contact with the non-Indian community. The church she attends, the Holy Ghost Church, has only one white member.[83]

Gloria Tom, another plaintiff, was born in 1958. She attended school in Cortez but left after the sixth grade because she got in a fight with a white boy and was expelled. "It fell back on racism at Cortez," she said, "where Indian kids would fight the white kids, and Indian kids would be blamed for anything that would happen. There was a lot of confrontation that went on." She has five children who attend school in Cortez, and two of them have also been expelled for fights with white students. She has virtually no Anglo friends and almost no contact with the white community.[84]

Joselina Lopez, another Ute plaintiff, went to the high school in Cortez but dropped out before her senior year. "I knew I wasn't going to make it," she explained. "I wasn't getting the attention I needed, but the more you ask for help the more frustrated the teacher gets." She transferred to an alternative school for Indians at Shiprock, New Mexico, and graduated with a high school diploma. She has very little contact with the non-Indian community.[85]

Marjorie Soto is a plaintiff and a member of the Ute Mountain Ute Tribe. She was born in 1953, and English is a second language for her. Her parents spoke only Ute, and she would have to interpret for her mother when they went to stores in Cortez. She attended junior high in Cortez but left during the ninth grade to attend an Indian boarding school in Chilocco, Oklahoma. "When I entered junior high I began to have problems," she said. "I became aware of prejudice against Indians and Hispanics. The teacher made us sit in the back of the class, and we were ignored. The teacher wouldn't help us, and we didn't learn much. Part of it is cultural. Ute people are not aggressive, and that can carry over into the school room. We are afraid when we go to school. We're Indian, and we're different. There is a fear of whites."

"Money talks," Soto said. "If you have money you're OK, but if you're poor they'll treat you as a subspecies. I was on food stamps at one time and was treated very shabbily in the stores. I don't think whites were treated the same way. We really are two different societies, and we don't intersect unless we have to. I have few contacts in the white community. There is a lot of prejudice against Indians in Cortez."

Soto has a degree as a licensed public nurse and applied for a job in a nursing home in Cortez but was not hired. "I could get a job as a maid in a motel, but it's very discouraging. You know that even if you get a degree, you can't get a job in Cortez. That causes a lot of fear and a sense of rejection for many Indians. Sometimes I feel embarrassed to say I am from Towaoc. Those who really suffer are the kids."

She worked for a year at the hospital in Cortez and said she saw discrimination against Indians. "On one occasion in 1993, the police brought in an intoxicated Indian who had been beaten by some white kids. The officers were laughing about Indians and Indian drunks and how we're no better than dogs."[86]

Janice Colorow was born in 1953 and has lived on the reservation her entire life. She grew up speaking Ute and did not learn English until she was in the fifth grade. Her parents were Ute speakers, and the family lived in a hogan. During the summer, they became nomadic sheep herders and lived in the surrounding hills and canyons in a tent. She attended the high school in Cortez for about a year and then transferred to the Ignacio Indian boarding school. "I went to boarding school basically because Indian kids could not get along with the white kids. The teachers were not helpful. Those of us who had problems usually tend to be put in the back of the room." She ran unsuccessfully for the board of education in 1991.[87]

Julian Lopez, who grew up on the reservation speaking Ute, also had negative experiences at the high school in Cortez. "They said I couldn't speak my own language in class. And when I needed help with my homework, they showed me once and that was it. But they would spend a lot of time with the Anglo kids and show them how to do it." Lopez also said the white students picked on Indians. He dropped out of the high school in the ninth grade. He now creates Indian art, paints, and makes pottery.[88]

Sarah Hatch, a tribal member, is the coordinator for the Johnson–O'Malley program, which provides federal funds to state schools attended by Indians to help meet their special education needs. She said Indian students begin to have problems when they get into middle school: "They start having problems academically and socially." Her son attended the junior high school in Cortez but left after the ninth grade and went to the Sherman Indian School in Riverside, California. "He felt isolated," she said. "He felt the teachers should have worked more with him, and that his academic work suffered at the school. A lot of Indian students go through the same thing. And I don't think it's a question of ability. My son did well at Sherman, and was always in the honor dorm."[89]

One of the non-Indians who testified at trial was Amanda Bandy, an anthropologist who worked for the Ute Mountain Ute Tribe for fifteen years as a social worker. She also served on the board of directors of the Colorado American Indian Foundation and was appointed by the governor to serve out a term in the Colorado State Senate. She said "racism is alive and well in southwest Colorado," and "the huge majority of people in each cultural community see themselves as separate and often in competition if not conflict."[90] Shortly after she went to work for the tribe, one of her first clients was a Ute Mountain Ute woman whom she said "had been attacked by a pickup-truck load of white Cortez youths who shoved a Coke bottle up her vagina. She had a number of ongoing medical and psychological problems resulting from that."

Bandy recalled another incident in 1990 when she went to a Wal-Mart with a young Ute male who needed to buy some things before going off to school. He went to the service desk to pay for the purchases from his Individual Indian Money account, also known as "eighteen money," and the assistant manager said loud enough for her to hear, "I just hate it when these kids get to go shopping on my tax money. This is bullshit." Bandy says she regularly hears people say things like, "Indians got their own land. The government takes care of them. The government pays their way. They're on the dole. They don't need to be here in Cortez." With rare exceptions, she said, candidates for state and county offices have not actively campaigned at Towaoc, and no public office holders conduct constituent meetings there.

Ernest House, a tribal member, graduated from the Cortez high school in 1965. His parents and grandparents were Ute speakers, and English is a second language for him. He was on the tribal council for fourteen years and served as chair for seven years. He was also appointed by the governor to the Four Corners Heritage Council and the White House Indian Education Board. But, he says ruefully, "I've been discriminated against from the day I was born until about two weeks ago, three weeks ago. Now, discrimination is real, and it's here in Cortez, and like any other border towns you're going to see—within an Indian reservation, you're going to see that." When he was at the high school in Cortez, "we used to have fights with Anglo kids every Friday evening," he said. "Discrimination is still here in Cortez. I don't think it will ever go away."[91]

William Thompson was the assistant principal of the only high school in the school district, which is located in Cortez. There were twelve separate schools in the district, but he could remember only one Indian who had ever been employed as a teacher. No Indians were employed in the administrative or secretarial and support staff at the district's central office. There was only one Indian assistant principal, and he had only recently been hired. Thompson acknowledged that Indian employees would be "good role models" for the Indian students but said few Indians were employed in the public schools. The few who were employed were bus drivers and custodial workers.[92] The school board has, however, adopted a career ladder program designed to encourage promotion of minority teachers up through the ranks. Its impact has yet to be determined.

George Schumpelt is director of the district's bilingual education program, which was first introduced in 1987. It teaches subjects in the students' native languages so they will learn the subject while also learning English. Approximately 80 percent of the students classified as Limited English Proficient (LEP) in the school district are Indian.[93] On the Iowa Test of Basic Skills, 81 percent of Indian students scored in the bottom quartile.

Schumpelt said there was a "cultural split" between Indian and white students that became more pronounced as the students grew older. "You watch kids play on the elementary playground, first three grades, and . . . [t]here is just no consciousness of culture." But as they grow older they polarize into different groups. "[O]ur cowboys polarize," he said. "Our band kids polarize."[94]

Allan Whitmer, one of the defendants, was elected to the school board in 1989. Since then there have been two vacancies on the board, both of which were filled by whites appointed by the remaining members. Whitmer said the fact that no Indians served on the board "don't concern me, no."[95]

Following a trial, the court made extensive findings of past and continuing discrimination against Indians and invalidated the at-large system. It found the following:

- During much of the nineteenth century "there was strong anti-Indian sentiment expressed in the press and by politicians."

- "The battle cry in Colorado seemed to be to exterminate the Indians."
- The anti-Indian sentiment precipitated a surprise attack by the state volunteers on a Cheyenne and Arapahoe village at Sand Creek in eastern Colorado. "Newspapers of the day greeted reports of the massacre with unanimous approval."
- Citing the persistent efforts of whites to exterminate and remove the Utes and expropriate their land, "[i]t is blatantly obvious" that American Indians "have been the victims of pervasive discrimination and abuse at the hands of the government, the press, and the people of the United States and Colorado in particular."
- The evidence revealed "a keen hatred for the Ute Indians and their way of life."
- There was "a history of discrimination—social, economic, and political, including official discrimination by the state and federal government."
- Indians had a depressed socioeconomic status caused in part by the past history of discrimination.
- There existed "substantial cultural and language barriers between the Native American and non-Indian communities in Montezuma County which clearly inhibit the effective participation of Native Americans in the community affairs and the political process."
- The "reticence of the Native American population of Montezuma County to integrate into the non-Indian population . . . is an obvious outgrowth of the discrimination and mistreatment of the Native Americans in the past."
- "The evidence in this case clearly indicates a polarization of the Native American and non-Indian communities in the Montezuma-Cortez-Towaoc area."[96]

The defendants had argued that Indians were not politically cohesive because they were divided by family rivalries. The court acknowledged that such rivalries existed but concluded "[i]t would be difficult to imagine any group of people constituting a more closely knit community, based upon their common history and shared social, political, and economic characteristics, than the residents of the Ute Mountain Ute Reservation.[97]

After the trial of the case, but before the court entered its opinion, an election was held for the school board in 1997. Tina Galyon, a Ute candidate, ran unopposed from District B and was elected, becoming the first Indian ever to serve on the school board. The defendants contended that her election showed Indian voting strength was not diluted, but the court disagreed. It held that because Galyon ran unopposed, "her election does nothing to counteract the findings of polarized voting and racial bloc voting."

The court concluded that American Indians in School District No. RE-1 were geographically compact and politically cohesive and that the candidates favored by Indians were usually defeated by whites voting as a bloc. As a remedy for the Section 2 violation, the court ordered into effect a single-member district plan for election of school board members, containing a majority-Indian district encompassing the reservation.

Today, the Ute Mountain Ute Reservation consists of about 597,000 acres in southwest Colorado, southeastern Utah, and northern New Mexico. It is governed by an elected tribal council of seven members. Tribal enrollment as of 1999 was 1,968.

Although Indians on the reservation continue to have a depressed socioeconomic status, the tribe owns and operates the Ute Mountain Tribal Park, a casino, a resort hotel, a pottery factory, and a commercial construction company. It is the reservation's biggest employer.

Arthur Cuthair, the lead plaintiff in the lawsuit against the school board, met an untimely and tragic fate. In the early afternoon of May 5, 2006, a fire started in the bedroom of his house trailer. He took his six-year-old son outside and went back in to fight the fire but succumbed to smoke inhalation and collapsed. He was taken to the hospital emergency room, where he was pronounced dead by the county coroner.[98]

Tim LaFrance, a lawyer from Durango who was on the legal team that represented the plaintiffs, said that Cuthair had left an important legacy: "There is a mechanism in place now for the tribe to elect one of their own to the school board for the benefit of their children." Or as Cuthair would have put it, "We all have an opportunity now to go up the ladder together."

CHAPTER 7

Nebraska

Thurston County, located in eastern Nebraska, is home to the Omaha and Winnebago tribes. Historically, the county elected its seven-member board of supervisors from single-member districts. Following the election of an Indian (Leonard Springer) in 1964 from a majority-Indian district, the county abandoned its district system and adopted at-large elections in 1971. This type of switch from district to at-large elections following increased minority registration or office holding was widespread in the South after the Voting Rights Act was passed in 1965. As the Supreme Court has noted, "[v]oters who are members of a racial minority might well be in the majority in one district, but in a decided minority in the county as a whole. This type of change [from district to at-large] could therefore nullify their ability to elect the candidate of their choice just as would prohibiting some of them from voting."[1] Following the change to at-large elections, no American Indian was elected to the Thurston County Board of Supervisors.

Seven years later, in 1978, the United States sued Thurston County, alleging that its adoption of at-large elections diluted Indian voting strength and was in violation of the Constitution and the Voting Rights Act. The county, while denying liability, entered into a consent decree returning to district voting and adopted a plan containing two (out of seven) majority-Indian districts. The county also consented to being placed under the preclearance provisions of Section 5 of the Voting Rights Act for five years so that its compliance with the court's order could be "more effectively monitored."[2] After the county reverted back to single-member districts, two American Indians—Edwin McCauley in 1980 and 1984 and Isaac Caramony in 1988 and 1992—were elected to the board from one of the majority-Indian districts.

The 1990 census showed the Indian population in Thurston County had grown to nearly 44 percent, and that the supervisor districts were malapportioned. The county adopted a new plan to comply with "one person, one vote," but the plan still contained only two majority-Indian districts. Indians were "packed" in those two districts at 88 percent and 97 percent respectively, leaving the other five districts majority white. The plan also protected the incumbents by keeping them in the districts from which they had previously been elected.

Omaha tribal members Hollis D. Stabler, Jr., and Sharon Freemont, together with two local organizations (the Omaha Tribal Historical Project and Red Feather Family Services) and represented by the ACLU and the Walthill Legal Aid Society, sued the county in 1993 alleging that the new plan for the board of supervisors diluted Indian voting strength in violation of the Voting Rights Act and the Constitution.[3] They sought the creation of a third majority-Indian district to reflect the increase in Indian population in the county. The plaintiffs also challenged at-large elections for the County School District 13 School Board and the Village of Walthill Board of Trustees, both of which were located in Thurston County. No American Indian had ever been elected to either governing body, despite numerous Indian candidacies.

Early History of the Omaha and Winnebago Tribes

It is thought that the Omaha, whose name means "those who go upstream" or "against the current," have lived near their present location in Nebraska for the past two centuries or more.[4] During the winter, they lived in earth lodges similar to those of other Missouri River tribes and grew beans, corn, squash, and melons. During their annual hunts on the plains for buffalo, deer, and other game, they lived in tepees made of buffalo skins.

In response to ever-increasing pressure from white settlers and miners who moved into their territory, the Omaha joined with other tribes in making treaties with the United States in 1830 and 1836 in which they extinguished title to their land lying east of the Missouri.[5] In 1854, Congress passed an act creating the territories of Kansas and Nebraska. To make room for white settlers, the Indian tribes were pressured into ceding more land and settling on smaller reservations. The Omaha ceded their hunting grounds in Nebraska, consisting of nearly 5 million acres, retaining for their own use a tract of 300,000 acres bordering the Missouri River.[6] The treaty contained a provision for the survey and allotment of land to Indians who desired to possess permanent homes.

The Winnebago historically lived in the area of Green Bay in northeast Wisconsin. Rev. Jedediah Morse, who undertook a study of American Indians for the secretary of war, visited the Winnebago in 1822 and wrote, "They have five villages on the Lake, and fourteen on Rock River. The country has abundance of springs, small lakes, ponds, and rivers, a rich soil, producing corn and all sorts of grain. The lakes abound with fine-flavored, firm fish. . . . They cultivate corn, potatoes, pumpkins, squashes, and beans, and are remarkably provident."[7]

American miners began to move into their territory during the mid-1820s, and as a result the Winnebago were forced in 1829 to relinquish to the United States their land in Illinois and Wisconsin south of the Fox and Wisconsin rivers.[8] In response to ever-increasing white encroachment, the Winnebago were forced again to cede a major portion of their territory in 1832 and accept a tract west of the Mississippi.[9] A third treaty signed in 1837 further reduced the size of the reservation by ceding to the United States all tribal land east of the Mississippi.[10]

J. D. Stevens, a missionary to the American Indians in the Northwest Territory in the late 1820s, noted the consequences of Indian dependence and how granting them the franchise would have a positive impact on their welfare. "They are politically a nonentity," he said. "The whole Indian race is not worth one white man's vote. If the Indian were raised to the right of giving his suffrage, a plenty of politicians on the frontiers would enter into plans to better him; whereas now the subject drags along like an incubus in Congress."[11]

Shortly before Iowa was granted statehood in 1846, the Winnebago were forced to sign yet another treaty ceding to the United States all the land assigned to them by the 1832 treaty, in exchange for land north of St. Peter's and west of the Mississippi.[12] This land proved unsuitable to them, and in 1855 they entered into another treaty ceding back to the United States the land previously allotted them and accepting in exchange an eighteen-square-mile tract on the Blue Earth River in Minnesota Territory.[13] This treaty provided that the land would be the Winnebago's "permanent home." But that did not prove to be the case.

In 1859, the tribe entered into another treaty with the United States; this one allotted land to individual tribal members, with the rest to be sold "to the highest bidder."[14] Hundreds of thousands of acres of former tribal land were thus open to purchase and settlement by whites. The increased presence of whites added to a growing sentiment that all Indians should be removed from the state. Actual removal took place in 1862 following a Sioux uprising in Minnesota in which more than 400 whites were killed. Although the Winnebago took no part in the killings, they were forcibly deported by steamboat down the Mississippi and then up the Missouri to the Crow Creek Reservation in South Dakota.

Living conditions in South Dakota were harsh. As Little Hill, a Winnebago Tribe member, described it: "It was not a good country. It was all dust. Whenever we cooked anything, it would be full of dust. We found out after a while we could not live there. . . . There was not enough to eat."[15] After six of his children died, Little Hill and other tribal members sought refuge in Nebraska, where they were finally given a reservation in 1865 when the United States purchased for them the northern portion of the Omaha Reservation.[16] Other Winnebago secretly returned to Wisconsin, where they remain today. Perhaps with unintended irony, one of the largest manufacturers of motor homes, with headquarters in Iowa, has adopted the name Winnebago.

In the late 1950s, the Indian Claims Commission determined that the amount paid the Omaha Tribe for the nearly 5 million acres ceded in 1854 was "unconscionable" and awarded it an additional $2,735,000.[17] Similar claims before the commission by the Winnebago for land it ceded in Wisconsin and Illinois in 1829, 1832, and 1837 were settled by an award of $4,600,000.[18]

Territorial and State Laws Affecting Indians

Nebraska was organized as a territory in 1854 after passage of the Kansas–Nebraska Act. Voting in territorial elections was limited to "free white male inhabitants."[19] The following year, the Legislative Assembly passed an act limiting voting to "free white male citizens of the United States, who have attained the age of twenty-one years."[20] The Nebraska Territory passed a number of other laws targeting American Indians for special treatment. In 1856, it made it unlawful "for any person to sell, give away, or in any way, manner, or subterfuge, traffic, trade, exchange or otherwise dispose of any intoxicating liquors to any Indian or Half Breed residing in, or passing through this Territory," and making it "the duty of all good citizens to enforce this law, and wherever liquor is found in the possession of Indians or half breeds, it is the duty of all citizens to destroy such liquor."[21] The preoccupation of whites with Indian consumption of alcohol was evident from the fact that versions of this law were reenacted in 1891, 1909, 1913, 1917, 1937, and 1943.[22]

The territory enacted another law in 1864 providing that "Indians and negroes who appear incapable of receiving just impressions of the facts respecting which they are examined, or of relating them intelligently and truly," were incompetent to testify in court.[23] The law was still in effect as of 1894.[24]

Nebraska became the thirty-seventh state on March 1, 1867. That year the Nebraska legislature amended its election laws to provide that "nothing in this act shall be construed to allow Indians to vote, except those who own real estate and are entirely freed from all tribal relations."[25] Six years later, the Nebraska legislature adopted a resolution requesting Congress to remove the Omaha, Otoe, and Pawnee tribes "to some place beyond the limits of Nebraska, or, otherwise, to secure the passage of a law which shall absolutely prevent them from leaving their reservation." Expressing disdain for the tribes, the resolution provided the following:

> These Indians are lawless in their conduct and indecent in their dress, and are a source of great annoyance to the settlement through which they pass, by begging from house to house, and frightening the women and children by their savage and uncouth appearance, and by stealing. . . . A continuance of such abuses will have a tendency to retard immigration, and will very soon lead to war and bloodshed between the abused white settlers and these lawless bands.[26]

Under the 1875 Nebraska Constitution, "Indians not taxed" were excluded from the numerical count used for the reapportionment of state house and senate districts.[27]

John Elk, a tribal member who had renounced his tribal affiliation, tried to register for an 1880 municipal election in Omaha but was refused. He brought suit, but the Supreme Court held he was not entitled to vote because he was not a "citizen" within the meaning of the U.S. Constitution.[28] According to the Court, a person could become a citizen only by birth or naturalization, and the "alien and dependent condition of the members of the Indian tribes could not be put off at their own will without the action or assent of the United States."[29] Because Elk was not subject to the jurisdiction of the United States at the time of his birth, and because he had not been naturalized by treaty or statute, he was not a citizen and not entitled to vote. Justice Harlan wrote a strong dissent. He argued that the decision of the majority robbed the Fourteenth Amendment of "its vital force" and meaning, with the result that "[T]here is still in this country a despised and rejected class of persons with no nationality whatever, who, born in our territory, owing no allegiance to any foreign power, and subject, as residents of the states, to all the burdens of government, are yet not members of any political community, nor entitled to any of the rights, privileges, or immunities of citizens of the United States."[30]

The Nebraska legislature, showing a continuing disdain for Indian culture and traditions, passed a law in 1913 that marriages and divorces among Indians according to Indian custom "shall be unlawful and shall be punished."[31]

Indian Land Allotments

Omaha tribal land was allotted in the 1880s pursuant to the treaties entered into in 1854 and 1865.[32] In 1881 a group of Omaha tribal members, described by more traditional Indians as "make-believe white men," requested Congress to give each family a clear and full title to its property. As one of them explained, "The road our fathers walked is gone, the game is gone, the white people are all about us. There is no use any Indian thinking of the old ways; he must now go to work as the white man does."[33] The allotments were opposed by more traditional members of the tribe, who were known as "those who live in earth lodges."

Alice Fletcher, an anthropologist, lobbied heavily for allotment. She was part of a movement known as "friends of the Indian" and believed strongly that Indian culture and traditions were becoming increasingly obsolete and that Indians must inevitably be assimilated into the culture of the white man. In part as a result of her efforts, Congress passed the Omaha Allotment Act of 1882,[34] which became the blueprint for the subsequent Dawes Allotment Act of 1887.[35]

The western section of the reservation was sold for settlement by whites in 1882. Under the terms of the allotment act, lands distributed to Indians were to be held in trust for a period of twenty-five years, after which the government would issue a deed of ownership to the allottees and release then from guardianship.

Even before the trust period expired, Indians who were unable to cultivate their lands for lack of ponies or other reasons leased them to whites without the consent of the Indian agent or the government. In 1894 the Indian Rights Association reported that "White men, who never expect to relax their hold, occupy them, and the Indians, for the most part, are in camps along the Missouri River, dancing and carousing."[36]

As the trust expiration date grew nearer, a local newspaper, the *Pender (Neb.) Times*, predicted that "[e]ventually all this desirable farm land, as good as the best in northeastern Nebraska, will fall into the hands of whites who have awaited the move."[37] The prediction proved to be substantially correct.

Historian Janet McDonnell reported that "[a]s the date of the trust termination approached, speculators descended on the reservation and maneuvered the Indians into fraudulent land transactions, sometimes plying them with liquor to secure their signatures on deeds." One particularly egregious case concerned Nazaenza Blackbird, a sixty-five-year-old Omaha woman who could neither speak, read, nor write English. A local merchant induced her to convey a deed to her eighty acres of farmland for $1.00.[38]

Many of the white settlers trespassed on Indian land. White traders also charged Indians exorbitant interest rates, and the increasingly impoverished Indians were forced to lease lands to whites at below market rates. Eventually, two-thirds of the acreage allotted to tribal members was lost or sold to neighboring white cattlemen and farmers.[39]

Land on the Winnebago Reservation was also allotted after enactment of the Dawes Act. As a result, from 1887 to 1934, the tribe lost more than three-fourths of its reservation land.[40]

The Reservation Today

Today, the Winnebago and Omaha reservations officially comprise the entire land area of Thurston County. However, according to a 1986 report of the Confederation of American Indians, non-Indians on the Omaha Reservation owned 67,495 acres, or 71 percent of the total acreage. American Indians owned a total of 27,413 acres, 8,553 of which were owned by the tribe and 18,860 of which had been allotted. The report also found that 71 percent of the Winnebago Reservation lands were similarly owned by non-Indians.[41]

Residential segregation in Thurston County is both checker-boarded and severe. Figures from the 1990 census revealed that nearly 95 percent of the county's American Indian population lived in majority-Indian census blocs, and over 67 percent lived in census blocs that were 90 percent or more American Indian. Over 92 percent of the county's white population lived in majority-white census blocs, and over 80 percent resided in census blocs that were 90 percent or more white. The villages of Macy and Winnebago were 97.7 percent and 90.5 percent Indian, respectively, whereas Pender, the county seat, was over 99 percent white.[42]

The Omaha Tribe reports 5,992 enrolled members, 5,227 of whom reside on the reservation.[43] The Winnebago Tribe numbers 3,736 members, 1,204 of whom reside on the reservation.[44]

Retrocession

One issue that has deeply divided the Indian and non-Indian communities in Thurston County is retrocession. As part of its then policy of terminating the reservation system and the distinctive relationship between the federal and tribal governments, Congress enacted legislation in 1953 allowing Nebraska to exercise jurisdiction over offenses committed by or against Indians on Indian reservations in the state.[45] But in 1968, in a reversal of the termination policy, Congress enacted legislation authorizing the federal government to accept "a retrocession" of jurisdiction over such offenses. Nebraska adopted a resolution ceding to the federal government all criminal jurisdiction over offenses committed by or against Indians, except motor vehicle offenses, and the resolution was accepted by the secretary of the interior as to the Omaha Reservation in October 1970. Despite this action by the state and federal governments, Thurston County law enforcement officers continued to arrest Indians for offenses committed on the Omaha Reservation, and those Indians were then tried by non-Indian county and municipal courts.[46]

The Omaha Tribe sued the Village of Walthill, Thurston County, and the state seeking to enforce retrocession. The Nebraska legislature, reversing itself, had adopted a resolution purportedly rescinding its offer of retrocession, and the Nebraska Supreme Court held the acceptance of retrocession by the United States over the Omaha Reservation was invalid.[47] The federal court, however, held the retrocession was proper, and the decision was affirmed on appeal.[48]

The Winnebago Tribal Council adopted a resolution in favor of retrocession in 1974. According to the resolution, "during the past year the Law and Order services provided by Thurston County Nebraska law enforcement organization to the Winnebago Indian people has reached a point of complete inadequacy and inefficiency, and . . . it is imperative that adequate, fair and equitable law and order services be provided on the Winnebago Indian Reservation at the earliest possible date."[49] The board of trustees of the Village of Walthill, expressing its opposition to retrocession, unanimously adopted a resolution in 1975 that federal authorities remove the village from the criminal jurisdiction of the United States.[50] The county board of supervisors also unanimously adopted a resolution that "none of the Civil or Criminal jurisdiction of the State of Nebraska be ceded to the United States for any purpose."[51] The state legislature authorized a study of the retrocession issue but took no further action.

As part of a broader anti-Indian movement in the West, an organization calling itself Concerned Citizens Council, Inc. was organized in Thurston County in 1976. One of its stated "principles" was to protect nontribal members from "the whims of the governing bodies of the tribe without voice or representation in that government."[52] It was also opposed to retrocession.

According to Hollis Stabler, the Concerned Citizens Council "was formed for the sole purpose of opposing Indians' rights."[53] Many local white elected officials were active members of the Concerned Citizens Council. Blair Richendifer, who served as a state representative from Thurston County and was a former mayor of Walthill, was employed by the Concerned Citizens Council and represented it at an eight-state conference held in Montana on "equal rights for all citizens." Duward Morgan, a member of the board of supervisors, served on the board of Concerned Citizens in 1977. Raymond Wingett, chair of the board of supervisors, was also a member of the board of the Concerned Citizens Council. James Rossiter, at one time a member of the board of trustees of the Village of Walthill as well as the board of supervisors, served as president of Concerned Citizens Council.[54] Roger Sailors, the president of a local bank, was also a member of the board of Concerned Citizens.[55]

In a June 17, 1976, article, the *Walthill Citizen*, which served as a voice for white residents and organizations in Thurston County, urged its readers to join the Interstate Congress on Equal Rights, a multistate organization committed to abolishing Indian reservations and federal ownership of land. On February 24, 1977, the paper ran an editorial praising the Concerned Citizens Council and saying, "We need this organization and we need it badly."[56] Later that year in an editorial it boasted, "We, as a newspaper, were the first to advance the concept of the White having rights."[57] The paper also complained bitterly about the enforcement of Indian treaties: "We have here, clear and simple, a case of the United States honoring treaties made obsolete when the ethnic group become citizens of the United States. What other citizen has a right to treat with his own country? It really doesn't make much sense, does it?"[58]

In 1985, some ten years after its first effort, the Winnebago Tribal Council adopted another resolution in favor of retrocession of civil and criminal jurisdiction to the United States.[59] Winnebago retrocession was again raised in the Nebraska legislature in the form of Legislative Resolution (LR) 57, sponsored by a state representative from outside Thurston County.

To express its continuing opposition to retrocession, Thurston County's board of supervisors adopted another resolution in 1985 that it "opposes the proposed retrocession plan and specifically opposes L.R. 57."[60] The board's resolution was approved by a vote of five to two. All the members from the majority-white districts voted in favor of the resolution; the two supervisors who resided in the majority-American Indian districts opposed it. The village board of Pender, at the request of the Concerned Citizens Council, adopted a resolution opposing Winnebago retrocession.[61]

Thurston County's representative in the Nebraska legislature, Sen. James Goll, opposed retrocession on the Winnebago Reservation. However, in testimony before the Nebraska State Judiciary Committee, he conceded that "[t]he racial discrimination faced by the Winnebago in Thurston County is a burden thrust on them by the white man for hundreds of years, and I would have to be blind or foolish to suggest that it doesn't exist on the Reservation today."[62]

The Concerned Citizens Council lobbied in opposition to Winnebago retrocession before the Nebraska Judiciary Committee in 1985.[63] The Thurston County sheriff also expressed public opposition to retrocession. This opposition included letters to the editor in the local newspaper in which he said "retrocession in Thurston County violates the constitutional rights of the non-Indian who live, reside, and own property in Thurston County by allowing people to be taxed and ruled without representation. Those who say it doesn't are very sadly mistaken and are not using very good judgment." In condemning the prior Omaha retrocession, he said "I am a victim, just like all of the residents of Thurston County."[64]

Despite local white opposition, the BIA endorsed the Winnebago Tribe's retrocession efforts, and retrocession was authorized in 1986.[65]

Continuing Polarization

In a 1971 report prepared by the Interchurch Ministries of Nebraska, the state's Indian commissioner Robert Mackey was quoted as saying that local community attitudes "range from total denial of any 'problem' to outright hostility with regard to Indians. . . . In too many places, the general attitude remains that the only good Indian is a dead Indian."[66]

American Indians boycotted businesses in Walthill in the 1970s. According to Hollis Stabler, they felt the merchants "just simply cared about the Indians' money and had no other concern for them socially, culturally, politically, whatever. It was simply a point of greed and no reciprocation in terms of employment opportunities. I think it was a general festering of all of those social degradations and that's what prompted it."[67]

Stabler has a bachelor's degree in business administration from the University of Nebraska at Lincoln. Both his father and grandmother were college graduates. He served in the Marine Corps and has worked as a police officer and as director of sales and marketing at the Dakota Sioux Casino in Watertown, South Dakota. He has also served on the Omaha Tribal Council. He said he is treated "very well, very politely, very professionally" by elected officials, but there is another side to relations with non-Indians in Thurston County. As he put it,

> Discrimination is oftentimes a feeling of uncomfortableness and disparate treatment. I believe if any Indian goes to Pender, they'll find both in short order. I've certainly experienced that myself over there. Just the looks. The stares. The attitude of throwing down a menu, as opposed to handing you a menu. The coldness. The unfriendliness. The unwelcomeness. There is a sign south of Pender that says, "You're entering the Omaha Reservation." There was a period of time in the 1970s and 80s when that sign was cut down five times until they put metal posts on it.[68]

The stereotypical and negative attitude of many whites toward Indians is evident from the local press. The *Walthill Citizen* printed a front-page letter to the editor on July 31, 1969, entitled "Seek Equal Rights" that was signed by "concerned citizens of Thurston County." The letter was an angry and bitter response to the rape a week earlier of a white woman by a group of American Indian men:

> I would guess that the criminals were gently reprimanded and reminded that this was a "no-no" and the Great White Father who doles out the monthly checks and commodities for this "Poor" misguided minority group was unhappy with them. But they received their checks the next month so they could stay drunk and continue their drunkenness and

> criminal acts. We who live in this community are getting just about all we can take of this favoritism; it is time we whites demand our equal rights. . . . If some of those "social workers" who have never seen or lived around the Indians, but still constantly bewail the plight of the "pitiful underprivileged Indian" could have changed places with this poor girl last Friday night, they might finally realize there are two sides to the picture.

Stabler said that in the early 1970s the *Walthill Citizen* carried an editorial saying that "Indians are so stupid they couldn't invent the wheel. And that was typical. I coughed, too, when I first read that."[69]

Sharon Freemont has lived on both the Omaha and Winnebago reservations and currently resides in Walthill. She is a graduate of Briarcliff College in Iowa, and she works in the payroll department of Casino Omaha in Onawa. She said Indians and non-Indians don't socialize much. As she explained, "it's uncomfortable, because in the Walthill community, it's an understanding that there is a fence, invisible fence, between the non-Indians and the Indians."[70] In 1981, the Walthill Village Board of Trustees unanimously adopted a resolution urging the federal government to make the fence more visible by excluding the village from the boundaries of the Omaha Reservation.[71]

Freemont tells the story of her twelve-year-old son Michael, who went to the Pump & Pack in Walthill to refill a gas can for their lawn mower. Several young white boys were standing outside the store and started laughing at him and called him a "little brown nigger." "I was very upset," she said, "but Michael said 'just don't worry about it, Mom.' But I went up and I talked to those boys. I said, 'don't your parents teach you anything? I don't appreciate you calling my son these names.' They laughed and they just walked away."[72]

Freemont also said Indians "have to go pay for our gas before we can get our gas. I've seen other individuals that are non-Indian, they don't—they wave to the window and the gas pump is turned on for them. I complained once—'why do we have to pay?' They shrug their shoulders."[73]

One exception to the Indians-pay-before-they-pump rule was Hollis Stabler and his wife. Stabler said because he and his wife are more than half white—he is 15/32 parts Indian—and are not as dark as full-bloods, they are treated differently. They are not required to pay before pumping gas at the Pump & Pack. "But if a full-blood walks in and he's speaking Omaha that person is treated very shabbily. They watch them and suspect them immediately of shoplifting."[74]

Segregated Churches

Elected officials, past and present, acknowledged that churches in Thurston County are largely segregated.[75] Freemont said, "I have never felt welcome going to any of the churches in Walthill. When you do go into the churches you are made to feel unwelcome. You are never greeted with a smile."[76]

Mark Kemling, a Nebraska native, became pastor of the First Methodist Church in Walthill in 1990. He tried to promote a dialogue between the American Indian and white communities and to address race relations in his work as a minister. He believed there was "very little contact between the two communities." He promoted a "Native American Awareness Sunday" for two years and invited an Indian to participate and play his drum at one of the services. After that, members of the pastor–parish relations committee from Walthill asked to meet with Kemling. They told him they were "embarrassed" by the Indian drummer "and didn't think there was any place for drums in the church." Kemling said that as a result of the meeting, "we no longer emphasized Native American Awareness Sunday." At a subsequent meeting, the committee said it was "concerned that I was spending too much time with Indians and that they wished I wouldn't preach about it."[77] Duward Morgan, a member of the First Methodist Church and a former member of the board of supervisors, said he thought Kemling "was taking too much interest in getting the Indians in the church."[78]

Kemling surveyed his congregation in 1993 to determine how it felt about ministry with American Indians and in general what it felt the church should be doing in the community. The members were interested in "bringing new people into the church," he said, but "interest in reaching out to Native Americans wasn't particularly high." Despite that, Kemling said he remained committed to "work toward a multicultural congregation in Walthill," and he participated in a racial reconciliation group that met periodically "to share a meal together and talk about ways of getting together and understanding one another."[79]

The filing of the tribal members' voting rights lawsuit increased tensions between Kemling and his congregation. The Nebraska Conference Board of Church and Society had given a grant of $250 to the Legal Aid Society so it could publically disseminate information about the reason the suit had been filed. Members of the Walthill congregation, in a meeting with Methodist church officials, expressed their displeasure with the grant and said it was "taking sides in a lawsuit." After that, according to Kemling, "church attendance dropped by two-thirds at least, and giving also dropped significantly." The pastor–parish relations committee subsequently voted unanimously that Kemling be transferred to another church. As a consequence, he was reassigned by the district superintendent to a Methodist church in Curtis.[80]

Kemling said there was one American Indian church member when he came to Walthill, and three joined while he was there. Charles Merrick, one of the Indian members, left the church when Kemling's removal was announced. Two other Indians who had been attending the church, Terry and Wynona St. Cyr, also left. Kemling said about the only interracial socialization he saw in Walthill was at sporting events at the local high school.[81]

Exclusion from Employment and Business

Indians have been largely excluded from local government employment. As of 1994, Thurston County had approximately fifty employees, only one of whom was an American Indian.[82] Walthill had seventeen employees, no more than one of whom was an American Indian.[83] School District 13 also had only one American Indian employee.[84]

Few American Indians owned their own businesses in Thurston County.[85] There was only one American Indian, a student, working in a business in Walthill.[86] Edwin McCauley, who is a tribal member and a farmer, knew of only two or three Indian farmers in the entire county.[87]

Civil Rights Complaints and Litigation

In addition to the two voting rights lawsuits, there have also been several judicial and administrative complaints of discrimination filed by Indians against the Village of Walthill. Desiree Johnson, an American Indian employee of Walthill, filed charges in 1984 with the Nebraska Equal Opportunity Commission (NEOC) and the U.S. Equal Employment Opportunity Commission (EEOC) alleging discrimination on the basis of race.[88] She filed a subsequent charge claiming retaliation by the village for filing the initial charge.[89] In 1985, the NEOC found that there was reasonable cause for the charge, and the parties reached a $2,000 settlement.[90] The following year the EEOC also issued findings that there was reasonable cause to believe the village had violated Johnson's civil rights.[91]

In 1990 and 1991, two lawsuits, one in federal court and the other in state court, were filed by Indians against Walthill and one of its police officers alleging racially motivated police brutality. In the state court case, the parties reached a $10,556 settlement. The federal case was also settled but is subject to a confidentiality agreement.[92]

School Board and Lack of Responsiveness

In April 1993, Stabler and several other tribal members went before the school board and made three requests: that it provide for Indian representation on the board; that it provide a class that would teach the Omaha language; and that employment opportunities be listed in *Indian Country Today*, a newspaper widely read in the Indian community. There was no response to the first request, Stabler said. As for the second, one of the board members (Ruth Newton) said "it will be a cold day in hell when we'll teach Indian language, the

Omaha language, at Walthill Public School."[93] Other board members nodded their heads in agreement. Roger Tremayne, one of the board members, said it was unnecessary to teach Omaha because "we currently offer a foreign language at school," which was Spanish. He also doubted that teaching Omaha would serve "any real purpose as far as the education of the children is concerned."[94] As for the third request, some notices of job openings did subsequently appear in *Indian Country Today*.

One of the comments Stabler got from a board member was, "'why can't we all be treated the same?' My response was, 'fine. Since you're on the Omaha Reservation let's all be treated like Omahas.' I was simply exemplifying the irony of that statement."[95]

Stabler and the former superintendent of School District 13 did a study and found that Indian students at all grade levels missed approximately twice as many days of school as non-Indian students, and that they performed approximately one letter grade below their non-Indian peers. The response to the report was "total apathy," he said, and the board took no action on it.[96]

Stabler said that one of the primary reasons for the lawsuit seeking representation on the school board was that "at the school here anything Indian has no value whatsoever to these people." There were no Indian teachers, no Indian administrators, and no Indian service or maintenance workers at the school.[97]

Disparate Socioeconomic Status

Socioeconomic data from the 1990 census showed great disparities between American Indians and non-American Indians in Thurston County. The per capita income of American Indians was 36 percent that of whites ($3,996 vs. $11,043); more than 57 percent of the American Indian households earned less than $15,000 compared with 35 percent of whites; 54.89 percent (1,643 persons) of American Indians were living below the federal poverty level compared with 11.97 percent (454) of whites; 70.25 percent of American Indian children below five years of age lived in families with incomes below the poverty level compared with 12.50 percent of white children; 31.52 percent of American Indians age sixteen and over in the labor force were unemployed compared with 3.03 percent of whites; 47.10 percent of American Indian households were female headed compared with 6.15 percent of whites; 36.65 percent of American Indians lived in owner-occupied housing compared with 72.14 percent of whites; 35.75 percent of American Indians had no high school diploma compared with 26.28 percent of whites; and 3.74 percent of American Indians had a bachelor's degree or higher graduate degree compared with 11.14 percent of whites.[98]

The poverty status of American Indians is also reflected in Indian Health Service statistics, which demonstrate that Indians in Thurston County have significantly elevated rates of morbidity and mortality compared with white residents. According to the Indian Health Service, for the period 1987–89, the infant mortality rate for the Omaha–Winnebago service unit was nearly twice that of the United States and of the state of Nebraska. The age-adjusted mortality rate from all causes was nearly three times that of the United States.[99]

Depressed Indian Turnout

A consistent pattern of depressed Indian turnout exists across elections in Thurston County. On the basis of data for six countywide elections from the 1988 primary to the 1992 general election, on average 20.2 percent of the county's American Indian VAP turned out, whereas 54.3 percent of the county's white VAP turned out, for an average racial differential in turnout of 34.1 percent.[100] On the basis of data for six school board elections from the 1990 primary to the 1994 general election, on average 16.2 percent of the American Indian VAP turned out whereas 52.6 percent of the white VAP turned out, for an average racial differential in turnout of 36.4 percent.[101]

There is a direct link between a minority group's reduced political participation and its depressed socioeconomic status. As the Supreme Court has recognized, "political participation tends to be depressed where minority group members suffer effects of prior discrimination such as inferior education, poor employment opportunities, and low incomes."[102] Numerous appellate and trial court decisions, including those from Indian Country, are to the same effect. In a case from South Dakota involving the Sisseton Independent School District, the court of appeals concluded that "[l]ow political participation is one of the effects of past discrimination."[103] And in a case from Montana, the court held "lower . . . social and economic factors hinder the ability of American Indians in Montana to participate fully in the political process."[104]

Michael Simpson, a lawyer who worked for the Walthill Legal Aid Society, said "you can't really overstate the negative effect of poverty on voter turnout. There is a huge number of people who are just living day to day and don't vote at all." Many Indians have also felt a sense of alienation from the white community and its political institutions, he said. The county seat of Pender, where the courthouse is located and where the county commission has its office, "was a place to be avoided at all costs. The town was seen by most as hostile and unwelcoming to Indians."[105]

Racial Bloc Voting

The fundamental differences between the Indian and non-Indian communities are reflected in the high levels of racial bloc voting in Thurston County. In seven countywide contests involving Indian candidates, the average level of Indian support for the Indian candidates was 86 percent. The average level of white crossover voting for the Indian candidates was only 11 percent. According to plaintiffs' expert Dr. Gordon Henderson, "the 11 percent of white crossover voting won't even come close to providing the number of votes that would be needed to enable an Indian candidate to get as many votes as the candidate of choice of white voters."[106]

Charles Merrick, an American Indian who twice ran unsuccessfully for the school board, said he never asked whites to vote for him because he knew they wouldn't. He would never run again under the at-large system, he said, because "we are outnumbered. There is more white voters than Indian voters in our district there. So an Indian will never make the school board under the conditions we have now."[107]

Merrick also believes he wasn't elected "because the non-Indians thought that once I or any Native American got on there the school district would deteriorate." He recounted a conversation with a neighbor in 1989: "he was out walking up the street one day and I talked with him and he asked me if I was running for the school board and I told him I was. He said, 'I'm fearing for the school board. If Indians get up there it's going to go to hell and I'm going to move.'"[108]

Sharon Freemont thinks the Indians who ran for the school board lost because whites feared if they were elected education would deteriorate: "It's felt that as Native-Americans coming into the community and into the school, village board, that we are going to be destroying a community; the education of the children will go downhill. It's just felt by myself that Indians are thought as less than human, if we are put on the school board or the village board, because it will destroy everything in the Walthill community."[109]

The first Indian elected to the school board was Edwin McCauley in 1994, more than a year after the voting rights lawsuit was filed. The election of a minority candidate after litigation has begun has happened in other cases but is generally discounted by the courts. As one court put it, to hold otherwise "will thwart successful challenges to electoral schemes on dilution grounds," and "would merely be inviting attempts to circumvent the Constitution."[110]

The predictions by Merrick and Freemont that some whites would leave the school system if Indians were elected to the board proved to be correct. The student body of School District 13 was 80 percent American Indian in 1994–95. During that academic year, and following the election of the first Indian to the school board, twenty-seven students, all but one of whom was white, opted out of the district to attend schools with majority-white student bodies. A large number of those who transferred were children of current and former members of the school board, including the president of the board when the litigation was filed.[111]

Local Elections Are Based on Status

Indian candidates, who lack the resources to finance media campaigns and who don't have meaningful access to the majority-white community, were seriously disadvantaged by the existing political system in Thurston County, which depends almost exclusively on a candidate's status in the majority community. Little or no advertising is done. Candidates do not put up yard signs, nor do they conduct door-to-door campaigning. What is important is who the candidate is and how well he or she is known in the community.

Raymond L. Storm, a public school employee, was a member of the village board for eight years. He has lived in Walthill since 1962 and in the county all of his life. "I just signed up and ran," he said. "I didn't really campaign any." He spent "Zero dollars" on his first campaign and "[n]one; nothing" on his second.[112]

Steve Dunn, chair of the village board, said he "never really did campaign. I just signed up. That's all I have ever done." He never spent any money to run for office, and doesn't believe anyone has ever campaigned door to door in village elections.[113]

Decision of the District Court

The defendants argued that American Indians, because of their depressed turnout, would have to be a supermajority in a district of about 75 percent to give them an effective voting majority, and that the plaintiffs' proposed plan for the county commission fell short of providing three such districts. The district court disagreed and concluded that it was sufficient if a proposed plan provided "the *potential* for a minority group to elect representatives of its choice—not the absolute guarantee."[114]

The defendants also argued that Indians had achieved some success in elections, and that an Indian had been hired as chief of police of the Village of Walthill. The district court, however, in ruling for the plaintiffs on their challenge to elections for the board of supervisors, found the following:

- "Native Americans vote together and choose Native American candidates when given the opportunity."
- "[W]hites vote for white candidates to defeat the Native American candidate of choice."
- "[I]t is obvious that Native Americans lag behind whites in areas such as housing, poverty, and employment."
- There was evidence of "overt and subtle racial discrimination in the community."[115]

The court invalidated the challenged plan under Section 2 of the Voting Rights Act and held that plaintiffs were entitled to a new plan creating a third majority-Indian district. The court, however, dismissed the challenges to School District 13 and the board of trustees of the Village of Walthill because American Indians were not sufficiently compact to form a majority in a single-member district. Both sides appealed, but the court of appeals affirmed the decision of the trial court.[116] In doing so, it affirmed the findings of the lower court, including that "racial polarization and minimal white crossover voting results in a legally significant white bloc vote to defeat Native American candidates of choice." It also concluded that "the white majority has little interaction with most Native American candidates, and, therefore, the opportunity to become known as a person and to be trusted with public office is not equal." And as important, the court held that "Thurston County maintained its current districting system with a discriminatory intent and thwarted Congress's purpose in amending §2 in 1982 to provide 'equally open' political processes."[117]

WHAT THE FUTURE MAY HOLD

Although American Indian turnout has been depressed in the past, the fact that numerous Indians have run for public office and received strong support from Indian voters, as well as the fact that two tribal organizations—the Omaha Tribal Historical Project and the Red Feather Family Service—were plaintiffs in the lawsuit challenging the method of elections for the county, the Village of Walthill, and School District 13, is evidence that many Indians want to participate in nontribal elections. Indeed, there are now three American Indians (Darren Wolfe, Paul Don Snowball, and Danelle Smith) on the county board of supervisors. Two tribal members (Vida Stabler and Kenna Robinson) are members of the board of School District 13, and all of the members of the school board in Macy, which is located on the reservation, are Indian.

Other hopeful signs are the tribes' commitments to economic development and the preservation of Indian languages and culture. Members of the Omaha Tribe have undertaken a concerted effort to preserve their traditions of music, gift giving, oratory, and powwows. They have also made a special effort to save their language. At the Tribe Head Start Program, preschoolers are taught Omaha names for colors, shapes, and numbers. The public school at Macy teaches the Omaha language as part of its curriculum.[118] Vida Stabler, a tribal member, teaches language classes at the Omaha Indian Reservation high school. "I know it's a struggle," she said. "But these young ones have good minds—with each day they produce more and more."[119]

According to anthropologist Robin Ridington, the Omaha are "bringing back old traditions as these fit into contemporary life. . . . [T]he Omaha are strong today rather than disadvantaged and demoralized, precisely because they have remained 'emotionally bound' to an Indian identity. They have taken elements of white culture that are of benefit, but they have also retained the cultural spirit their ancestors spoke of."[120]

Despite the efforts to preserve Indian culture and gains in office holding, Vida Stabler says relationships between the Indian and non-Indian communities "are no better today than in the past. And it's based on misunderstanding. People have to have shared experiences to know each other, but unfortunately we don't have that. Still, Indians have grown to understand that voting in local elections is about empowerment. The opportunity to make decisions is what we want. And I believe my vote does make a difference."[121]

Dennis Hastings, a tribal member and coauthor of a book on Omaha tribal culture,[122] takes a cautiously optimistic view of Indians' prospects for the future:

> I think we will continue to live here and expand our economic development. . . . And I think there is a greater interest in participating in non-tribal elections, because that is tied to economic development. As Omaha, we get along with people, but they don't always get along with us. The white people need to take a look at themselves and see if they are thinking as in the old times and are not changing. When you are dealing with hard core prejudice it doesn't flake off. But we have a tendency to work and think things will get better. It will take time. We fall down and get back up. Hopefully, the white people will come with us. It's going to get better. If it weren't, I wouldn't be here.[123]

The American Indian population in Thurston County is growing at a faster rate than the non-Indian population. On the basis of the 2000 census, Indians are now a slight majority (52 percent) of the county's population.[124] If the American Indian population continues to grow as it has over the past decades, then despite continued racial division and polarization in voting, Indians will have even greater opportunities to participate in township, school board, and county elections and to elect the candidates of their choice.

CHAPTER 8

Wyoming

The Wind River Indian Reservation in Wyoming, located on the eastern slope of the Wind River Mountains and southwest of the Owl Creek Mountains, lies in one of the most protected and scenic valleys in the American West. But Indians on the reservation, Eastern Shoshone and Northern Arapaho, have had a long and troubled history of encroachment by white settlers as well as discrimination by territorial, state, and federal governments. The traditional land base of Indians was systematically diminished, they were forced onto the reservation, they were denied the rights of citizenship and the right to vote, their culture was denigrated, they were reduced to abject poverty, and their children were made to attend schools where they were not permitted to speak their native language and where many died from the diseases of the white man. The legacy of the past remains and takes the form today of a seriously depressed socioeconomic status, racially polarized voting, and the isolation of Indians from significant contact with the white community.

The reservation contains 3,525 square miles, approximately 90 percent of which is in Fremont County, with the remainder extending into Hot Springs County. Virtually all of the American Indians in Fremont County live on the reservation, and more than half live in a fairly concentrated area in the communities of Fort Washakie, Ethete, and Arapaho. The county itself has 9,250 square miles and is larger than six states and only slightly smaller than New Hampshire.

Each tribe has a separate general council, consisting of all the tribe's members, and a business council, consisting of six members. Business council members are elected by tribal members in even-numbered years by plurality vote. Matters concerning the entire reservation, which is owned and jointly occupied by the tribes, are determined by a joint business council, which consists of the two business councils.

In 2005, tribal members filed suit challenging at-large elections for the five-member Fremont County Commission as diluting Indian voting strength.[1] Although Indians were 20 percent of the county's population of 35,804, no Indian had ever been elected to the commission despite numerous Indian candidates who had the overwhelming support of Indian voters. As a remedy, they sought single-member districts. Given the concentration of Indian population on the reservation, a majority-Indian district could easily be drawn that was compact and contiguous and that complied with traditional redistricting principles.

Early Treaties and White Encroachment

In determining whether a voting practice dilutes minority voting strength, a court must consider the history and extent of discrimination against the minority group and its impact on the group's ability to participate in the political process.[2] Among the darkest chapters of the history of discrimination against the Eastern Shoshone and Northern Arapaho is the taking of Indian land and efforts to assimilate, and in some instances exterminate, tribal members.

The Treaty of Fort Laramie of 1851 was the first effort by the United States to confine the Central Plains Indians to specified boundaries in order to facilitate western movement by white settlers.[3] The Arapaho and Cheyenne were assigned over 100,000 square miles (sixty-four million acres) of territory in parts of present-day Colorado, Wyoming, Nebraska, and Kansas. In response to increasing encroachment by settlers, however, the tribes were pressured to cede additional territory and entered into a new treaty in 1861, the Treaty of Fort Wise, which established a reservation of some three million acres.[4]

One of the early organized assaults against the Shoshone, known as the Battle of Bear River or the Bear River Massacre, took place on a bitter cold day in January 1863, near Preston in present-day Franklin County, Idaho. Troops under the command of Col. Patrick Connor, in retaliation for attacks by the Indians on settlers who had moved into the Cache Valley, surrounded a Shoshone village and killed approximately 250 people, including ninety women and children. After the slaughter, some of the soldiers went through the camp raping women and bashing the heads of children.[5]

Later that year, the United States entered into a treaty with the Eastern Shoshone that described and set aside "the boundaries of the Shoshone country, as defined and described by said nation," consisting of 44,672,000 acres in present-day Wyoming, Colorado, Utah, and Idaho.[6] The United States reserved the right to use the territory for travel routes, military agricultural settlements, military posts, telegraph lines, railways, and ferries, in exchange for an annuity of $10,000 for twenty years and provisions and clothing amounting to $6,000.

One of the most bitterly remembered massacres took place in 1864 at Sand Creek in present-day Colorado. The Arapaho and Cheyenne were camped on land established for them by the Treaty of Fort Wise of 1861. Despite the fact that an American flag and a white flag of truce were flying, an irregular group of miners, ranchers, and townsmen led by Col. John Chivington attacked the camp, killing between 250 and 500 elders, women, and children.[7]

The Arapaho scattered into three bands in northern Colorado, central Wyoming, and South Dakota, but they continued to be hunted down. In 1865, U.S. troops, again under the command of Col. Patrick Conner, attacked another camp of Arapaho led by Chief Black Bear at Tongue Creek near the Wyoming–Montana border. The encampment was destroyed, and between thirty-five and sixty Arapaho men were killed.[8]

Gen. Philip Sheridan was appointed head of the Department of the Missouri in 1867, and his job was to pacify the Plains Indians and keep them confined to the reservations. The author of the statement, "the only good Indian is a dead Indian," Sheridan adopted a policy that any Indians caught off the reservations would be considered hostile and taken under military control.[9]

As westward migration by whites gained momentum following the Civil War, the U.S. government determined that the size of the region set aside for the Indians was too large. On July 3, 1868, the Eastern Shoshone were induced to cede the vast empire that was theirs and enter into the Second Treaty of Fort Bridger.[10] Pursuant to the treaty, they received 3,054,182 acres in the Wind River Valley in Wyoming.[11] The treaty provided that the land would be "set apart for the absolute and undisturbed use and occupation of the Shoshone Indians . . . and for such other friendly tribes or individual Indians as from time to time they may be willing, with the consent of the United States, to admit amongst them." In exchange, they received an annuity of $10 "for each Indian roaming, and twenty dollars for each Indian engaged in agriculture" for ten years as well as provisions and clothing. The treaty, as did others, required Indian children to attend school and be instructed in "English education."

Wyoming became a territory in 1868, and the right of suffrage and of holding office was limited to male citizens of the United States above the age of twenty-one years (though the following year Wyoming became the first territory to grant women residents the right to vote).[12] Because Indians were not deemed to be citizens, they were necessarily excluded from participating in territorial political affairs.

South Pass in Fremont County was used by whites as a route around the Wind River Mountains to Oregon and California. As long as there were no white settlements there, the Indian tribes remained fairly peaceful. However, when the 1868 gold rush brought the first real white settlement to South Pass and Indians could see their land being taken, hostilities broke out. Between 1867 and 1870, 5,000 non-Indians also moved onto the Wind River Indian Reservation, establishing towns and grazing their cattle, horses, and sheep.[13]

The Northern Arapaho, who were essentially homeless, came to the Shoshone reservation in 1870. The Shoshone permitted them to stay temporarily, with the understanding that the U.S. government would provide them with a permanent home elsewhere.[14]

A major confrontation between the white settlers at South Pass and Indians took place in 1870. The details, as related by Capt. Herman G. Nickerson, who was a participant, were reported in a *Lander Evening Post* story published in 1921. In response to attacks and depredations by Indians, which were blamed on the Arapaho, a man named Smith, described as "a noted desperado who afterwards was killed in a saloon fight," was chosen to lead sixty-one mounted men in an attack on the Arapaho. Captain Nickerson was to follow down the river with one hundred footmen. Before they reached the Arapaho camp, the mounted men encountered a group of Indians on their way to trade in Lander. Although there was nothing to indicate the group was hostile, the mounted men attacked them, killing sixteen Indians, including Chief Black Bear and two "squaws." The mounted men and Nickerson's group met near Lander, where they killed several other Indians. Later, at Nickerson's ranch, the group met and killed nine other Indians and captured five Indian children. Shortly thereafter, the Arapaho left the reservation. Nickerson, ironically, was later appointed as a federal agent on the Wind River Reservation.[15]

During their first years on the reservation, the Eastern Shoshone were dependent on the buffalo as the mainstay of their life, but as the herds diminished they began to try to rely on agriculture. Valuable minerals had been discovered in the southern part of the reservation, which resulted in the Brunot Cession Agreement of 1872, in which the Shoshone ceded 700,642 acres south of the north fork of the Popo Agie River to the United States for the sum of $25,000.[16]

Another attack on the Arapaho, known as Bates Battle, took place in 1874 in Wyoming's Washakie and Hot Springs counties. U.S. troops led by Capt. A. E. Bates, with a contingent of Shoshone, attacked Chief Black Coal's camp of 600 to 700 people. The Arapaho won the better part of the battle in terms of human lives, but the destruction of their lodges and the loss of horses forced them to leave for Oklahoma or South Dakota.[17] Not having found a permanent home elsewhere, the Northern Arapaho were moved to the Wind River Indian Reservation permanently by the government in 1878. Since 1878, the Eastern Shoshone Tribe and the Northern Arapaho Tribe have been regarded as the equitable owners in common of the Wind River Reservation.[18]

The Wyoming Territorial Legislature made repeated requests of Congress to grant it easements or roads over Indian land, to extinguish Indian title to reservation lands, and to secure ownership of reservation land to white settlers. In 1879, it asked Congress for an appropriation to open and establish a military wagon road from Fort Washakie in the Wind River Valley to the Yellow Stone National Park and Fort Ellis in Montana.[19] In another memorial, it prayed for "the extinguishment of the Indian title to the eastern part of the Shoshone, Bannock and Crow reservations" to allow a route of travel and communication between Wyoming and Montana.[20] In a third memorial, it asked Congress for relief and remuneration for settlers on the Shoshone reservation "who defend[ed] their property and lives against bands of warlike and hostile savages," "or else that the titles of these lands and ranches be secured and made good to the aforesaid settlers, their heirs and assignees."[21]

In 1890, when Wyoming became a state, the legislature added a literacy test to its citizenship requirement for voting.[22] The same year it sent a resolution to Congress that "as the game has nearly all been killed, . . . the only use to which arms are put by these savages on their excursions is the killing of the cattle of the settlers and menacing them and their families," and it requested Congressional legislation "as will result in the complete disarming of the Indians, and in keeping them on their reservations."[23]

The ongoing hostility of white settlers to Indians was apparent in an 1890 memorial to Congress by the Wyoming legislature seeking reparations for "victims of Indian avarice, malevolence, robbery, murder and other crimes of the most hideous character committed by numerous bands of Indians inhabiting the country lying west of the Missouri River."[24] Another memorial from the legislature requested Congress to adjudicate and pay claims of settlers and travelers who "sustained losses by reason of Indian outrages and deprivations committed without provocation."[25]

The 1895 minutes of the Fremont County Commission noted "difficulties existing between the white settlers and the Indians arising from conflict between the Shoshone Indians Treaty and the Wyoming state laws governing hunting upon the unoccupied land" and directed the county attorney to confer with the Indian agent "for the adjustment of the matter."[26] Two weeks later, the minutes recounted that white trappers in Fremont County had fired on some Indians, who then undertook to retaliate. The confrontation ended up in court and was settled by an agreement that "in the future, no Indians should be permitted to leave the said Indian Reservation and go upon the said upper Big Wind River lands unless accompanied by one or more Indian Police."[27]

The agricultural economy of the Indians was also failing, and by 1895 the Indians on the reservation were totally dependent on the government for food, clothing, and shelter.[28] The social and economic misfortunes compelled the Indians to sell more land to the United States. The First McLaughlin Agreement, or Thermopolis Purchase, was concluded in 1896. The Big Horn Hot Springs, approximately 75,000 acres in the northeast corner of the reservation (the so-called Ten-Miles Square), was the main feature of the land ceded to the United States for $60,000 cash payment.[29] Indians were compelled by the Second McLaughlin Agreement of 1905 to cede an additional 1,438,633 acres of reservation land north of the Big Wind River to the United States.[30] The government offered the ceded lands for sale to whites under the provisions of the homestead, town site, coal, and mineral land laws.[31]

By the early 1900s most of the best land in the region was occupied by ranches or irrigated farms. Yet white settlers continued to arrive, forcing gradual expansion onto the dry basin floors and prompting the development of many irrigation projects, often sponsored jointly by private citizens and the United States. The arrival of the homesteaders in the Wind River Basin significantly altered the American Indian's economic base. As the number of settlers and their farms increased, the number of Indians working their own farms and ranches decreased, and they began to rent and eventually to sell their land while hiring themselves out as laborers.[32]

Diseases of the white man—smallpox, measles, diphtheria, and influenza—which Indians had little resistance to, had taken a significant toll on tribal members on the Wind River Reservation. In 1829, the Arapaho population in Colorado and Wyoming was estimated to be 6,000. By 1900 less than 1,000 Arapaho, and a similar number of Shoshone, remained on the reservation.[33] One historian has said that by 1900, only 841 Shoshone and 801 Arapahoe were alive, a net population loss since 1878 of over 32 percent of Shoshone and 14.6 percent of Arapaho.[34]

In 1934, all the remaining lands that had been ceded to the United States by the 1905 agreement were reserved from non-Indian settlement. In 1940, the secretary of interior began a series of restoration of certain undisposed lands to tribal ownership. These lands again became part of the Wind River Reservation. In addition, the United States later reacquired, in trust for the tribes, additional ceded land and certain lands north of the Big Wind River that previously had passed into private ownership.[35]

John Herrick, assistant to the commissioner of Indian service, in testimony before a Senate committee in 1941, said the Eastern Shoshone and Northern Arapaho

> by the policy of a white Government and the acquisitiveness of a white society, were progressively deprived of the land from which they must derive their livelihood. They were crowded into a bare corner of the land left to them. They were in danger only a few years ago of becoming a perpetual public charge. . . . I don't believe that any other reservation better illustrates the progress of the deprivation of the Indians of their landed resources.[36]

Life on the Reservation

In the first part of the twentieth century, Indians on the Wind River Reservation often lived in dire conditions, a result of the loss of their land and the history of discrimination. A white resident of the reservation reported in 1914, "It has been pretty hard on the Indians. Counting up I find that we gave no less than 405 meals last winter and 190 pints of milk, all to Indians and free of charge. It is about all that stood between some of them and starvation. It comes hard on the family purse, but we can't see the poor people starve to death."[37] Another person reported, "We have here about 800 Arapahoes chiefly pagan and possibly as backward and destitute as any tribe under the care of this government. Last winter there were several deaths from no other cause than lack of nutrition and unavoidable exposure. I myself made the coffin and dug graves for four."[38] The following year, the superintendent of the Shoshone Agency wrote the commissioner of Indian affairs that "[t]hese Indians have been very poor and there is, every winter, more or less suffering, a good deal of it on account of their improvidence."[39]

J. Norris, superintendent of the Shoshone Agency, wrote the commissioner of Indian affairs on December 4, 1915, concerning reports that destitute Indians were eating carcasses of sheep drowned in mud holes:

> Looking at the matter from the standpoint of a white person, it is true that there is always more or less partial distress and destitution for the reason that many of the Indians are as yet improvident and cannot learn to save a part of their crop and a part of their funds to tide them over during the long winter months. . . . I have heretofore reported to the Office, these Indians are like practically all of the tribes, a great many of them will eat the carcasses of a cow, horse or sheep any time they can find it on the range. This custom has prevailed, as you know, always among many of the Indians.[40]

On the Wind River Reservation, entire families—up to ten people—often lived in a canvas tent or one-room shack. The floors were dirt, and insulation consisted of cardboard boxes. The crowded living conditions led to the spread of disease, as did contaminated water in streams and ditches.[41]

The Indian Citizenship Act of 1924 conferred citizenship on all non-citizen Indians born within the United States, which in theory included the right to vote. However, Wyoming maintained its literacy test for voting, which blunted the impact of the new citizenship law. After its enactment, the superintendent of the Crow Agency wrote to the superintendent at Fort Washakie requesting a copy of the Wyoming law containing "an educational requirement for voters." As he pointed out, "I am inclined to think that this is a very good thing in this case, as there are certainly many Indians on your reservation and on my reservation who are utterly incapable of voting intelligently."[42] The superintendent at Fort Washakie replied quoting state law: "No person shall have the right to vote who shall not be able to read the constitution of this state."[43]

Sara Wiles, a resident of Lander, has a collection of more than 25,000 photographs she has taken on the Wind River Indian Reservation. In the 1980s, she located a collection of photographs that was housed at the BIA office at Fort Washakie. She made copies of the photographs and with the help of local Indians was able to identify the people who appeared in the pictures. Many of the photographs were of Civilian Conservation Corps projects, she said, "so we assumed that a lot of them were taken in connection with the Indian New Deal programs in the 1930s."[44]

Many of the photographs from the 1930s were taken in the winter and show the ground covered with snow and Indians living in canvas tents or dilapidated one-room cabins. Gary Collins, one of the plaintiffs in the voting rights lawsuit, was born in 1948 and lived on the reservation with his parents and his brother in a one-room log cabin for his first nine years. They had no running water and initially had no electricity or telephone.[45]

Two of the pictures collected by Wiles show the segregated outhouses at the old railroad depot at Arapaho, Wyoming. "Indians" is written on the door of one of the outhouses and "Whites" on the other. The railroad, which went from Riverton through Arapaho and to Lander, was discontinued in the 1950s after automobiles became more available.

The Catholic Church also discriminated against American Indians. Father Prendergast, a priest on the Wind River Reservation, had a policy in the 1940s of excommunicating any Catholic tribal member who attended an Indian Sun Dance. Two sisters, Annette Belle and Louella White, along with other family members, were excommunicated under the priest's policy after they attended a Sun Dance. Belle added, "they wouldn't even bury my little brother when he died because of that."[46]

Wyoming Rep. William Henry Harrison was one of the leaders of the movement in the 1950s to terminate the tribes and reservations. He declared it was the intention of Congress to "terminate at the earliest possible time, all Indians." The Wind River Reservation was slated for termination, but representatives from the Northern Arapaho and Eastern Shoshone Business Councils asked that the reservation be exempted because of its poverty and poor educational level, and it was spared.[47]

The state legislature reenacted its requirement that only those may vote "who shall be able to read the constitution of this state" in 1943 and again in 1951.[48] The test was not repealed until 1971 and was repealed then only because passage of amendments to the Voting Rights Act in 1970 made the ban on literacy requirements nationwide.[49]

Segregation and Polarization off the Reservation

Public accommodations were segregated off the reservation as late as the 1960s. When Indians went to shop in Lander and Riverton, they were met with signs that said "No Dogs or Indians Allowed" or simply "No Indians Allowed."[50] The signs, said Patricia Bergie, one of the plaintiffs in the voting rights lawsuit, "reinforced what I already up to that point knew about the racist attitudes and behaviors of the people."[51]

Lucille McAdams, another plaintiff, was born in 1932 in Fremont County. She remembers seeing the signs "No Dogs or Indians

Allowed" in Riverton. Once she went into a café with her father, her sister, and a non-Indian friend, and "they told my dad they couldn't serve us. So we all had to leave." She also overheard remarks people made about "dirty Indians."[52]

James Large, another of the plaintiffs, said when he was a little boy his mother took him to town to buy a pair of shoes. As they walked by the New Way Café they saw a sign that said, "No Indians and Dogs Allowed." His mother pointed at the sign and said, "they don't like Indians in here, so don't try to ever go in there."[53]

Betty Friday is a Northern Arapaho and remembers seeing the sign "No Dogs or No Indians Allowed" at a restaurant in Lander. She was not raised, she said, "to be hateful" but "to be proud of who we were and to hold our head up." The experience of seeing the sign "was a eyeopener" and gave her the first insight into "the non-Indian's way of thinking of the Indian people."[54]

The "No Dogs or Indians Allowed" signs have come down, but Fremont County remains a largely segregated society, deeply divided along racial lines in virtually all areas of life. Churches and civic organizations tend to be segregated, and there is little social contact between the Indian and white communities.

Indians frequently complain about being followed and denied service in businesses and places of public accommodation. Sara Wiles recalled a "really bad experience" she had in 1997 when she went to a restaurant in Hudson in Fremont County with an Indian family and was refused service. "I tried to be the peacemaker and convince the people at the restaurant they needed to serve us. And they did eventually, but it took us all night. I had to ask for every single glass of water and every single piece of bread and every single dish, personally ask them to be brought to the table."[55]

Most of the prejudice against Indians is "subtle," Wiles said,

> sort of pretending they're not there or ignoring them in stores. Or I will go into stores or a restaurant with Indian friends, and the white people will address me, but they won't address the Indians. With a lot of people in Lander they're not really interested in learning about the reservation. They ask me questions like: "Aren't you afraid to go out there? Why

> are you doing that? There's, you know, nothing out there. There's no culture but alcoholism on the reservation." . . . White people who work on the reservation are interested and concerned about Indians . . . [but] I get the feeling that most people who are outside of that circle of acquaintances aren't really interested in the reservation or really learning more about what people think and how people feel there.[56]

Keja Whiteman, a tribal member, believes racism exists in Fremont County. She bought a CD at the Wal-Mart in Riverton, but when she got to her car and opened the package there wasn't a CD in the case. She immediately went back into the store, and the lady at the customer service stand said, "You people are always trying stuff like this." Whiteman said, "I felt as if it was a racial discrimination." The incident made her feel "embarrassed and angry." Whiteman's children have had similar experiences in Fremont County. A white girl told her daughter she didn't want to play with her "because she was an Indian." The comment was "hurtful to my daughter. It was hurtful to me as her mom," Whiteman said. As a result of her past experiences, she said, "I'm not good at initiating contact with non-Indians often. In a store setting, in a social setting that's harder for me than I think it is for some people." She has friends who are members of both tribes, but she has only "acquaintances" who are non-Indian and does not "socialize" with them.[57]

Betty Friday has experienced discrimination at stores in Riverton. In December 2005, she bought groceries at the local Wal-Mart and then later bought a DVD player, which she put on a credit card. On her way out of the store she was stopped by a Wal-Mart employee, "and she took a scanner, and she went through everything in my cart and then proceeded to tell me that the DVD player was not on that list." Friday showed the store employee the separate receipt she had for the DVD but told her "that I would never again let her do that to me." Friday has never gone back to the Wal-Mart store and says she was "humiliated" by the experience, "because I saw non-Indian people going out of the store with their carts, and they were not being stopped." Friday experienced similar treatment at a U-Haul office in Lander. She was returning a trailer when "another man came in with a big U-Haul truck, and the guy just left us standing there while he went out and took care of him. So we had to wait for 15 or 20 minutes for him to come back and take care of us."[58]

Ivan Posey, the chair of the Eastern Shoshone Business Council, said there was racism today in Fremont County. He has experienced lack of service in restaurants "and people following you around in stores."[59] He was also a member of the Lander Chamber of Commerce for eight months in 1993 but left in "frustration" after local merchants refused to observe a Native American Appreciation Day. As he explained, "we looked at an appreciation day to have the vendors maybe mark things down 10 percent or something, just for a day to acknowledge the contributions of the American Indians in Lander spending their money or going to Safeway or whatever. And we could never get it done." The merchants remained opposed to an appreciation day even "without discounts or anything."[60]

Michelle Hoffman, a non-Indian, is the superintendent of Fremont County School District No. 14, which includes the Wyoming Indian High School at Ethete. She has been in stores in Lander and Riverton where Indians were ahead of her but she has been waited on first. She also said, "I have been in rest rooms where people will not go in and use the stall if a Native comes out of there." She says discrimination against Indians has not improved much over the past twenty years.[61]

Richard Brannan is a former chair of the Northern Arapaho Business Council. He and his family rented a townhouse in Riverton from a local realty company. After they moved in, the owner of the townhouse found out the family was Indian and "he harassed us constantly until we moved out of there," said Brannan.[62] He has "no relationship" with non-Indians off the reservation, other than the mayor of Riverton. "It's like two different worlds," he said.[63]

Helsha Acuna, a member of the Apache Tribe, is a professor of American Indian Studies at Central Wyoming College, where she has been employed for ten years. When she first came to Fremont County in the late 1990s, she rented a trailer from a white couple who owned property near Riverton. She and her daughter cleaned the trailer and moved some of their belongings in; however, before she could take up residence, Acuna got a call from the owner, who said the rental wasn't going to work. "We've had Indians out here before who have worked for us," he said, "and it's never worked out real well, and we just don't know that we'll be able to sleep at night with you on the property." Acuna then called the wife to see if she could resolve things, but the wife was adamant that she move. "'You know what, Helsha?'" Acuna reported the woman said, "'We're not the niggers here. You may not be from here, you may be an Apache, but you're no better than these F-ing Arapahos or F-ing Shoshones that are out here.'"[64]

Acuna had to hire an attorney to make arrangement to pick up her belongings from the trailer. When she returned to the trailer, all her belongings had been placed outside in the snow and rain. Several people were also there, one of whom was leaning against the side of the trailer with his hand around the barrel of a shotgun. Acuna eventually rented a small house in Lander, where she lives today.[65]

Acuna said one of the problems with Indian–white relations is "the conspiracy of silence." White students don't learn anything about Indian culture, and "what happens is that they are walking around with, well, unfortunately, stereotypes of what they think an Indian is, and they truly believe it." They think Indians "are drunk, they are lazy, they just get welfare checks." There is an "institutionalized racism, institutionalized prejudice," and it affects people of both races, Acuna said. The damage of stereotypes "has gone both ways. That there is among many Indian people a deep anger and resentment, and therefore there is a lot of stereotypes and prejudice about those white people out there."[66]

Tom Throop lives in Lander and is the former director of the Equality State Policy Center, a Wyoming public interest organization. He described Indian–white relations today in Fremont County as "disappointingly bad. I continue to be surprised at how much stress and strain and ill will there is between Native Americans and white Americans in Fremont County." In Lander, Throop said, "rarely do you see whites and Native Americans exchanging pleasantries in the street, but you will see Native Americans engaging, you will see whites engaging."[67]

Todd Guenther, who teaches anthropology and history at Central Wyoming College, agreed that "I don't see a great deal of improvement in race relations in the Valley over the years."[68] Valerie Thomas, a former member of the county commission and an attorney in Lander, says "there's such a gulf still of misunderstanding and miscommunication" between Indians on the reservation and non-Indians off the reservation in Fremont County.[69]

John Vincent, a local attorney, was elected mayor of Riverton in 2002. When he was sworn in, he had an American Indian cedaring ceremony, in which those in attendance are blessed with cedar smoke. Afterward he spoke at a Martin Luther King, Jr., Day rally and was presented with an Indian blanket, which he hung in the council chambers in the Riverton City Hall. In response, he has gotten complaints "that I was favoring Native American people over Riverton residents." He has also been criticized in letters to the editor in the newspaper for participating in the cedaring ceremony and placing the Indian blanket in the council chambers.[70]

Former county commissioner Gary Jennings says he has no social contact with tribal members on the reservation.[71] Another former commissioner, Lanny Applegate, also had very little contact with the reservation. As he put it, "I had no reason to go out there over the years." He doesn't belong to any social or business clubs or groups. He belongs to a church, but could only identify one person he thinks is Indian who is a member.[72] Commissioner Douglas Thompson agreed "there are people in the county that are racially prejudiced. I think people are aware of race. You know, it's an obvious thing."[73]

Indian Boarding Schools

Part of the history of discrimination that continues to polarize the Indian and white communities involves the Indian boarding schools. Dr. Martha Hipp, a school psychologist at the Wyoming Indian High School, has studied the history of Indian education in Fremont County, including the boarding school years and the establishment in more modern times of the Wyoming Indian School. The study was funded in part by a grant from the Wyoming Council for the Humanities. In conducting her study, she interviewed some fifty-three people, including those who had attended boarding schools and those who had participated in the formation of the Wyoming Indian School.[74]

Arapaho were among the first to attend the Carlisle Indian Training School in Pennsylvania. Between 1881 and 1894, seventy-three Arapaho and Shoshone children were sent on trains to Carlisle, Santee, or Genoa boarding schools. Only twenty-six survived. The rest died of diseases such as tuberculosis, measles, and flu. One of those who died in April 1882 and was buried at the cemetery at Carlisle rather than returned home for burial by his family was Hayes Friday, a Northern Arapahoe.[75]

Richard Brannan is the great-great-grandson of Chief Black Coal, the last recognized chief of the Arapaho. Brannan said two of Black Coal's children were sent to Carlisle, where they died and are buried today.[76]

Burton Hutchinson, who served as chair of the Northern Arapaho Business Council for twenty years and whose grandparents were sent to boarding school, said "they just picked them. 'All right, you get ready tomorrow. We're going to ship you off.'" He also said "they didn't bring them home every year. They had to complete eight years before they come home."[77]

A second phase of the boarding school system was in-state schools. Four boarding schools opened on the Wind River Reservation between 1883 and 1913, three of which were government/church mission schools. The commissioner of Indian Affairs issued orders in 1886 that "no school will be permitted on the reservation in which the English language is not exclusively taught."[78] Initially, children as young as age four were kept in these schools for years at a time. The boarding schools were characterized by overcrowding, lack of adequate sanitation, inadequate water supply, contagious diseases (such as trachoma), hard manual labor, poor nutrition, excessive punishment for infraction of school rules, and the disparagement of Indian culture and identity. More important, Indian children were deprived of the care and affection of their parents, which, Hipp says, had "devastating effects" on them. Between 1892 and 1902, the death rate of the children in the schools was 50 percent, which prompted school officials to give the students some holiday visits home.[79] Rev. John Roberts, who ran both the government boarding school at Fort Washakie and the Episcopal mission boarding school nearby, was reported as saying, "I don't understand why so many of them die."[80]

Indian children frequently ran away from the boarding schools, and when they were caught they were returned and subjected to very harsh punishment. There were cells in the cellar at Fort Washakie where recalcitrant Indian children were put in solitary confinement and kept in chains.[81] At St. Stephens as late as the 1940s, school officials would cut strips from rubber tires, tie them to wooden handles, and beat the children with them. At the government school, school officials would discipline the students by making them walk around in circles carrying heavy posts on their shoulders.[82]

Burton Hutchinson was born in 1929, was raised by his grandparents on the reservation, and attended boarding school at St. Michael's Mission in Ethete. He grew up speaking Arapaho. "We didn't know how to speak English," he said. "I was taught the old way, the culture, traditions. My grandma and grandpa always spoke to us in Arapaho. Grandma used to make biscuits for us every morning, gravy. Because that's all they could afford. My grandfather later on, when he got about in his 60s, 70s, he started drawing money, but it was only $21 a month."[83]

The boarding school "was tough for us," Hutchinson said. "Like when they took me that day, it was on a Sunday, I didn't know what they were saying." The school had "disciplinarians," and it was run "like a military-type school." It "took a long time before we could really understand English. By the time we got through the eighth grade they had taught us how to read English." If the disciplinarians caught you speaking Arapaho, they would say, "'You, you, you. Get extra duty.' That's the way they punished us." They would make the children sweep, mop, and clean up, inside and outside, and pick up trash, mow the grass, and shovel snow. The older male students worked outside on the farm milking cows. The girls worked in the kitchen. The disciplinarians also had "big sticks," Hutchinson said, and "if you didn't understand and you done something else, they'd really get after you. If you didn't listen, why, you got a swat right in the butt." They also taught the students Christian religion, and it was "mandatory. You had to learn the Bible and all the stories." Officials at the boarding school cut Hutchinson's braids. "I didn't like that when they cut my hair," he said.[84]

Both of Patricia Bergie's parents attended boarding schools on the Wind River Reservation. Her mother went to the Shoshone Indian Mission School and her father to the Fort Washakie Government School. "They were forced to be there," she said, and "it was probably very traumatic for them. My mother doesn't really talk about it, so that leaves a lot just her being silent about it." Bergie's parents were also forced to speak English and punished if they spoke Shoshone. As a consequence, they made no effort to make her fluent in Shoshone "because of their experience with washing out their mouth and being hit and stuff like that." The boarding school experiences of her parents and her own experiences growing up on the reservation have made Bergie "very distrustful of the white people." It has also "caused a lot of self-esteem problems, so just not being confident in that large society."[85]

James Large was raised primarily by his grandparents, who had also attended Indian boarding schools. Although Arapaho was spoken around the house, he said, his grandparents "really didn't want me to learn a lot of it and speak it all the time because they had gotten punished so much in boarding schools that they didn't want me to go through the same punishment that they did."[86]

The Johnson O'Malley Act of 1934 provided funding to the states for education of Indian children who lived on land that was not taxed and thus helped lead to the gradual demise of the traditional Indian boarding schools.[87] Martha Hipp, in summarizing the boarding school experience, said "the results of these abusive experiences have been passed down in various forms from one generation to the next. The harsh punishments and prolonged emotional neglect with the direct injunction not to show a reaction enforced helplessness and distance from any possible caregivers in the environment." Boarding school children, who were prevented from speaking their own language and were forced to learn a new language, were effectively inhibited from being fluent in any language, she said.[88]

Richard Brannan attended modern-day public schools but says he continues to be haunted by the boarding school experience of his ancestors. He has a five-year-old grandson and wonders what he would do if suddenly strangers came and took the child away and "I didn't know where he was, I didn't know if he was going to come back or not, and I never get to enjoy being with him." But that, he said, is "what happened to the Arapaho children and the Arapaho parents. They were taken away, and they never got to experience the feelings of love by their parents. It was cruel punishment that they received at the hands of the federal government and many churches. What they did to us is unconscionable. They tried genocide. They tried to wipe us out totally from the face of the earth. When they couldn't do that, then they implemented the boarding schools to kill the Indian inside the child so we would become as non-Indians. But they haven't been successful because we're still here today."[89]

Public Schools: Tension and Conflict

In modern times, Indian students have continued to suffer from discrimination in the public schools at the hands of teachers and white students. After leaving boarding school, Burton Hutchinson attended high school in Lander in the 1940s but only for one year. The white kids "thought they were really different from you, because them being white and us were this color," he said, pointing to his face. It was "kind of a racist thing." In class, "it wasn't that equal thing. We were kind of set aside. You weren't really recognized because you were Indian, you know. I noticed that. A lot of us gave up the first year. I felt that it wasn't no good."[90]

Patricia Bergie attended the Fort Washakie Elementary School in the 1950s. All of the children enrolled in the school were Indian, but all of the teachers were white. She described her experience at the school as "one of just intimidation." The students were not allowed to wear braids, and the teachers had low expectations for the students. After finishing elementary school, Bergie went to Lander High School in the 1960s. The experience was one of "real culture shock." Although she was not a remedial student, she was placed in a remedial class. She did well on academics but was not recognized as an achiever. "Most of the time," she said, "they just didn't acknowledge an Indian person as excelling." In one of her science classes, in which she was the only Indian student, her teacher said "what a blessing it was and a privilege for white people to be white." Bergie said, "I didn't know what to do. I knew I was not wanted."[91]

Gary Collins, whose father was Northern Arapaho but whose mother was Swedish, attended Lander High School in the 1960s. He did not have a lot of problems at the school, but he said "many of my Indian friends and relatives who looked more Indian than I do did receive innuendos and slurs and racial actions." The white students "would call us spear chuckers or wagon burners, just in a verbiage that was condescending, there would be displays of some people walking like they were inebriated to mimic an Indian person." In response, "many tribal members would withdraw into their own little segments of the community at school. It was visually segregated in terms of where they felt their comfort zone was." Many of the Indian students dropped out of school because "the sudden change and the different kinds of attributes within the school community made it difficult to learn. So they, they dropped out."[92]

Patrick Goggles, a Northern Arapaho, is currently a member of the state legislature elected from majority-Indian House District 33. His family name in Arapaho means Iron Eyes, but it was changed to Goggles to accommodate the white man. He attended the high school in Lander in the 1960s and said there was "a lot of tension, fights between the young men. Just a general dislike for one another." He also said Indian students experienced harsher discipline and in-school suspension: "If a Native kid skipped a class, he got three days or she got three days. And the non-Native kids got a day." Most Indian students sat in the back of the classroom, and "if you didn't excel in athletics, you were sort of like not there," Goggles said. But it was hard to participate in athletics and other after-school activities because of a lack of transportation. Indian students either had to hitch a ride or walk or run home in the evening.[93]

Betty Friday attended school in Lander from 1960 to 1963. She said, "I felt like I was invisible." The teachers never encouraged her or the other Indian students to go to college. She had an uncle "who was very good in math, but I never heard the teachers tell him you should go to school and be a math instructor." Her senior year, Friday's business teacher wrote something in shorthand in one of her books. She did not know shorthand at the time, but later after she went to business school and learned shorthand she went back to the book, "and it told me, 'Good luck,' and in shorthand it said, 'You'll need it.' And I never forgot that." She took the message to mean, "You're gonna need all the luck you can get because you're not going to make it."[94]

Sandra C'Bearing, a tribal member, attended school in Lander in 1968. Even though she held up her hand to answer the teacher's questions, she said "I never, never got called upon." Other Indian students were similarly ignored. When she indicated she wanted to run for class office, the class sponsor said she should try out for the class mascot instead, because it would disguise her identity: "We're having try-outs for the tiger (the class mascot). You could try out for that. That way, no one could see you." C'Bearing declined the invitation.[95]

Richard Brannan also attended schools in Lander in the 1960s and 70s. His experiences were similar to other Indian students'. There were "fisticuffs, fighting" with the white students, he said. They would call you "redskin," and "it would lead to get you angry." Ultimately, he said, "I had to put up a veil or a difference face. I couldn't show my true feelings. I had to put on what you'd call like armor to protect myself." He estimated he had confrontations with more than half of the white students at school.[96]

In 1970, a fight broke out at the Lander High School between white and Indian students, which culminated in approximately 200 white and Indian students confronting each other at Sinks Canyon several miles south of town. The crowd dispersed when some white students showed up with guns.[97]

As late as September 1972, the Lander and Dubois schools had an explicit policy of not recognizing the special needs of Indian children. According to the Fremont County School Organization Committee, "District 6 and LVHS District categorically reject the principle of special recognition of ethnic differences or needs in favor of educational policies applicable to all students regardless of racial origin. Accordingly, it is extremely difficult . . . to single out programs specifically designed to meet the special educational needs of the county's Indian children."[98] To the extent that history of the American West was taught in the county's public schools, it "was taught totally from the point of view of the pioneers," Hipp said.[99]

Ivan Posey attended high school in Lander in 1974, but he didn't last the year. He left to attend an Indian school in Chilocco, Oklahoma, because of racial slurs from white students, "racial tension," and "fights," he said. The confrontations continued after regular school hours and it was common at "football games and stuff to have fights going on." Posey discussed the problems he was having with white students with the Lander school counselors, and they said "I could probably do better in a boarding school."[100]

James Large, who was born in 1945, attended a number of schools, including those in Lander and Riverton. He has been called names, such as "dirty Indian, F-ing Indian." He got into fights over the name calling. Large also attended the Mill Creek School on the Wind River Reservation, where all the teachers were non-Indian. He said the white teachers gave the students "swats" for speaking Arapaho. The teachers "would have a paddle in their room," and if you said something in Arapaho "that was a cause for swats. It was almost a daily occurrence with me."[101]

Sara Wiles has two children who attended school in Lander. She knows a lot of the teachers in the Lander school district and has heard comments from them "over the years about the Indian students, and they're things like 'they're dirty, they come to school unclean, they're not prepared, they aren't doing well in this environment, they can't learn, they're stupid,' things like that."[102]

Todd Guenther said Indian and white children in the elementary schools "don't seem to notice race very often." But when they get to high school, "there seems to be a real separation between the groups. There's not a great deal of fraternization. They don't seem to go to each other's homes on Friday and Saturday nights."[103]

Betty Friday served on the Johnson O'Malley parent committee in Fremont County on and off from 1977 to 2004 and has heard complaints from Indian students that they were treated rudely by their white teachers. When Indian students were two or three minutes late getting to a class at the school in Lander because of the distance they had to travel from one classroom to another, they were told they would be put on the absenteeism list, whereas white students who did the same thing were not. Friday called the different treatment of Indian students by school officials "a double standard." A lot of Indian students dropped out of the Lander school. During one six-month period, "we probably lost about 20 or 30 students," Friday said.[104]

Although Lander school personnel claim a low Indian dropout rate—7.5 percent to 32 percent—Indians insist it was as high as 60 percent. Hipp got Indian students to identify Indians in class graduation pictures from the Lander paper for 1970 and 1971. On the basis of the identifications, she concluded that the number of Indians "that actually graduated appears to be only 20 to 30 percent."[105]

Wyoming Indian High School: Racial Taunts and Slurs

In an effort to address the discrimination and other problems Indian students were experiencing in the public schools, tribal members began in 1966 to try to establish a high school on the reservation. They formed an organization called the Wind River Education Association that was composed of Arapaho and Shoshone as well as mixed-blood American Indians.[106] As James Large explained, the purpose of the school "was to absorb the pushout rate, what we used to call it, of Lander and Riverton and the other surrounding schools when kids would go to school and not be able to fit in to the system."[107]

The education association met opposition from the white community. James Large said the opposition "was primarily by the non-Indian people in both Lander and Riverton, Shoshoni, Dubois districts, because they thought if we formed our own district out there they wouldn't have as many Indians to count in and receive Indian impact money into their school system."[108]

Two predominantly white reservation property owner groups—Parents Interested in Education (PIE) and Property Owners on the Reservation (POOR)—also opposed the idea of a high school on the reservation because they said it would lead to racial "segregation." No one, however, objected to the all-white schools that existed in the county as being segregated. According to Hipp, the concern over segregation "was kind of a propaganda campaign." That the stated concern over segregation was a pretext, and that the real objection was to funneling money to the reservation, is apparent from the minutes of a 1971 meeting of POOR. When someone said the proposed Indian school would provide jobs and more money on the reservation, another replied: "What would the Indians do . . . spend more money for gas and in the bars? Anyway, they won't know nothing when they graduate."[109]

In 1972, a high school on the reservation, the Wyoming Indian High School, was approved as a BIA school. It remained a BIA contract school until 1983, when the community voted for it to become a public school. The Indian school district became a unified K–12 public school district in 1983, and a new building for the Wyoming Indian High School was completed in 1987. Admission is open to all students.[110]

The graduation rate of Indian students from the Wyoming Indian School is higher today than in previous years. In 2004–2005 it was 59 percent, which was still lower than the Wyoming average graduation rate, which was 81 percent in 2004–2005. In 2005–2006, the graduation rate for Indian students was still 23 percent lower than the state's graduation rate. Indian children today perform poorly in English on the Measures of Academic Progress test. And because there are deficiencies in English, "there are deficiencies in every academic class. Students become discouraged, and they drop out," said Hipp. According to Hipp, Indian children continue to "have conflict about taking part in the white educational system that's still largely assimilationist."[111]

From the very beginning Indian sports teams from the Wyoming Indian School experienced discrimination when they played white teams off the reservation. Al Redman, who later became a coach, recalled when he was driving the team school bus some men drove up in a truck behind him and threw bottles, hitting the bus. "I almost put the brakes on," he said, "but someone would have got hurt. So they passed and kept throwing bottles. Once they put a dead deer in the bus at Meteetsee. Once we drove up to a gas station and they said, 'Oh, f ___, here come those Indians again.'"[112]

Michelle Hoffman said students from the Wyoming Indian High School today experience two kinds of discrimination, "one is social discrimination, and one is institutional discrimination." The social discrimination occurs when Indian students are out in the non-Indian community; this discrimination "is very easy to see." One such incident occurred in Lander when the school had a picnic to celebrate the end of the school year. "Carloads of other children pulled up alongside and did war whoops and yelled, 'Go back to the reservation.'"[113]

According to Hoffman, Indian students attending a regional basketball tournament at Riverton heard "people in the stands yelling out, 'white chocolate,' 'black Indian boy,' and 'go back to the res.'" "White chocolate" refers to "a student that would be half Native and half white," Hoffman said. She has heard name calling from both white students and adults. Hoffman has also heard her students called, "and I hate this word, I hate this word, 'prairie niggers.' Why should we have our children have to put up with that? Do we ask any other children to be strong, accept slurs like that?" When mainly white students are competing at athletic events you may hear "trash talk, but talk that includes any racial slurs you probably wouldn't hear," Hoffman said. The racial slur "sets itself apart." Indian students attending a state tournament in Casper were also called names when they went to a local mall.[114]

A documentary film entitled *Chiefs* was released in 2002; it followed the Wyoming Indian High School Chiefs basketball team through two seasons. The film portrayed, among other things, "racist taunts" that were made toward the Indian ball players.[115]

The institutional discrimination, Hoffman said, was in the form of textbooks selected by the state department of education for use in the public schools. The textbooks "cover very little history background on Native Americans," she said. Out of six high school textbooks, "there's approximately 20 pages that talk about Native Americans, and in those 20 pages half the pages talk about Sacagawea, a page and a half talks about casinos, the summary for one of the chapters talks about how disadvantaged Native Americans are, they live in poverty, squalor, and that most of them live in automobiles. That's the kind of institutionalized racism that we see in schools, and we're teaching this to our children all across the state."[116]

Pioneer Museum Exhibits

The Fremont County Pioneer Museum and its treatment of Indian artifacts and exhibits further reveals the divide between the Indian and non-Indian communities. A Pioneer Association was organized in the county in 1885 and began construction of a museum in 1909. Its mission was to preserve the history and heritage of central Wyoming for the benefit of residents and tourists. In its early years, Indians and mixed-bloods participated in the affairs of the Pioneer Association. However, beginning in the 1940s the participation of American Indians diminished to next to nothing. The cause for that, according to Todd Guenther, a former director of the Fremont County Pioneer Museum, was that American Indians found the exhibits at the museum "to be very insulting and didn't want to participate or visit." The things that most offended American Indians were exhibits "that referred to Indian women as squaws and Indian men as bucks." Those terms were interpreted by American Indians as derogatory and "as being very akin to a black person being called a nigger," Guenther said.[117]

Guenther was hired as director of the museum in 1995 by the museum's board of directors, who are appointed by the county commission. Guenther sought and was awarded a $10,000 grant from the Wyoming Council for the Humanities to begin replacing and improving the care of the exhibits and to "remove some of the racist connotations that were incorporated in them," he said. To assist in this project, he recruited students from Wyoming Indian High School, Fort Washakie Junior High, and the Lander schools. The museum board of directors and the Pioneer Association were supportive of Guenther's efforts, with the notable exception of Crosby Allen, who was a member of both the board and the Pioneer Association and was later elected to the county commission. Following a meeting of the Pioneer Association at which Guenther announced the receipt of the grant from the Wyoming Council for the Humanities, Allen asked for more information about the project that was to be undertaken. According to Guenther, "when I explained that to him, he terminated the meeting by slamming his notebook shut and saying, 'I hate the goddamn Indians, and I won't have anything to do with this.'"[118]

Guenther also undertook a project to repair the original museum buildings, build a new museum complex, and relocate the museum to another site within the City of Lander. According to Guenther, Crosby Allen, who was on the county commission by this time, was "very hostile to our efforts to get the museum building either repaired or replaced and became a major obstacle to our making progress in the first few years of that undertaking."[119]

As director of the museum, Guenther gave public lectures and slide shows on historic topics and the museum project. On occasion, he said, people came up to him and said, "'I'll support the museum if you don't emphasize those prairie niggers,' which is a slur that's heard around the area referring to Native Americans."[120]

One-Shot Antelope Hunt: Dancing with "Squaws"

Lander, the Fremont County seat, is home to the annual One-Shot Antelope Hunt. It is a major event in the county, and participants have included governors, astronauts, a Metropolitan Opera singer, and other celebrities. All the participants in the hunt itself have been white men.[121] Teams compete, and those that fail to kill an antelope with one shot are required to dress as, and dance with, Indian women. As the *Wyoming State Journal* put it in an article, with accompanying photograph, in September 1970, "Carl Browall, Lander's One-Shot team member, is undaunted even after suffering the humiliation of being dressed up by (complete with rouge!) and dancing with the squaws, as pennance [*sic*] for his failure to bring down an antelope with one shot."[122] Similar photographs and stories about the One-Shot Antelope Hunt with the losing team members dressed as "squaws" have regularly appeared in local newspapers.

Sara Wiles once attended the One-Shot Antelope Hunt's Saturday-night banquet in Lander and found it "pretty offensive." She said it "seemed like sort of a throwback to minstrel show days when Indians were expected to perform in a certain way and act in a certain way, to fall in line with the good ol' boy stereotypes. The whole thing seemed really anachronistic to me. It seemed like something that should have happened 80 year[s] ago, but it still is continuing."[123]

Disputes over Natural Resources

Ownership and use of land and resources on the Wind River Reservation have been a continuing source of contention between the tribes, white landowners, and the state. In a memorial to Congress in 1941, the legislature noted that "beginning in the year 1939 the Department of the Interior . . . initiated a policy of buying back 'in trust' all the lands heretofore sold on the 'ceded' portion of the reservation as well as some lands not a part of the reservation" and requested Congress to enact legislation that will provide Fremont and Hot Springs Counties taxes lost on property "which has been re-purchased in trust for Indians."[124]

In the early 1940s, white ranchers in Fremont County urged members of Congress to preserve their grazing rights on the reservation. In one letter, Mrs. L. A. Phillips wrote the following:

> The white people who bought farms and made homes on the Indian Reservation are entitled to help to get grazing rights for live stock like we used to have. . . . They don't give us equal rights with the Indians. . . . We pay the taxes that keeps the Indian service going too, and we pay the salaries of these Indian officials who are denying us any rights. We say we are as good as any Indians, yet these Indian officials treat us like we were some kind of rats. . . . We can use our tomahawks and get a few scalps too so keep an eye on us next election.[125]

In another similar letter, Lawrence Raymond wrote, "The white land owners on the Indian Reservation here in Fremont County need your help in getting the relief by act of Congress to give us grazing rights."[126]

In 1941, the Wind River Indian Reservation Land Owners' Council petitioned Congress to provide grazing opportunities for white landowners. "Sentimentality for the Indian has no place in this development," they said. "They may insist this is their reservation. It is not." "The white man cannot be oppressed in Wyoming, simply because he is on lands that the Indians once owned, any more that they can in Ohio, Illinois, and other states."[127] Members of Congress acknowledged that "[t]he situation on the ceded portion of the Wind River Reservation is highly controversial."[128] The use of water resources on the reservation has been the subject of protracted litigation and remains an ongoing dispute between the tribes, the county, the state, and white ranchers. Following a 1904 U.S. government order, the Bureau of Reclamation developed the nation's first federal irrigation district on the Wind River Indian Reservation. It presently extends along both sides of the reservation's major river, the Wind River, and provides water for farms and ranches in a 335,000-acre zone of the reservation. This is the most productive portion of the reservation, but for the most part it is owned and/or operated by non-Indians who acquired the parcels of land from the time of the Dawes Act of 1887 to the 1930s.[129]

The state of Wyoming filed suit in 1977 against the United States to determine water rights in the Big Horn River drainage system.

The litigation resulted in, among other things, a finding that the intent of the Treaty of Fort Bridger of 1868 was to reserve water rights to the Wind River Indian Reservation from appropriation under state law, and that the measure of the tribes' reserved water rights was the water necessary to irrigate practicably irrigable acreage.[130]

Gary Collins, who has served as the tribal water engineer, said "it seems like every time there would be a dispute about water it would heighten everybody's awareness about Indian versus non-Indian."[131] John Vincent thinks the controversy over water rights "probably has been the single largest stressor" in Indian–white relations.[132]

Indians' Depressed Socioeconomic Status

Aside from ongoing controversies and racial polarization, another factor that contributes to the inability of Indians to participate effectively in the at-large system of elections is their depressed socioeconomic status, a continuing effect of past discrimination. Dr. Garth Massey, a professor of sociology and international studies at the University of Wyoming, conducted a comprehensive study in 1998 of socioeconomic conditions on the reservation for the Joint Business Council. He and his colleague Audie Blevins conducted a reservation-wide household count rather than a sample survey. Their purpose was to produce data that could be used by the tribes for program evaluation, grant writing, and other needs.

In conducting the survey, Massey employed thirty interviewers, all of whom were American Indians and residents of the reservation. They conducted 2,700 interviews with Indian households, and approximately 560 interviews with non-Indian households. An "Indian" for purposes of the survey was anyone who self-identified as an Indian. According to Massey, "we interviewed 95 percent of the households on the reservation, representing what we think is probably about 95 percent of the people" on the reservation.[133]

Massey described the needs of Indians on the Wind River Reservation as "dramatic." Among his findings were the following:

- Median annual income for Indian households was $11,929, which was approximately half the amount reported by the 2000 census ($22,656).
- Fifty-six percent of all Indian households and 58.3 percent of all Indians on the reservation were living in poverty. The national poverty rate was about 13 percent.
- Forty percent of all Indian households shared a domicile.
- Sixty percent of Indian homes on the reservation were in need of major repair, and 50 percent were substandard. About 20 percent of the Indian domiciles were not inhabited because they were in need of repair for one reason or another.
- The reservation was almost entirely lacking in manufacturing and assembly operations, with few private-sector service jobs and few jobs requiring professional and technical expertise. About half of those on the reservation who were employed worked in public-sector jobs.
- Of those able and available to work, more than one-third were unemployed. The unemployment rate was more than seven times higher than the national average and three to four times the level for many depressed rural areas.
- Little retail business was done on the reservation itself.
- Other factors contributing to unemployment and poverty on the reservation included low wages, job insecurity, health problems, lack of availability of a vehicle, unpaved roads, and lack of snow removal in winter.
- Health on the reservation was a serious problem. A third of all Indian persons ages eighteen to fifty-four reported having diabetes as did 42 percent of those ages fifty-five and over. Nearly 50 percent of children and youths reported having asthma.
- About 40 percent of the domiciles occupied by Indians didn't have a land-line for telephone service.[134]

Although many things influence political behavior, there is a strong link between socioeconomic status and voting. As Massey explained,

> The socioeconomic (SES) model of political participation is nowhere as obviously applicable as on the WRIR [Wind River Indian Reservation]. A high degree of social isolation, along with rurality, minority ethnic status of the Indians, lower levels of educational and occupational attainment, unemployment, low income and a high rate of poverty all conform to the relevant model by suppressing political participation, including that most basic form of participation: voting. Add to this the other difficulties of the Indians on the WRIR—poor health, substandard housing, uncertainty of reliable transportation, and a history of marginalization and discrimination—and it is no wonder that political participation is low.[135]

The poor and unemployed, Massey said, "don't have the luxury of being involved in civic affairs, in political life, to the extent that more affluent or more comfortable or people with a more secure lifestyle have."[136]

White Resentment of Indian "Entitlements"

Even though American Indians in Fremont County have a depressed socioeconomic status, the fact that they receive per capita payments from oil and gas resources on the reservation, as well as federal health benefits, is a source of resentment among many whites in the county. The oil and gas royalties are divided equally among the two tribes. The monthly per capita payment for members of the Eastern Shoshone Tribe for January 2008 was $250. For members of the Northern Arapaho Tribe, whose numbers are greater, the per capita payment was $100. Former commissioner Gary Jennings acknowledged there was a "clash in cultures" between Indians on the reservation and whites off the reservation. As he explained, "certain people get per capita and others do not get a per capita, so you have different attitudes develop from that and other things."[137]

Scott Ratliff said there is "this notion that Indian people are paid because they're Indian, and that isn't the case. They're paid because of royalties that come off of their land. But I think that resentment exists." There was also "some resentment that there's a land that many people feel like they can better utilize if it weren't controlled by Indian people."[138]

Whites have also complained that American Indians do not pay taxes. But as Ivan Posey pointed out, Indians pay taxes when they shop in Lander and Riverton, and federal income taxes are collected from oil, gas, and mineral extraction.[139]

Discrimination in Law Enforcement

Law enforcement in Fremont County has been a divisive issue. Helsha Acuna has been stopped several times by the police in Riverton for alleged traffic violations. On one occasion she talked to a county judge and asked him to explain why she was being stopped so frequently. "It's because you're Indian," he said. "If you're an Indian and there's a reason to pull you over, they will, to check to see if you have insurance, if you even have a driver's license, and, of course, to check to see if you've been drinking." The judge said he didn't approve of the practice, but "this is what goes on with the police department."[140]

Valerie Thomas, who has worked as a public defender in Fremont County, believes "the judicial system uses factors that are not overtly racial, but the impact of them is extraordinarily racial." In addition, "there's just no venue to discuss and resolve these matters that I know." Bail, for example, is routinely denied to Indian defendants and granted to white defendants, she said. As a public defender, in reviewing the files of white defendants it was usual to find consent forms to the taking of blood samples or breathalyzer tests, but it was not unusual for such forms to be missing from the files of American Indians.[141]

Since he has been mayor, John Vincent has gotten complaints of racial discrimination in law enforcement committed by the Riverton police. The complaints were sufficiently serious that he requested the FBI to conduct an investigation. The U.S. Department of Justice also assigned two people to conduct a series of public meetings in Riverton in an effort to resolve the existing problems. The meetings were attended by tribal officials and members, local citizens, and members of the police department. As a result of the investigations and meetings, Riverton has adopted a policy of "community policing," which is designed to encourage people, particularly members of the Indian and minority community, to feel comfortable in communicating with the police. Vincent thinks the new policy has improved policing in Riverton.[142]

Unresponsive County Officials

A significant lack of responsiveness of elected officials to the particular needs of minorities is also relevant evidence of vote dilution.[143] Fremont County officials have generally been unresponsive to the needs of the American Indian community, and Indians say they are simply ignored by the county government.

Few Indians, for example, have been hired by the county as poll workers. Julie Freese, the county clerk, said American Indians were, and always have been, "severely underrepresented" as poll workers. There are eight voting precinct on the reservation and thirty-eight poll worker positions. At the last election, only three of the thirty-eight poll workers were American Indians.[144]

Very few Indians have been employed by Fremont County. In 2005, a total of 282 people were employed full time by the county, but only six (.02 percent) were American Indian. There were eleven part-time or temporary employees, none of whom was Indian. There were forty new hires during the 2005 fiscal year, and none was an American Indian.[145] The workforce at the county courthouse is virtually all white. The employment of Indians by the county in earlier years was no better. The various county agencies recommend people for vacancies, but the ultimate decision to hire is made by the county commission.[146] Julie Freese admitted that Indians were "severely underrepresented" in county employment.[147] She said qualified Indians had applied for county jobs, but "I can't tell you why they're not being hired."[148]

In fact, members of the county commission have said they are unconcerned about, and have never investigated, racial imbalance in county hiring. Former commissioner Jennings said he wouldn't have knowledge of Indians who had been hired to work for the county "unless I investigated it. And I don't do that."[149] Commissioner Patrick Hickerson doesn't know how many Indians are employed by Fremont County, but it is not something he is concerned about investigating.[150] Commissioner Douglas Thompson could identify only three Indians who had been appointed to local boards by the county commission.[151]

The tribal Joint Business Council asked the county commission in 1972 to appoint one member of each tribe to the Governing Hospital Board. Hospitals in Fremont County are supported in part by grants from the Indian Health Service (IHS). In the past, the IHS had given $230,000 to the hospital board. A new grant of $280,000 was being proposed by the IHS, but if the request for Indian membership on the hospital board were denied, the Joint Tribal Council indicated it "shall ask the Indian Health Service to withdraw any current and future support of Fremont County Hospitals Construction projects."[152]

The county commission adopted a resolution that "although previously inadequately expressed, [the commission] does appreciate the past, and hopefully the future, aid and assistance of the individual members of the Shoshone and Arapahoe Tribes and their Joint Business Council in making fine, new, well-equipped hospitals available to the people of Fremont County, and is desirous of recognizing such aid and assistance and honoring the request made by" the Tribal Council. But saying that no vacancies were available, it agreed only to "appoint one member each of the Shoshone and Arapahoe Tribes to act as representatives of their respective Tribes as ex-officio members of the Board of trustees."[153]

Because the commissioners refused to appoint tribal members to the board, the IHS withheld the grant at the tribes' request.[154] A year later, a vacancy on the hospital board did occur, but rather than appointing a tribal member the county commission appointed someone from Riverton to have a "balance" between Lander and Riverton.[155]

During the 1992 county elections, a referendum was on the ballot for adopting single-member districts for the county commission. Despite the fact that residents of the Wind River Reservation supported the referendum as a way of enhancing Indian political participation, defendant Freese opposed it because she said it would be too much trouble to prepare ballots for the districts and would impose administrative burdens on her office.[156]

In a resolution adopted in 1993, the county commission opposed a legislative bill (SF 172) requiring that full faith and credit be afforded by the state of Wyoming to the decisions of the Tribal Court of the Eastern Shoshone and Northern Arapaho Tribes. The commission said "[t]he people of Fremont County would be directly and adversely affected should SF 172 be enacted into law."[157]

Scott Ratliff, who served several terms in the state legislature, ran for the county commission in 2000 because "I thought there was a lot of disparities going on and had hoped to make a difference." Although there were senior citizen centers in many communities in the county, there were none on the reservation. Ratliff also did not think the reservation received a fair share of sales tax distribution. "The infrastructure on the reservation is really in disarray," he said. He felt he could have contributed to improvements if he could have gotten elected. Ratliff doesn't think the county commission has adequately represented the reservation. "I spend a fair amount of my time, my working days, on the reservation somewhere," he said, "and I, I can't honestly remember ever seeing a County Commissioner at anything that I go to that's physically out where the Indian people live. And I think unless you're out in those areas you don't really know what those communities need."[158]

In 2002, the tribes asked the county commission to provide a letter of support for the tribes' application to the Environmental Protection Agency (EPA) for a Wind River Watershed Initiative grant. The amount of the grant was approximately a million dollars, $250,000 of which would have gone to support nonreservation, non-Indian landowners. Stephanie Kessler, an environmental policy specialist who was hired by the Joint Business Council to help prepare the grant proposal, made a formal presentation to the county commission. The tribes were not seeking any money from the county, simply a letter of support. The commission took the request under advisement. Several weeks later, Commissioner Lanny Applegate advised Kessler that the request for a letter of support for the EPA grant application had been denied. The reason he gave was "they didn't think there was enough money going to nonreservation or non-Native American individuals written into the grant," Kessler said. According to Kessler, "even if a quarter of it was to go for non-Indians, it wasn't good enough for this County Commission. They wanted more."[159]

Kessler also did a comprehensive study, funded by a grant from the EPA, of water quality on the Wind River Reservation from 2000 to 2005. Among the study's findings were that reservation drinking water appeared less safe than drinking water in other communities in Wyoming. Trends showed a greater level of health-based violations, with 40 percent of reservation systems having violations in 2004 affecting possibly 61 percent of the population served by all systems, a rate eight times greater than the rest of Wyoming. The violations were related to inadequate treatment and the presence of coliform bacteria in the water supply. There were numerous "boil orders," meaning that water users had to boil their water before drinking it. During the summer of 2003, the community of Fort Washakie was on boil orders for two and a half months. Kessler also said the problems reservation residents have had with contaminated drinking water, which were regularly reported in local papers, would have been addressed sooner if the affected community had been off the reservation. "It just wouldn't have been allowed to go on for so long," she said. "It's something that should rise to the level of local government to be concerned about."[160]

In December 2002, a representative of the Northern Arapaho Tribe asked the county commission to sponsor the tribe's Community Development Block Grant for a shelter for victims of domestic violence. The commission refused to do so.[161]

In 2004, the county commission refused to endorse a $300,000 Community Development Block Grant from the state to build a charter school on the reservation. Commissioner Jennings told the proposed new principal of the school, "I applaud you, but you're a dreamer. I'm opposed to it. I'll tell you why, because this is the latest in a long line of ideas that have gone nowhere. You're only treating the symptoms. We keep throwing money at problems. We're going nowhere except we're spending millions of dollars."[162]

Jennings also served in the state legislature for four terms. During his time in office the legislature considered a bill allowing the Arapaho language to be taught in the public schools. Jennings opposed the bill. He said teaching French or Spanish or Latin in the public schools was "okay," but teaching Arapaho was not. It should "not be force-fed through the public schools," he said.[163]

The Wyoming Senate adopted a resolution in 2006 proposing to amend the state constitution to allow the state to make appropriations directly to the business councils of the Eastern Shoshone and Northern Arapaho tribes as well as to the Joint Business Council.[164] Although the county commission did not take a formal position on the resolution, individual commission members opposed it on the grounds that the tribes could not be held accountable. Gary Jennings opposed the resolution because he disapproved "of giving money to folks that don't necessarily have any accountability for the expenditure of the money."[165] Fremont County treasurer Scott Harnsberger and Commissioner Thompson testified in opposition to the bill in the Wyoming House on similar grounds.[166]

Ivan Posey characterized opposition to the direct funding bill as "racism for the most part, just the uneducated biased view of a person." He said the Shoshone Business Council has "an accounting firm that comes and does our audits every year, and they're current."[167] Richard Brannan also denied there was no tribal accountability for funds received. "We have to have an entity-wide audit done every fiscal year," he said. "And that's inclusive of all state, federal, tribal funding. So there is accountability there."[168]

Commissioner Thompson has made no effort to increase Indian participation in county politics. As he put it, "I do not encourage participation in any governmental affairs or committees or anything on the basis of race."[169] None of the social programs the county commission supports has an office or physical presence on the reservation. Commissioner Hickerson said the county commission has never undertaken any specific projects on the reservation, "not a project, no."[170]

One of the reasons the county commission has been unresponsive to the needs and concerns of American Indians is that the members are generally ignorant of Indians and are unconcerned about conditions on the reservation. Valerie Thomas admitted that prior to running for the county commission in 1992, she had never even visited the Wind River Reservation. "To be perfectly honest with you," she said, "if I had to get gas, I would have been hesitant to stop on the reservation." She was fearful there would be "animosity between whites and Native Americans." During her campaigning for the county commission, however, Thomas visited the reservation and said she was "very well" received. She has subsequently done work for the Eastern Shoshone Tribe.[171]

Former commissioner Gary Jennings was unaware of any discrimination against American Indians in Wyoming or Fremont County by the U.S. government, the state of Wyoming, or private individuals. He had no knowledge of whether Indians had ever been denied the right to vote or if the state ever had a literacy test for voting. He was unaware of the experiences American Indians had in the boarding schools. He did not think Indians had any greater needs in education, employment, and health care than whites living off the reservation. Jennings did, however, think that whites had been discriminated against in employment. "Different nationalities have been discriminated against," he said. "No doubt about that."[172]

Former commissioner Applegate was similarly unaware of any discrimination against American Indians in Wyoming or Fremont County by the U.S. government, the state of Wyoming, or private individuals. He was not aware that Indians were ever refused service in restaurants in Fremont County. He was unaware that Indians had ever been denied the right to vote in Wyoming. He was unaware whether Indians on the reservation today suffer in any way from the effects of past discrimination. He was unaware if Indians had any special needs in the areas of education, business development, water management, health care, unemployment, and job training. Applegate did not know if American Indians had a distinctive language or culture. As he put it, "I don't know what they have out there, their differences. I'm not familiar with their cultures."[173]

Commissioner Douglas Thompson said he was "not personally aware" of any discrimination that may have been practiced by the federal government, state government, county government, or private individuals against American Indians in Wyoming or Fremont County. As he put it, "I'm not in a position to judge whether it was racial discrimination or not." Thompson does not think the government's taking of land from Indians in Fremont County had a negative impact on the tribes because "it put money in their tribal coffers." He estimated the Indian population of Fremont County to be between "8 to 10 percent," half of its actual size. He had no knowledge of the income level of Indians on the reservation. He did not know if Indians had a lower life expectancy than non-Indians. He did not think Indians had any special needs or concerns. He does not attend any events on the reservation.[174]

Commissioner Patrick Hickerson similarly had no knowledge of any discrimination that may have been practiced against American Indians in Fremont County. He has never attended any cultural events on the reservation and has no social contacts on the reservation.[175]

Valerie Thomas said she and the other commissioners "dealt ignorantly with the reservation." They did not understand the tribal form of government, and "we would come up against brick walls or else be terribly insulting to them. And so we didn't get much business accomplished with the reservation, not surprisingly, and I don't think there's been much since." Thomas said members of the county commission, in speaking about Indians, would say things "like 'drunk Indians—well, you can't ever get any business done with Indians.'"[176]

Other Governmental Conflicts

Patrick Goggles said some members of the state legislature opposed the resolution to allow the tribal government to receive direct grants from the state because they believed "the tribes should become political subdivisions, should become a part of Wyoming's state jurisdiction." Although the dispute was largely jurisdictional, Goggles said it had "racial underpinnings." Some of the discussions were about "those Indians." "'If they would become like us, you know, become part of a political subdivision, we wouldn't have these discussions. But you know, they want to maintain their sovereignty.'"[177]

The tribes commissioned a study by the National Economic Research Association of New York to determine the amount of revenues derived by Wyoming and Fremont County from residents and businesses on the reservation and the amount of expenditures by Wyoming and Fremont County for services returned to the reservation. The report was released in June 1988 and concluded that for the years 1979 to 1987, the disparity between tax revenues flowing off the Wind River Reservation to state and county governments and services returned to the reservation by those governments was nearly $73 million.[178] The tribes provided the county commission with a copy of the report, but it took no action.[179]

The Joint Tribal Council sought another accounting in 2003 from Charles River Associates, who found that in a fifteen-year period, from 1988 through 2002, there was a forty-six–million-dollar disparity in revenues derived by Wyoming and Fremont County from residents and businesses on the reservation and the amount of expenditures for services returned to the reservation. The total loss to the reservation in interest and revenues since 1979 was reported to be $282 million.[180] This disparity between revenues and expenditures has never been resolved.

Polarized Voting and Few Indians Elected

The extent that minorities have been elected to office and the extent of racially polarized voting are the two most important factors in a vote dilution challenge.[181] Only one American Indian, Keja Whiteman, a member of the Turtle Mountain Band of Chippewa Indians in North Dakota, has ever been elected to the Fremont County Commission, and she was elected in 2006 after the voting rights lawsuit was filed. And notably, Whiteman ran on a platform of opposition to single-member districts. During the course of the campaign, she said, the issue of the "division of Fremont County" came up, and "that did not appeal to me at all, and so I took, I think, a real open stand that I was running to unify rather than divide the county." She told people, "I didn't appreciate the idea of dividing Fremont County." Her support of at-large elections, she said, "got me a lot of attention from people at the grocery store, from people at forums. Whenever I was out and about people were really interested in the idea of unifying the county."[182]

Whiteman acknowledged that the objections she heard to district elections came from the "non-Indian community." There was "more resentfulness" by whites to majority-Indian districts, she said, and "the majority of the racism that I see is coming from the non-Native community."[183]

James Large was of the opinion that the pendency of the voting rights lawsuit "had a lot of impact" on Whiteman's election. He believes her election was going to be used "to defuse the issue of the lawsuit."[184]

It has frequently happened that a minority gets elected after a voting rights lawsuit has been filed. Both the legislative history of Section 2 and decisions of the courts, however, have discounted such elections because to hold otherwise would provide the white majority the opportunity to evade Section 2 "by manipulating the election of a 'safe' minority candidate" who was committed to keeping an existing discriminatory system in place.[185] In addition, the standard under Section 2 is not whether minorities are ever able to elect a candidate of their choice, but whether they usually fail to do so.[186]

There have been a total of eight American Indian candidacies for the Fremont County Commission: Keja Whiteman and W. O. Goggles in 2006; Ratliff and Allen Whiteman in 2000; McAdams in 1996; and Large, Collins, and McAdams in 1986. The plaintiffs' statistical evidence showed that although Whiteman was a candidate of choice of Indian voters in the 2006 general election, the first choice of Indian voters in the Democratic primary was Indian candidate Goggles, who got 70 percent of the Indian vote in that primary election, compared with Whiteman's 68 percent. In the general election, Whiteman did not receive a majority of the non-Indian votes, but she received more non-Indian votes (42 percent) than any Indian candidate had ever received before. All other Indian candidates for the county commission have been defeated.[187]

In the 2000 election, Ratliff was the overwhelming choice of Indian voters, with 85 percent of their vote in the Democratic primary and 88 percent in the general election. But he got only 34 percent of the non-Indian vote in the general election and was defeated. Allen Whiteman was the second choice of Indian voters in the Democratic primary, with 42 percent of the Indian vote, but he came in last among white voters with 19 percent of their vote.[188]

In the 1996 election, McAdams was the strong choice of Indian voters, with 79 percent of the Indian votes in the Democratic primary and 90 percent of the Indian vote in the general election. In the general election she was the last choice of non-Indian voters, with only 24 percent of their vote, and was defeated. In the 1996, 2000, and 2006 general elections, the Indian candidates got on average 87 percent of the Indian vote but only a third of the non-Indian vote.[189]

In the 1986 Democratic primary for a four-year seat, Large was the first choice of Indian voters in an eight-candidate field, with 49 percent of the Indian vote; however, he was the last choice of non-Indian voters, with only 7 percent of their vote, and was defeated. In the 1986 Democratic primary for a two-year seat, Collins was the first choice of Indian voters in a six-candidate field, with 47 percent of the Indian vote, but he got only 11 percent of the non-Indian vote and was defeated.[190]

In the general elections for the county commission from 1986 to 2006, Indians cast a majority of their votes for twenty-four individual candidates, nineteen of whom were white and five of whom were Indian. Of the twenty-four candidates preferred by Indian voters, nineteen (79 percent) were defeated, further indicating the dilutive effect of the at-large method of elections.[191]

No American Indian has ever been elected to city government in Lander or Riverton, the two largest towns in Fremont County. Indians, however, have been elected to local school boards, which are not elected countywide but from their respective school districts. Three of the school districts are predominantly Indian, Districts 14, 21, and 38. Thus it is not surprising that Indians have regularly been elected in these three districts. Patrick Goggles was elected to the state legislature from Fremont County, but the district from which he was elected, House District 33, is majority Indian. American Indians have also been elected to the board of trustees of Wyoming Central College, but it is elected from residency districts.[192] It is readily apparent that countywide at-large elections and white bloc voting have had a negative impact on minority office-holding.

Aside from the statistical evidence, those involved in local politics in Fremont County agree that voting is polarized along racial lines. Gary Collins said "polarization was evident in the voting process." Scott Ratliff agreed whites tend to vote cohesively for white candidates, and that voting was racially polarized. "There are people that would vote against me because I'm Native," he said. "I think they don't like Indians." Richard Brannan thinks whites vote as a bloc for white candidates, and that "our vote is diluted" under the at-large system. Indians tend to vote for Indian candidates, he said, because "they have the same background and they understand the needs that we have." Ivan Posey said people in Fremont County vote along racial lines "for the most part," and that Indians tend to vote for Indian candidates and whites for white candidates. Lucille McAdams agreed that voting is racially polarized and that whites tend to vote for white candidates in county elections. Indians tend to vote for Indian candidates, she said, "primarily if they know the person."[193]

James Large was pessimistic about his chances when he ran for the county commission in 1986. He felt he would not get good white support, because "there's some people still fighting the old settler fights, you know, circle the wagon trains. And I think that it had a bearing on whether they was going to vote for an Indian or not." He also thought his "pro-Indian" stance hurt him with non-Indian voters. Gary Jennings assumed Indian candidates got support from Indian voters because "we tend to support our own."[194]

Michelle Hoffman has been actively involved in politics, having been elected to the board of Fremont County School District No. 1 and having served as chair of the Fremont County Democratic Party for six years. She also ran for state superintendent of public instruction in 2006. Although she carried Fremont County, she lost statewide.

She said she was told on at least five occasions that she had three strikes against her—"I was a woman, a Democrat in Wyoming, and I lived on the reservation." On the basis of her experience as chair of the county Democratic Party, Hoffman said "it seemed that votes were cast based upon racial identity." American Indians "ran good races, hard races for the county commission, but came up short in the voting. I don't know if there was ever a chance there."[195]

Tom Throop said whites and American Indians in Fremont County "vote differently." They are "separate communities of interest, without a question. They view the world differently. They have different issues. I think as a result ethnic voting patterns play themselves out in the county." Although he has not done a study of voting patterns, John Vincent says "given the comments I've heard from time to time there are some people who certainly" vote on racial lines. Vincent thinks Patrick Goggles got elected to the legislature because House District 33 was majority Indian. "Well, he's Native American. It's a Native American district. I do think there's a connection."[196]

Racial Issues and Appeals in Political Campaigns

Overt or subtle racial appeals in campaigns are further evidence of polarization and minority vote dilution.[197] Such appeals are characteristic of elections in Fremont County and have further divided the Indian and non-Indian communities. Scott Ratliff was first elected to the state legislature in 1980. When he ran for reelection in 1982, a political action committee known as the Committee to Defeat Scott Ratliff was formed in Fremont County. The committee took out ads, Ratliff said, one of which "was a reminder that Scott Ratliff was an enrolled member and that he would be voting on water issues." Ratliff also got hate letters saying the only reason he was running "was either to take care of my family or the Indian community."[198] Patrick Goggles thinks Ratliff was hurt in his subsequent campaign for the county commission because "he had long hair," and he "advocated a lot for Indian education. That type of thing."[199]

The editor of the *Lander Journal* told Lucille McAdams during her campaign that people in Fremont County probably would not vote for her because several years ago a boy named McAdams had shot a non-Indian boy in Sinks Canyon. During her campaign she had problems with people taking down her campaign signs. In Lander, her brother-in-law caught some kids, whom she assumed were white because Lander is predominantly white, destroying some of her signs.[200]

Gary Collins ran for the county commission in 1986 "to provide the Indian perspective and to support the reservation initiatives that I saw was in need," such as the provision of public services, environmental concerns, tourism, economic development, and access to utilities. But he thinks he got a negative response from white voters who took him "to be a threat to the non-Indian community that somebody was actually moving forward in the tribal arena." Collins's mother, who is Swedish and worked in a store in Riverton, heard comments from people that "we've got to watch Gary Collins, he's going to take our water."[201]

Valerie Thomas decided to run for the county commission in 1992 in part in protest over the commission's decision to consider the location of a nuclear waste dump in the county as a form of economic development. She campaigned "on the basis that there was little to no accountability on the Board of Commissioners." Another of Thomas's big campaign issues was calling for a referendum on adopting single-member district elections for the county commission. She believed Lander and the southern part of the county were not adequately represented on the commission, all of whose members came from the northern half of the county. Residents of the reservation supported the adoption of district elections, whereas non-Indians off the reservation frequently opposed it. Some thought they would have more influence voting for five commissioners, but about half of those who objected and refused to sign her petition to hold a referendum, Thomas said, did so because "the risk would be that there would be a representative from the reservation." The referendum on single-member districts made it on the 1992 general election ballot but was defeated by a vote of 55 percent to 45 percent.[202]

During one of John Vincent's campaigns for mayor, someone went door to door in Riverton warning people not to vote for Vincent "because if elected I was going to give Riverton back to the Indians," he said.[203]

Enhancing Factors

Other factors that have been recognized as enhancing the dilution effect of at-large elections include an unusually large district size and the use of staggered terms of office.[204] Fremont County contains 3,525 square miles and is larger than six states, which makes it very difficult to campaign countywide, especially for Indian candidates who lack financial resources. James Large said campaigning at-large in Fremont County was "a big problem." There was not only the large size of the county to contend with, but "people within the county are spread all over the county." Lucille McAdams says the at-large system also discourages Indians from being candidates. "I think the cost is probably a big deterrent," she said.[205]

Commissioner Gary Jennings agreed that running countywide imposes a hardship in campaigning for the county commission "in the sense you have more ground to cover if you want to cover all the ground." Commissioner Thompson said because of the large size of Fremont County, it would be an "immense task" to campaign door to door, and that "it would harm my ranching profession" even to attempt to do it. Commissioner Hickerson agreed that the large size of the county is a disadvantage in campaigning to those who have a poor financial situation. He also said the at-large system of elections made it more difficult for Indian voters to elect candidates of their choice to the county commission. "The cost of running a campaign could be an issue," he said. Another thing that would make it harder for Indians to get elected at-large is they would "have to appeal to a broader community."[206]

Fremont County uses staggered terms for county commission elections: two members are elected in presidential election years and three members are elected in off-years. Staggered terms limit minority voters' opportunity to use single-shot voting to attempt to elect candidates of their choice. Indian voters, for example, would have a much better chance of electing a candidate of their choice in a five-seat contest, where they could concentrate their vote on a single candidate and where the white vote would likely be dispersed, than in a two-seat contest, where the white vote would be more cohesive.

Tenuous Policy Underlying At-Large Elections

Another factor relevant in determining if an at-large system dilutes minority voting strength is the tenuousness of the policy underlying its use.[207] At-large voting is the exception in Fremont County as well as in the state of Wyoming.

Both Lander and Riverton, the two largest municipalities in Fremont County, elect their municipal governments from wards or districts, rather than at-large. There are eleven fire districts in the county, and their boards are elected by the residents of each district rather than from the county at-large. The board of commissioners of the LeClair Irrigation District is also elected from single-member districts. The board of trustees of Central Wyoming College in Riverton is elected at-large but uses residency districts in order to ensure geographic representation.

The state legislature is elected entirely from single-member districts. Fremont County encompasses six state house districts, four of which are entirely within the county. There are four state senate districts in Fremont County. Two are entirely within the county: Districts 25 and 26. State law also expressly authorizes single-member districts for county commissions. Districts must be as nearly equal in population as practicable and take into account "the geographic, economic and social characteristics of the county."[208]

Ironically, although they oppose single-member districts for the county commission, members of the Fremont County Commission support districts for other elected bodies. Commissioner Hickerson supports the district method of elections for the fire district boards because "the citizens of the district should have the election oversight."

He also thinks as a general matter that "community interests that are significantly different should have an opportunity for a representative." But despite that view, he doesn't think the reservation should be a district for purposes of electing the county commission.[209]

Former commissioner Lanny Applegate also said he is opposed to districts for the county commission but paradoxically says, "I'm a firm believer of local control," and he thinks local communities should have their own representatives. He also approves of district elections for the City of Lander.[210]

Commissioner Thompson is also a firm advocate of "local control," which he said means that "all of the citizens have an equal say in the decisions, the activities of that government." But he does not think Indians on the reservation should have local control over who they elect to the county commission. "I don't believe that's the same situation," he said. "We're talking about county government."[211]

Mayor John Vincent thinks ward elections for the Riverton City Council work. "It provides everybody kind of equal access to an elected representative. It also assures that each part of the community is going to have somebody elected from that part." Vincent also favors single-member districts for the county commission for the same reasons. "If you want to have consistent representation from a broad spectrum of your society or your group, then the way you do that is by requiring it to be done just like we do in the state legislature or we do in city government. It would be pretty difficult for me to say that's not a good way to do things when it's the way the City of Riverton has done it since it was created."[212]

The county's own expert, Dr. Keith Gaddie, agreed that at-large elections have been a significant impediment to minority political participation. He concurred that minority voters have better opportunities to elect candidates of their choice from districts in which they, the minority group members, comprise a majority of the population (a "majority minority district"), as opposed to an at-large system where they are in the minority. As he put it, "when you don't concentrate minority voters, you do make it harder for them to win—you make it harder for them to pick the candidate that they want."[213]

Gaddie also acknowledged that the opposition to creating majority minority districts "has come from communities that were usually white majority that were trying to preserve their electoral systems."[214] In the case of Fremont County, the opposition to single-member districts for the county commission has come almost exclusively from the white community.

District elections would have a positive impact on Indian political participation. According to Massey, including the reservation in a single-member district "would likely foster a sense of empowerment and political significance that could have a self-fulfilling effect, somewhat mitigating and possibly reversing the entropic effects of the poor socioeconomic conditions of the reservation."[215]

Massey's view was echoed by Tom Throop, the former director of the Equality State Policy Center (ESPC). During the 2004 election, ESPC became actively engaged in voter education, registration, and get-out-the-vote efforts on the Wind River Reservation. Throop wrote a report, "Wind River Reservation (Wyoming) Voter Registration Project," on the voter registration efforts undertaken by the two business councils and the ESPC. On the basis of his experience, Throop said American Indians "have been interested in local, state, and federal elections if they're convinced that there's some relevancy to their lives." Throop was also convinced that the existence of a majority-Indian house district played "the central role" in the increased registration, turnout, and political participation of Indians in the 2004 general election. As he explained, "for the first time there was a broad perception among enrolled members of the Tribes that they actually had an opportunity to elect one of their own and have someone who understands their issues, understands their culture and their history representing them in the Wyoming legislature."[216]

During the 2004 election, the Northern Arapaho Tribe also organized a voter registration campaign and coordinated its efforts with the National Congress of American Indians. The tribe gave voters rides to the polls and distributed T-shirts saying, "I'm Native American and I Vote."[217]

Although there is currently only one American Indian, Patrick Goggles, in the state legislature, his presence has had an undeniable impact on the legislative process. At its 2003 session, for example, the legislature passed several bills directly benefitting Indians on the Wind River Reservation. One established a tribal liaison position in the governor's office to help coordinate programs between the state and tribal governments. Another bill allowed tribal clerks to register voters. Another allowed the tribes to receive state funds directly for programs funded through severance taxes on minerals. And another provided an appropriation to the Joint Business Council to address the needs of Indian students on the reservation.[218]

Ratliff also said that being a minority on an elected body did not mean you were ineffective, were isolated, and provided no representation to your constituents. Citing his own experience as the only Indian member of the legislature, he said, "I don't think I would have been reelected if that were the case." He cited several bills he had sponsored that were passed, including legislation authorizing an increase in the number of county commission members and the adoption of single-member districts by local referendum.[219]

Efforts to Maintain Indian Culture and Traditions

Despite the isolation of the Indian community and its depressed socioeconomic status, there is a renewed effort on the reservation to preserve and practice Indian traditions and culture. For more than two decades, there has been a program to revive the Arapaho and Shoshone languages, and children are instructed in those languages in elementary school. The Shoshone have established a culture center to preserve and perpetuate the culture of the Eastern Shoshone Tribe. According to Massey, "the Indian traditions and cultures are a major reason that people live on the reservation."[220]

Sara Wiles said, "there has been a tremendous effort on the reservation" to maintain Indian language and cultural traditions. Since 1987, "there have been events on the reservation called language and culture camps. And at these camps a variety of different traditional activities are taught in addition to language, music, crafts, dancing, traditions, stories, things like that." Recent photographs taken by Wiles show traditional Arapaho ceremonies on the reservation, including a giveaway, powwows, the grand entry at a powwow, a powwow parade, a women's traditional dance, dancing to the drum, a men's traditional dance, a boy's team dance, hoop games, a shinny game, and a Heritage Day at Wyoming Indian High School. Wiles says, "the powwow tradition, the music tradition, the dancing tradition, are very, very much alive and much participated in by a number of people, a number of children. And children start dancing when they're very, very young." The Sun Dance, a traditional Indian religious ceremony, is also held annually by each of the tribes on the reservation.[221]

Defenses Raised by the Defendants

The defendants initially moved to dismiss the plaintiffs' case on the grounds that Section 2 of the Voting Rights Act as applied to a county, such as Fremont, that was not covered by the special preclearance provisions of Section 5 was unconstitutional. The court, however, rejected that argument, noting that the constitutionality of Section 2 as applied in non-Section 5 jurisdictions had been consistently upheld.[222]

Defendants also argued that American Indians were defeated in elections for the county commission because they did not campaign and were not as qualified as their white opponents. Indians not only campaigned and received strong support from Indian voters, but they were highly qualified for office. Lucille McAdams has two master's degrees, one in public health and another in education. She has worked for the Joint Business Council as tribal secretary, worked for the tribes in realty, worked for the IHS, worked with the tribes in implementing Johnson O'Malley education programs, and given training for Head Start programs on Indian reservations in Montana, Wyoming, and Idaho. She has also served on the Wyoming Civil Rights Commission.[223]

When McAdams ran for the county commission in 1996, she campaigned extensively. She attended rallies, was in parades in Lander and Riverton and at the county fair, attended powwows, had ads on the radio and in the newspaper, and had signs and matchbooks as well as magnetic signs for vehicles. She described herself as a "serious" candidate.[224]

Scott Ratliff was also clearly qualified as a candidate for the county commission. He has a master's degree in guidance and counseling from the University of Wyoming. He has worked for the Riverton High School as an Indian home school coordinator, worked for the Wyoming Department of Education as a coordinator of Indian education, and worked twenty-five years at Central Wyoming College as a counselor and outreach coordinator. Before running for the county commission in 2000, he had served six terms in the state legislature.[225]

Ratliff also conducted a vigorous campaign. He put up big, yellow 4′ x 8′ signs with "Ratliff" painted on them around the county. He took out ads in the paper and ran spots on the radio. He attended forums, he was in a parade, and he campaigned throughout the county.[226]

Gary Collins was also a well-qualified candidate for the county commission. He has a bachelor's degree in geology from the University of Wyoming. He has served as a natural resource specialist for the Joint Business Council and as tribal water engineer. He has worked for the Northern Arapaho Tribe on their tribal farm project. He was elected to the Northern Arapaho Business Council in 1986 and served as chair. He has served on the national Royalty Minerals Advisory Council and has worked on programs undertaken by the Bureau of Reclamation Department of Energy and the National Academy of Sciences. He also served on the Fremont County Solid Waste Board and the Wyoming Vocational Rehabilitation Council.[227]

James Large was also a qualified candidate for the county commission. He has a degree in education from the University of Wyoming. He served in Vietnam in the 101st Airborne Division and received two Purple Hearts. He is active in the American Legion and is a member of the color guard. He also makes jewelry and does leatherwork. He has taught in school, worked as activity coordinator in the Wyoming State Penitentiary in Rawlins, Wyoming, and as job director for the Tribal Employment Rights Office. He was also elected to the board of the Wyoming Indian High School in the late 1980s.

He was appointed by the Arapaho Business Council to serve on the Legal Services Board and the Wind River Housing Commission.[228]

Another argument raised by defendants was that Indians on the Wind River Reservation were not politically cohesive because they were composed of two independent tribes with different histories and traditions. Although the Eastern Shoshone and Northern Arapaho historically were adversaries, that relationship has changed significantly over the years. The two tribes are now strongly connected by years of intermarriage, indicating a vigorous and new growth in the larger Indian community. As explained by Patrick Goggles, "when you say Arapaho and you say Shoshone, there's a group that's going to be larger than those two put together some day, and those are the children of the intermarried parents. They call them Sho-Raps. Half Arapaho and Half Shoshone. And there's a large number of them and right now, they've really crossed traditional boundaries, cultural boundaries as well. When we're focusing just on tribal membership, you know, we're missing the point."[229]

James Large is a Sho-Rap. He is a member of the Northern Arapaho Tribe on his father's side, but his mother and brother are both enrolled members of the Eastern Shoshone Tribe. He doesn't draw a sharp distinction between the tribes. He says, "it behooves me to be pro-Indian from both sides of the fence, so to speak."[230]

It is not unusual today for a family to have children who are members of different tribes. Richard Brannan has grandchildren who are Sho-Raps. Burton Hutchinson's first wife was an Eastern Shoshone. His children, however, are Arapaho. Hutchinson is also related to various Shoshone families.[231]

There is intermarriage not only between the Arapaho and Shoshone, but among other tribes as well. Patricia Bergie, for example, was married to a tribal member from Montana who was Chippewa and Lakota. Ivan Posey, a member of the Eastern Shoshone Tribe, also has Arapaho blood through his father. His mother was an enrolled member of the Northern Cheyenne Tribe in Montana. Posey's wife was a member of the Northern Arapaho Tribe. In addition to Shoshone and Arapaho, residents on the Wind River Reservation self-identified on the 2000 census as members of some twenty-two other tribes.[232]

There is a lot of social and business contact between members of the Shoshone and Arapaho tribes. Patricia Bergie, who is a member of the Shoshone Tribe, is a deacon in an Arapaho Church. All American Indians have a common and related socioeconomic status. As Massey put it, although Indians on the Wind River Reservation are members predominantly of the Shoshone and Arapaho Tribes, it would be "misleading to treat them as two very distinct groups. In almost all respects they are very, very similar in terms of employment, employment history, levels of poverty, and certainly the needs that they have."[233]

Richard Brannan foresees a day when, because of intermarriage and other factors, the two tribes will merge into one tribal government. As he explained, "as you live close to each other as neighbors, your characteristics become much closer aligned to each other. We both have common goals, common interests, protecting the reservation, protecting our children. So there's commonalities that happen over time." James Large also thinks that "maybe a hundred years from now there would be so much intermarriage that there will be no tribal distinction and it will be as one."[234]

Courts, moreover, have found American Indian political cohesion and Section 2 violations in counties similar to Fremont where two separate tribes occupied the same reservation.[235] The courts have also found American Indian cohesion and Section 2 violations in counties containing parts of two distinct reservations.[236]

Decision of the District Court

Following extensive discovery, the challenge to at-large elections for the county commission was tried over a two-week period in February 2007 in Casper, Wyoming. The parties filed post-trial proposed findings and conclusions in May 2007, and the case is awaiting decision on the merits. There is little doubt, given the importance of voting rights, that the decision will have significant impact on both the Indian and non-Indian communities in Fremont County.

CHAPTER 9

Increasing Importance of the Indian Vote

All of the states discussed in the preceding chapters adopted devices that had the purpose or effect of denying or diluting American Indians' votes. Colorado, Montana, South Dakota, and Wyoming limited voting to citizens, which by definition excluded noncitizen Indians. Montana and South Dakota also excluded noncitizens from holding elected office. Three states, Montana, South Dakota, and Nebraska, limited voting to taxpayers or landowners, which further denied Indians the franchise. South Dakota also excluded from voting those American Indians who were members of a tribe or who received support from the government. Wyoming adopted a literacy test for voting in 1890, which had an obvious detrimental impact on Indians for whom English was a second language. Montana and South Dakota prohibited polling places on reservations, and Colorado and Montana had laws whereby residency on a reservation did not establish residence in the state for purposes of voting. Nebraska excluded Indians from the count used for reapportionment, and Montana required the re-registration of all voters in 1937 and provided that registrars be citizens as well as taxpayers. All of these laws, which are summarized in table 3, contributed significantly to the depressed levels of Indian registration and turnout.

Table 3
Passage of Restrictive Voting Laws

Restriction	Col.	Mont.	Neb.	S. Dak.	Wyo.
Limiting voting to citizens	1859	1865	1855	1861	1868
Limiting voting to taxpayers		1891		1890	
Limiting voting to landowners		1889	1864		
Literacy test for voting					1890
Excluding from voting tribal members and Indians who received support from the govt.				1890	
Prohibiting polling places on reservations		1871		1895	
Limiting office holding to citizens		1889		1861	
Residence on a reservation does not establish residence in the state	1966	1911			
Excluding Indians from count used for reapportionment			1875		
Requiring re-registration of all voters		1937			
Requiring registrars to be citizens		1893			
Requiring registrars to be taxpayers		1937			

Many of these jurisdictions, however, have argued that it was the reservation system, not state laws or practices, that resulted in the lack of Indian participation in the larger political process.

"Reservation Defense"

South Dakota conceded in the lawsuit over its 1996 interim legislative redistricting plan that American Indians were not equal participants in elections in District 28 but argued that it was the "reservation system" and "not the multimember district which is the cause of [the] 'problem' identified by Plaintiffs."[1] According to defendants, Indians' loyalty was to tribal elections; they simply didn't care about participating in elections run by the state. The argument overlooked the fact that the state, by historically denying Indians the right to vote, had itself been responsible for denying Indians the opportunity to develop a "loyalty" to state elections.

Factually, however, defendants were wrong. Although Indian political participation was undeniably depressed, Indians did care about state politics. Indians were candidates for the South Dakota house and senate in 1992 and 1994 and received overwhelming support from Indian voters. An Indian ran for treasurer of Dewey County in 1992 and received 100 percent of the Indian vote. Indians have also run for and been elected to other offices in District 28A. If Indians didn't care about state politics they would not have run for office nor would they have supported the Indian candidates.

Furthermore, more Indians undoubtedly would have run for office had they believed the state system was fair and would provide them with a realistic chance of being elected. As one court has explained, the lack of minority candidates "is a likely result of a racially discriminatory system."[2] Another court pointed out that white bloc voting "undoubtedly discourages [minority] candidates because they face the certain prospect of defeat."[3]

The Cheyenne River Sioux have decided to conduct elections for the tribe and the state at the same time, a measure designed to increase Indian participation in state elections. The litigation discussed in chapter 5—the Sisseton–Wahpeton case, the suits brought by Indians in 1986 protesting the failure of county officials to provide sufficient polling places for elections and voter registration cards, the challenge to the 1996 legislative redistricting, the Section 5 enforcement lawsuit, the challenge to the 2001 redistricting plan, and the dilution claims filed in Charles Mix County, Buffalo County, and the city of Martin—further shows that Indians in South Dakota do care about participating in state and local elections.

The state's reservation defense was not, of course, new. An alleged lack of Indian interest in state elections was also advanced as a defense by South Dakota in the cases involving denying residents of the unorganized counties the right to vote or run for county office. In the first case, the state sought to justify denying residents in unorganized counties the right to vote for officials in the organized counties to which they were attached on the ground that a majority of the residents were "reservation Indians" who "do not share the same interest in county government as the residents of the organized counties."[4] The court rejected the defense, noting that a claim that a particular class of voters lacks a substantial interest in local elections should be viewed with "skepticism," because "'[a]ll too often, lack of a 'substantial interest' might mean no more than a different interest, and '[f]encing out' from the franchise a sector of the population because of the way they may vote.'" The court concluded that Indians residing on the reservation had a "substantial interest" in the choice of county officials, and it held the state scheme unconstitutional.[5]

In the second case, the state argued that denying residents in unorganized counties the right to run for office in organized counties was justifiable because most of them lived on an "Indian Reservation and hence have little, if any, interest in county government." Again, the court disagreed. It held that the "presumption" that Indians lacked a substantial interest in county elections "is not a reasonable one."[6]

The reservation defense has been raised—and rejected—in other voting cases brought by American Indians in the West. In the suit by Crow and Northern Cheyenne in Big Horn County, Montana, the county argued that Indian dual sovereignty, not at-large voting, was the cause of reduced Indian participation in county politics. The court disagreed, noting that Indians had run for office in recent years and were as concerned about issues relating to their welfare as white voters. According to the court, "[r]acially polarized voting and the effects of past and present discrimination explain the lack of Indian political influence in the county, far better than existence of tribal government."[7]

In a similar manner, regarding the case in Montezuma County, Colorado, the court found that Indian participation in elections was depressed and noted "the reticence of the Native American population of Montezuma County to integrate into the non-Indian population." But instead of counting this "reticence" against a finding of vote dilution, the court concluded it was "an obvious outgrowth of the discrimination and mistreatment of the Native Americans in the past."[8]

The claim that Indians didn't care about state politics was familiar for another reason. It was virtually identical to the argument that whites in the South made in an attempt to defeat challenges brought by blacks to election systems that diluted their voting strength. "It's not the method of elections," they said in cases from Arkansas to Mississippi, "black voters are just apathetic." But as the court held in a case from Marengo County, Alabama, "[b]oth Congress and the courts have rejected efforts to blame reduced black participation on 'apathy.'" The real cause of the depressed level of political participation by blacks in Marengo County was "racially polarized voting; a nearly complete absence of black elected officials; a history of pervasive discrimination that has left Marengo County blacks economically, educationally, socially, and politically disadvantaged; polling practices that have impaired the ability of blacks to register and participate actively in the electoral process; election features that enhance the opportunity for dilution; and considerable unresponsiveness on the part of some public bodies.[9]" The court could have been writing about Indians in the West.

In a case from Mississippi, the court rejected a similar "apathy" defense. "Voter apathy," it said, "is not a matter for judicial notice." According to the court, "[t]he considerable evidence of the socioeconomic differences between black and white voters in Attala County argues against the . . . reiteration that black voter apathy is the reason for generally lower black political participation."[10] It is convenient and self-reassuring for a jurisdiction to blame the victims of discrimination for their condition, but it is not a defense to a claim of minority vote dilution.

The basic purpose of the Voting Rights Act is "to banish the blight of racial discrimination in voting."[11] To argue, as South Dakota and other states have frequently done, that the depressed levels of minority political participation preclude claims under the act would reward jurisdictions with the worst records of discrimination by making them the most secure from challenge. Congress could not have intended such an inappropriate result. In *Gingles* the Court said, "The essence of a § 2 [vote dilution] claim is that a certain electoral law, practice, or structure interacts with social and historical conditions to cause an inequality in the opportunities enjoyed by black and white voters to elect their preferred representatives."[12] There can be no serious doubt that social and historical conditions, whatever their causes, have created a condition under which at-large voting and other election practices dilute the voting strength of American Indian voters. As one court put it, "the long history of discrimination against Indians has wrongfully denied Indians an equal opportunity to get involved in the political process."[13]

Sea Change in Indian Political Participation

Tribal members' litigation challenging discriminatory election practices is evidence of the importance American Indians place on the vote. Further evidence is provided by the dramatic growth in Indian participation in recent elections. In the 2000 presidential election, the average turnout for Buffalo, Dewey, Shannon, and Todd counties in South Dakota was 42.7 percent. Turnout in the same counties in the 2004 election, which was driven almost exclusively by Indian voters, grew to 65.2 percent, an increase of 22.5 percent, whereas turnout for the state as a whole grew by only 9.9 percent.[14] In 2004, turnout on the Fort Belknap Reservation in Montana topped 80 percent of eligible voters, far ahead of the state average of 67 percent.[15] Similar increases in Indian turnout were reported for reservation areas in other states, including Arizona, Minnesota, New Mexico, and Wisconsin.

In 2004, the National Congress of American Indians (NCAI) launched a Native Vote Campaign to register Indian voters and increase turnout. According to NCAI president Joe Garcia, "increasing civic participation among American Indian and Alaska Native communities is imperative to protecting sovereignty and ensuring Native issues are addressed on every level of government."[16] The NCAI said it would "ramp up our voter participation in 2008," and it targeted eighteen states, from Alaska to Wyoming.

Jonathan Windy Boy, an American Indian and a member of the Montana House of Representatives, said in the past there has been a lot of skepticism, even cynicism, among Indians about the idea of voting. "Some people didn't vote as a point of pride—defiance, even," he said. "But that's all changed. There's much more of a sense today that we can work within this system."[17]

Many things are driving the increased Indian political participation—business development, new wealth from casinos, the need to interact with nontribal governments, and obtainment of state and federal funds for health clinics, education improvements, water-reclamation projects, and cleanup of old mining areas. According to Jefferson Keel, an officer of both the Chickasaw Nation in Oklahoma and the NCIA, "there's been a sea change in my lifetime . . . people feel a real stake in the system."[18] Patrick Goggles, who in 2005 became the first Northern Arapaho elected to the Wyoming state legislature, says "you have to participate in this political process. You can't just step back and complain about it."[19]

An organization known as the Indigenous Democratic Network (INDN's List) was formed in 2005 to encourage and train Indians on how to run for political office. In 2006, INDN's List supported twenty-six candidates from twelve states, representing twenty-one tribes. The organization's founder, Kalyn Free, a member of the Choctaw Nation of Oklahoma, said that twenty of the candidates were elected to office, nine of whom were elected to office for the first time.

Another tribal organization called "Prez on the Rez" was formed to get Democratic presidential candidates to campaign on the reservations and meet with tribal leaders and members.[20] "More than ever before," said Prez on the Rez, "Indians are speaking." And that candidates were listening was evident from the fact that for the first time in history presidential candidates campaigned on reservations in Montana. Sen. Barack Obama visited the Crow Reservation in May 2008 and called it "one of the most important events we've had in this campaign."[21] He was adopted into the Crow Tribe and given an Indian name, "One who helps people throughout the land." Crow Chairman Carl Venne explained the Indian interest in the presidential campaign by saying, "we want to become self-sufficient and be part of this great society."[22]

A week later, Sen. Hilary Clinton campaigned on the Flathead Indian Reservation. Joe MacDonald, the president of the Salish Kootenai College, gave her a beaded necklace and a pair of moccasins sewn by a tribal elder. "You have gone a million miles for American Indian people," he said, "so here's a pair of moccasins to help you on your journey."[23] To enthusiastic cheers from the crowd of some 1,200 supporters, Clinton promised that if she were elected president, she would have a representative of Indian Country inside the White House to confer with on a daily basis. Both Clinton and Obama also made historic campaign visits to the Wind River Indian Reservation in Wyoming and the Pine Ridge Indian Reservation in South Dakota.[24]

Indian Country Today reported in June 2008 that "American Indian voters, eager to shed a mistaken image of powerlessness, will play an important role in selecting the next president of the United States."[25] That role was evident from the increase in the number of Indian delegates to the 2008 Democratic National Convention. In 1996, there were fifty Indian delegates to the convention. In 2000 there were seventy-five, and in 2004 there were seventy-six. But in 2008, the number rose to one hundred and fifty delegates and four super delegates. Indians also had an unprecedented six members on the Democratic National Convention Standing Committees. Frank LaMere, chairman of the Native American Caucus and a Nebraska super delegate, described the convention as "a red-letter day for native people from across the country."[26]

Wind River Intergovernmental Agreement

Another significant example of American Indians' desire to participate in the larger governmental process was the intergovernmental agreement entered into on April 29, 2008, by the Northern Arapaho and Eastern Shoshone Tribes of the Wind River Reservation in Wyoming and the City of Riverton, whose population is overwhelmingly white. The agreement provides that the tribes and the city will deal with one another on a "government-to-government" basis and pursue "agreements for the benefit of our citizens, including efforts to improve the local economy and job opportunities and to create or expand community programs and services." The agreement also included a "reservation of rights" provision that it "does not constitute a waiver of sovereign immunity by either Tribe or the City of Riverton."[27]

The signing of the agreement at the Riverton City Hall was an emotional event and represented a significant departure from the often divisive confrontations that had characterized relations between the town and the tribes in the past. Harvey Spoonhunter, a member of the Northern Arapaho Business Council, said it was "a historic moment, a unique occurrence, and shows what can be accomplished by cooperation and knocking down barriers." Ivan Posey, a member of the Eastern Shoshone Business Council, said "there have been times when we struggled to get along, but we have come together to work together for a common good. This agreement is taking us in the right direction." John Vincent, the Mayor of Riverton, who was a strong supporter of the agreement, said it was "one of the happiest times in my life, a way to solidify our relationships for the future." These comments were echoed by Diana Mahoney, a member of the city council. "What a happy day for Fremont County," the beaming council member said.[28]

But as much of a step forward as the agreement was, or seemed to be to those who had signed it, it triggered a backlash from some non-Indians. At a meeting of the city council on June 3, 2008, Vincent announced that the county attorney had sent him a series of e-mails in which he objected to a phrase in the agreement that the City of Riverton "is within the exterior boundaries of the Wind River Indian Reservation," and said it would allow the tribes to tax residents of Riverton, exercise criminal jurisdiction over them, and implement land use planning. "The county attorney said I was stupid and couldn't read," Vincent said, "and that 'I'm going to sue you unless you take that language out of the agreement.'"[29]

Others present at the meeting also spoke against the agreement. One elderly woman spoke forcefully that "this agreement would be the camel's nose under the tent. We need to kill the BIA and make the reservations deader than a doornail. Nobody loves Indian people more than I do, and I know they have been mistreated, but they can't be productive citizens under the existing system. Many are in prison, they're dead, drunk, or on drugs. I plead with you to do away with the reservations." Others in the audience nodded their heads in agreement.[30]

Vincent pointed out that Riverton had been carved out from the Wind River Reservation but was, in fact, still located within its exterior boundaries. He denied that the exterior-boundaries language was intended to cede jurisdiction over Riverton to the tribes or would have that effect, and he was undoubtedly correct. As a general proposition, a tribe loses jurisdiction over reservation land that has been conveyed to a non-Indian.[31] That rule would be particularly applicable where the ceded land had become a separately incorporated town, such as Riverton. Vincent stressed that "the purpose of the agreement was to help people get over a division that has long existed and build bridges that have not always been there in the past."[32] But to placate the objectors, the city council and the Northern Arapaho agreed to remove the exterior-boundaries language from the agreement. And despite the white backlash, the leadership of the city and the tribes remained committed to pursuing agreements that would benefit all of their citizens.

Influence of the Indian Vote on Election Outcomes

Although American Indians are a numerically small group, there is general agreement that the Indian vote has played an important role in recent elections. Vine Deloria, Jr., has identified several congressional elections where the Indian vote made the difference—Sen. George McGovern in South Dakota, Sen. Lee Metcalf in Montana, Sen. Frank Church in Idaho, and Sen. Howard Cannon in Nevada.[33]

In the 2002 U.S. Senate election in South Dakota, Democrat Tim Johnson defeated Republican John Thune by only 524 votes, a margin of victory generally credited to the increase in the number of Indian voters. An exceptional Indian turnout in Arizona helped Janet Napolitano win the governor's race in 2002. "Without the American Indians," she said, "I wouldn't be standing here today."[34] Democrat Brian Schweitzer beat Republican Bob Brown for governor of Montana in 2004 by four percentage points. Russ Lehman, the author of a national survey of the Indian vote and its impact, said "Schweitzer was able to win because of the impact of the tribal vote. It was huge, huge."[35] The Indian vote was also considered critical in the 2006 election in Montana for the U.S. Senate, in which Jon Tester narrowly defeated the incumbent Conrad Burns.[36]

Significance of Indian Office Holding

Social science data confirm what should be obvious: increased minority office holding results in greater political and social responsiveness to minority interests and greater minority influence over decision making.[37] A study of ten cities in California found that minority (black and Hispanic) political participation was "associated with important changes in urban policy—the creation of police review boards, the appointments of more minorities to commissions, the increasing use of minority contractors, and a general increase in the number of programs oriented to minorities." The report also found that the mere presence of black and Hispanic council members tended to break down polarization and racial stereotyping and "has increased minority access to councils and changed decision-making processes."[38]

A 1979 study in Alabama similarly found "a causal relationship between growth and black political participation and policy change: the greater the change in political mobility, the greater the change in social welfare policy."[39] A study of Newark, New Jersey, concluded that under a minority mayor, "more blacks were appointed to high-level positions," there was increased minority employment, and "general political activity focused, as never before, on the black community in Newark."[40] A similar study of Tuskegee, Alabama, and Durham, North Carolina, reached comparable conclusions: increased minority political participation had a positive impact on the distribution of services.[41]

That increased Indian participation can significantly influence decision making was apparent from the actions taken by the 2002 districting commission in Montana, which for the first time included an Indian member. Not only were the deliberations of the commission free of the anti-Indian slurs that characterized prior commissions, but the plan adopted by the 2002 commission provided American Indians a greater opportunity to elect candidates of their choice than under any previous plan.

At the November 2008 general election in Montana, Denise Juneau, daughter of state representative Carol Juneau, was elected superintendent of public instruction, the first American Indian woman ever elected to a statewide executive position.[42] Juneau will oversee more than 400 school districts, the education of some 140,000 school children, and a budget that comprises almost half of the state's total budget. The importance of her position to Indians, as well as the entire population of the state, is apparent. Juneau described her election as "historic" and said she was "feeling pretty good" about the considerable challenges that lay before her.[43]

In other 2008 elections, twenty-two American Indians from sixteen tribes and eleven states (Alaska, Arizona, California, Colorado,

Montana, Nevada, Oklahoma, Pennsylvania, South Dakota, Washington, and Wyoming) won their state and local contests. Kalyn Free, the president of INDN's List, said "tribal members are engaged at all levels of government in an unprecedented manner. To shape history, you have to be willing to make it."[44]

Increased Indian office holding and political participation has certainly not redressed all of the legitimate grievances of the Indian community nor realized all the goals of the modern movement for Indian self-determination, but it has conferred undeniable benefits. It has made it possible for American Indians to participate in and influence elections as well as elect candidates of their choice. It has made it possible for Indians to pursue careers in politics and make the values and resources of Indians communities more available to society as a whole. It has provided Indian role models, conferred racial dignity, and helped dispel the myth that Indians are incapable of political leadership. It has also required whites to deal with Indians more nearly as equals, a change in political relationships with profound implications.

Some Indians, for a variety of reasons, have undoubtedly felt their participation in state and federal elections would be meaningless, or even counterproductive. But the importance of the Indian vote in recent elections has convinced most there is no downside to participating in elections that affect the welfare of the Indian community. As the Indian population increases in the West, and despite continued resistance from the non-Indian population, American Indians will play an increasingly important role in state and national politics.

Abbreviations

Ariz.	Arizona Supreme Court
C.F.R.	*Code of Federal Regulations*
ch.	chapter
Cir.	Circuit Court
Civ.	Civil
Cl.	Claims
Ct.	Court
D.	District
Def. Ex.	Defendant's Exhibit
F.	*Federal Reporter*
F.2d	*Federal Reporter, Second Series*
F.3d	*Federal Reporter, Third Series*
F. Supp.	*Federal Supplement*
HR Rep.	U.S. House of Representatives Report
HR Res.	U.S. House of Representatives Resolution
Ind. Cl. Comm	Indian Claims Commission
M.D.Ala.	Middle District of Alabama
NA	National Archives
N.W.2d	*North Western Reporter, Second Series*
P.2d	*Pacific Reporter, Second Series*

Pl. Ex.	Plaintiff's Exhibit
Pub. L.	Public Law
slip op	slip opinion (opinion not published in case reporter but separately printed)
S. Rep.	U.S. Senate Report
S. Res.	U.S. Senate Resolution
Stat.	*United States Statutes at Large*
Stats at Large of USA	*Statutes at Large of the United States of America, 1789–1873*
Tr. Trans.	Trial Transcript
U.S.	*United States Supreme Court Reports*
USCCAN	*U.S. Code Congressional and Administrative News*

Notes

Preface

1. "Indian country" is defined in 18 *U.S. Code* §1151 (1948) as land under the supervision of the United States set aside for the use of Indians. The phrase is used more broadly here to mean areas in the West with significant Indian populations.

Introduction

1. *Yick Wo v. Hopkins*, 118 U.S. 356, 370 (1886).
2. *Voting Rights Act of 1965*, 79 *Stat*. 437, 42 *U.S. Code* §1973, et seq.

1. Evolution of Federal Policy toward American Indians

1. *Johnson v. McIntosh,* 21 U.S. 543 (1823).
2. Ibid at 572–73.
3. Ibid. at 591.
4. *Cherokee Nation v. Georgia*, 30 U.S. 1, 20 (1831).
5. Ibid. at 17.
6. *Worcester v. Georgia*, 31 U.S. 515, 556–57 (1832).
7. Ibid. at 557.
8. *Indian Removal Act*, 4 *Stat*. 411 (1830).
9. Jackson, "First Annual Message."
10. Deloria, *American Indian Policy in the Twentieth Century*, 242.

11. Foreman, *Indian Removal.*

12. See Kappler, *Indian Affairs.*

13. Deloria, and Lytle, *American Indians, American Justice*, 3–4.

14. *Elk v. Wilkins*, 112 U.S. 94, 103 (1884).

15. Ibid. at 104–05.

16. Ibid. at 105.

17. Indian Peace Commission, *Proceedings of the Great Peace Commission of 1867–1868*, 86–87, quoted in Prucha, *Indians in American Society*, 18.

18. Quoted in Prucha, *Indians in American Society*, 41.

19. "Second Treaty of Fort Laramie of 1868," 15 *Stat*. 635.

20. Quoted in Nabokov, *Native American Testimony*, 118.

21. Deloria and Lytle, *American Indians, American Justice*, 5.

22. Manypenny, *Annual Report of the U.S. Commissioner of Indian Affairs (1856)*, reprinted in Prucha, *Documents of United States Indian Policy*, 89–92.

23. Cox, *Annual Report of the Secretary of the Interior* (1868), reprinted in Prucha, *Documents of United States Indian Policy*, 129–30.

24. See, e.g., Szasz, *Education and the American Indian*, 9.

25. *Act of April 10, 1869*, ch. 16, §4, 16 *Stat*. 16, 40.

26. U.S. Board of Indian Commissioners, *Report of the Board of Indian Commissioners (1869)*, reprinted in Prucha, *Documents of United States Indian Policy*, 131–34.

27. House debate on the Wheeler–Howard Bill, *Congressional Record* 78, pt. 11: 724–44.

28. *Indian Claims Commission Act*, 60 *Stat*. 1049–50 (1946).

29. U.S. Indian Claims Commission, *Final Report* (1979), 1.

30. *Indian Appropriation Act of March 3, 1871*, 16 *Stat*. 566 (1871), 25 *U.S. Code* §71.

31. Chaudhur, "American Indian Policy," in Deloria, *American Indian Policy in the Twentieth Century*, 17. According to Deloria, "various commissions continued making treaties with the tribes until 1914, when the Ute Mountain Utes signed the last major agreement with the United States. But these treaties, because of the prohibition by Congress, had to be called 'agreements' when being presented for ratification." Deloria & Lytle, *American Indians, American Justice*, 5.

32. For a discussion of the federal regulation of tribal members during this period, see Prucha, *Great Father*; Tyler, *History of Indian Policy*; and Pevar, *Rights of Indians and Tribes.*

33. *United States v. Kagama*, 118 U.S. 375, 383 (1886).

34. Price, *Annual Report of the Commissioner of Indian Affairs* (1881), 156.

35. Teller, *Annual Report of the U.S. Secretary of the Interior* (1883), reprinted in Prucha, *Documents of United States Indian Policy*, 160–62.

36. Commissioner of Indian Affairs, "Indian Department Rules," No. 492 §237 and No. 497, 4th & 6th Rules. See also Bradley, *After the Buffalo Days*, vol. 1, 45–49.

37. *Windy Boy v. County of Big Horn, Montana*, No. CV-83-225-BLG (D. Mont.), Joe Medicine Crow, Tr. Trans. vol. 1, 112.

38. Dixon, *Vanishing Race*, p. xx.
39. *Large v. Fremont County, Wyoming*, No. 05-CV-270J (D. Wyo.), Martha Hipp, Tr. Trans., 217.
40. Ibid.
41. Quoted in Marriott and Rachlin, *American Indian Mythology*, 138–39.
42. *Major Crimes Act of 1885*, 23 *Stat*. 385, 18 *U.S. Code* §1153.
43. Sen. George Vest, speaking during Senate debate on the Indian Appropriation Bill (Feb. 16, 1885), *Congressional Record* 48, 1732–36.
44. *United States v. Kagama*, 118 U.S. at 384.
45. *Elk v. Wilkins*, 112 U.S. at 102.
46. Ibid.
47. "Treaty of July 3, 1868," 15 *Stat*. 673.
48. *Act of July 25, 1868*, 15 *Stat*. 178.
49. *Ward v. Race Horse*, 163 U.S. 504 (1896).
50. American Indian Policy Review Commission, *Final Report*, 63–64.
51. Atkins, *Annual Report of the Commissioner of Indian Affairs (1887)*, reprinted in Prucha, *Documents of United States Indian Policy*, 174–76.
52. Ibid.; and Pevar, *Rights of Indians and Tribes*, 4–5.
53. United States Commission on Civil Rights, *Indian Tribes*, 34.
54. *Large v. Fremont County*, Martha Hipp, Tr. Trans., 221.
55. Quoted in Dixon, *Vanishing Race*, 68.
56. Ibid. at 93.
57. *Large v. Fremont County*, Stephen Thernstrom, Tr. Trans., 843–44.
58. U.S. Senate, *Indian Education: A National Tragedy—A National Challenge*.
59. U.S. American Indian Policy Review Commission, *Final Report 1977*, 63–64.
60. *General Allotment Act of 1887*, 24 *Stat*. 388, 25 *U.S.C.* §§331–58.
61. *Draper v. United States*, 164 U.S. 240, 246 (1896).
62. *United States v. Nice*, 241 U.S. 591, 601 (1916).
63. *Burke Act of 1906*, 34 *Stat*. 182.
64. U.S. American Indian Policy Review Commission, *Final Report 1977*, 66–67.
65. Wolfley, "Jim Crow, Indian Style,"176–78.
66. Morgan, *Annual Report of the Commissioner of Indian Affairs 1889*, reprinted in Prucha, *Documents of United States Indian Policy*, 177–78.
67. *Lone Wolf v. Hitchcock*, 187 U.S. 553, 566 (1903).
68. *United States v. Winans*, 198 U.S. 371, 381 (1905).
69. Sells, *Declaration of Policy in the Administration of Indian Affairs*, 1–2
70. U.S. American Indian Policy Review Commission, *Final Report 1977*, 69.
71. Horsman, "Scientific Racism and the American Indian," 168.
72. Dixon, *Vanishing Race*, 3.
73. *Ex Parte Crow Dog*, 109 U.S. 556, 571 (1883).
74. *Missouri, Kansas and Texas Railway Company v. Roberts*, 152 U.S. 114, 117 (1894).
75. U.S. American Indian Policy Review Commission, *Final Report 1977*, 74.

76. *Indian Territory Naturalization Act*, 26 *Stat*. 81.

77. *Act of March 3, 1901*, 31 *Stat*. 1447.

78. *Act of November 6, 1919*, ch. 95, 41 *Stat*. 350.

79. *Act of March 3, 1921*, 41 *Stat*. 1249–50.

80. *Indian Citizenship Act of 1924*, 43 *Stat*. 253.

81. For a discussion of the society, see Nabokov, *Native American Testimony*, 275–79.

82. Quoted in Nabokov, *Native American Testimony*, 281.

83. See Porter, "Demise of the Ongwehoweh," 127.

84. *Ex parte Green*, 123 F.2d 862, 864 (2d Cir. 1941).

85. Houghton, "Legal Status of Indian Suffrage," 520.

86. Chas. H. Burke to superintendents and others, July 10, 1924, NA, Rocky Mountain Region, Denver, Colo.

87. See, e.g., *Montana Laws* 1937, p. 527, requiring deputy voter registrars to be "taxpaying" residents of their precincts; and *Montana Laws* 1937, p. 523, requiring re-registration of all voters.

88. *Buckanaga v. Sisseton Independent School District*, 804 F.2d 469, 474 (8th Cir. 1986).

89. Wolfley, "Jim Crow, Indian Style," 185.

90. *Harrison v. Laveen*, 67 Ariz. 337, 196 P.2d 456, 463 (1948).

91. *Allen v. Merrell*, 352 U.S. 889 (1956); and Act of Feb. 14, 1957, ch. 38, *1957 Utah Laws* 89–90. See also *Allen v. Merrell*, 353 U.S. 932 (1957), vacating the state court decision as moot.

92. Meriam and Associates, *Problem of Indian Administration*, 3–9, 20–23, 86–89.

93. *Indian Reorganization Act of 1934*, 48 *Stat*. 984, 25 *U.S. Code* §461 et seq.

94. Philip, *Indian Termination Policy*, 5.

95. Rep. Edgar Howard, speaking during House debate on the Wheeler–Howard Bill, *Congressional Record* 78, pt. 11, 724–44.

96. *Indian Reorganization Act of 1934*, 25 *U.S. Code* §461.

97. U.S. House, *Readjustment of Indian Affairs*, HR Rep. 1804, 6.

98. Collier, *Indians of the Americas*, 226.

99. Deloria & Lytle, *American Indians, American Justice*, 15.

100. Comments of Ramon Roubideaux, quoted in Nabokov, *Native American Testimony*, 329.

101. Ibid. at 307, 324.

102. U.S. House, *Indians*, HR Res. 108, 1.

103. Rep. Lee Metcalf, quoted in Peterson, "American Indian Political Participation," 116–26.

104. Pevar, *Rights of Indians and Tribes*, 7.

105. U.S. Commission on Civil Rights, *Indian Tribes: A Continuing Quest for Survival*, 23.

106. Nabokov, *Native American Testimony*, 356.

107. *Act to Confer Jurisdiction on the State of California, Minnesota, Nebraska, Oregon, and Wisconsin*, 67 *Stat.* 588, 589 (1953), 18 *U.S. Code* §1162, 28 *U.S. Code* §1360.

108. For example, the *Relocation Act of 1956*, Pub. L. 959.

109. U.S. Commission on Civil Rights, *Indian Tribes: A Continuing Quest for Survival*, 33.

110. *Jurisdiction over Criminal and Civil Actions*, 82 *Stat.* 78–80 (1968), 25 *U.S. Code* §§1321–23, 1326.

111. Johnson, "Forgotten American," 440.

112. U.S. Senate, *Indian Education*, S. Rep. 501, 21 and 53.

113. U.S. House, Interior and Insular Affairs Committee, HR Rep. 907, 1, 6–7.

114. U.S. House, Interior and Insular Affairs Committee, HR Rep. 1026, 15.

115. U.S. House, Interior and Insular Affairs Committee, HR Rep. 1308, 4.

116. U.S. House, Interior and Insular Affairs Committee, HR Rep. 1386, 9.

117. Nixon, "President's Message to the Congress," 1.

118. *Indian Financing Act of 1974*, 88 *Stat.* 77 (1974), 25 *U.S. Code* §1451.

119. *Indian Self-Determination and Education Assistance Act of 1975*, 88 *Stat.* 2203 (1975), 25 *U.S. Code* §450a.

120. *Voting Rights Act Amendments of 1975*, 89 *Stat.* 400 (1975), 42 *U.S. Code* §1973b(f).

121. *Indian Health Care Improvement Act of 1976*, 90 *Stat.* 1400 (1976), 25 *U.S. Code* §1601.

122. *American Indian Religious Freedom Act of 1978*, 92 *Stat.* 469 (1978), 42 *U.S. Code* §1996.

123. *Indian Child Welfare Act of 1978*, 92 *Stat.* 3069 (1978), 25 *U.S. Code* §1901.

124. *Indian Mineral Development Act of 1982*, 25 *U.S. Code* §§2101–8.

125. *Indian Tribal Government Tax Status Act of 1982*, 96 *Stat.* 2607.

126. *Indian Gaming Regulatory Act of 1988*, 25 *U.S. Code* §§2701–21.

127. *The Native American Business Development, Trade Promotion, and Tourism Act of 2000*, 114 *Stat.* 2012, 25 *U.S. Code* §4301(a)(2).

128. *United States v. Wheeler*, 435 U.S. 313, 323 (1978).

129. Clinton, "Government-to-Government Relations."

130. Clinton, Executive Order no. 13175.

131. Bush, "Memorandum for the Heads of Executive Departments."

132. *Billings (Mont.) Gazette*, "Crow Tribe Adopts Candidate Obama in Historic Visit," May 20, 2008.

133. *Worcester v. Georgia*, 31 U.S. at 556–57.

2. Voting Rights Act: How It Works

1. This history is discussed in many places, e.g., Key, *Southern Politics in State and Nation*; Woodward, *Origins of the New South, 1877–1913*; Kousser, *Shaping of Southern Politics*; and Fonner, *Reconstruction*.

2. *South Carolina v. Katzenbach*, 383 U.S. 301, 308 (1966).

3. *Voting Rights Act of 1965*, 79 *Stat.* 437, 42 *U.S. Code* §1973.

4. Ibid., 42 *U.S. Code* §§1973b(e), h & j.

5. *South Carolina v. Katzenbach*, 383 U.S. at 315.

6. *Voting Rights Act of 1965*, 42 *U.S. Code* §1973(b).

7. Senate Committee on Judiciary, *Voting Rights Act Extension*, S. Rep. 295, 12, reprinted in 1975 USCCAN 774.

8. *Voting Rights Act of 1965*, 42 *U.S. Code* §1973a(c).

9. Ibid., §1973b(a).

10. Senate Committee on Judiciary, *Voting Rights Act Extension*, S. Rep. 295, 12 n.4, reprinted in 1975 USCCAN 774, 778.

11. *Voting Rights Act of 1965*, 42 *U.S. Code* §§1973b, 1973aa.

12. Ibid., §1973c.

13. Ibid., §§1973d & f.

14. *Allen v. State Board of Elections*, 393 U.S. 544, 566–67 (1969).

15. Regarding redistricting plans, see *Beer v. United States*, 425 U.S. 130 (1976); for annexations, see *City of Richmond v. United States*, 422 U.S. 358 (1975); for setting the date for a special elections, see *Henderson v. Harris*, 804 F. Supp. 288 (M.D.Ala. 1992); and for a polling place move, see *Perkins v. Matthews*, 400 U.S. 379, 387–90 (1971).

16. *Allen v. State Board of Elections*, 393 U.S. at 555–56, n. 19.

17. *Beer v. United States*, 425 U.S. at 141.

18. *South Carolina v. Katzenbach*, 383 U.S. at 328.

19. *Perkins v. Matthews*, 400 U.S. at 396.

20. *Voting Rights Act of 1965*, 42 *U.S. Code* §§1973j(d) and (f).

21. Ibid., §1973j(a).

22. *South Carolina v. Katzenbach*, 383 U.S. at 359–60.

23. *Allen v. State Board of Elections*, 393 U.S. at 595.

24. *South Carolina v. Katzenbach*, 383 U.S. at 309.

25. House Committee on the Judiciary, *Voting Rights Act Extension*, HR Rep. 227, 36; and *McDaniel v. Sanchez*, 452 U.S. 130, 151 (1981), which said that "centralized review enhances the likelihood that recurring problems will be resolved in a consistent and expeditious way".

26. Senate Committee on the Judiciary, *Voting Rights Act Extension*, S. Rep. 417, 58, reprinted in 1982 USCCAN 236.

27. House Judiciary Committee, HR Rep. 439, 15, reprinted in 1965 USCCAN 2446.

28. House Committee on the Judiciary, *Voting Rights—Tests*, HR Rep. 397, reprinted in 1970 USCCAN 3281.

29. Senate Committee on the Judiciary, *Voting Rights Act Extension*, S. Rep. 295, 13, n. 5, reprinted in 1975 USCCAN 779 & n. 5.

30. Ibid.

31. Ibid.

32. *Georgia v. United States*, 411 U.S. 526, 531 (1973).

33. Senate Committee on the Judiciary, *Voting Rights Act Extension*, S. Rep. 295, 15, 17–18, reprinted in 1975 USCCAN 781, 783–84.

34. *Voting Rights Act Extension*, 42 *U.S. Code* §1973aa–1a(e).

35. Senate Committee on the Judiciary, *Voting Rights Act Extension*, S. Rep. 295, 47–48, reprinted in 1975 USCCAN 813–14.

36. Procedures for the Administration of Section 5, *Code of Federal Regulations* 28, §51, Appendix to Part 51—Jurisdictions Covered under Section 4(b) of the Voting Rights Act, As Amended.

37. *Voting Rights Act Extension*, 42 *U.S. Code* §1973aa–1a.

38. Senate Committee on the Judiciary, *Voting Rights Act Extension*, S. Rep. 295, 38–39, reprinted in 1975 USCCAN 804–806.

39. *City of Rome v. United States*, 446 U.S. 156, 180 (1980).

40. Ibid. at 179, 182.

41. *Voting Rights Act of 1965*, 42 *U.S. Code* §1973.

42. *Morton v. Mancari*, 417 U.S. 535, 554 n. 24 (1974), which said that the preference in BIA hiring was "political rather than racial in nature."

43. *Rice v. Sioux City Memorial Park Cemetery*, 349 U.S. 70, 76 (1955).

44. *Klahr v. Williams*, 339 F. Supp. 922, 927 (D. Ariz. 1972); *United States v. Iron Moccasin*, 878 F.2d 226 (8th Cir. 1989); and *Natonabah v. Board of Education*, 355 F. Supp. 716, 724 (D. N.Mex. 1973).

45. Rep. Peter Rodino, speaking for amendment of the Voting Rights Act, *Congressional Record* 121, p. 16,244.

46. Rep. Drinan, speaking for amendment of the Voting Rights Act, *Congressional Record* 121, p. 16,262.

47. *Klahr v. Williams*, 339 F. Supp. at 927, cited in House Judiciary Committee, Subcommittee on Civil and Constitutional Rights, *Extension of the Voting Rights Act*, hereafter cited as "1975 House Hearings."

48. *Oregon v. Mitchell*, 400 U.S. 112, 147 (1970), J. Douglas concurring, cited in *Congressional Record* 121, p. 16,245 (statement of Rep. Edwards).

49. *Goodluck v. Apache County*, cited in 1975 House Hearings, Appendix 1225–30, and in *Congressional Record* 121, p. 16,250 (statement of Rep. Young).

50. House Committee on the Judiciary, *Voting Rights Act Extension*, HR Rep. 196, 30.

51. Sen. William Scott, speaking for the amendment of the Voting Rights Act, *Congressional Record* 121, p. 13,603.

52. Senate Committee on the Judiciary, *Voting Rights Act Extension*, S. Rep. 295, 25, 29, reprinted in 1975 USCCAN 791, 795.

53. Senate Committee on the Judiciary, *Voting Rights Act Extension*, S. Rep. 417, 10, reprinted in 1982 USCCAN 187.

54. *Voting Rights Act Extension*, 42 *U.S. Code* §1973aa–6.

55. Ibid., §1973b(a); and Senate Committee on the Judiciary, *Voting Rights Act Extension*, S. Rep. 417, 43–6, reprinted in 1982 USCCAN 221–24.

56. *City of Mobile v. Bolden*, 446 U.S. 55 (1980).

57. *Thornburg v. Gingles*, 478 U.S. 30, 44 (1986), quoting the legislative history.

58. Ibid. at 47.

59. Senate Committee on the Judiciary, *Voting Rights Act Extension*, S. Rep. 417, 28–29, reprinted in 1982 USCCAN 206–207.

60. *Thornburg v. Gingles*, 478 U.S. at 48 n.15, 50–51.

61. *Johnson v. De Grandy*, 512 U.S. 997, 1012 & n.10, 1018 (1994).

62. *Thornburg v. Gingles*, 478 U.S. at 56.

63. Ibid. at 53 n. 21, internal quotation marks omitted.

64. Ibid. at 56.

65. Ibid. at 48–49 n. 15.

66. *County Council of Sumter County, S.C. v. United States*, 555 F. Supp. 694, 707 (D.D.C. 1983).

67. Ibid.

68 Ibid. at 707 n. 13. In *South Carolina v. Katzenbach*, the plaintiffs made a similar argument that the coverage formula was defective because it was "awkwardly designed . . . and that it disregards various local conditions which have nothing to do with racial discrimination." The Court held "[t]hese arguments . . . are largely beside the point," and that the trigger was not a mathematical formula but was designed "to describe these areas . . . relevant to the problem of voting discrimination" (383 U.S. at 329).

69. House Committee on the Judiciary, *Voting Rights Language Assistance*, H. Rep. 655, reprinted in 1992 USCCAN 767.

70. Ibid.

71. Ibid. at 771 n. 18.

72. Ibid. at 771–75.

73. *Lopez v. Monterey County*, 525 U.S. 266, 282 (1999).

74. Ibid. at 282–83.

75. Ibid. at 283.

76. *United States v. Blaine County, Montana*, 363 F.3d 897, 904–05 (9th Cir. 2004).

77. *Blaine County, Montana v. United States*, 544 U.S. 992 (2005).

78. *Fannie Lou Hamer, Rosa Parks, and Coretta Scott King Voting Rights Act Reauthorization and Amendments Act of 2006*, Pub. L. 109-246, 120 *Stat.* 577.

79. Ibid., §§2(b)(8) and (9).

80. *Reno v. Bossier Parish School Board*, 528 U.S. 320, 341 (2000).

81. *Voting Rights Act Reauthorization and Amendments Act of 2006*, 120 *Stat.* 577, §5(3)(c).

82. *Georgia v. Ashcroft*, 539 U.S. 461, 482–83 (2003).

84. *Voting Rights Act Reauthorization and Amendments Act of 2006*, 120 *Stat.* 577, §5(1)(d).

84. *Northwest Austin Municipal Utility District Number One v. Mukasey*, 557 F. Supp.2d 9 (D. D.C. 2008).

85. *Northwest Austin Utility District Number One v. Holder*, 129 S.Ct. 2504 (2009).

86. Procedure for the Administration of Section 5, *Code of Federal Regulations* 28, pt. 51, app. (2002).

87. Covered Areas for Voting Rights Bilingual Election Materials—2000. *Federal Register* 67 (2002): 48871.

88. See, e.g., Davidson & Grofman, *Quiet Revolution in the South*; and McDonald, "Quiet Revolution in Minority Voting Rights."

89. Matthew Fletcher, conversation with author, Jan. 31, 2008.

3. Montana I

1. *Windy Boy v. County of Big Horn*, 647 F. Supp. 1002 (D. Mont. 1986).

2. U.S. Bureau of the Census, *1980 Census of Population*, sec. *PC 80-1-B28*.

3. *Thornburg v. Gingles*, 478 U.S. 30, 47 (1986).

4. Leitch, *Concise Dictionary of Indian Tribes*, 141–44; Oswalt, *This Land Was Theirs*, 282–93; and *United States v. Montana*, 457 F. Supp. 599 (D. Mont. 1978).

5. Denig, *Five Indian Tribes of the Upper Missouri*, 146.

6. Hodge, *First Americans, Then and Now*, 193–213; and Hoebel, *Cheyennes*, 120–133.

7. "Treaty with the Crow Tribe, 1825," 7 *Stat*. 266; and "Treaty with the Cheyenne Tribe, 1825," 7 *Stat*. 255.

8. Cohen, *Handbook of Federal Indian Law*, 41.

9. "First Treaty of Fort Laramie with the Sioux, Cheyenne, Arapahoes, Crows, Assinaboines, Gros-Ventre, Mandans and Arickaras of 1851," 11 *Stat*. 749.

10. Royce, *Indian Land Cessions in the United States*; and *Montana v. United States*, 450 U.S. 544, 557–58 (1981).

11. *Act of 1864*, 13 *Stat*. 85.

12. Memorial Relative to Proposed Treaty with Snake and Crow Indians (1864), *Laws of the Territory of Montana, 1st Legislative Assembly*, 721.

13. *Act of March 3, 1865*, ch. 127, 13 *Stat*. 541, 559.

14. Act Amendatory of an Act Entitled "Act Regulating the Holding of Elections in Montana Territory," *Laws of the Territory of Montana, 4th Sess.*, 875–76.

15. Quoted in Spence, *Montana*, 56.

16. *Act of 1867*, 14 *Stat*. 426; and An Act Concerning Jurors, *Law of the Territory of Montana, 4th Sess.* (1867), 69–70.

17. Resolved by the Legislative Assembly of the Territory of Montana, *Laws of the Territory of Montana, 4th Sess.*, 273.

18. "Second Treaty of Fort Laramie of 1868," 15 *Stat*. 649.

19. *United States v. State of Montana*, 457 F. Supp. at 603.

20. Memorial Praying for a Treaty with the Crow Indians, Protecting the Rights of the Citizens of Montana in the Valley of the Yellow Stone (Jan. 11, 1869), *Laws of the Territory of Montana, 5th Sess*. (1869), 119.

21. *Crow Tribe of Indians v. United States*, 284 F.2d 361, 362–63 (Ct. C1. 1960).

22. *Northern Cheyenne Indians of the Tongue River Reservation, Montana v. United States*, No. 329-C (Ind. Cl. Comm. Nov. 27, 1963).

23. No Precinct Opened at Indian Agencies or in Unorganized Counties, *Laws of the Territory of Montana, 7th Sess.* (1871), 459–60, 471, 506; and *Laws of the Territory of Montana, Extraordinary Sess.* (1873), 87.

24. *Montana Territorial Laws 1872,* 303, 308–09.

25. To His Excellency—the President of the United States, *Laws of the Territory of Montana, 9th Sess.* (1876), 208.

26. House Joint Memorial in Relation to Restoring a Portion of the Crow Indian Reservation to the Public Domain, *Laws of the Territory of Montana, 10th Sess.* (1877), 441–42.

27. Ibid., *Laws of the Territory of Montana, 11th Sess.* (1879), 136–37.

28. Ibid., 130–31.

29. Agreement with the Crows of 1880, unratified; and *Act of April 11, 1882,* 22 *Stat.* 42.

30. House Joint Memorial Concerning Leasing and Reduction of the Crow Indian Reservation, *Laws of the Territory of Montana, 14th Sess.* (1885), 236–37.

31. *Windy Boy,* Testimony of Joe Medicine Crow, Tr. Trans., 111.

32. Ibid. at 111–12.

33. Council Joint Memorial Concerning the Executive Order of the President of the United States Setting Apart Certain Lands in Montana as a Reserve for the Cheyenne Indians, *Laws of the Territory of Montana, 14th Sess.* (1885), 237–38.

34. *Windy Boy,* Declaration of C. Adrian Heidenreich, 8–9, 28.

35. Price, *Report of Commissioner of Indian Affairs* (1883), excerpted in Washburn, *American Indian and the United States*, 352–54.

36. U.S. Commissioner of Indian Affairs, *Annual Report* (1886), 418.

37. *Montana Enabling Act of February 22, 1889,* 25 *Stat.* 676.

38. *Montana Laws 1889,* 124; and "Rights of Suffrage and Qualifications to Hold Office" in Montana Constitution, Art. IX, Sec. 2.

39. Act to Amend an Act Entitled "An Act to Provide for the Registration of the Names of Electors, and to Prevent Fraud at Elections," *Laws of the State of Montana, 3rd Sess.* (1893), 78–91.

40. Thomas Jefferson Morgan, *Annual Report of the Commissioner of Indian Affairs,* reprinted in Prucha, *Documents of United States Indian Policy*, 177.

41. Maj. James Brisbin (1889), reprinted in the Montana Historical Society, *Not in Precious Metals Alone*, 67–68.

42. *Act of 1891,* 26 *Stat.* 989. See *United States v. Finch,* 395 F. Supp. 213, 218 (D. Mont. 1975), map showing the ceded portion of the reservation.

43. Senate Joint Memorial to the Honorable, the [U.S.] Senate and House, *Laws of the State of Montana, 2d Sess.* (1891), 316–17.

44. *Act of June 10, 1896,* ch. 398, 29 *Stat.* 321, 341–42.

45. Senate Joint Memorial to the Honorable, the [U.S.] Senate and House, in *Laws of the State of Montana, 6th Sess.* (1899), 153.

46. Senate Joint Memorial to the Honorable, the [U.S.] Senate and House, in *Laws of the State of Montana, 7th Sess.* (1901), 210–11; and Senate Joint Memorial to

the Honorable, the [U.S.] Senate and House, in *Laws of the State of Montana, 8th Sess.* (1903)., 351–52.

47. *Act of 1904,* 33 *Stat.* 352; and *United States v. Finch,* 395 F. Supp. at 219.

48. "Are Pushing Canal Work," *Hardin (Mont.) Tribune,* April 24, 1908.

49. "Pass Bill in Senate," *Hardin (Mont.) Tribune,* May 22, 1908.

50. House Joint Memorial no. 4, *Laws of the State of Montana, 11th Sess.* (1909), 385–86.

51. Senate Joint Memorial no. 1, *Laws of the State of Montana, 12th Sess.* (1911), 554–55; and Senate Joint Memorial no. 2, *Laws of the State of Montana, 14th Sess.* (1915), 465–66.

52. Montana Constitution, Art. V, §3 Legislative Department; Art. VII, §3 Executive Department; Art. VIII, §10 Judicial Departments; Art. XIV, §1 Military Affairs; Act to Amend Section 1880 of School Laws of Montana, *Laws of the State of Montana, 2nd Sess.* (1891), 243–45; Act Relating to Municipal Indebtedness, *Laws of the State of Montana, 5th Sess.* (1897), 226–28; Act to Amend Section 1331 of Political Code, Relating to Primary Elections, *Laws of the State of Montana, 7th Sess.* (1901), 29, 115–16; Act Relating to Granting of Franchises by Cities and Town, *Laws of the State of Montana, 8th Sess.* (1903), 158–59; Act Prohibiting the Selling of Intoxicating Liquors to Habitual Drunkards or to Minors or to Indians, *Laws of the State of Montana, 14th Sess.* (1915), 60; Act to Amend Section 499, Relative to Establishment of Voting Precincts in Indian Country, *Laws of the State of Montana, 16th Sess.* (1919), 235; and Act to Prohibit Possession of and Traffic in Peyote and Mescal Buttons, *Laws of the State of Montana, 18th Sess.* (1923), 40. See *State v. Big Sheep, Montana,* 243 P. 1067 (1976), holding that Indians on the Crow Reservation were subject under some circumstances to prosecution in the Hardin Justice Court for possession of peyote.

53. An Act Providing for Creation of Election Precincts and Registration of Electors, *Laws of the State of Montana, 12th Sess.* (1911), 223.

54. 1 *Opinions of the Montana Attorney General* 362 (1906); 5 *Opinions of the Montana Attorney General* 240 (1913); and 8 *Opinions of the Montana Attorney General* 195 (1919).

55. "Indians Can't Vote," *Hardin (Mont.) Tribune,* July 4, 1913.

56. "List of Registered Voters," *Hardin (Mont.) Tribune,* Oct. 16, 1914.

57. Resolution by the Crow Indian Council, Nov. 22, 1915, reprinted in Robert Yellowtail, "Why the Crow Indian Reservation Should Not Be Opened," *The Red Man,* Apr. 1916, 265–69.

58. 1 *Opinions of the Montana Attorney General* 60 (1905); and 5 *Opinions of the Montana Attorney General* 460 (1914).

59. *Crow Allotment Act of 1920,* 41 *Stat.* 751.

60. "Crow Allotments Made," *Hardin (Mont.) Tribune,* May 4, 1923.

61. See *Montana v. United States,* 450 U.S. at 559 n. 9.

62. Lowie, *Crow Indians,* xxi.

63. Heidenreich, "Persistence of Values among the Crow Indians."

64. *United States v. Montana*, 604 F.2d 1162, 1164 n. 3 (9th Cir. 1979).

65. Hodge, *First Americans, Then and Now*, 206.

66. Northern Cheyenne Constitution of 1936; and Crow Tribe Constitution of 1948.

67. *Indian Citizenship Act of 1924*, 8 *U.S. Code* §1401(a)(2).

68. C.H. Asbury to the commissioner of Indian affairs, June 9, 1924, NA, Rocky Mountain Region, Denver, Colo.

69. The story of black disfranchisement in the South in the aftermath of Reconstruction is told in many places, e.g., Key, *Southern Politics in State and Nation*; Kousser, *Shaping of Southern Politics*; and Franklin, *Reconstruction after the Civil War*.

70. Houghton, "Legal Status of Indian Suffrage," 520.

71. "900 Montana Indians May Vote," *Hardin (Mont.) Tribune*, June 20, 1924.

72. "737 More Voters Register to Date," *Hardin (Mont.) Tribune*, July 25, 1924.

73. "Crow Indian Tribe in First Political Council," *Hardin (Mont.) Tribune*, Aug. 15, 1924.

74. "A Real American for Congressman," *Hardin (Mont.) Tribune*, Aug. 15, 1924; and "Only Two Democrats on County Ticket Elected," *Hardin (Mont.) Tribune*, Nov. 7, 1924.

75. "Official Returns Primary Nominating Election Held on July 17, 1928," *Hardin (Mont.) Tribune*, July 27, 1928.

76. "Official Returns General Election Held on Tuesday Nov. 8, 1932," *Hardin (Mont.) Tribune*, Nov. 18, 1932.

77. "Official Returns Primary Nominating Election Held on July 17, 1934," *Hardin (Mont.) Tribune*, July 24, 1934.

78. "Many Crows Are Seen; Another Spring Sign," *Billings (Mont.) Gazette*, Feb. 14, 1924.

79. "Plain Bull's Squaw Now Susie Alcohol," *Billings (Mont.) Gazette*, Feb. 14, 1924.

80. "Medicine Man Names Miss Crow Feathers," *Billings (Mont.) Gazette*, Jan. 13, 1924.

81. "Will Remove Indian Vagrants to Reserve," *Billings (Mont.) Gazette*, Feb. 1, 1925.

82. Act to Amend Sections 555, 557, 561 and 570 of Chapter 61 of the Revised Codes of Montana, Relating to Who May Register, *Laws of the State of Montana, 25th Legislative Assembly* (1937), 527.

83. Act to Amend Section 23-3003, Pertaining to Deputy Registrars, *Laws of the State of Montana, 44th Sess.* (1975), ch. 205.

84. Act to Amend Sections 555, 557, 561 and 570, *Laws of the State of Montana, 25th Legislative Assembly* (1937), 523–27. And see, "If you Don't Register You Won't Be Able to Vote," *Hardin (Mont.) Tribune–Herald*, June 18, 1937, reporting that all voter registrations had been purged and identifying deputy registrars, none of whom were Indian and none of whom were at Crow Agency.

85. "Official Returns General Election, November 8, 1938," *Hardin (Mont.) Tribune–Herald*, Nov. 24, 1938, reflecting the decline in voter participation at reservation precincts.

86. *State v. Kemp*, 106 Mont. 449, 78 P.2d 585 (1938).

87. 16 *Opinions of the Montana Attorney General* 42 (1935).

88. 17 *Opinions of the Montana Attorney General* 12 (1937).

89. 19 *Opinions of the Montana Attorney General* 789 (1942); and 20 *Opinions of the Montana Attorney General* 147 (1943).

90. Section 8890. Who Competent to Act as Juror, *Laws of the State of Montana, 26th Sess.* (1939), 510.

91. *Windy Boy*, Declaration of C. Adrian Heidenreich, 17.

92. "Riley, Greenwald, Kalberg and Iverson Nominated," *Hardin (Mont.) Tribune–Herald*, July 22, 1954, reporting that Yellowtail got 20 percent of the vote in Big Horn County.

93. "Hawks and Miller Win Nomination," *Hardin (Mont.) Tribune–Herald*, June 7, 1956, reporting that Wall got 35 percent of the vote in Big Horn County.

94. "The Candidates Speak," *Hardin (Mont.) Tribune–Herald*, May 28, 1970.

95. Crow Service Unit, *Environmental Health Profile and Priority Projection*, 7; and U.S. Department of the Interior, BIA, *Local Estimates of Resident Indian Population*, 7.

96. U.S. Bureau of the Census, *1980 Census of Population*, p. 28-147.

97. Crow Tribe of Indians, *Crow Tribe Housing Condition Survey, 1985.*

98. U.S. Bureau of the Census, *1980 Census of Population*, p. 28-262.

99. Ibid., p. 28-214.

100. Dyche, "English Achievement of Seventh Grade Crow Indian Students," 34–35.

101. Brophy & Aberle, *Indian: America's Unfinished Business*, 140.

102. Senate Joint Resolution no. 2, *Laws of the State of Montana, 44th Sess.* (1975), 1723–24.

103. *Windy Boy,* Testimony of Joe Medicine Crow, Tr. Trans., 112–13.

104. *Windy Boy,* Testimony of Janine Windy Boy, Tr. Trans., 199.

105. *Windy Boy,* Testimony of Jim Kindness, Tr. Trans., 283.

106. *Windy Boy,* Testimony of Dan Half, Tr. Trans., 730.

107. *Windy Boy,* Testimony of Clo Small, Tr. Trans., 484–87.

108. *Windy Boy,* Testimony of Leo Hudetz, Tr. Trans., 620–22.

109. U.S. Bureau of the Census, *1980 Census of Population*, p. 28-214.

110. *Windy Boy,* Testimony of Harvey Pitsch, Tr. Trans., 571.

111. *Windy Boy,* Testimony of Janine Windy Boy, Tr. Trans., 211.

112. *Windy Boy,* Testimony of Tyrone Ten Bear, Tr. Trans., 514, 519.

113. Dan Brown, conversation with author, Oct. 2, 1985.

114. *Windy Boy,* Testimony of Dale Old Horn, Tr. Trans., 531–33.

115. Ibid. at 536.

116. Eloise Pease, conversation with author, June 1985.

117. *Windy Boy,* Testimony of Sharon Peregoy, Tr. Trans., 643–44.
118. *Windy Boy,* Testimony of Carlene Old Elk, Tr. Trans., 862.
119. *Windy Boy,* Testimony of Katie Pretty Weasel, Tr. Trans., 721–24.
120. *Windy Boy,* Testimony of Dessie Bad Bear, Tr. Trans., 422–23.
121. *Windy Boy,* Testimony of Henry Ruegamer, Tr. Trans., 662.
122. *Windy Boy,* Testimony of Morley Langdon, Tr. Trans., 435, 439, 441–42.
123. *Windy Boy,* Testimony of Gary Howey, Tr. Trans., 733.
124. *Montana v. United States,* 450 U.S. 544.
125. *Windy Boy,* Declaration of C. Adrian Heidenreich, 22.
126. Big Horn County Local Government Study Commission, *Final Report,* 8.
127. U.S. Commission on Civil Rights, *Indian Tribes: A Continuing Quest for Survival,* 1.
128. *Windy Boy,* Testimony of Joe Medicine Crow, Tr. Trans., 113.
129. U.S. Commission on Civil Rights, *Indian Tribes: A Continuing Quest for Survival,* 5.
130. Jim Ruegamer, conversation with author, Sept. 2, 1985.
131. Ibid.
132. *Windy Boy,* Testimony of Jim Ruegamer, Tr. Trans., 332.
133. Ibid. at 335.
134. Pius Real Bird, conversation with author, Sept. 30, 1985.
135. *Windy Boy,* Testimony of James Ruegamer, Tr. Trans., 336–37.
136. *Windy Boy,* Testimony of Leo Hudetz, Tr. Trans., 615.
137. *Windy Boy,* Pl. Exs. 171, 179.
138. *Windy Boy,* Testimony of James Ruegamer, Tr. Trans., 340.
139. *Windy Boy,* Def. Ex. 19.
140. *Windy Boy,* Testimony of James Ruegamer, Tr. Trans., 342–43.
141. *Windy Boy,* Testimony of Leo Hudetz, Tr. Trans., 615–16.
142. *Windy Boy,* Testimony of James Ruegamer, Tr. Trans., 342–44; and "Attention! VOTERS!" July 1982, paid political advertisement, Laurence Koebbe and Edithe McCleary, co-chairmen, Bipartisan Campaign Committee.
143. Pius Real Bird, conversation with author, Sept. 30, 1985.
144. *Windy Boy,* Testimony of Robert Ruegamer, Tr. Trans., 160.
145. *Windy Boy,* Testimony of James Ruegamer, Tr. Trans., 333, 390, 392.
146. *Windy Boy,* Testimony of Janine Windy Boy, Tr. Trans., 221.
147. Pius Real Bird, conversation with author, Sept. 30, 1985.
148. *Windy Boy,* Testimony of Patrick Doss, Tr. Trans., 455–56, 459, 462.
149. *Windy Boy,* Testimony of Janine Windy Boy, Tr. Trans., 230–31.
150. *Windy Boy,* Testimony of Dessie Bad Bear, Tr. Trans., 418–20.
151. *Windy Boy,* Testimony of Tim Bernardis, Tr. Trans., 317.
152. *Windy Boy,* Testimony of Tyrone Ten Bear, Tr. Trans., 507–08.
153. *Windy Boy,* Testimony of Clarence Belue, Tr. Trans., 164–65.
154. *Windy Boy,* Testimony of Gail Small, Tr. Trans., 448–49.

155. *Windy Boy*, Def. Ex. 7, pp. 4–57.

156. *Windy Boy*, Testimony of Gail Small, Tr. Trans., 446.

157. *Windy Boy*, Testimony of Mark Small, Tr. Trans., 473.

158. *Windy Boy*, Testimony of Frank Back Bone, Tr. Trans., 716.

159. *Windy Boy*, Testimony of Mark Small, Tr. Trans., 476–77.

160. *Windy Boy*, Testimony of Joe Floyd, Tr. Trans., 774.

161. *Windy Boy*, 647 F. Supp. at 1011, 1017, 1020.

162. Ibid. at 1008–09, 1013, 1016–18, 1022.

163. *Citizens Equal Rights Alliance v. Johnson*, CV-07-74 BLG-RFC (D. Mont.).

164. Nellie Little Light, conversation with author, June 26, 2007.

165. James Ruegamer, conversation with author, Feb. 2008.

166. The history of the formation of the Fort Belknap Reservation is discussed in chapter 4.

167. *United States v. Blaine County, Montana*, No. CV 99-122-GF-DWM (D. Mont.).

168. Ibid., 363 F.3d 897, 900, 909–11 (9th Cir. 2004).

169. Ibid. at 913–14.

170. For a further discussion of the Blaine County litigation, see McCool, Olson, and Robinson, *Native Vote*, 111–130.

171. The history of the formation of the Fort Peck and Flathead reservations is discussed in chapter 4.

172. *Alden v. Rosebud County Board of Commissioner*, Civ. No. 99-148-BLG (D. Mont. May 10, 2000); *United States v. Roosevelt County Board of Commissioners*, No. 00-CV-54 (D. Mont. Mar. 24, 2000); and *Matt v. Ronan School District*, Civ. No. 99-94 (D. Mont. Jan. 13, 2000).

4. Montana II

1. "Treaty of Fort Laramie of 1851," Sept. 17, 1851, 11 *Stat.* 749.

2. "Treaty of Hell Gate," July 16, 1855, 12 *Stat.* 975.

3. "Lame Bull's Treaty," Oct. 17, 1855, 11 *Stat.* 657.

4. Memorial and Joint Resolution to the Honorable Secretary of the Interior, *Laws of the Territory of Montana, 1st Legislative Assembly* (1864), 721.

5. To the Honorable Senate and House of Representatives of the United States, *General Laws of the Territory of Montana, 4th Sess.* (1867), 268–69.

6. Resolved by the Legislative Assembly of the Territory of Montana, *General Laws of the Territory of Montana, 4th sess.* (1867), 278.

7. Joint Memorial to the Congress of the United States, *General Laws of the Territory of Montana,* 5th Sess. (1869), 119–120.

8. "Treaty between the United States and the Blackfoot Nation of Indians, Etc.," Nov. 16, 1865 (unratified); "Treaty with the Assiniboines, July 18, 1866" (unratified); "Agreement with the Gros Ventre, July 13, 1868" (unratified); and "Treaty with the Blackfoot, Etc.," Sept. 1, 1868 (unratified).

9. *Act of June 5, 1872*, 17 *Stat.* 226.

10. Grant, Executive Order of July 5, 1873.

11. *Act of April 15, 1874*, 18 *Stat.* 28.

12. Hayes, Executive Order of July 13, 1880.

13. *Act of May 15, 1886*, ch. 333, 24 *Stat.* 29, 44.

14. *Act of May 1, 1888*, 25 *Stat.* 113.

15. *United States v. Kipp*, 369 F. Supp. 774, 776 (D. Mont. 1974).

16. Senate Joint Memorial to the Honorable Senate and House, *Laws of the State of Montana, 4th Sess.*, (1895), 65–66; Senate Joint Memorial to the Honorable the Senate and House, *Laws of the State of Montana, 6th Sess.* (1899), 154; and House Joint Memorial to the Senate and the House, *Laws of the State of Montana, 8th Sess.* (1903), 355.

17. Senate Joint Memorial to the Honorable the Senate and House, *Laws of the State of Montana, 6th Sess.* (1899), 155; and Senate Joint Memorial to the Honorable Senate and House, *Laws of the State of Montana, 9th Sess.* (1905), 354.

18. House Joint Memorial No. 1, *Laws of the State of Montana, 10th Sess.* (1907), 592–93.

19. *Flathead Allotment Act*, Pub. L. 159, 33 *Stat.* 302 (1904). See also Taft, "Presidential Proclamation of May 22, 1909," opening the Flathead Reservation to settlement.

20. *Fort Peck Allotment Act*, Pub. L. 177, 35 *Stat.* 558 (1908). See also Wilson, "Presidential Proclamation of July 25, 1913," opening the Fort Peck Reservation to settlement.

21. *Fort Belknap Allotment Act*, ch. 135, 41 *Stat.* 1355 (1921).

22. *Act of May 13, 1896*, ch. 175, 29 *Stat.* 117.

23. *Act of April 30, 1908*, 35 *Stat.* 70, 83–84.

24. *Act of Sept. 7, 1916*, ch. 452, 39 *Stat.* 739.

25. *Blackfeet and Gros Ventre Nations v. United States*, 81 Ct. Cl. 101, 131 (1935).

26. *Act of May 1, 1888*, ch. 213, 25 *Stat.* 113.

27. *Agreement of 1895*, 29 *Stat.* 354, art. 5; and *Act of Mar. 1, 1907*, Pub. L. 154, 34 *Stat.* 1015, 1035–36.

28. *Confederated Salish and Kootenai Tribes v. United States*, 437 F.2d 458, 463, 468, 469 (Ct. Cl. 1971).

29. *Stephens v. Nacey*, 141 P. 649, 651 (Mont. 1914).

30. *Blackfeet et al. Nations v. United States*, 81 Ct. Cl. 101 (1935).

31. *Fort Peck Reservation v. United States*, 18 Ind. Cl. Comm. 241 (1967); *Blackfeet and Gros Ventre Tribes of Indians and Assiniboine Tribes of Indians v. United States*, 19 Ind. Cl. Comm. 361 (1968); and *United States v. Assiniboine Tribes of Indians*, 428 F.2d 1325 (Ct. Cl. 1970).

32. *Confederated Salish and Kootenai Tribes of the Flathead Reservation, Montana v. United States*, 16 Ind. Cl. Comm. 1, 79–80 (1965); and *Confederated Salish and Kootenai Tribes of the Flathead Reservation, Montana v. United States*, 8 Ind. Cl. Comm. 40 (1959).

33. *Confederated Salish and Kootenai Tribes of the Flathead Reservation, Montana v. United States*, 437 F.2d 458 (Ct. Cl. 1971).

34. Senate Joint Memorial no. 7, *Laws of the State of Montana, 27th Sess.* (1941), 473; Senate Joint Memorial no. 3, *Laws of the State of Montana, 31st Sess.* (1949), 662; Senate Joint Memorial no. 1, *Laws of the State of Montana Passed, 32nd Sess.* (1951), 754–55; and House Joint Memorial no. 8, *Laws of the State of Montana, 34th Sess.* (1955), 900–901.

35. *Old Person v. Cooney*, No. CV-96-004-GF (D. Mont.); and *Windy Boy*, Report of C. Adrian Heidenreich, "Perspective on Discrimination against Indians in Montana" (report), Pl. Ex. 73, p. 33.

36. Plaintiffs also challenged redistricting in the area encompassed by the Fort Peck, Fort Belknap, and Rocky Boy Reservations but subsequently withdrew those claims.

37. Constitution of Montana, Art. V, Sec. 14.

38. *Old Person v. Cooney*, Oct. 27, 1998, slip op. at 4–5.

39. Ibid. at 8, 11–12.

40. Ibid. at 5, 11–13.

41. *Old Person v. Cooney*, Pl. Ex. 25, p. 2.

42. Ibid., Pl. Ex. 23, p. 10; and Def. Ex. 515, p. 1931.

43. Ibid., Pl. Ex. 23, p. 17.

44. Ibid., Pl. Ex. 33, p. 3; and Def. Ex. 515, p. 1942.

45. Ibid., Pl. Ex. 38, p. 2.

46. Ibid. at 5.

47. Ibid. at 3.

48. Ibid. at 4.

49. Ibid. at 8.

50. Ibid. at 15–16.

51. Ibid.

52. Ibid., Pl. Exs. 38, 43, 44, 45.

53. Ibid., Pl. Ex. 45.

54. Ibid., Pl. Ex. 43.

55. Ibid.

56. Ibid., Pl. Ex. 47, p. 2.

57. Ibid., Pl. Ex. 4, p. 6.

58. Ibid., Testimony of Seldens Frisbee, Tr. Trans. vol. 7, pp. 1033–34.

59. Ibid., Pl. Ex. 49.

60. Ibid., Pl. Ex. 52.

61. Ibid., Pl. Ex. 52.

62. Ibid., D. Ex. 518, p. 29; and D. Ex. 525.

63. Ibid., D. Ex. 525.

64. Ibid. Pl. Ex. 74, p. 8.

65. Ibid., Pl. Ex. 74.

66. *Elk v. Wilkins*, 112 U.S. 94, 5 S. Ct. 41, 44 (1884). See *Delaware Indians v. Cherokee Nation*, 193 U.S. 127, 144 (1905), in which Indians "are recognized as a distinct

political community"; and *Morton v. Mancari*, 417 U.S. 535, 553–54 (1974), in which Indians are "members of quasi-sovereign tribal entities".

67. *Old Person v. Cooney*, Pl. Ex. 176.

68. Ibid., Pl. Ex. 177.

69. Ibid., Pl. Ex. 46, p. 10.

70. Ibid., Testimony of Joe MacDonald, Tr. Trans., vol. 1, p. 178.

71. Ibid., Testimony of Margaret Campbell, Tr. Trans., vol. 4, p. 650.

72. See http://www.constituionparty.com/ustp-p1.html.

73. *Old Person v. Cooney*, Report of Steven P. Cole, p. 18, table 1; p. 20, table 3.

74. Ibid., Pl. Ex. 77 (Fair Housing Assistance Program, *Final Report*, 1989), 7.

75. Ibid. at 15.

76. House Joint Memorial no. 14, *Laws of the State of Montana, 35th Sess.* (1957), 768–70.

77. Senate Joint Memorial no. 5, *Laws of the State of Montana, 35th Sess.* (1957), 785–86.

78. House Joint Resolution no. 35, *Laws of the State of Montana, 40th Sess.* (1967), 1201–02. See also House Joint Resolution no. 22, *Laws of the State of Montana, 41st Sess.* (1969), 1166–68.

79. House Joint Resolution no. 57, *Laws of the State of Montana, 44th Sess.* (1975), 1737–38.

80. *Old Person v. Cooney*, 230 F.3d 1113, 1121, 1127, 1128–29 (9th Cir. 2000).

81. *Old Person v. Cooney*, Oct. 27, 1998, slip op. at 39.

82. Ibid. at 42, 44.

83. Ibid. at 51.

84. *Old Person v. Cooney*, 230 F.3d at 1131.

85. Ibid. at 1121, 1127, 1129, 1130–31.

86. Ibid. at 1130.

87. *Old Person v. Cooney*, on remand sub nom. *Old Person v. Brown*, Pl. Ex. 3, p. 14.

88. *Old Person v. Brown*, Pl. Ex. 3, 20, 28.

89. Ibid., Expert Report for Susan Byorth Fox, Attachment 1.

90. *Old Person v. Brown*, 182 F. Supp.2d 1002, 1012 (D. Mont. 2002).

91. Ibid., 312 F.3d 1036, 1039, 1046, 1050 (9th Cir. 2002).

92. Ibid., Response to Appellants' Petition for Rehearing and Rehearing En Banc, Exhibit (Adopted House and Senate District, December 2002).

93. Joint Legislative Committee on Districting and Apportionment, *Minority Report on SR 2 and HR 3.*

94. Resolution of the House of Representatives of Montana Rejecting the Legislative Plan That the Montana Districting and Apportionment Commission Submitted (Mont. H. Res. 3), 1–2.

95. Resolution of the Senate of Montana Rejecting Legislative Plan the Montana Districting and Apportionment Commission Submitted, (Mont. S. Res. 2), 1–2.

96. Montana House of Representatives, Bill for an Act Entitled "Act Providing a Population Criterion for Redistricting of Legislative Districts," House Bill no. 309, 58th Legislature, 2003.

97. *Brown v. Montana Districting and Reapportionment Commission*, No. ADV-2003-72 (Mont. 1st Jud. Dist. Ct. Lewis & Clark County).

98. *Old Person v. Brown*, 540 U.S. 1016 (2003).

99. Governor's Office of Indian Affairs, American Indian Caucus, 2007 Legislature, http://governor.mt.gov; and "Native Americans Are Finding Their Voice in Government," *Los Angeles Times*, April 22, 2007, http:www.latimes.com.

5. South Dakota

1. Gibbon, *Sioux*, 2–6; Ostler, *Plains Sioux and U.S. Colonialism*, 21–23.

2. "Treaty with the Sioux, Sept. 23, 1805," in *Laws Relating to Indian Affairs*, 316.

3. "Treaty with the Teeton Tribe, 1815," 7 *Stat.* 125; "Treaty with the Sioux of the Lakes, 1815," 7 *Stat.* 126; "Treaty with the Sioux of St. Peter's River, 1815," 7 *Stat.* 127; "Treaty with the Yankton Sioux, 1815," 7 *Stat.* 128; and "Treaty with the Laway Tribe, 1815," 7 *Stat.* 136. Also see "Treaty with the Sioux, 1816," 7 *Stat.* 143.

4. "Treaty with the Teton, Yancton, and Yanctonies Sioux, 1825," 7 *Stat.* 250; "Treaty with the Sioune and Oglala Tribes, 1825," 7 *Stat.* 252; and "Treaty with the Hunkpapa Band of the Sioux Tribe, 1825," 7 *Stat.* 257.

5. Ostler, *Plains Sioux and U.S. Colonialism*, 32.

6. "Treaty with the Sioux, 1837," 7 *Stat.* 538.

7. Ostler, *Plains Sioux and U.S. Colonialism*, 34.

8. "First Treaty of Fort Laramie, 1851,"11 *Stat.* 749. Also, see *United States v. Sioux Nation of Indians*, 448 U.S. 371, 374 n. 1 (1980).

9. "Treaty with the Sioux—Sisseton and Wahpeton Bands, 1851," 10 *Stat.* 949; "Treaty with the Sioux—Mdewakanton and Wahpakoota Bands, 1851," 10 *Stat.* 954; and "Treaty with the Yankton Sioux, 1858," 11 *Stat.* 743.

10. *Act of Congress of March 2, 1861*, 12 *Stat.* 239, sec. 5.

11. Act to Provide Temporary Government for the Territory of Dakota, *Dakota Territorial Laws 1862*, 21. See also Act to Regulate Elections (January 14), *Dakota Territorial Laws 1864*, ch. 19, §51; and Act to Establish a Civil Code, *Dakota Territorial Laws 1866*, §26, 1, 4 (providing that Indians cannot vote or hold office).

12. Act to Prevent Indians from Trespassing upon Ceded Lands, *Dakota Territorial Laws 1862*, ch. 46, 319.

13. An Act Respecting Jurors, *Dakota Territorial Laws 1862*, ch. 52, 374.

14. Memorial and Joint Resolution [Relative to a Proposed Treaty with the Brule Sioux Indians], *Dakota Territorial Laws 1862*, ch. 99, 503.

15. Memorial to Congress Asking for a Treaty with Chippewa Indians of Red Lake and Pembina on the Red River of the North, *Dakota Territorial Laws 1862*, ch. 100, 505.

16. Preface to an Act to Provide a Temporary Government for the Territory of Dakota, *Dakota Territorial Laws 1862*, preface.

17. Bryant and Murch, *History of the Great Massacre*, 479; and Gibbon, *Sioux*, 110.

18. *Forfeiture Act of February 16, 1863*, 12 *Stat.* 652.

19. Memorial Praying for the Establishment of a Military [Post] on the Big Sioux River, *Dakota Territorial Laws 1863*, ch. 66, 267.

20. Memorial and Joint Resolution to the Secretary of War, Commanding Generals Pope and Sully, *Dakota Territorial Laws 1866*, ch. 49, 565; Memorial Praying for the Establishment of a Military Post on the Vermillion River, *Dakota Territorial Laws 1866*, ch. 51, 569; and Memorial to the Secretary of War Praying for the Erection of a Military Post at the North Base of the Black Hills of Dakota, *Dakota Territorial Laws 1866*, ch. 50, 566.

21. Memorial and Joint Resolution Relative to Appointment of an Indian Agent, *Dakota Territorial Laws 1866*, ch. 38, 551.

22. Act Prohibiting Harboring of Indians within the Organized Counties, *Dakota Territorial Laws 1866*, ch. 19, 482.

23. See, e.g., "Treaty with the Sioux—Sans Arcs Band, 1865," 14 *Stat.* 731; and "Treaty with the Sioux—Upper Yanktonai Band, 1865," 14 *Stat.* 743.

24. Brown, *Bury My Heart at Wounded Knee*, 119.

25. Olson, *Red Cloud and the Sioux Problem*, 27–51; and Brown, *Bury My Heart at Wounded Knee*, 117–42.

26. Memorial to Secretary of War, Asking Further Protection from Indian Invasions, *Dakota Territorial Laws 1867*, ch. 16, 119; Memorial to Gen. U. S. Grant, relative to Indian Matters in the Northwest, *Dakota Territorial Laws 1867*, ch. 17, 120; Memorial to Commissioner of General Land Office Praying for Extension of Public Land Surveys out the White River Valley to Pine Lands of Black Hills, *Dakota Territorial Laws 1867*, ch. 20, 125; *Dakota Territorial Laws 1867*, 125; and Memorial to Secretary of War, Praying for Erection of Military Post at North Base of Back Hills, *Dakota Territorial Laws 1867*, ch. 21, 127.

27. "Second Treaty of Fort Laramie of 1868," 15 *Stat.* 635.

28. Olson, *Red Cloud and the Sioux Problem*, 76–81; and Brown, *Bury My Heart at Wounded Knee*, 140–41.

29. Memorial and Joint Resolution Relative to Indian Affairs in Dakota Territory, *Dakota Territorial Laws 1868*, 275.

30. Memorial to Secretary of War, Praying for Construction of Military Post in the Red River Valley, *Dakota Territorial Laws 1868*, 285.

31. Memorial to President of the U.S. Relative to Removal of the Pembina Band of Chippawa [*sic*] Indians to White Earth Agency, *Dakota Territorial Laws 1871*, 585; and Memorial to President of the U.S. Relative to the Pembina Band of Chippewa Indians, *Dakota Territorial Laws 1873*, 218.

32. Memorial to Congress, Asking the Valuable Lands Lying West of the Missouri River, May Be Opened to Settlement, *Dakota Territorial Laws 1873*, 204.

33. Memorial to the Honorable, the Senate and House of Representatives of the U.S., *Dakota Territorial Laws 1875*, 347.

34. Brown, *Bury My Heart at Wounded Knee*, 268–72.

35. Welch, *Killing Custer*, 149–77; Gibbon, *Sioux*, 116–17; Brown, *Bury My Heart at Wounded Knee*, 278–82; and Ostler, *Plains Sioux and U.S. Colonialism*, 338–60.

36. *Act of Feb. 28, 1877*, 19 *Stat.* 254; *United States v. Sioux Nation of Indians*, 448 U.S. at 383 n. 14; and Brown, *Bury My Heart at Wounded Knee*, 283–84.

37. *United States v. Sioux Nation of Indians*, 448 U.S. at 424.

38. Brown, *Bury My Heart at Wounded Knee*, 283.

39. Ostler, *Plains Sioux and U.S. Colonialism*, 83; and Gibbon, *Sioux*, 117.

40. Brown, *Bury My Heart at Wounded Knee*, 394; and Welch, *Killing Custer*, 257–58.

41. Joint Resolution Praying for Speedy Passage of Law Providing for Opening of Devil's Lake Indian Reservation, *Dakota Territorial Laws 1887*, 402; and Joint Resolution and Memorial for Passage of Pending Bill Opening to Settlement a Portion of the Sioux Indian Reservation in Dakota, *Dakota Territorial Laws 1889*, 178.

42. *Act of March 2, 1889*, 25 *Stat.* 896.

43. *Rosebud Sioux Tribe v. Kneip*, 430 U.S. 584, 589 (1977).

44. Memorial to Congress, Praying for Opening to Settlement under Homestead Law of the Yankton Indian Reservation, *South Dakota Laws 1890*, 327; and Memorial to Congress, Praying for Opening to Settlement under Homestead Law of the Crow Creek Indian Reservation, *South Dakota Laws 1890*, 327.

45. Ostler, *Plains Sioux and U.S. Colonialism*, 243–49.

46. Accounts of the Sioux and their battles with settlers and the army are told in many places, e.g., Lazarus, *Black Hills*; Carlson, *Plains Indians*; Brown, *Bury My Heart at Wounded Knee*; Ostler, *Plains Sioux and U.S. Colonialism*; Gibbon, *Sioux*; Andrist, *Long Death*; and Russell, "Indians and Soldiers of the American West."

47. *Act of April 23, 1904*, 33 *Stat.* 254; *Act of March 2, 1907*, 34 *Stat.* 1230; and *Act of May 30, 1910*, 36 *Stat.* 448. See *Rosebud Sioux Tribe v. Kneip*, 430 U.S. at 585.

48. Proposing an Amendment to the Constitution (March 8, 1890), *South Dakota Laws 1890*, ch. 45, 118. The South Dakota Constitution of 1899 provided that voting was restricted to male resident "Citizens of the United States" (S.Dak. Constitution, Article VII, sec. 1, Elections and Rights of Suffrage). State statutory law provided that "Indians resident within this state . . . cannot vote or hold office" (S.Dak. Stat. sec. 3424, Parsons 2d rev. ed., 1901).

49. Ibid.

50. Providing for Elections in Unorganized Counties (March 12, 1895), *South Dakota Laws 1895*, ch. 84, 88.

51. Providing for the Manner of Selecting Jurors, *South Dakota Laws 1901*, ch. 168, 270.

52. Relating to Instruction in Other than the English Language, *South Dakota Laws 1921*, ch. 203, 307; and Act Revising School Laws of the State of South Dakota, *South Dakota Laws 1931*, 108, 175.

53. Joint Resolution and Memorial Requesting Congress to Treat with Indians for Cession and Opening for White Settlement that Portion of Rosebud Indian Reservation Lying Within Boundaries of Gregory County, *South Dakota Laws 1901*, ch. 147, 248.

54. *Rosebud Sioux Tribe v. Kneip*, 430 U.S. at 615–16.

55. *Indian Citizenship Act of 1924, 8 U.S. Code* §1401(a)(2).

56. *Buckanaga v. Sisseton Independent School District*, 804 F.2d 469, 474 (8th Cir. 1986).

57. *Little Thunder v. South Dakota*, 518 F.2d 1253, 1255–57 (8th Cir. 1975).

58. *United States v. South Dakota*, 636 F.2d 241, 244–45 (8th Cir. 1980).

59. *South Dakota Codified Laws* §§16.0701-0706 (1939).

60. *Bone Shirt v. Hazeltine*, 336 F. Supp.2d 976, 1024 (D. S.Dak. 2004).

61. Act of Mar. 27, 1973, *South Dakota Laws 1973*, ch. 70, 111.

62. *Voting Rights Act of 1965—Extension*, Pub. L. 94-73, *Federal Register* 41 (Jan. 5, 1976): 784.

63. Ibid. (July 20, 1976): 30002. Eighteen counties in the state are currently required to conduct bilingual elections. See chapter 2.

64. *South Carolina v. Katzenbach*, 383 U.S. 301, 328 (1966).

65. Janklow, William. *1977 South Dakota Opinions of the Attorney General* 175; 1977 Westlaw 36011 (S.Dak. Attorney General).

66. *United States v. Tripp County, South Dakota*, Civ. No. 78-3045 (D. S.Dak. Feb. 6, 1979), ordering the state to submit reapportionment plan for preclearance; and *United States v. South Dakota*, Civ. No. 79-3039 (D. S.Dak. May 20, 1980), enjoining implementation of law revising system of organized and unorganized counties absent preclearance.

67. U.S. Bureau of the Census, *Census 2000 Summary File 3*.

68. South Dakota Advisory Committee to the U.S. Commission on Civil Rights, *Native Americans in South Dakota*, 6.

69. Ibid. at 6–7.

70. U.S. Bureau of the Census, *Census 2000 Summary File 3*.

71. Ibid.

72. *Thornburg v. Gingles*, 478 U.S. 30, 69 (1986).

73. *Buckanaga*, 804 F.2d at 474.

74. South Dakota Advisory Committee to the U.S. Commission on Civil Rights, *Native Americans in South Dakota*, 38–9.

75. *Buckanaga*, 804 F.2d at 473–76.

76. For a discussion of the settlement and the use of cumulative voting, see Wolfley, "Jim Crow, Indian Style," 200.

77. *American Horse v. Kundert*, Civ. No. 84-5159 (D. S.Dak. Nov. 5, 1984).

78. *Black Bull v. Dupree School District*, Civ. No. 86-3012 (D. S.Dak. May 14, 1986).

79. *Fiddler v. Sieker*, No. 85-3050 (D. S.Dak. Oct. 24, 1986).

80. South Dakota Task Force on Indian–State Government Relations, *April Staff Report*, 17, 25.

81. *Bone Shirt*, 336 F. Supp.2d at 980-81.

82. South Dakota Advisory Committee to the U.S. Commission on Civil Rights, *Native American Participation in South Dakota's Political System*, 35, 52.

83. *Bone Shirt*, 336 F. Supp.2d at 981.

84. An Act to Redistrict the Legislature, *South Dakota Laws 1991, 1st Spec. Sess.*, ch. 1, p. 1 codified as amended at *South Dakota Code of Laws* §§2-2-24 through 2-2-31.

85. Ibid. §5, 1, 5.

86. *Emery v. Hunt*, 272 F.3d 1042, 1044 (8th Cir. 2001).

87. An Act to Eliminate the Single-Member House Districts in District 28, *South Dakota Laws 1996*, ch. 21, 45, amending *South Dakota Code of Laws* §2-2-28.

88. Minutes of (S.Dak.) House State Affairs Committee, *House State Affairs Committee Minutes, 1/29/96*, p. 5. The name of the amending act was HB 1282.

89. *Emery*, 272 F.3d at 1044.

90. Constitution of South Dakota, Article III, Sec. 5, Legislative Reapportionment.

91. *In re Legislative Reapportionment*, 246 N.W. 295, 297 (S.Dak. 1933).

92. *In re State Census*, 62 N.W. 129, 130 (S.Dak. 1895). Other states have similar constitutional provisions, and courts have interpreted them in the same way. See, e.g., *Exon v. Tiemann*, 279 F. Supp. 603, 608 (D. Neb. 1967), per curiam, three-judge court, interpreting the Nebraska Constitution; *Legislature of California v. Deukmejian*, 669 P.2d 17 (Cal. 1983), per curiam; and *In re Interrogatories*, 536 P.2d 308 (Colo. 1975).

93. South Dakota Legislative Research Council, Issue Memorandum 95-36, Sept. 12, 1995, p. 6.

94. South Dakota Legislative Research Council, Issue Memorandum 99-12, Apr. 29, 1998, p. 5.

95. *Emery*, Civ. No. 00-3008 (D. S.Dak.), Report of Steven P. Cole, tables 1 & 2. Dr. Cole used two standard techniques for determining the existence of cohesion and racial bloc voting: BERA and homogeneous precinct analysis.

96. Ibid.

97. Ibid., table 3.

98. Ibid., tables 1 & 3.

99. *Clarke v. City of Cincinnati*, 40 F.3d 807, 457 (6th Cir. 1994), "[w]hen white bloc voting is 'targeted' against black candidates, black voters are denied an opportunity enjoyed by white voters, namely, the opportunity to elect a candidate of their own race"; and *RWTAAAC v. Sundquist*, 29 F. Supp.2d 448, 457 (W.D. Tenn. 1998), affirmed, 209 F.3d 835 (6th Cir. 2000).

100. *Emery*, Civ. no. 00-3008 (D. S.Dak.), Report of Steven P. Cole, table 3.

101. South Dakota Advisory Committee to the U.S. Commission on Civil Rights, *Native Americans in South Dakota*, 3.

102. *Emery*, 615 N.W.2d 590, 597 (S.Dak. 2000).

103. *Bone Shirt*, 336 F. Supp.2d at 1028.

104. Ibid. at 984–85, 991, 1011, 1040.

105. Ibid. at 984.

106. Ibid. at 985.
107. Ibid.
108. *Bone Shirt*, 200 F. Supp.2d 1150, 1154 (D. S.Dak. 2002).
109. *Bone Shirt*, 336 F. Supp.2d at 1019, 1025–26.
110. Ibid. at 1026.
111. Ibid.
112. Ibid.
113. Ibid.
114. Ibid.
115. Ibid., quoting Rep. Stanford Addelstein.
116. Ibid. at 1028.
117. Ibid. at 1035.
118. Ibid. at 1030.
119. Ibid. at 1029–30.
120. Ibid. at 1031.
121. Ibid. at 1046.
122. Ibid. at 1041, 1046.
123. Ibid. at 1032, 1036.
124. Ibid. at 1035–36, 1046, comments of Rep. John Teupel.
125. Ibid. at 1035.
126. Ibid. at 1032.
127. Ibid.
128. Ibid. at 1033.
129. Ibid.
130. Ibid.
131. *Rogers v. Lodge*, 458 U.S. 613, 627 (1982).
132. Act to Allow Municipalities to Establish Individual Contests When More than One Seat is Vacant in a Municipal Election, *South Dakota Laws 1996*, ch. 59, 104; and Act to Provide for Secondary Election, *South Dakota Laws 1985*, ch. 110, 295.
133. *City of Rome, Georgia v. United States*, 446 U.S. 156, 183–84 (1980).
134. *Quick Bear Quiver v. Hazeltine*, Civ. No. 02-5069 (D. S.Dak.).
135. Ibid., Dec. 27, 2002, slip op. at 3.
136. For a discussion of noncompliance with Section 5 by covered jurisdictions in the South, see McDonald, "1982 Extension of Section 5."
137. *United States v. Day County, South Dakota*, No. CV 99-1024 (D. S.Dak. June 16, 2000).
138. *Weddell v. Wagner Community School District*, Civ. No. 02-4056 (D. S.Dak. Mar. 18, 2003).
139. *United States v. Blackpipe State Bank*, No. 93-5115 (D. S.Dak.).
140. *Wilcox v. City of Martin*, No. 02-5021 (D. S.Dak.).
141. *Cottier v. City of Martin*, 445 F.3d 1113, 1116 (8th Cir. 2006).
142. Ibid. at 1117

143. Ibid. at 1115–16.

144. *Cottier*, 446 F. Supp.2d 1175, 1184–88 (D. S.Dak. 2006).

145. *Cottier*, 475 F. Supp.2d 932, 936 (D. S.Dak. 2007).

146. *Kirkie v. Buffalo County, South Dakota*, Civ. No. 03-3011 (D. S.Dak. Feb. 12, 2004).

147. *Blackmoon v. Charles Mix County*, Civ. 05-4017 (D. S.Dak.).

148. Decennial Revision of Commission Districts—At-Large Elections, *South Dakota Code of Laws* §7-8-10.

149. South Dakota House Bill 1265.

150. *Quick Bear Quiver v. Nelson*, 387 F. Supp.2d 1027, 1031, 1034 (D. S.Dak. 2005).

151. *Blackmoon v. Charles Mix County*, 2005 Westlaw 2738954 (D. S.Dak.).

152. *Blackmoon v. Charles Mix County*, Dec. 4, 2007, consent decree.

153. Grace Chung Becker, acting assistant attorney general, to Sara Frankenstein, Feb. 11, 2008.

154. Ibid. at 2–3.

6. Colorado

1. *Cuthair v. Montezuma-Cortez, Colorado School District No. RE-1*, 7 F. Supp.2d 1152 (D. Colo. 1998).

2. *Evans v. Cornman*, 398 U.S. 419 (1970); and Duke W. Dunbar, attorney general of Colorado, to Byron A. Anderson, secretary of state, July 31 1970, Archives, Colorado Attorney General (who wrote that in light of *Evans v. Cornman*, "Colorado cannot deny the right of suffrage to a bona-fide domiciliary of the state simply because he lives on a federal reservation").

3. Act of Dec. 7, 1859, *1860 Jefferson Territory Session Laws*, ch. 13, §5, 198.

4. Act of Nov. 6, 1861, *1861 Colorado Territory Session Laws*, §1, 72, 73; Act of Feb. 18, 1881, *1881 Colorado Session Laws*, §1, 113, 114, reenacting citizenship and residency qualifications for voting; and Colorado Constitution, Art. VII, sec. 1 (1918), limiting the franchise in all state elections to citizens of the United States.

5. Opinion of the Attorney General of Colorado, no. 343, *1921–1922 Colorado Attorney General Biennial Report*, 133–37.

6. Byron G. Rogers, attorney general of Colorado, to D. H. Wattson, superintendent, Consolidated Ute Agency, Nov. 24, 1936, Archives of Colo. Attorney General. See also Opinion of the Attorney General of Colorado, no. 1323–48, *1947–1948 Colorado Attorney General Biennial Report*, 142, which said that "[p]ersons residing within the confines of . . . land over which the United States has exclusive jurisdiction" are not residents of Colorado "within the meaning of our election laws."

7. Opinion of the Attorney General of Colorado, no. 60-3444, *1959–1960 Colorado Attorney General Biennial Report*, 79.

8. Colorado Senate Joint Memorial no. 3, *1966 Colorado Session Laws*, 241.

9. "Treaty with the Utah," Sept. 9, 1849, 9 *Stat.* 984. The history of the Utes and their settlement on various reservations is recounted in *Cuthair*, 7 F. Supp.2d at 1155–61.

10. Smith, *Birth of Colorado*, 75.

11. *Weekly Rocky Mountain (Colo.) News*, Apr. 24, 1861 and June 27, 1860; and Svaldi, *Sand Creek and the Rhetoric of Extermination*, 147.

12. Svaldi, *Sand Creek and the Rhetoric of Extermination*, 164–65; *Cuthair*, Report of Richard N. Ellis, 4; and *Rocky Mountain (Colo.) News*, Mar. 24, 1863, and Mar. 26, 1863.

13. Memorial of Aug. 15, 1862, *1862 Colorado Territorial Session Laws*, 155.

14. "Tabequache Treaty," Mar. 25, 1864, 13 *Stat.* 673.

15. Smith, *Birth of Colorado*, 210.

16. *Cuthair*, Report of Richard N. Ellis, 6; and *Rocky Mountain (Colo.) News*, Aug. 10, 1864.

17. *Rocky Mountain (Colo.) News*, April 9, 1863, and August 31, 1864; and Athearn, *Coloradans*, 73.

18. *Cuthair*, Report of Richard N. Ellis, 6; and *Rocky Mountain (Colo.) News*, Aug. 10, 1864.

19. U.S. Congress, Joint Committee on the Conduct of the War, testimony of John S. Smith.

20. Andrist, Long Death, 89.

21. Kennedy, "Colorado Press and the Red Man," 75.

22. *Cuthair*, Report of Richard N. Ellis, 8, citing "Notes and Documents," *New Mexico Historical Review*26 (April 1951): 156–57.

23. Joint Memorial of Feb. 8, 1865, *1865 Colorado Territorial Session Laws*, 149.

24. Joint Memorial of Feb. 5, 1866, *1866 Colorado Territorial Session Laws*, 180.

25. Joint Memorial and Resolution of Jan. 10, 1867, *1867 Colorado Territorial Session Laws*, 152.

26. *Cuthair*, Report of Richard N. Ellis, 8; and *Central City (Colo.) Register*, Jan. 5, 1865; Jan. 8, 1865; Jan. 11, 1865; and Jan. 18, 1865.

27. *Cuthair*, Report of Richard N. Ellis, 9; and *(Colo.) Trans.*, June 5, 1867.

28. *Cuthair*, Report of Richard N. Ellis, 9; and *Rocky Mountain (Colo.) News*, Oct. 2, 1867.

29. *Cuthair*, Report of Richard N. Ellis, 9; and *(Pueblo, Colo.) Chieftain*, Sept. 17, 1868.

30. "Treaty with the Ute," Mar. 2, 1868, 15 *Stat.* 619.

31. Delaney, *Ute Mountain Utes*, 45.

32. Vandenbusche and Smith, *Land Alone*.

33. *Act of June 8, 1872*, ch. 354, 17 *Stat.* 339.

34. Memorial of Jan. 26, 1872, *1872 Colorado Territorial Session Laws*, 227.

35. Board of Indian Commissioners, *Fourth Annual Report*, 94.

36. *Cuthair*, Report of Richard N. Ellis, 19–20; and *Denver (Colo.) Tribune*, Mar. 26, 1873.

37. "Brunot Agreement with Ute Nation—1874," ch. 136, 18 *Stat.* 36 (1874).

38. Delaney, *Ute Mountain Utes*, 46.

39. Memorial of Jan. 28, 1876, *1876 Colorado Territorial Session Laws*, 203.

40. *Cuthair*, Report of Richard N. Ellis, 25.

41. *Act of May 3, 1878*, ch. 87, 20 *Stat.* 48.

42. Brown, *Bury My Heart at Wounded Knee*, 376; and Smith, *Song of the Hammer and Drill*, 46.

43. Brown, *Bury My Heart at Wounded Knee*, 388.

44. *Cuthair*, Report of Richard N. Ellis, 27.

45. Ibid. at 28; and *Denver (Colo.) Daily Times*, Oct. 14, 1879.

46. *Cuthair*, Report of Richard N. Ellis 28; and *Dolores (Colo.) News*, Oct. 25, 1879.

47. *Cuthair*, Report of Richard N. Ellis, 30; and *Rocky Mountain (Colo.) News*, Apr. 24, 1880.

48. *Act of June 15, 1880*, ch. 223, 21 *Stat.* 199.

49. Teller, *Resolution on Opening Ute Lands for Homesteading*, S. Misc. Doc. 63, 3.

50. Delaney, *Ute Mountain Utes*, 65.

51. Joint Memorial of Mar. 11, 1885, *1885 Colorado Session Laws*, 406; Joint Memorial of Feb. 16, 1887, *1887 Colorado Session Laws*, 456; and House Joint Memorial I, *1887 Colorado Session Laws*, 466.

52. Parkhill, *Last of the Indian Wars*, 38–40.

53. *Act of May 1, 1888*, ch. 213, §4, 25 *Stat.* 113, 133.

54. *Act of Feb. 20, 1895*, ch. 113, 28 *Stat.* 677.

55. Delaney, *Ute Mountain Utes*, 73–74.

56. Chapin, *Land of the Cliff-Dwellers*, 107–08, 113.

57. Delaney, *Ute Mountain Utes*, 79.

58. Jenet Mason to Indian Agent, Ignacio, Colo., Nov. 27, 1917, NA, Rocky Mountain Region, Denver, Colo.

59. *Cuthair*, Report of Richard N. Ellis, 55.

60. Board of Indian Commissioners, *23rd Annual Report*, 16–17.

61. Delaney, *Ute Mountain Utes*, 92, 95.

62. Order of Restoration, Southern Ute Indian Reservation, *Federal Register* 2, (1937): 1403; and Confederated Bands of the Ute Tribe, Order of Restoration, *Federal Register* 2 (1937): 1404. See also *Act of June 28, 1938*, Pub. L. 75-754, 52 *Stat.* 1209, modifying the land restoration orders of the secretary of the interior; declaring all lands within the 1868 Ute Reservation north of the Ute Mountain Ute Reservation to be the absolute property of the United States; prohibiting the restoration of any more territory north of the existing reservation; and conferring jurisdiction on the U.S. Court of Claims to hear cases arising from federal mismanagement of Ute lands.

63. *Confederated Bands of Ute Indians v. United States*, 117 Ct. Cl. 433 (1950). In 1962 the Indian Claims Commission held that the consideration paid to the Utes for lands ceded in the Brunot agreement was so inadequate as to be unconscionable. *Confederated Bands of Ute Indians v. United States*, 11 Ind. Cl. Comm. 180, 303 (1962).

64. Delaney, *Ute Mountain Utes*, 101.

65. Ibid. at 100; James R. Mosier to Gov. Edwin C. Johnson, 1955, Governor's Papers, Box 66081, File: Report on Ute Indian Liquor Problem to Gov. Johnson by James Mosier; and Arthur Cuthair, interview with author, April 1, 1889.

66. Delaney, *Ute Mountain Utes*, 100, 106–07; and *Cuthair*, Report of Amanda Bandy, 10.

67. *Cuthair*, Supplemental Report of Richard N. Ellis, 3–4.

68. Ibid. at 2–4, 7.

69. Ibid. at 8–9.

70. *Cuthair*, Deposition of Richard Ellis, 57.

71. *Cuthair*, Supplemental Report of Richard N. Ellis, 15–21.

72. Ibid. at 22–24.

73. Delaney, *Ute Mountain Utes*, 106–07.

74. Carrier, *West of the Divide*, 160–61.

75. Montezuma-Cortez School District No. RE-1, PAC, *Recommendations and Responses* (Feb. 9, 1994). The board, however, has more recently adopted a mission statement that includes "explor[ing] and embrac[ing] cultural differences." See www.cortez.k12.co.us.

76. Clyde Benally, conversation with author, April 1996.

77. *Cuthair*, Report of Amanda Bandy, 7.

78. U.S. Bureau of the Census, *1990 Census*, Summary Tape File 3.

79. *Cuthair*, 7 F. Supp.2d at 1155.

80. The quotes from Arthur Cuthair are taken from *Cuthair*, Deposition of Arthur Cuthair, Feb. 26, 1997, and from the author's interview notes.

81. *Cuthair*, 7 F. Supp.2d at 1163.

82. The quotes from Jocelyn Dutchie are taken from the author's interview notes.

83. The quotes from Angela Badback are taken from *Cuthair*, Deposition of Angela Badback, Feb. 27, 1997, and from the author's interview notes.

84. The quotes from Gloria Tom are taken from *Cuthair*, Deposition of Gloria Tom, Feb. 27, 1997, and from the author's interview notes.

85. The quotes from Joselina Lopez Arthur are taken from *Cuthair*, Deposition of Joselina Lopez, Feb. 27, 1997, and from the author's interview notes.

86. The quotes from Marjorie Soto are taken from *Cuthair*, Deposition of Marjorie Soto, Feb. 26, 1997, and from the author's interview notes.

87. The quotes from Janice Colorow are taken from *Cuthair*, Deposition of Janice Colorow, Feb. 26, 1997, and from the author's interview notes.

88. The quotes from Julian Lopez are taken from *Cuthair*, Deposition of Julian Lopez, Feb. 27, 1997, and from the author's interview notes.

89. The quotes from Sarah Hatch are taken from *Cuthair*, Deposition of Sarah Hatch, Feb. 26, 1997, and from the author's interview notes.

90. *Cuthair*, Report of Amanda Bandy, 9.

91. The quotes from Ernest House are taken from *Cuthair*, Deposition of Ernest House, Feb. 27, 1997, and the author's interview notes.

92. *Cuthair*, Deposition of William R. Thompson, 7.

93. *Cuthair*, Deposition of George Schumpelt, 22.

94. Ibid. at 39.

95. *Cuthair*, Deposition of Allan Whitmer, 25.

96. *Cuthair*, 7 F. Supp.2d at 1156–57, 1160–62, 1169–70.

97. Ibid. at 1161.

98. *Cortez (Colo.) Journal*, "Fire Kills Former Ute Tribal Leader," May 6, 2006.

7. Nebraska

1. *Allen v. State Board of Elections*, 393 U.S. 544, 569 (1969).

2. *United States v. Thurston County, Nebraska*, Civ. No. 78-0-380 (D. Neb. May 9, 1979).

3. *Stabler v. County of Thurston, Nebraska*, 8:CV93-00394 (D. Neb. 1993).

4. See generally Fletcher, *Historical Sketch of the Omaha Tribe*.

5. "Treaty with the Omaha, Oct. 15, 1836," 7 *Stat.* 524.

6. "Treaty with the Omaha, Mar. 16, 1854," 10 *Stat.* 1043.

7. Jedediah Morse, quoted in NaNations, "Native American Nations, The Winnebago Indian Tribe," http://www.nanations.com/dishonor/winnebago-indian-tribe.htm.

8. "Treaty with the Winnebago, Aug. 1, 1829," 7 *Stat.* 323.

9. "Treaty with the Winnebago, Sept. 15, 1832," 7 *Stat.* 370.

10. "Treaty with the Winnebago, Nov. 1, 1837," 7 *Stat.* 544.

11. J. D. Stevens, quoted in NaNations, "Native American Nations, The Winnebago Indian Tribe," http://www.nanations.com/dishonor/winnebago-indian-tribe.htm.

12. "Treaty with the Winnebago, Oct. 13, 1846," 9 *Stat.* 878.

13. "Treaty with the Winnebago of Feb. 27, 1855," 10 *Stat.* 1172.

14. "Treaty with the Winnebago of Apr. 15, 1859," 12 *Stat.* 1101.

15. Little Hill, quoted in Nabokov, *Native American Testimony*, 163.

16. "Treaty with the Omaha, March 6, 1865," 14 *Stat.* 667; and "Treaty with the Winnebago, Mar. 8, 1865," 14 *Stat.* 671. And see Fowler, *Columbia Guide to American Indians*, 189.

17. *The Omaha Tribe of Nebraska v. United States*, 6 Ind. Cl. Comm. 730, 759 (1958); and *The Omaha Tribe of Nebraska v. United States*, 7 Ind. Cl. Comm. 572-c (1959).

18. *The Winnebago Tribe and Nation of Indians v. United States*, 8 Ind. Cl. Comm. 78 (1959); *The Winnebago Tribe and Nation of Indians v. United States*, 16 Ind. Cl. Comm. 81 (1965); *The Winnebago Tribe and Nation of Indians v. United States*, 23 Ind. Cl. Comm. 464 (1970); and Lurie, "Winnebago," 705.

19. *Act to Organize the Territories of Nebraska and Kansas* (May 30, 1854), NA, pp. 32–33.

20. Act Regulating Elections (Jan. 1855), *Laws, Joint Resolutions, and Memorials of the Territory of Nebraska, 1st General Assembly*, 176.

21. Act to Prevent Use of Intoxicating Liquors among Indians, or Half Breeds (Jan. 26, 1856), *Laws of Territory of Nebraska, 2nd Sess.* (1856), , 186.

22. Act to Make Selling or Giving Away of Fire-arms to Any Indian Not a Citizen, a Felony (Apr. 8, 1891), *Nebraska General Laws*, ch. 29; Act to Amend Sections 7159 and 7160 of Chapt XXII Entitled "Liquors" (April 6, 1909), *Nebraska General Laws*, ch. 71; Act to Make Selling or Giving Away Intoxicating Drinks, to an Indian, an Offense (April 8, 1913), *Nebraska General Laws*, ch. 67; Act to Regulate Restrict and Prohibit Manufacture, Sale, Giving Away of Intoxicating Liquors, *Nebraska Laws*, 1917, ch. 187; Act to Amend Sec. 38 Chap 116, Relating to Liquors; to Prohibit Sale Thereof to Indians, *Nebraska Session Laws*, 1937, ch. 125; and Act to Amend Sec. 53-338, Relating to Liquor Control to Prohibit Selling, Giving Away of Alcoholic Liquor to Minors or Persons Who Are Mentally Incompetent, *Nebraska Session Laws*, 1943, ch. 121.

23. Act to Amend Sec. 310, Relative to Competency of Witnesses (Feb. 15, 1864), *Nebraska General Laws*, 129.

24. "Practices in Justices' Court," in *Treatise on Powers and Duties*, 255.

25. Act to Amend Sec. 23 of Chap. 17, Entitled "Elections" (Feb. 18, 1867), *Nebraska General Laws*, 20.

26. Memorial and Joint Resolution to Congress (Feb. 26, 1873), *Memorials and Joint Resolutions*, 100.

27. Census; Legislative Apportionment, *Proceedings of the Nebraska Constitutional Convention 1919–1920*, art. XIX, sec. 2.

28. *Elk v. Wilkins*, 112 U.S. 94, 109 (1884).

29. Ibid. at 100.

30. Ibid. at 122–23.

31. Act to Provide for and Regulate Marriages and Divorces Among Certain Indians and to Define Rights of Indian Children (Apr. 8, 1913), *Nebraska General Laws*, ch. 68.

32. Milner, *With Good Intentions*, 183.

33. Du Bamo Thi, quoted in Nabokov, *Native American Testimony*, 239, which cited Fletcher and La Flesche, *Omaha Tribe*, 636.

34. *Omaha Allotment Act of 1882*, 22 *Stat.* 341, ch. 434.

35. *General Allotment Act of 1887*, 24 *Stat.* 388.

36. Otis, *Dawes Act and the Allotment of Indian Lands*, 128.

37. Quoted in McDonell, "Land Policy on the Omaha Reservation," 401.

38. Ibid. at 401–402, 405–406.

39. Nabokov, *Native American Testimony*, 238.

40. Hoxie, *Encyclopedia of North American Indians*, 683.

41. Confederation of American Indians, *Indian Reservations*, 135, 138.

42. U.S. Bureau of the Census, *1990 Census*, Pub. L. 94-171.

43. NaNations, "Omaha Tribe of Nebraska: Community Environmental Profile," http://www.mnisose.org/profiles/omaha.htm (accessed Nov. 2008).

44. NaNations, "Winnebago Tribe of Nebraska, Community Environmental Profile," http://www.mnisose.org/profiles/winnebag.htm (accessed Nov. 2008).

45. *Act to Confer Jurisdiction on California, Minnesota, Nebraska, Oregon, and Wisconsin* (Aug. 15, 1953), 67 *Stat.* 588.

46. *Omaha Tribe of Nebraska v. Village of Walthill*, 334 F. Supp. 823, 828 (D. Neb. 1971).

47. *State (Neb.) v. Goham*, 187 Neb. 35, 187 N.W.2d 305 (1971).

48. *Omaha Tribe of Nebraska v. Village of Walthill*, 460 F.2d 1327 (8th Cir. 1972).

49. Winnebago Tribe of Nebraska, "Resolution no. 74-35."

50. Village of Walthill, Nebraska, "Resolution, Dec. 9, 1975."

51. Thurston County, Nebraska, "Resolution, Jan. 27, 1976."

52. "Concerned Citizens Council, Inc.," *Walthill (Neb.) Citizen*, April 8, 1976.

53. *Stabler v. County of Thurston*, Deposition of Hollis Stabler 67.

54. "Church Studies Unique Problem," *Walthill (Neb.) Citizen*, June 17, 1976.

55. *Stabler*, Deposition of Hollis Stabler 67.

56. Editorial, *Walthill (Neb.) Citizen*, Feb. 24, 1977.

57. Editorial, *Walthill (Neb.) Citizen*, May 12, 1977.

58. "The Citizen Speaks Out" (editorial), *Walthill (Neb.) Citizen*, May 26, 1977.

59. Winnebago Tribe of Nebraska, "Resolution no. 85-31."

60. Thurston County, Nebraska, "Resolution no. 168" (March 5, 1985).

61. "Winnebago Tribe's Retrocession Idea Is Opposed by County Board," *Pender (Neb.) Times*, April 18, 1985.

62. Sen. James Goll, speaking to the Nebraska Legislature Judiciary Committee, *Hearing on Legislative Resolution 57*, on April 17, 1985, pp. 6–11, 93.

63. Nebraska Legislature Judiciary Committee, *Hearing on Legislative Resolution 57*, pp. 38, 106.

64. Sheriff Clyde Storie, letter to the editor, *Pender (Neb.) Times*, April 18, 1985, and May 1, 1986.

65. Cora L. Jones, acting superintendent, to Sen. Peter Hoagland, April 16, 1985, U.S. Dept. of Interior, BIA, Winnebago Agency, Neb.; and Resolution by the Nebraska Legislature Regarding Winnebago Retrocession, *Legislative Journal of Nebraska* (1986), vol. 1, 91–92.

66. Interchurch Ministries of Nebraska, Inc., "American Indian in Nebraska," 16.

67. *Stabler,* Deposition of Hollis Stabler, 63.

68. Ibid. at 81.

69. Ibid. at 64.

70. *Stabler,* Sharon Freemont, Tr. Trans., 129.

71. Village of Walthill, Nebraska, "Resolution, Mar. 10, 1981."

72. *Stabler*, Deposition of Sharon Freemont, 20–21.

73. Ibid. at 36–37.

74. *Stabler,* Deposition of Hollis Stabler, 84.

75. See, e.g., *Stabler*, Deposition of Roger Tremayne, 13; Deposition of Steve Dunn, 19–20; and Deposition of Mark Casey, 42–43.

76. *Stabler*, Sharon Freemont, Tr. Trans., 126.

77. *Stabler*, Mark Kemling, Tr. Trans., 318, 322–23.

78. *Stabler*, Deposition of Duward Morgan, 10.

79. *Stabler*, Mark Kemling, Tr. Trans., 325, 332.

80. *Stabler*, Tr. Trans., 329, 336.

81. *Stabler*, Mark Kemling, Tr. Trans., 333, 346–48.

82. *Stabler*, Deposition of Mark Casey, 39–40.

83. *Stabler*, Deposition of Steve Dunn, 29–31.

84. *Stabler*, Deposition of Roger Tremayne, 28.

85. *Stabler*, Sharon Freemont, Tr. Trans., 127; Charles Merrick, Tr. Trans., 303–04; and Edwin McCauley, Tr. Tran., 362.

86. *Stabler*, Sharon Freemont Tr. Trans., 127; and Charles Merrick, Tr. Trans., 303.

87. *Stabler*, Edwin McCauley, Tr. Trans. 374.

88. *Johnson v. Village of Walthill*, Case no. NEB 1-84/85-9-8730.

89. Ibid., Case no. NEB 1-84/85-12-9030.

90. State of Nebraska Equal Opportunity Commission, *Conciliation Agreement, June 1985.*

91. Equal Opportunity Commission, Determinations, Feb. 5, 1986, Feb. 11, 1986.

92. *Parker v. Village of Walthill and Cameron Arthur*, CV90-0-238 (D. Neb. 1990); and *Saunsoci v. Cameron Arthur and the Village of Walthill*, Case No. 8601 (Dist. Ct. of Thurston County).

93. *Stabler,* Deposition of Hollis Stabler, 86, 97.

94. *Stabler*, Deposition of Roger Tremayne, 49–50.

95. *Stabler*, Deposition of Hollis Stabler, 94.

96. Ibid. at 108, 111.

97. Ibid. at 91, 98–99.

98. U.S. Bureau of the Census, *1990 Census*, Summary Tape File 3.

99. Aberdeen Area Indian Health Service, *Mortality Charts*, September 1994; and Annie E. Casey Foundation, *Kids Count Data Book*, 1993.

100. *Stabler v. County of Thurston*, Pl. Ex. 157.

101. Ibid., Def. Ex. 597.

102. *Thornburg v. Gingles*, 478 U.S. 30, 69 (1986).

103. *Buckanaga v. Sisseton Independent School District*, 804 F.2d 469, 475 (8th Cir. 1986).

104. *Old Person v. Cooney*, 230 F.3d 1113, 1129 (9th Cir. 2000). In accordance, see *Windy Boy v. County of Big Horn*, 647 F. Supp. 1002, 1016-017 (D. Mont. 1986), which states that "[r]educed participation and reduced effective participation of Indians in local politics can be explained by many factors . . . but the lingering effects of past discrimination is certainly one of those factors".

105. Michael Simpson, conversation with author, July 28, 2008.

106. *Stabler*, Gordon Henderson, Tr. Trans., 200.

107. *Stabler*, Charles Merrick, Tr. Trans., 307–08, 312.

108. Ibid. at 311–12.

109. *Stabler*, Sharon Freemont, Tr. Trans., 133.

110. *Zimmer v. McKeithen*, 485 F.2d 1297, 1307 (5th Cir. 1973).

111. *Stabler,* Keith Maheny, Tr. Trans., 387–88; Deposition of Roger Tremayne, 6–9; and Deposition of M. Jeannie Gaer, 5.

112. *Stabler,* Raymond L. Storm, Tr. Trans., 659–63.

113. *Stabler,* Steve Dunn, Tr. Trans., 726–27.

114. *Stabler v. County of Thurston*, Aug. 29, 1995, slip op. at 13–14.

115. Ibid. at 14–16.

116. *Stabler v. County of Thurston*, 129 F.3d 1015 (8th Cir. 1997).

117. Ibid. at 1022–23.

118. Ibid. at 95–97.

119. Vida Stabler, quoted in "Keeping Alive a Language and a Culture," *JournalStar (Lincoln, Neb.)*, Aug. 26, 2004.

120. Robin Ridington, "Omaha Survival: A Vanishing Indian Tribe That Would Not Vanish," University of Nebraska, Lincoln, Institute of Museum and Library Services, http://omahatribe.unl.edu/etexts/oma.0020/index.html.

121. Vida Stabler, conversation with author, Aug. 2008.

122. Ridington and Hastings, *Blessing For a Long Time*.

123. Dennis Hastings, conversation with author, Aug. 2008.

124. U.S. Bureau of the Census, *Census 2000,* Summary File 1.

8. Wyoming

1. *Large v. Fremont County, Wyoming*, No. 05-CV-270J (D. Wyo.).

2. *Thornburg v. Gingles*, 478 U.S. 30, 36–37 (1986).

3. "Treaty of Fort Laramie of 1851," 11 *Stat.* 749. See Washburn, *American Indian and the United States*, 4:2477.

4. "Treaty of Fort Wise," 12 *Stat.* 1163.

5. Madsen, *Shoshone Frontier and the Bear River Massacre*, 190–92; *Utah History Encyclopedia*, s.v. "Bear River Massacre, Utah," http://www.OnlineUtah.com (accessed Jan. 6, 2009); and *Large*, Report of Martha Hipp, 9.

6. "First Treaty of Fort Bridger of July 2, 1863," 18 *Stat.* 685. See *United States v. Shoshone Tribe of Indians*, 304 U.S. 111, 113 (1938); and *Shoshone Tribe of Indians v. United States*, 299 U.S. 476, 485–86 (1937).

7. Andrist, *Long Death*, 89; Kennedy, "The Colorado Press and the Red Man," 75; and Hoig, *Sand Creek Massacre*.

8. Russell, "Indians and Soldiers of the American West," 222; and *Large*, Report of Martha Hipp, 10.

9. *Large*, Martha Hipp, Tr. Trans., 219.

10. "Second Treaty of Fort Bridger of July 3, 1868," 15 *Stat.* 673.

11. *United States v. Shoshone Tribe of Indians*, 304 U.S. at 113; and *Shoshone Tribe of Indians*, 299 U.S. at 485.

12. *An Act to Provide a Temporary Government for the Territory of Wyoming* (July 25, 1868), 15 *Stat.* 178.

13. "South Pass Had Uneasy Beginning With 1868 Marked By Indian Raids," *Wyoming State Journal*, June 29, 1950; and Stamm, *People of the Wind River*, 46–47.

14. *Shoshone Tribe of Indians*, 299 U.S. at 486–91.

15. "The Famous Raid on the Arapahoe Indians in April 1870 as Related by One Who Took a Principal Part," *Lander Evening Post*, Nov. 17, 1921; *Large*, Martha Hipp, Tr. Trans., 260–61; and Stamm, *People of the Wind River*, 57, 244.

16. "Brunot Cession Agreement of 1872," 18 *Stat.* 291 (ratified in 1874); and *Shoshone Tribe of Indians*, 299 U.S. at 487.

17. *Large*, Report of Martha Hipp, 7.

18. *Shoshone Tribe of Indians*, 299 U.S. at 486–91; *Eastern Shoshone Tribe v. Northern Arapaho Tribe*, 926 F. Supp. 1024, 1027 (D. Wyo. 1996); and "W.I.N.D.S. Project: Wind River Indian Needs Determination Study."

19. Council Joint Memorial and Resolution no. 11, *Session Laws of Wyoming Territory 1879*, ch. 94, 160.

20. Council Resolution and Joint Memorial no. 15, *Session Laws of Wyoming Territory 1879*, ch. 99, 166.

21. House Joint Resolution and Memorial no. 2, *Session Laws of Wyoming Territory 1879*, ch. 102, 167.

22. Wyoming Constitution, *Session Laws of Wyoming, 1890*, 51.

23. Disarmament of the Indians, *Session Laws of Wyoming, 1890*, 413.

24. Indian Depredation Claims, *Session Laws of Wyoming, 1890*, 211.

25. Claims Arising from Indian Depredation, *Session Laws of Wyoming, 1890*, 419.

26. *Large*, "Minutes of Meeting, Fremont County Commission," Mar. 4, 1895.

27. Ibid., Mar. 28, 1895.

28. *Wyoming v. Owl Creek Irrigation District*, 753 P.2d 76, 83 (Wyo. 1988).

29. *Articles of Agreement on 21 April 1896 between James McLaughlin, on the Part of the U.S., and Shoshone and Arapaho Tribes* (hereafter cited as *First McLaughlin Agreement of 1896)*, 30 *Stat.* 93 (ratified in 1897); and *Wyoming v. Owl Creek Irrigation District*, 753 P.2d at 83–84.

30. *Act to Ratify and Amend Agreement with Indians Residing on Shoshone or Wind River Indian Reservation* (hereafter cited as *Second McLaughlin Agreement of 1905)*, 33 *Stat.* 1016.

31. *Wyoming v. Owl Creek Irrigation District*, 753 P.2d at 84.

32. Ibid.

33. *Large*, Report of Martha Hipp, 12.

34. Stamm, *People of the Wind River*, 238–39.

35. *Wyoming v. Owl Creek Irrigation District*, 753 P.2d at 84.

36. U.S. Senate, Subcommittee of the Committee on Public Lands and Surveys, *Statement of John Herrick, Assistant to the Commissioner, Indian Service*, testimony of John Herrick, p. 602.

37. Memorandum to Commissioner Sells, quoting extract from letter from Arapahoe Reservation, Wyoming, May 13, 1914, NA, Rocky Mountain Region.

38. Ibid., quoting extract from letter from Arapahoe Reservation, Wyoming, Sept. 10, 1914, NA, Rocky Mountain Region.

39. J. Norris, superintendent Shoshone Agency, to commissioner of Indian Affairs, Jan. 20, 1915, NA, Rocky Mountain Region.

40. Ibid., Dec. 4, 1915.

41. *Large*, Martha Hipp, Tr. Trans., 238–39; and *Large*, Pl. Exs. 242–57 (photos of Indian tents and shacks on the Wind River Reservation from the 1930s).

42. C. H. Asbury, superintendant of Crow Agency, to R. P. Haas, superintendant of Ft. Washakie, June 9, 1924, NA, Rocky Mountain Region.

43. R. P. Haas to C. H. Asbury, June 26, 1924, quoting sec. 9, art. 6, *Wyoming Compiled Statutes* (Annotated 1910), NA, Rocky Mountain Region.

44. *Large*, Sara Wiles, Tr. Trans., 1132–33.

45. *Large*, Gary Collins, Tr. Trans., 574.

46. *Large*, Report of Martha Hipp, 41.

47. Ibid. at 32, and *Large*, Martha Hipp, Tr. Trans., 241.

48. Act of Feb. 5, 1943, *1943 Wyoming Session*, ch. 27, 25; and Election Law Revision Act, 1951 *Wyoming Session*, ch. 127, 197.

49. Act of Feb. 27, 1971, *1971 Wyoming Sessions*, ch. 178, 236.

50. *Large*, Martha Hipp, Tr. Trans., 241.

51. *Large*, Patricia Bergie, Tr. Trans., 654.

52. *Large*, Emma Lucille McAdams, Tr. Trans., 996–97.

53. *Large*, James Large, Tr. Trans., 1057–58.

54. *Large*, Betty Friday, Tr. Trans., 1112.

55. *Large*, Sara Wiles, Tr. Trans., 1127–28.

56. Ibid. at 1126–27.

57. *Large*, Keja Whiteman, Tr. Trans., 1495, 1517, 1522–23, 1535–36.

58. *Large*, Betty Friday, Tr. Trans., 1117.

59. *Large*, Ivan Posey, Tr. Trans., 946–47.

60. Ibid. at 957–59.

61. *Large*, Michelle Hoffman, Tr. Trans., 1092–93, 1096, 1100.

62. *Large*, Richard Brannan, Tr. Trans., 882.

63. Ibid. at 878–79.

64. *Large*, Helsha Acuna, Tr. Trans., 1314–15.

65. Ibid. at 1315–17.

66. Ibid. at 1325, 1327–28.

67. *Large*, Tom Throop, Tr. Trans., 1183–84.

68. *Large*, Todd Guenther, Tr. Trans., 1219.

69. *Large*, Valerie Thomas, Tr. Trans., 1248–49.
70. *Large*, John Vincent, Tr. Trans., 1748.
71. *Large*, Deposition of Gary Jennings, 36, 38.
72. *Large*, Deposition of Lanny Applegate, 17, 26.
73. *Large*, Douglas Thompson, Tr. Trans., 1402.
74. *Large*, Martha Hipp, Tr. Trans., 199, 272, 289.
75. Stamm, *People of the Wind River*, 234; *Large*, Report of Martha Hipp, 18; *Large*, Martha Hipp, Tr. Trans., 221; *Large*, Pl. Ex. 19 (photo of gravestone of Hayes Friday); and *Large*, Pl. Exs. 17 and 18 (photos of the graveyard at the Carlisle Indian School).
76. *Large*, Richard Brannan, Tr. Trans., 885.
77. *Large*, Deposition of Burton Hutchinson, 15.
78. J. D. C. Atkins, *Annual Report of the Commissioner of Indian Affairs* (1887), reprinted in Prucha, *Documents of United States Indian Policy*, 175.
79. *Large*, Report of Martha Hipp, 19–22; *Large*, Martha Hipp, Tr. Trans., 225, 227; and *Large*, Todd Guenther, Tr. Trans., 1221.
80. *Large*, Tr. Trans., Todd Guenther, 1221.
81. Ibid. at 1224.
82. *Large*, Martha Hipp, Tr. Trans., 229.
83. *Large*, Deposition of Burton Hutchinson, 8, 10–12, 31, 33.
84. Ibid. at 12–14, 19–20.
85. *Large*, Patricia Bergie, Tr. Trans., 650–51.
86. *Large*, James Large, Tr. Trans., 1038–39.
87. *Large*, Report of Martha Hipp, 30.
88. *Large*, Martha Hipp, Tr. Trans., 233–34.
89. *Large*, Richard Brannan, Tr. Trans., 886.
90. *Large*, Deposition of Burton Hutchinson, 22–23.
91. *Large*, Patricia Bergie, Tr. Trans., 652–56.
92. *Large*, Gary Collins, Tr. Trans., 574, 576–78.
93. *Large*, Deposition of Patrick Goggles, 15–16, 18–19.
94. *Large*, Betty Friday, Tr. Trans., 1110–12.
95. *Large*, Report of Martha Hipp, 37.
96. *Large*, Richard Brannan, Tr. Trans., 865–68.
97. *Large*, Report of Martha Hipp, 38; and *Large*, Martha Hipp, Tr. Trans., 250.
98. *Large*, Report of Martha Hipp, 39.
99. *Large*, Martha Hipp, Tr. Trans., 250.
100. *Large*, Ivan Posey, Tr. Trans., 930–33.
101. *Large*, James Large, Tr. Trans., 1037–41.
102. *Large*, Sara Wiles, Tr. Trans., 1129.
103. *Large*, Todd Guenther, Tr. Trans., 1218–19.
104. *Large*, Betty Friday, Tr. Trans., 1114–16.
105. *Large*, Report of Martha Hipp, 39; and *Large*, Martha Hipp, Tr. Trans., 251.
106. *Large*, Martha Hipp, Tr. Trans., 253.

107. *Large,* James Large, Tr. Trans., 1053.

108. Ibid.

109. *Large,* Report of Martha Hipp, 45–48; and *Large,* Martha Hipp, Tr. Trans., 253–54, 256.

110. *Large,* Report of Martha Hipp, 51, 59; and *Large,* Martha Hipp, Tr. Trans., 257.

111. *Large,* Report of Martha Hipp, 60; and *Large,* Martha Hipp, Tr. Trans., 235, 259–60.

112. *Large,* Report of Martha Hipp, 52.

113. *Large,* Michelle Hoffman, Tr. Trans., 1084–85, 1092–93.

114. Ibid. at 1084–86, 1093–94, 1106.

115. *Large,* Sara Wiles, Tr. Trans., 120–21.

116. *Large,* Michelle Hoffman, Tr. Trans., 1103–04, 1086.

117. *Large,* Todd Guenther, Tr. Trans., 1206–07.

118. Ibid. at 205–06, 1208–10.

119. Ibid. at 1210, 1212–13.

120. Ibid. at 1219.

121. *Large,* Sara Wiles, Tr. Trans., 1153.

122. *Wyoming State Journal,* ". . . and One Who Missed!" Sept. 21, 1970.

123. *Large,* Sara Wiles, Tr. Trans., 1130–31.

124. House Joint Memorial no. 4, *1941 Wyoming Sessions,* 216.

125. Sen. H. H. Schwartz to Sen. Elmer Thomas, Jan. 8, 1942, with letter from Mrs. L. A. Phillips to Sen. H. H. Schwartz, Dec. 24, 1941, NA, Rocky Mountain Region, Denver, Colo.

126. Sen. H. H. Schwartz to Sen. Lawrence Raymond, Jan. 9, 1942, with letter from Sen. Lawrence Raymond to Sen. H. H. Schwartz, Dec. 26, 1941, NA, Rocky Mountain Region, Denver, Colo.

127. Wind River Indian Reservation Land Owners' Council to Congress of the U.S. (1941), NA, Rocky Mountain Region, Denver, Colo.

128. Sen. H. H. Schwartz to Sen. Elmer Thomas, Dec. 31, 1941, NA, Washington, D.C.

129. *Large*, Report of Garth Massey, 8; *Large*, Garth Massey, Tr. Trans., 59–60; and Stamm, *People of the Wind River,* 243.

130. *Wyoming v. Owl Creek Irrigation District*, 753 P.2d at 100–01.

131. *Large*, Gary Collins, Tr. Trans., 594–95.

132. *Large*, John Vincent, Tr. Trans., 1759.

133. *Large*, Garth Massey, Tr. Trans., 47–48, 50, 56.

134. *Large*, Report of Garth Massey, 9–11, 15–17, 19–23, 25–26; and Garth Massey, Tr. Trans., 50, 66, 68, 72–75.

135. *Large*, Report of Garth Massey, 28.

136. *Large*, Garth Massey, Tr. Trans., 77–78.

137. *Large*, Deposition of Gary Jennings, 32.

138. *Large*, Scott Ratliff, Tr. Trans., 698.

139. *Large*, Ivan Posey, Tr. Trans., 941.
140. *Large*, Helsha Acuna, Tr. Trans., 1302, 1304–05, 1321.
141. *Large*, Valerie Thomas, Tr. Trans., 1249–50, 1252.
142. *Large*, John Vincent, Tr. Trans., 1741–42, 1746–47.
143. *Thornburg v. Gingles*, 478 U.S. at 37.
144. *Large*, Julie Freese, Tr. Trans., 1714, 1717–18.
145. *Large*, "Fremont County, Wyoming, 2005 EEO-4 Report."
146. *Large*, Deposition of Gary Jennings, 61.
147. *Large*, Julie Freese, Tr. Trans., 1722–23.
148. Ibid. at 1725.
149. *Large*, Deposition of Gary Jennings, 62.
150. *Large*, Patrick Hickerson, Tr. Trans., 1642–43.
151. *Large*, Douglas Thompson, Tr. Trans., 1474–75.
152. *Large*, "Minutes of Meeting, Fremont County Commission, Feb. 18, 1972," 557; and Report of Martha Hipp, 58.
153. *Large*, "Minutes of Meeting, Fremont County Commission, Feb. 18, 1972," 557.
154. *Large*, Report of Martha Hipp, 58; and Martha Hipp, Tr. Trans., 247–48.
155. *Large*, Martha Hipp, Tr. Trans., 248.
156. *Large*, Valerie Thomas, Tr. Trans., 1246; and Julie Freese, Tr. Trans., 1698–99.
157. *Large*, "Minutes of Meeting, Fremont County Commission, Feb. 16, 1993," 104.
158. *Large*, Scott Ratliff, Tr. Trans., 705–07.
159. *Large*, "Minutes of Meeting, Fremont County Commission, Nov. 12, 2002"; and Stephanie Kessler, Tr. Trans. 745–50.
160. *Large*, Stephanie Kessler, Tr. Trans., 750–53, 757–58.
161. *Large*, "Minutes of Meeting, Fremont County Commission, Dec. 12, 2002."
162. *Large*, Deposition of Gary Jennings, 56.
163. Ibid. at 33–34.
164. Senate Joint Resolution no. SJ0002 (2006).
165. *Large*, Gary Jennings, Deposition, 63.
166. *Large*, Richard Brannan, Tr. Trans., 906.
167. *Large*, Ivan Posey, Tr. Trans., 964, 985.
168. *Large*, Richard Brannan, Tr. Trans., 906.
169. *Large*, Douglas Thompson, Tr. Trans., 1476.
170. *Large*, Patrick Hickerson, Tr. Trans., 1625, 1637.
171. *Large*, Valerie Thomas, Tr. Trans., 1237, 1240–41, 1252.
172. *Large*, Deposition of Gary Jennings, 10–11, 23–25, 27–29, 31.
173. *Large*, Deposition of Lanny Applegate, 9–10, 12, 14–15, 22–23.
174. *Large*, Douglas Thompson, Tr. Trans., 1437–41, 1468, 1470.
175. *Large*, Patrick Hickerson, Tr. Trans., 1634–35, 1637.
176. *Large*, Valerie Thomas, Tr. Trans., 1246–47, 1263.
177. *Large*, Deposition of Patrick Goggles, 105, 108.

178. National Economic Research Associates, "Preliminary Estimate of Revenues Derived."

179. *Large*, Gary Collins, Tr. Trans., 605–06.

180. *Large*, Report of Martha Hipp, 58.

181. *Thornburg v. Gingles*, 478 U.S. at 48 n. 15.

182. *Large*, Keja Whiteman, Tr. Trans., 1500.

183. Ibid. at 1519, 1526–27.

184. *Large*, James Large, Tr. Trans., 1065.

185. Senate Committee on the Judiciary, *Voting Rights Act Extension*, S. Rep. 417, 29 n.115, 1982, quoting *Zimmer v. McKeithen*, 485 F.2d 1297, 1307 (1973).

186. *Thornburg v. Gingles*, 478 U.S. at 76, where a challenged plan "generally works to dilute the minority vote, it cannot be defended on the ground that it sporadically and serendipitously benefits minority voters".

187. *Large*, Reports of Steven P. Cole, Pl. Ex. 239, table 2, Pl. Ex. 240, table 2.

188. Ibid.

189. Ibid.

190. Ibid.

191. *Large*, Reports of Steven P. Cole, summary table A4; and Steven P. Cole, Tr. Trans., 142–45.

192. *Large*, William Cooper, Tr. Trans., 28; and Patrick Hickerson, Tr. Trans., 1642.

193. *Large*, Gary Collins, Tr. Trans., 608; Scott Ratliff, Tr. Trans., 697, 710; Richard Brannan, Tr. Trans., 884–85; Ivan Posey, Tr. Trans., 952–53; and Emma Lucille McAdams, Tr. Trans., 1010–11.

194. *Large*, James Large, Tr. Trans., 1061, 1072; and Deposition of Gary Jennings, 34.

195. *Large*, Michelle Hoffman, Tr. Trans., 1080–84.

196. *Large*, Tom Throop, Tr. Trans., 1182–83; and John Vincent, Tr. Trans., 1741–42, 1757.

197. *Thornburg v. Gingles*, 478 U.S. at 37.

198. *Large*, Scott Ratliff, Tr. Trans., 697–98, 701.

199. *Large*, Deposition of Patrick Goggles, 91.

200. *Large*, Emma Lucille McAdams, Tr. Trans., 1009–10, 1017.

201. *Large*, Gary Collins, Tr. Trans., 600–03.

202. *Large*, Valerie Thomas, Tr. Trans., 1238–40, 1242, 1244–46.

203. *Large*, John Vincent, Tr. Trans., 1752.

204. *Thornburg v. Gingles*, 478 U.S. at 37.

205. *Large*, James Large, Tr. Trans., 1061; and Emma Lucille McAdams, Tr. Trans., 1008.

206. *Large*, Deposition of Gary Jennings, 42; Douglas Thompson, Tr. Trans., 1468–69; and Patrick Hickerson, Tr. Trans., 1638–40.

207. *Thornburg v. Gingles*, 478 U.S. at 37.

208. Composition; Election for Increasing the Number; Term; Quorum; Election for Districting; Procedures, *Wyoming Statutes* §18-3-501.

209. *Large*, Patrick Hickerson, Tr. Trans., 1629–31.
210. *Large*, Deposition of Lanny Applegate, 39, 41–42.
211. *Large*, Douglas Thompson, Tr. Trans., 1441–42.
212. *Large*, John Vincent, Tr. Trans., 1761–63.
213. *Large*, Keith Gaddie, Tr. Trans., 565–67.
214. Ibid. at 567.
215. *Large*, Report of Garth Massey, 29.
216. *Large*, Tom Throop, Tr. Trans., 1170, 1179–81.
217. *Large*, Deposition of Patrick Goggles, 75–76, 78.
218. *Large*, Sarah Gorin, Tr. Trans., 1280–81.
219. *Large*, Scott Ratliff, Tr. Trans., 711, 739.
220. *Large*, Patricia Bergie, Tr. Trans., 651–52; and Garth Massey, Tr. Trans., 60.
221. *Large*, Sara Wiles, Tr. Trans., 1123–24, 1146–51; and Pl. Exs. 258–68.
222. *Large v. Fremont County*, Jan. 26, 2007. See, e.g., *United States v. Blaine County*, 363 F.3d 897 (9th Cir. 2004).
223. *Large*, Emma Lucille McAdams, Tr. Trans., 997, 999–1001.
224. Ibid. at 1005–07.
225. *Large*, Scott Ratliff, Tr. Trans., 695–96.
226. Ibid. at 729.
227. *Large*, Gary Collins, Tr. Trans., 578–79, 582, 587–89.
228. *Large*, James Large, Tr. Trans., 1050–52; and author's interview notes.
229. *Large*, Deposition of Patrick Goggles, 131.
230. *Large*, James Large, Tr. Trans., 1038.
231. *Large*, Richard Brannan, Tr. Trans., 872; and Deposition of Burton Hutchinson, 10, 34.
232. *Large*, Patricia Bergie, Tr. Trans., 648; Ivan Posey, Tr. Trans., 929; and Garth Massey, Tr. Trans., 51.
233. *Large*, Patricia Bergie, Tr. Trans., 673, 689; and Garth Massey, Tr. Trans. 45.
234. *Large*, Richard Brannan, Tr. Trans., 873; and James Large, Tr. Trans., 1065.
235. See, e.g., *United States v. Blaine County, Montana,* where two separate tribes, the Gros Ventre and Assiniboine, occupy the Fort Belknap Reservation in Blaine County.
236. See, e.g., *Windy Boy v. County of Big Horn*, 647 F. Supp. 1002, 1004 (D. Mont. 1986), where two separate tribes and reservations, the Crow and Northern Cheyenne, occupy Big Horn County; and *Stabler v. County of Thurston*, 129 F.3d 1015, 1018 (8th Cir. 1997), where two separate tribes and reservations, the Omaha and Winnebago, occupy Thurston County.

9. Increasing Importance of the Indian Vote

1. *Emery v. Hunt*, Civ. No. 00-3008 (D. S.Dak.), Defendants' Response, 26.
2. *McMillan v. Escambia County*, 748 F.2d 1037, 1045 (11th Cir. 1984).

3. *Hendrix v. McKinney*, 460 F. Supp. 626, 632 (M.D.Ala. 1978).

4. *Little Thunder v. South Dakota*, 518 F.2d 1253, 1255 (8th Cir. 1975).

5. Ibid. at 1256.

6. *United States v. South Dakota*, 636 F.2d 241, 244–45 (8th Cir. 1980).

7. *Windy Boy v. County of Big Horn*, 647 F. Supp. 1002, 1021 (D. Mont. 1986).

8. *Cuthair v. Montezuma-Cortez, Colorado School Dist. No. RE–1*, 7 F. Supp.2d 1152, 1161 (D. Col. 1998).

9. *United States v. Marengo County Commission*, 731 F.2d 1546, 1568, 1574 (11th Cir. 1984).

10. *Teague v. Attala County, Miss.*, 92 F.3d 283, 294–95 (5th Cir. 1996). Other courts have similarly rejected "apathy" as the cause for low minority voter political participation, e.g., *Whitfield v. Democratic Party of State of Arkansas*, 890 F.2d 1423, 1431 (8th Cir. 1989); and *Kirksey v. Board of Supervisors of Hinds County, Miss.*, 554 F.2d 139, 145, and n. 13 (5th Cir. 1977), rejecting the apathy defense and listing past discrimination, socioeconomic disparities, and bloc voting as causes for nonregistration.

11. *South Carolina v. Katzenbach*, 383 U.S. 301, 308 (1966).

12. *Thornburg v. Gingles*, 478 U.S. 30, 47 (1986).

13. *Bone Shirt v. Hazeltine*, 336 F. Supp.2d 976, 1022 (D. S.Dak. 2004).

14. First American Education Project, *Native Vote 2004*, 37.

15. "Indian Vote Could Be the Difference," *Great Falls (Mont.) Tribune*, Nov. 1, 2006.

16. Quoted in "NCAI to Launch Updated Native Vote Web Site," *Indian Country Today*, Jan. 11, 2008.

17. Quoted in "Native Americans Are finding Their Voice in Government," *Los Angeles Times*, Apr. 22, 2007.

18. Ibid.

19. Quoted in "The Indian Vote: When Candidates Come Calling," *Special Report of Reznet News (Univ. of Mont.)*, Apr. 8, 2008, http://reznetnews.org.

20. "American Indians Seize Moment to Make Political Voices Heard," *Denver Post*, June 18, 2008.

21. "Crow Tribe Adopts Candidate in Historic Visit," *Billings (Mont.) Gazette*, May 20, 2008.

22. Ibid.

23. "Talking to Tribes: Democratic Hopeful Courts Montana's Native Vote," *Missoulian (Missoula, Mont.)*, May 28, 2008.

24. "The Indian Vote: When Candidates Come Calling," *Special Report of Reznet News*, Apr. 8, 2008; and "Dems Woo Native American Vote," *Politico*, June 18, 2008, http://reznetnews.org.

25. "A Clear Winner: Indians," *Indian Country Today*, June 6, 2008.

26. Quoted in "American Indians Seize Moment to Make Political Voices Heard," *Denver Post*, June 18, 2008.

27. City of Riverton and the Northern Arapaho and Eastern Shoshone Tribes, *Intergovernmental Agreement between the City of Riverton.*

28. Riverton City Council, *City Council Meeting of April 29, 2008*, DVD.

29. Riverton City Council, *City Council Meeting of June 3, 2008*, DVD.

30. Ibid.

31. *Plains Commerce Bank v. Long Family Land*, 128 S. Ct. 2709, 2719 (2008).

32. Riverton City Council, *City Council Meeting of June 3, 2008*, DVD.

33. McCool, "Indian Voting," 129.

34. Quoted in McCool, Olson, and Robinson, *Native Vote*, 177. And see "60 Years Ago in Arizona, Indians Won Right to Vote," *Tucson (Ariz.) Citizen*, July 25, 2008.

35. "Indian Vote Could Be the Difference," *Great Falls (Mont.) Tribune*, Nov. 1, 2006.

36. "Native Americans Are Finding Their Voice in Government," *Los Angeles Times*, April 22, 2007.

37. Morris, "Black Electoral Participation," 164, 180; and McCool, Olson, & Robinson, *Native Vote*, 165–75.

38. Browning, Marshall, and Tabb, *Protest Is Not Enough*, 141, 168.

39. Hamilton, "Political Access, Minority Participation," 15.

40. Yatrakis, "Delivering the Goods," 15.

41. Keech, *Impact of Negro Voting*, 2, 93.

42. "22 Natives from 11 States, 16 Tribes Win Elections," *Reznet News (Univ. of Mont.)*, Nov. 5, 2008, http://reznetnews.org.

43. "Browning's Juneau New Schools Superintendent," *Great Falls Tribune*, Nov. 5, 2008.

44. "22 Natives from 11 States, 16 Tribes Win Elections," *Reznet News (Univ. of Mont.)*, Nov. 5, 2008, http://reznetnews.org.

Bibliography

The bibliography is organized in sections as follows: federal treaties and statutes in chronological order; other federal documents; court decisions; territorial, state, and municipal memorials, laws, and enactments in chronological order; opinions of state attorneys general by state and in chronological order; depositions, trial transcripts, exhibits, and witness interviews by case; and other sources.

Federal Treaties and Statutes (in Chronological Order)

United States. "Treaty with the Sioux, September 23, 1805." In *Indian Affairs: Laws and Treaties. Vol. 2, Treaties,* compiled and edited by Charles J. Kappler, 1031. Washington, D.C.: G.P.O, 1904.

United States. "Treaty with the Teeton Tribe, 1815." 7 *Stats at Large of USA* 125 (1815).

United States. "Treaty with the Sioux of the Lakes, 1815." 7 *Stats at Large of USA* 126 (1815).

United States. "Treaty with the Sioux of St. Peter's River, 1815." 7 *Stats at Large of USA* 127 (1815).

United States. "Treaty with the Yankton Sioux, 1815." 7 *Stats at Large of USA* 128 (1815).

United States. "Treaty with the Laway Tribe, 1815." 7 *Stats at Large of USA* 136 (1815).

United States. "Treaty with the Sioux, 1815." 7 *Stats at Large of USA* 143 (1815).

United States. "Treaty with the Teton, Yancton, and Yanctonies Sioux, 1825." 7 *Stats at Large of USA* 250 (1825).

United States. "Treaty with the Sioune and Oglala Tribes, 1825." 7 *Stats at Large of USA* 252 (1825).

United States. "Treaty with the Cheyenne Tribe, 1825." 7 *Stats at Large of USA* 255 (1825).

United States. "Treaty with the Hunkpapa Band of the Sioux Tribe, 1825." 7 *Stats at Large of USA* 257 (1825).

United States. "Treaty with the Crow Tribe, 1825." 7 *Stats at Large of USA* 266 (1825).

United States. "Treaty with the Winnebago, August 1, 1829." 7 *Stats at Large of USA* 323.

Indian Removal Act. 4 *Stats at Large of USA* 411 (1830).

United States. "Treaty with the Omaha." July 15, 1830. 7 *Stats at Large of USA* 328.

United States. "Treaty with the Winnebago, September 15, 1832." 7 *Stats at Large of USA* 370.

United States. "Treaty with the Omaha, October 15, 1836." 7 *Stats at Large of USA* 524.

United States. "Treaty with the Sioux." 7 *Stats at Large of USA* 538 (1837).

United States. "Treaty with the Winnebago, November 1, 1837." 7 *Stats at Large of USA* 544.

United States. "Treaty with the Winnebago, October 13, 1846." 9 *Stats at Large of USA* 878.

United States. "Treaty with the Utah." September 9, 1849. 9 *Stats at Large of USA* 984.

United States. "Treaty with the Sioux—Sisseton and Wahpeton Bands." 10 *Stats at Large of USA* 949 (1851).

United States. "Treaty with the Sioux—Mdewakanton and Wahpakoota Bands." 10 *Stats at Large of USA* 954 (1851).

United States. "First Treaty of Fort Laramie with the Sioux, Cheyenne, Arapahoes, Crows, Assinaboines, Gros-Ventre, Mandans and Arickaras of 1851." 11 *Stats at Large of USA* 749.

United States. "Treaty with the Omaha, March 16, 1854." 10 *Stats at Large of USA* 1043.

Act to Organize the Territories of Nebraska and Kansas. 33rd Cong., 1st sess. (May 30, 1854). National Archives. General Records of the U.S. Government. Interior and Insular Affairs Committee and Its Predecessors, 1805–1988. RG 11.

United States. "Treaty with the Winnebago of February 27 1855." 10 *Stats at Large of USA* 1172.

United States. "Treaty of Hell Gate with the Flathead, Kootenai, and Upper Pend d'Oreille." 12 *Stats at Large of USA* 975 (1855).

United States. "Lame Bull's Treaty." 11 *Stats at Large of USA* 657 (1855).

United States. "Treaty with the Yankton Sioux." 11 *Stats at Large of USA* 743 (1858).

United States. "Treaty with the Winnebago of April 15, 1859." 12 *Stats at Large of USA* 1101.

Act of Congress of March 2, 1861. 12 *Stats at Large of USA* 239.

United States. "Treaty of Fort Wise." 12 *Stats at Large of USA* 1163 (1861).

Forfeiture Act of February 16, 1863. 12 *Stats at Large of USA* 652.

United States. "First Treaty of Fort Bridger of July 2, 1863." 18 *Stats at Large of USA* 685.

Act of 1864. 13 *Stats at Large of USA* 85.

United States. "Tabequache Treaty." March 25, 1864. 13 *Stats at Large of USA* 673.

Act of March 3, 1865. Ch. 127, 13 *Stats at Large of USA* 541, 559.
United States. "Treaty with the Omaha, March 6, 1865." 14 *Stats at Large of USA* 667.
United States. "Treaty with the Winnebago, March 8, 1865." 14 *Stats at Large of USA* 671.
United States. "Treaty with the Sioux—Sans Arcs Band." 14 *Stats at Large of USA* 731 (1865).
United States. "Treaty with the Sioux—Upper Yanktonai Band." 14 *Stats at Large of USA* 743 (1865).
United States. "Treaty between the United States and the Blackfoot Nation of Indians, etc." November 16, 1865 (unratified).
Act of May 15, 1866. Ch. 333, 24 *Stats at Large of USA* 29, 44.
United States. "Treaty with the Assiniboines." July 18, 1866 (unratified).
Act of 1867. 14 *Stats at Large of USA* 426.
United States. "Treaty with the Ute." March 2, 1868. 15 *Stats at Large of USA* 619.
United States. "Second Treaty of Fort Laramie of 1868." 15 *Stats at Large of USA* 635, 649.
United States. "Second Treaty of Fort Bridger of July 3, 1868." 15 *Stats at Large of USA* 673.
United States. "Agreement with the Gros Ventre." July 13, 1868 (unratified).
An Act to Provide a Temporary Government for the Territory of Wyoming (July 25, 1868). 15 *Stats at Large of USA* 178.
United States. "Treaty with the Blackfoot, etc." September 1, 1868 (unratified).
Act of April 10, 1869. Ch. 16, 16 *Stats at Large of USA* 16, 40.
Indian Appropriation Act of March 3, 1871. 16 *Stats at Large of USA* 566 (1871), 25 U.S.C. §71.
Act of June 5, 1872. 17 *Stats at Large of USA* 226.
Act of June 8, 1872. Ch. 354, 17 *Stats at Large of USA* 339.
United States. "Brunot Cession Agreement of 1872." 18 *Stats at Large of USA* 291 (ratified in 1874).
Act of February 11, 1874. 18 *Stat*. 15.
Act of April 15, 1874. Ch. 97, 18 *Stat*. 28.
United States. "Brunot Agreement with Ute Nation—1874." Ch. 136, 18 *Stat*. 36 (1874).
Act of February 28, 1877. 19 *Stat*. 254.
Act of May 3, 1878. Ch. 87, 20 *Stat*. 48.
Act of June 15, 1880. Ch. 223, 21 *Stat*. 199.
United States. "Agreement with the Crows of 1880" (unratified).
Act of April 11, 1882. 22 *Stat*. 42.
Omaha Allotment Act of 1882. 22 *Stat*. 341.
Major Crimes Act of 1885. 23 *Stat*. 385.
Act of May 15, 1886. Ch. 333, 24 *Stat*. 29.
General Allotment Act of 1887. 24 *Stat*. 388, 25 *U.S. Code* §§331–58.
Act of February 15, 1887. Ch. 130, 24 *Stat*. 402

Act of May 1, 1888. Chap. 213, § 4, 25 *Stat*. 113, 133.
Montana Enabling Act of February 22, 1889. 25 *Stat*. 676.
Act of March 2, 1889. Ch. 391, 25 *Stat*. 871.
Act of March 2, 1889. 25 *Stat*. 896.
Indian Territory Naturalization Act of 1890. 26 *Stat*. 81.
Act of 1891. 26 *Stat*. 989, 1091.
Act of February 20, 1895. Ch. 113, 28 *Stat*. 677.
Agreement of 1895. 29 *Stat*. 354, art. 5.
Act of May 13, 1896. Ch. 175, 29 *Stat*. 117.
Act of June 10, 1896. Ch. 398, 29 *Stat*. 321, 341–42, 350–58.
Articles of Agreement on 21 April 1896 between James McLaughlin, on the Part of the U.S., and Shoshone and Arapaho Tribes (known as the *First McLaughlin Agreement of 1896)*. 30 *Stat*. 93.
Act of July 1, 1898. Ch. 571, 30 *Stat*. 571.
Act of March 3, 1901. 31 *Stat*. 1447.
Act of April 23, 1904. 33 *Stat*. 254.
Flathead Allotment Act. Pub. L. 159, 33 *Stat*. 302 (1904).
Act of 1904. 33 *Stat*. 352.
Act to Ratify and Amend Agreement with Indians Residing on Shoshone or Wind River Indian Reservation (known as the *Second McLaughlin Agreement of 1905)*. 33 *Stat*. 1016.
Burke Act of 1906. 34 *Stat*. 182.
Act of March 1, 1907. 34 *Stat*. 1015, 1035–36.
Act of March 2, 1907. 34 *Stat*. 1230.
Act of April 30, 1908. 35 *Stat*. 70.
Act of May 29, 1908. Pub L. 156, 35 *Stat* 444, 448–50.
Fort Peck Allotment Act. Pub. L. 177, 35 *Stat*. 558 (1908).
Act of May 30, 1910. 36 *Stat*. 448.
Act of September 7, 1916. ch. 452, 39 *Stat*. 739.
Act of November 6, 1919. ch. 95, 41 *Stat*. 350.
Crow Allotment Act of 1920. 41 *Stat*. 751.
Act of March 3, 1921. 41 *Stat*. 1249–50.
Fort Belknap Allotment Act, Ch. 135, 41 *Stat*. 1355 (1921).
Indian Citizenship Act of 1924. 43 *Stat*. 253, 8 *U.S. Code* § 1401.
Indian Reorganization Act of 1934, 48 *Stat*. 984, 25 *U.S. Code* § 461.
Order of Restoration, Southern Ute Indian Reservation, Colorado (July 17, 1937). *Federal Register* 2 (1937): 1403.
Confederated Bands of the Ute Tribe of Indians, Colorado, Order of Restoration (Nov. 13, 1937). *Federal Register* 2 (1937): 1404.
Act of June 28, 1938, 52 *Stat*. 1209.
Indian Claims Commission Act. 60 *Stat*. 1049 (1946).
Indian Country Defined. 18 *U.S. Code* §1151 (1948).

Act to Confer Jurisdiction on the State of California, Minnesota, Nebraska, Oregon, and Wisconsin. 67 *Stat*. 588 (1953), 18 *U.S. Code* § 1162.

Menominee Reservation. 67 *Stat*. 589 (1953), 28 *U.S. Code* §1360.

The Relocation Act of 1956. Pub. L. 959.

Voting Rights Act of 1965. 79 *Stat*. 437, 42 *U.S. Code* §1973.

Jurisdiction over Criminal and Civil Actions, 82 *Stat*. 78–80 (1968), 25 *U.S. Code* §§1321–23, 1326.

Indian Financing Act of 1974. 88 *Stat*. 77, 25 *U.S. Code* §1451.

Indian Self-Determination and Education Assistance Act of 1975. 88 *Stat*. 2203, 25 *U.S. Code* §450a.

Voting Rights Act Amendments of 1975. 89 *Stat*. 400–02, 42 *U.S. Code* §1973b(f).

Indian Health Care Improvement Act of 1976. 90 *Stat*. 1400, 25 *U.S. Code* §1601.

American Indian Religious Freedom Act of 1978. 92 *Stat*. 469, 42 *U.S. Code* §1996.

Indian Child Welfare Act of 1978. 92 *Stat*. 3069, 25 *U.S. Code* §1901.

Indian Mineral Development Act of 1982. 25 *U.S. Code* §§2101–8.

Indian Tribal Government Tax Status Act of 1982. 96 *Stat*. 2607.

Indian Gaming Regulatory Act of 1988. 25 *U.S. Code* §§2701–21.

The Native American Business Development, Trade Promotion, and Tourism Act of 2000. 114 *Stat*. 2012, 25 *U.S. Code* §4301(a)(2).

Fannie Lou Hamer, Rosa Parks, and Coretta Scott King Voting Rights Act Reauthorization and Amendments Act of 2006. 120 *Stat*. 577.

Other Federal Documents

American Indian Policy Review Commission. *Final Report*. Washington, D.C.: GPO: 1977.

Atkins, J.D.C. *See* U.S. Department of the Interior, Bureau of Indian Affairs.

Becker, Grace Chung, acting assistant attorney general, to Sara Frankenstein, February 11, 2008. U.S. Department of Justice. http://www.usdoj.gov/crt/voting/sec_5/ltr/l_021108.php.

Bush, George W. "Memorandum for the Heads of Executive Departments and Agencies: Government-to-Government Relationship with Tribal Governments," Office of Press Secretary, September 23, 2004. *Weekly Compilation of Presidential Documents* (September 27, 2004).

Clinton, William J. "Government-to-Government Relations with Native American Tribal Governments." Presidential Memorandum of April 24, 1994, *Federal Register* 59 (1994): 22951.

Cohen, Felix S. *Handbook of Federal Indian Law*. Washington, D.C.: GPO, 1942.

Commissioner of Indian Affairs. "Indian Department Rules" (nos. 492 and 497). In *Rules Governing the Court of Indian Offenses*, by Hiram Price. Washington, D.C., 1983.

Congressional Record. 48th Cong., 2nd sess., 1885 (Senate Debate on the Indian Appropriations Bill). Vol. 16, 1732–36.

Congressional Record. 73rd Cong., 2nd sess., 1934 (House debate on the Wheeler–Howard Bill). Vol. 78, pt. 11: 724–44.

Congressional Record. 94th Cong., 1st sess., 1975. Vol. 121, pp. 13,603, 16,244–45, 250 & 262.

Covered Counties in States Not Covered as a Whole. *Federal Register* 41 (January 5, 1976): 784.

Cox, Jacob D. *See* U.S. Department of the Interior.

Crow Service Unit. *Environmental Health Profile and Priority Projection for Crow Indian Reservation*. Crow Agency, Mont.: Crow Service Unit, 1985.

Grant, Ulysses S. Executive Order of November 14, 1871, Bitter Root Valley Reserve. In *Indian Affairs. Laws and Treaties,* compiled and edited by Charles J. Kappler, vol. 1, 854–55. Washington, D.C.: GPO, 1904.

Grant, Ulysses S. Executive Order of July 5, 1873. In *Indian Affairs. Laws and Treaties,* compiled and edited by Charles J. Kappler, vol. 1, 855–56. Washington, D.C.: GPO, 1904.

Grant, Ulysses S. Executive Order of August 19, 1874. In *Indian Affairs. Laws and Treaties,* compiled and edited by Charles J. Kappler, vol. 1, 856. Washington, D.C.: GPO, 1904.

Hayes, Rutherford. Executive Order of July 13, 1880. In *Indian Affairs. Laws and Treaties,* compiled and edited by Charles J. Kappler, vol. 1, 883. Washington, D.C.: GPO, 1904.

Implementation of the Provisions of the Voting Rights Act Regarding Language Minority Groups. *Federal Register* 41 (July 20, 1976): 30002.

Indian Peace Commission. *Proceedings of the Great Peace Commission of 1867–1868*. Washington, D.C.: Institute for the Development of Indian Law, 1975. Quoted in Prucha, *Indians in American Society*, 18.

Jackson, Andrew. "First Annual Message." In *A Compilation of the Messages and Papers of the Presidents,* edited by James D. Richardson, 1005–25. New York: Bureau of National Literature, 1897.

Johnson, Lyndon B. "The Forgotten American, The President's Message to the Congress on Goals and Programs for the American Indian." *Weekly Compilation of Presidential Documents* 4, no. 10 (March 6, 1968).

Manypenny, George W. *See* U.S. Department of the Interior, Bureau of Indian Affairs.

Morgan, Thomas Jefferson. *See* U.S. Department of the Interior, Bureau of Indian Affairs.

Nixon, Richard M. "The President's Message to the Congress of the United States on the American Indians" (July 8, 1970). *Public Papers of the President of the United States: Richard Nixon, 1970*. Washington, D.C.: GPO, 1970, 564–67, 776.

President. Executive Order no. 13175. "Consultation and Coordination with Indian Tribal Governments," Presidential Memorandum of November 6, 2000. *Federal Register* 65 (2000): 218.

Price, Hiram. *See* U.S. Department of the Interior, Bureau of Indian Affairs.

Procedures for the Administration of Section 5 of the Voting Rights Act of 1965, As Amended. *Code of Federal Regulations* 28, pt. 51 (2002).

Sells, Cato. *See* U.S. Department of the Interior, Bureau of Indian Affairs.

Taft, William H. "Presidential Proclamation of May 22, 1909." 36 *Stat*. pt. 2, 2494.

Teller, Henry M. *Resolution on Opening Ute Lands for Homesteading*. 47th Cong., 1st sess., 1883. S. Misc. Doc. 63.

Teller, Henry M. *See* U.S. Department of the Interior.

U.S. American Indian Policy Review Commission. *Final Report: Submitted to Congress, May 17, 1977*. Washington, D.C.: GPO, 1977.

U.S. Board of Indian Commissioners. *Fourth Annual Report*. Washington, D.C.: GPO, 1872.

U.S. Board of Indian Commissioners. *Report of the Board of Indian Commissioners (1869)*.Washington, D.C.: GPO, 1869. Reprinted in Prucha, *Documents of United States Indian Policy*, 131–34.

U.S. Board of Indian Commissioners. *23rd Annual Report*. Washington, D.C.: GPO, 1922.

U.S. Bureau of the Census. *1980 Census of Population, General Population Characteristics, Montana, Table PC 80-1-B28*. Washington, D.C.: U.S. Bureau of the Census, 1981

U.S. Bureau of the Census. *1990 Census*. Pub. L. 94-171.

U.S. Bureau of the Census. *Census 2000*: Summary Files 1–4. Washington, D.C.: U.S. Census Bureau, 2002.

U.S. Commission on Civil Rights. *Indian Tribes: A Continuing Quest for Survival* Washington, D.C.: GPO, 1981.

U.S. Commissioner of Indian Affairs. *Annual Report*. Washington, D.C.: GPO, 1886.

U.S. Commissioner of Indian Affairs. *Report*. Washington, D.C.: GPO, 1883.

U.S. Congress. Joint Committee on the Conduct of War. *Hearing before the Joint Committee on the Conduct of War*. 39th Cong., 1st sess., March 14, 1865.

U.S. Department of the Interior. *Annual Report of the Secretary of the Interior (1868)*, by Jacob D. Cox. Washington, D.C.: GPO, 1869. Reprinted in Prucha, *Documents of United States Indian Policy*.

U.S. Department of the Interior. *Annual Report of the U.S. Secretary of the Interior (1883)*, by Henry M. Teller. Washington, D.C.: GPO, 1884. Reprinted in Prucha, *Documents of United States Indian Policy*.

U.S. Department of the Interior. Bureau of Indian Affairs. *Annual Report of the Commissioner of Indian Affairs (1881, 1883)*, by Hiram Price. Available in the Congressional Serial Set, SuDocs Number I 20.1.

U.S. Department of the Interior. Bureau of Indian Affairs. *Annual Report of the Commissioner of Indian Affairs (1887)*, by J. D. C. Atkins. Washington, D.C.: GPO, 1887. Reprinted in Prucha, *Documents of United States Indian Policy*.

U.S. Department of the Interior. Bureau of Indian Affairs. *Annual Report of the Commissioner of Indian Affairs (1889)*, by Thomas Jefferson Morgan. Washington, D.C.: GPO, 1889. Reprinted in Prucha, *Documents of United States Indian Policy*.

U.S. Department of the Interior. Bureau of Indian Affairs. *Annual Report of the U.S. Commissioner of Indian Affairs (1856)*, by George W. Manypenny. Washington, D.C.: GPO, 1857. Reprinted in Prucha, *Documents of United States Indian Policy*.

U.S. Department of the Interior. Bureau of Indian Affairs. *Declaration of Policy in the Administration of Indian Affairs (April 17, 1917)*, by Cato Sells. National Archives, Rocky Mountain Region.

U.S. Department of the Interior. Bureau of Indian Affairs. *Local Estimates of Resident Indian Population and Labor Force Status: January 1985*. Washington, D.C.: GPO 1985.

U.S. House. Committee on the Judiciary. 89th Cong., 1st sess., 1965. HR Rep. 439.

U.S. House. Committee on the Judiciary. *Voting Rights—Tests*. 91st Cong., 2nd sess., 1970. HR 397.

U.S. House. *Indian Reorganization Act*. 73rd Cong., 2nd sess., 1934. HR Rep. 1804.

U.S. House. *Indians*. HR Res. 108. 83rd Cong., 1st sess. (August 1953). 67 *Stat*. B122.

U.S. House. Interior and Insular Affairs Committee, 93rd Cong., 2nd sess., 1974. HR Rep.907

U.S. House. Interior and Insular Affairs Committee, 94th Cong., 2nd sess., 1976. HR Rep. 1026.

U.S. House. Interior and Insular Affairs Committee, 95th Cong., 2nd sess., 1978. HR Rep.1308.

U.S. House. Interior and Insular Affairs Committee, 95th Cong., 2nd sess., 1978. HR Rep. 1386.

U.S. House. Judiciary Committee, Subcommittee on Civil and Constitutional Rights. *Extension of the Voting Rights Act: Hearings before the Subcommittee on Civil and Constitutional Rights of the House Judiciary Committee*. 94th Cong., 1st sess., 1975, appendix 1225–30.

U.S. House. Judiciary Committee. *Voting Rights Language Assistance Act of 1992*. 102nd Cong., 2nd sess., 1999. HR Rep. 655.

U.S. House. *Voting Rights Act Extension*. 94th Cong., 1st sess., 1975. HR Rep. 196.

U.S. House. *Voting Rights Act Extension*. 97th Cong., 1st sess., 1981. HR Rep. 227.

U.S. Indian Claims Commission. *Final Report*. Washington, D.C.: GPO, 1970.

U.S. Senate. Committee on the Judiciary. *Voting Rights Act Extension*. 94th Cong., 1st sess., 1975. S. Rep. 295.

U.S. Senate. Committee on the Judiciary. *Voting Rights Act Extension*. 97th Cong., 2d sess., 1982. S. Rep. 417.

U.S. Senate. *Indian Education: A National Tragedy—A National Challenge*. 91st Cong., 2d sess., 1969. S. Rep. 501.

U.S. Senate. Subcommittee of the Committee on Public Lands and Surveys. *Statement of John Herrick, Assistant to the Commissioner, Indian Service*. 77th Cong., 1st sess., September 1941.

Voting Rights Act Amendments of 1992, Determinations under Section 203. *Federal Register* 67 (2002): 48871.

Wilson, Woodrow. "Presidential Proclamation of July 25, 1913." 38 *Stat*. 1952.

Court Decisions

Alden v. Rosebud County Board of Commissioners, Civ. No. 99-148-BLG (D. Mont. May 10, 2000).
Allen v. Merrell, 352 U.S. 889 (1956); 353 U.S. 932 (1957).
Allen v. State Board of Elections, 393 U.S. 544 (1969).
American Horse v. Kundert, Civ. 84-5159 (D. S.Dak. Nov. 5, 1984).
Beer v. United States, 425 U.S. 130 (1976).
Black Bull v. Dupree School District, Civ. 86-3012 (D. S.Dak. May 14, 1986).
Blackfeet and Gros Ventre Tribes of Indians and Assiniboine Tribes of Indians v. United States, 19 Ind. Cl. Comm. 361 (1968).
Blackfeet et al. Nations v. United States, 81 Ct. Cl. 101 (1935).
Blackmoon v. Charales Mix County, 2005 Westlaw 2738954 (D. S.Dak. 2005).
Blaine County, Montana v. United States, 544 U.S. 992 (2005).
Bone Shirt v. Hazeltine, 200 F. Supp.2d 1150 (D. S.Dak. 2002), subsequent decision 336 F. Supp.2d 976 (D. S.Dak. 2004).
Brown v. Montana Districting and Reapportionment Commission, No. ADV-2003-72 (Mont. 1st Jud. Dist. Ct. Lewis & Clark County).
Buckanaga v. Sisseton Independent School District, 804 F.2d 469 (8th Cir. 1986).
Cherokee Nation v. Georgia, 30 U.S. 1 (1831).
Citizens Equal Rights Alliance v. Johnson, CV-07-74 BLG-RFC (D. Mont.).
City of Mobile v. Bolden, 446 U.S. 55 (1980).
City of Richmond v. United States, 422 U.S. 358 (1975).
City of Rome, Georgia v. United States, 446 U.S. 156 (1980).
Clarke v. City of Cincinnati, 40 F.3d 807 (6th Cir. 1994).
Confederated Bands of Ute Indians v. United States, 117 Ct. Cl. 433 (1950).
Confederated Bands of Ute Indians v. United States, 11 Ind. Cl. Comm. 180, 303 (1962).
Confederated Salish and Kootenai Tribes of the Flathead Reservation, Montana v. United States, 8 Ind. Cl. Comm. 40 (1959).
Confederated Salish and Kootenai Tribes of the Flathead Reservation, Montana v. United States, 16 Ind. Cl. Comm. 1 (1965).
Confederated Salish and Kootenai Tribes v. United States, 437 F.2d 458 (Ct. Cl. 1971).
Cottier v. City of Martin, 445 F.3d 1113 (8th Cir. 2006), on remand, 446 F. Supp.2d 1175 (D. S.Dak. 2006), adopting remedial plan, 475 F. Supp.2d 932 (D. S.Dak. 2007), granting rehearing en banc, 551 F.3d 733 (8th Cir. 2008).
County Council of Sumter County, S.C. v. United States, 555 F. Supp. 694 (D. D.C. 1983).
Crow Tribe of Indians v. United States, 284 F.2d 361 (Ct. Cl. 1960).
Cuthair v. Montezuma-Cortez, Colorado School District No. RE-1, 7 F. Supp.2d 1152 (D. Col. 1998).
Delaware Indians v. Cherokee Nation, 193 U.S. 127 (1905).
Draper v. United States, 164 U.S. 240 (1896).
Eastern Shoshone Tribe v. Northern Arapaho Tribe, 926 F. Supp. 1024 (D. Wyo. 1996).

Elk v. Wilkins, 112 U.S. 94 (1884).
Emery v. Hunt, 615 N. W. 2d 590 (S.Dak. 2000).
Emery v. Hunt, 272 F.3d 1042 (8th Cir. 2001).
Evans v. Cornman, 398 U.S. 419 (1970).
Exon v. Tiemann, 279 F. Supp. 603 (D. Neb. 1967).
Ex Parte Crow Dog, 109 U.S. 556 (1883).
Ex Parte Green, 123 F.2d 862 (2d Cir. 1941).
Fiddler v. Sieker, no. 85-3050 (D. S.Dak. Oct. 24, 1986).
Fort Peck Reservation v. United States, 18 Ind. Cl. Comm. 241 (1967).
Georgia v. Ashcroft, 539 U.S. 461 (2003).
Harrison v. Laveen, 196 P.2d 456 (1948).
Henderson v. Harris, 804 F. Supp. 288 (M.D. Ala. 1992).
Hendrix v. McKinney, 460 F. Supp. 626 (M.D. Ala. 1978).
In re Interrogatories, 536 P.2d 308 (Colo. 1975).
In re Legislative Reapportionment, 246 N.W. 295 (S.Dak. 1993).
In re State Census, 62 N.W. 129 (S.Dak. 1895).
Johnson v. De Grandy, 512 U.S. 997 (1994).
Johnson v. McIntosh, 21 U.S. 543 (1823).
Johnson v. Village of Walthill, Case No. Neb. 1-84/85-9-8730.
Johnson v. Village of Walthill, Case No. Neb. 1-84/85-12-9030.
Kirkie v. Buffalo County, South Dakota, Civ. No. 03-3011 (D. S.Dak. Feb. 12, 2004).
Kirksey v. Board of Supervisors of Hinds County, Mississippi, 554 F.2d 139 (5th Cir. 1977).
Klahr v. Williams, 339 F. Supp. 922 (D. Ariz. 1972).
Large v. Fremont County, Wyoming, No. 05-CV-270J (D. Wyo.).
Legislature of California v. Deukmejian, 669 P.2d 17 (Cal. 1983)
Little Thunder v. South Dakota, 518 F.2d 1253 (8th Cir. 1975).
Lone Wolf v. Hitchcock, 187 U.S. 553 (1903).
Lopez v. Monerey County, 525 U.S. 266 (1999).
Matt v. Ronan School District, Civ. No. 99–94 (D. Mont. Jan. 13, 2000).
McDaniel v. Sanchez, 452 U.S. 130 (1981).
McMillan v. Escambia County, 638 F.2d 1239 (5th Cir. 1981), subsequent opinion, 748 F.2d 1037 (11th Cir. 1984).
Missouri, Kansas and Texas Railway Company v. Roberts, 152 U.S. 114 (1894).
Montana v. United States, 450 U.S. 544 (1981).
Morton v. Mancari, 417 U.S. 535 (1974).
Natonabah v. Board of Education, 355 F. Supp. 716 (D. N.Mex. 1973).
Northern Cheyenne Indians of the Tongue River Reservation, Montana v. United States, No. 329-C (Ind. Cl. Comm. Nov. 27, 1963).
Northwest Austin Municipal Utility District Number One v. Mukasey, 573 F. Supp.2d 221 (D. D.C. 2008), reversed and remanded, 129 S.Ct. 2504 (2009).
Old Person v. Brown, 182 F. Supp.2d 1002 (D. Mont. 2002), affirmed, 312 F.3d 1036 (9th Cir. 2002).

Old Person v. Cooney, No. CV-96-004-GF (D. Mont. Oct. 27, 1998), reversed and remanded, 230 F.3d 1113 (9th Cir. 2000).

Omaha Tribe of Nebraska v. United States, 6 Ind. Cl. Comm. 730 (1958).

Omaha Tribe of Nebraska v. United States, 7 Ind. Cl. Comm. 572-c (1959).

Omaha Tribe of Nebraska v. United States, 8 Ind. Cl. Comm. 392 (1960).

Omaha Tribe of Nebraska v. Village of Walthill, 334 F. Supp. 823 (D. Neb. 1971), affirmed, 460 F.2d 1327 (8th Cir. 1972).

Oregon v. Mitchell, 400 U.S. 112 (1970).

Parker v. Village of Walthill and Cameron Arthus, CV90-0-238 (D. Neb. 1990).

Perkins v. Matthews, 400 U.S. 379 (1971).

Plains Commerce Bank v. Long Family Land, 128 S. Ct. 2709 (2008).

Quick Bear Quiver v. Hazeltine, Civ. No. 02-5069 (D. S.Dak. Dec. 27, 2002).

Quick Bear Quiver v. Nelson, 387 F. Supp.2d 1027 (D. S.Dak. 2005).

Reno v. Bossier Parish School Board, 528 U.S. 320 (2000).

Rice v. Sioux City Memorial Park Cemetery, 349 U.S. 70 (1955).

Rogers v. Lodge, 458 U.S. 613 (1982).

Rosebud Sioux Tribe v. Kneip, 430 U.S. 584 (1977).

RWTAAAC v. Sundquist, 29 F. Supp.2d 448 (W.D. Tenn. 1998).

Saunsoci v. Cameron Arthur and the Village of Walthill, Case 8601 (Dist. Ct. Thurston County).

Shoshone Tribe of Indians v. United States, 299 U.S. 476 (1937).

South Carolina v. Katzenbach, 383 U.S. 301 (1966).

Stabler v. County of Thurston, Nebraska, 8:CV93-00394 (D. Neb. Aug. 29, 1995), affirmed 129 F.3d 1015 (8th Cir. 1997).

State (Mont.) v. Kemp, 78 P.2d 585 (1938).

State (Neb.) v. Goham, 187 N.W.2d 305 (1971).

State v. Big Sheep, Montana, 243 P. 1067 (1976).

Stephens v. Nacey, 141 P. 649 (Mont. 1914).

Teague v. Attala County, Mississippi, 92 F.3d 283 (5th Cir. 1996).

Thornburg v. Gingles, 478 U.S. 30 (1986).

United States v. Assiniboine Tribes of Indians, 428 F.2d 1325 (Ct. Cl. 1970).

United States v. Blackpipe State Bank, no. 93-5115 (D. S.Dak.).

United States v. Blaine County, Montana, CV 99-122-GF-DWM (D. Mont.), affirmed, 363 F.3d 897 (9th Cir. 2004).

United States v. Day County, South Dakota, No. CV 99-1024 (D. S.Dak. June 16, 2000).

United States v. Finch, 395 F. Supp. 213 (D. Mont. 1975).

United States v. Iron Moccasin, 878 F.2d 226 (8th Cir. 1989).

United States v. Kagama, 118 U.S. 375 (1886).

United States v. Kipp, 369 F. Supp. 774 (D. Mont. 1974).

United States v. Marengo County Commission, 731 F.2d 1546 (11th Cir. 1984).

United States v. Montana, 457 F. Supp. 599 (D. Mont. 1978), reversed and remanded, 604 F.2d 1162 (9th Cir. 1979).

United States v. Nice, 241 U.S. 591 (1916).
United States v. Roosevelt County Board of Commissioners, 00-CV-54 (D. Mont. March 24, 2000).
United States v. Shoshone Tribe of Indians, 304 U.S. 111 (1938).
United States v. Sioux Nation of Indians, 448 U.S. 371 (1980).
United States v. South Dakota, Civ. 79-3039 (D. S.Dak. May 20, 1980).
United States v. South Dakota, 636 F.2d 241 (8th Cir. 1980).
United States v. Thurston County, Nebraska, Civ. No. 78-0-380 (D. Neb. May 9, 1979).
United States v. Tripp County, South Dakota, Civ. No. 78-3045 (D. S.Dak. Feb. 6, 1979).
United States v. Wheeler, 435 U.S. 313 (1978).
United States v. Winans, 198 U.S. 371 (1905).
Ward v. Race Horse, 163 U.S. 504 (1896).
Weddell v. Wagner Community School District, Civ. No. 02-4056 (D. S.Dak. Mar. 18, 2003).
Whitfield v. Democratic Party of State of Arkansas, 890 F.2d 1423 (8th Cir. 1989)
Wilcox v. City of Martin, No. 02-5021 (D. S.Dak.).
Windy Boy v. County of Big Horn, 647 F. Supp. 1002 (D. Mont. 1986).
Winnebago Tribe and Nation of Indians v. United States, 8 In. Cl. Comm. 78 (1959).
Winnebago Tribe and Nation of Indians v. United States, 16 In. Cl. Comm. 81 (1965).
Winnebago Tribe and Nation of Indians v. United States, 23 In. Cl. Comm. 464 (1970).
Worcester v. Georgia, 31 U.S. (6 Pet.) 515 (1832).
Wyoming v. Owl Creek Irrigation District. 753 P.2d 76 (Wyo. 1988).
Zimmer v. McKeithen, 485 F.2d 1297 (5th Cir. 1973).

Territorial, State, and Municipal Memorials, Laws, and Enactments (by State, in Chronological Order)

Colorado

1860 Jeff. Territory Session Laws.
1861 Colorado Territory Session Laws.
1862 Colorado Territorial Session Laws.
1865 Colorado Territorial Session Laws.
1866 Colorado Territorial Session Laws.
1867 Colorado Territorial Session Laws.
1872 Colorado Territorial Session Laws.
1876 Colorado Territorial Session Laws.
1881 Colorado Session Laws.
1885 Colorado Session Laws.
1887 Colorado Session Laws.
Colorado Constitution, Article VII, §1 (1918).
1966 Colorado Session Laws.

Montana

Laws, Resolutions and Memorials of the Territory of Montana, Passed at the First Legislative Assembly (1864).Virginia City, Mont. Territory: D.W. Tilton & Co., 1866.

General Laws, Resolutions and Memorials of the Territory of Montana, Passed at the Fourth Session of the Legislative Assembly (1867). Virginia City, Mont. Territory: D.W. Tilton & Co., 1868.

General Laws, Resolutions and Memorials of the Territory of Montana, Passed at the Fifth Session of the Legislative Assembly (1869). Helena, Mont. Territory: Montana Post Publishing Co., 1869.

Laws, Memorials, and Resolutions of the Territory of Montana Passed at the Seventh Session of the Legislative Assembly (1871). Deer Lodge, Mont. Territory: James H. Mills, Public Printer, 1872.

Laws, Memorial, and Resolutions of the Territory of Montana (1872).

Laws, Memorials, and Resolutions of the Territory of Montana, Extraordinary Session (1873). Helena, Mont. Territory: Robert E. Fisk, Public Printer, 1874.

Laws, Memorials, and Resolutions of the Territory of Montana, 9th Sess. (1876). Helena, Montana Territory: Robert E. Fisk, Public Printer, 1876.

Laws, Memorials, and Resolutions of the Territory of Montana (1877).

Laws, Memorials, and Resolutions of the Territory of Montana (1879).

Laws, Memorials, and Resolutions of the Territory of Montana (1883).

Laws, and Memorials and Resolutions of the Territory of Montana, 14th Sess. (1885).

Constitution of the State of Montana, as adopted by the Constitutional Convention held at Helena, Montana, July 4, 1889. Articles V, VII, VIII, IX, and XIV. Helena, Mont.: Independent Publishing Co., 1889.

Laws, Memorials, and Resolutions of the Territory of Montana (1889).

Laws, Resolutions and Memorials of the State of Montana, 2nd Sess., Montana Laws 1891, pp. 243–45, 316–17.

Laws, Resolutions and Memorials of the State of Montana, 3rd Sess. (1893).

Laws, Resolutions and Memorials of the State of Montana, 4th Sess. (1895), pp. 65–6.

Laws, Resolutions and Memorials of the State of Montana, 5th Sess. (1897). Helena, Mont.: State Publishing Co., 1897.

Laws, Resolutions and Memorials of the State of Montana, 6th Sess. (1899).

Laws, Resolutions and Memorials of the State of Montana, 7th Sess. (1901).

Laws, Resolutions and Memorials of the State of Montana, 8th Sess. (1903).

Laws, Resolutions and Memorials of the State of Montana, 9th Sess. (1905).

Laws, Resolutions and Memorials of the State of Montana, 10th Sess. (1907).

Laws, Resolutions and Memorials of the State of Montana, 11th Sess. (1909).

Laws, Resolutions and Memorials of the State of Montana, 12th Sess. (1911).

Laws, Resolutions and Memorials of the State of Montana, 13th Sess. (1913).

Laws, Resolutions and Memorials of the State of Montana, 14th Sess. (1915).

Laws, Resolutions and Memorials of the State of Montana, 16th Sess. (1919).

Laws, Resolutions and Memorials of the State of Montana, 17th Sess. (1921).
Laws, Resolutions and Memorials of the State of Montana, 18th Sess. (1923).
Laws, Resolutions, and Memorials of the State of Montana, 25th Sess. (1937).
Laws, Resolutions and Memorials of the State of Montana, 26th Sess. (1939).
Laws, Resolutions and Memorials of the State of Montana 27th Sess. (1941).
Laws, Resolutions and Memorials of the State of Montana, 31st Sess. (1949).
Laws, Resolutions and Memorials of the State of Montana, 32nd Sess. (1951).
Laws, Resolutions and Memorials of the State of Montana, 34th Sess. (1955).
Laws, Resolutions and Memorials of the State of Montana, 35th Sess. (1957).
Laws and Resolutions of the State of Montana, 40th Sess. (1967).
Laws and Resolutions of the State of Montana, 41st Regular and Extraordinary Sess. (1969).
Laws and Resolutions of the State of Montana, 44th Sess. (1975).
Joint Legislative Committee on Districting and Apportionment. *Minority Report on SR 2 and HR 3 Regarding the Recommendation to the Montana Districting and Apportionment Commission*. Helena, Mont.: January 29, 2003.
Montana Senate. Senate Res. 2. 58th sess. February 4, 2003, 1–2.
Montana House. House Res. 3. 58th sess. February 4, 2003, 1–2.

Nebraska

Laws, Joint Resolutions, and Memorials Passed at the Regular Session of the First General Assembly of the Territory of Nebraska (1855).
Laws, Joint Resolutions, and Memorials Passed at the Second Session of the Legislative Assembly of the Territory of Nebraska (1856).
Nebraska General Laws (1864).
Nebraska General Laws (1867).
Memorials and Joint Resolutions of the State of Nebraska (1873).
Laws, Joint Resolutions, and Memorials of the State of Nebraska (1891).
"Practices in Justices' Courts." In *A Treatise on the Powers and Duties of Justices of the Peace, Sheriffs, Coroners, and Constables in the State of Nebraska*, chap. 29. Lincoln, Neb.: State Journal Co., Law Publishers, 1894.
Nebraska General Laws (1909).
Nebraska General Laws (1913).
Nebraska Laws (1917).
Census; Legislative Apportionment. *Proceedings of the Nebraska Constitutional Convention 1919–1920*, art. XIX, sec. 2. Nebraska Archives RG32. Constitutional Conventions Records: 186601929.
Nebraska Session Laws, 1937.
Nebraska Session Laws, 1943.
Village of Walthill, Nebraska. "Resolution, December 9, 1975." In *Minutes of Meetings of the Board of Supervisors.* Pender, Neb., 1975.
Thurston County, Nebraska. "Resolution, January 27, 1976." In *Minutes of Meetings of the Board of Supervisors.* Pender, Neb., 1976.

Village of Walthill, Nebraska. "Resolution, March 10, 1981." In *Minutes of Meetings of Municipal Government of Walthill, Neb.* Walthill, Neb., 1981.
Thurston County, Nebraska. "Resolution no. 168" (March 5, 1985). In *Minutes of Meetings of the Board of Supervisors.* Pender, Neb., 1985.
Nebraska Legislature. Judiciary Committee. *Hearings on Legislative Resolution 57.* 89th Leg., 1st sess., April 17, 1985.
Legislative Journal of the State of Nebraska, 89th Legislature, 2nd sess. vol. 1 (1986).

South Dakota

Constitution of South Dakota. Article III, sec. 5. http://legis.state.sd.us/statutes/Constitution.aspx.
Dakota Territorial Laws, 1862.
Dakota Territorial Laws, 1863.
Dakota Territorial Laws, 1864.
Dakota Territorial Laws, 1866.
Dakota Territorial Laws, 1867.
Dakota Territorial Laws, 1868.
Dakota Territorial Laws, 1871.
Dakota Territorial Laws, 1873.
Dakota Territorial Laws, 1875.
Dakota Territorial Laws, 1887.
Dakota Territorial Laws, 1889.
South Dakota Laws, 1890.
South Dakota Laws, 1895.
South Dakota Laws, 1901.
South Dakota Laws, 1921.
South Dakota Laws, 1931.
South Dakota Codified Laws (Michie 1939).
South Dakota Laws, 1973.
South Dakota Laws, 1985.
South Dakota Laws, 1991, 1st Spec. Sess.
South Dakota Legislative Research Council. Issue Memorandum 95-36 (September 12, 1995). Pierre, S.Dak.: Archives of Legislative Research Council.
Minutes of (S.Dak.) House State Affairs Committee. *House State Affairs Committee Minutes 1/29/96*, p. 5.
South Dakota Laws, 1996.
South Dakota Code of Laws, §7-8-10, §§16.0701–0706.
South Dakota Laws, 1996.
South Dakota Legislative Research Council. Issue Memorandum 99-12 (April 29, 1998). Pierre, S.Dak.: Archives of Legislative Research Council.
South Dakota House Bill 1265 (March 7, 2005). An Act to Provide for Redistricting of Boards of County Commissioners.

Utah

1957 Utah Laws.

Wyoming

Session Laws of Wyoming Territory, Passed by the 6th Legislative Assembly (1879). Cheyenne, Wyo. Territory: Leader Stearn Book & Job Print, 1879.
Session Laws of Wyoming, 1890, 1st State Legislature.
Session Laws of Wyoming, 1941.
Session Laws of Wyoming, 1943.
Session Laws of Wyoming, 1951.
Session Laws of Wyoming, 1971.
Composition; Election for Increasing the Number; Term; Quorum; Election for Districting; Procedures, *Wyoming Statutes* §18-3-501.
Senate Joint Resolution no. SJ0002 (2006). Funding for Tribal Entities.

Opinions of State Attorneys General (by State, in Chronological Order)

Colorado

Opinion of the Attorney General of Colorado, No. 343. *1921–1922 Colorado Attorney General Biennial Report*, pp. 133–37.
Opinion of the Attorney General of Colorado, No. 1323-48. *1947–1948 Colorado Attorney General Biennial Report*, p. 142.
Opinion of the Attorney General of Colorado, No. 60-3444. *1959–1960 Colorado Attorney General Biennial Report*, p. 79.

Montana

1 *Opinions of the Montana Attorney General* 60 (1905).
1 *Opinions of the Montana Attorney General* 362 (1906).
5 *Opinions of the Montana Attorney General* 240 (1913).
5 *Opinions of the Montana Attorney General* 460 (1914).
8 *Opinions of the Montana Attorney General* (1919).
16 *Opinions of the Montana Attorney General* 42 (1935).
17 *Opinions of the Montana Attorney General* 12 (1937).
19 *Opinions of the Montana Attorney General* 789 (1942).
20 *Opinions of the Montana Attorney General* 147 (1943).

South Dakota

Janklow, William. Official Opinion No. 77-73, Voting Rights Act of 1965, as amended by Public Law 94-73; Bilingual Elections. *1977 South Dakota Opinions of the Attorney General* 175.

Depositions, Trial Transcripts, Exhibits, and Witness Interviews (by Case)

Bone Shirt v. Hazeltine

Black Horse, Charlene: interview and trial testimony.
Black Lance, Belva: interview and trial testimony.
Bradford, James, Rep.: interview and trial testimony.
Brandis, Arlene: interview and trial testimony.
Dillon, Craig: interview and trial testimony.
Drapeaux, Monica: interview and trial testimony.
McCool, Dan: expert report, interview, and trial testimony.
Meeks, Elsie: interview and trial testimony.
Van Norman, Tom, Rep.: interview and trial testimony.
Young, Lyla: interview and trial testimony.

Cuthair v. Montezuma-Cortez

Badback, Angela: interview.
Bandy, Amanda: report, interview, and trial testimony.
Colorow, Janice: interview.
Cuthair, Arthur: interview and trial testimony.
Dutchie, Jocelyn: interview.
Ellis, Richard N.: interview, expert reports, and trial testimony.
Hatch, Sarah: interview.
House, Ernest: interview.
Lopez, Joselina: interview.
Lopez, Julian: interview.
Montezuma-Cortez School District No. RE-1, P.A.C. Recommendations and Responses, February 9, 1994.
Schumpelt, George: deposition.
Soto, Marjorie: interview.
Thompson, William R.: deposition and trial testimony.
Tom, Gloria: interview.
Whitmer, Allan: deposition.
www.cortez.k12.co.us.

Emery v. Hunt

Cole, Steven P.: Report.

Large v. Fremont County, Wyoming

Acuna, Helsha: interview and trial testimony.

Applegate, Lanny: deposition.

Bergie, Patricia: interview and trial testimony.

Brannan, Richard: interview and trial testimony.

Collins, Gary: interview and trial testimony.

Cooper, William: expert report and trial testimony.

Freese, Julie: trial testimony.

"Fremont County, Wyoming, 2005 EEO-4 Report."

Friday, Betty: interview and trial testimony.

Gaddie, Keith: trial testimony.

Goggles, Patrick, Rep.: deposition.

Gorin, Sarah: interview and trial testimony.

Guenther, Todd: interview and trial testimony.

Hickerson, Patrick: trial testimony.

Hipp, Martha: interview, expert report, and trial testimony.

Hoffman, Michael: interview and trial testimony.

Hutchinson, Burton: interview and deposition.

Jennings, Gary: deposition.

Kessler, Stephanie: interview and trial testimony.

Large, James: interview and trial testimony.

Massey, Garath: interview, expert report, and trial testimony.

McAdams, Emma Lucille: interview and trial testimony.

"Minutes of Meeting, Fremont County Commission," March 4, 1895; March 28, 1895; October 7, 1937; February 18, 1972; March 6, 1990; December 1, 1992; January 12, 1993; February 16, 1993; August 12, 1997; November 12, 2002; and December 12, 2002.

Plaintiffs Exhibits: 17-9, 242-57.

Posey, Ivan: interview and trial testimony.

Ratliff, Scott: interview and trial testimony.

Thernstrom, Stephen: Tr. Trans. 843–44.

Thomas, Valerie: interview and trial testimony.

Thompson, Douglas: trial testimony.

Throop, Tom: interview and trial testimony.

Vincent, John: interview and trial testimony.

Whiteman, Keja: trial testimony.

Wiles, Sarah: interview and trial testimony.

"W.I.N.D.S. Project: Wind River Indian Needs Determination Study," August 1988.

Old Person v. Cooney

Campbell, Margaret: interview and trial testimony.
Cole, Steven P.: expert report and trial testimony.
constitutionparty.com.
Defendants' Exhibits: 518, 525.
Fox, Susan Byorth: expert report and trial testimony.
Frisbee, Seldens: trial testimony.
MacDonald, Joe: interview and trial testimony.
Plaintiffs' Exhibits: 3, 4, 23, 25, 33, 38, 43-6, 47, 49, 52, 73-4, 77, 176-77.

Stabler v. County of Thurston

Casey, Mark: deposition.
Defendants' Exhibit 597.
Dunn, Steve: deposition and trial testimony.
Freemont, Sharon: deposition and trial testimony.
Gaer, M. Jeannie: deposition.
Henderson, Gordon: expert report and trial testimony.
Kemling, Mark: trial testimony.
McCauley, Edwin: trial testimony.
Merrick, Charles: trial testimony.
Morgan, Duward: deposition.
Plaintiffs' Exhibit 157.
Stabler, Hollis: deposition.
Storm, Raymond: trial testimony.
Tremayne, Roger: deposition

Windy Boy v. County of Big Horn, Montana

Back Bone, Frank: interview.
Bad Bear, Dessie: interview and trial testimony.
Belue, Clarence: interview.
Bernardis, Tim: interview.
Brown, Dan: interview.
Defendants' Exhibits: 7, 19.
Doss, Patrick: interview.
Floyd, Joe: expert report and trial testimony.
Half, Dan: trial testimony.
Heidenreich, C. Adrian: interview, expert report, and trial testimony.
Hudetz, Leo: interview and trial testimony.
Kindness, Jim: trial testimony.
Langdon, Morley: trial testimony.
Medicine Crow, Joe: interview and trial testimony.
Old Elk, Carlene: interview and trial testimony.

Old Horn, Dale: interview and trial testimony.
Pease, Eloise: interview.
Peregoy, Sharon: trial testimony.
Pitsch, Harvey: interview and trial testimony.
Plaintiffs Exhibits: 171, 179.
Pretty Weasel, Katie: trial testimony.
Real Bird, Pius: interview and trial testimony.
Ruegamer, Henry: interview and trial testimony.
Ruegamer, James: interview and trial testimony.
Ruegamer, Robert: interview.
Small, Clo: interview and trial testimony.
Small, Gail: interview and trial testimony.
Ten Bear, Tyrone: trial testimony.
Windy Boy, Janine: interview and trial testimony.

Other Sources

Aberdeen Area Indian Health Service. *Mortality Charts*. Aberdeen, S.Dak., September 1994.

Andrist, Ralph K. *The Long Death: The Last Days of the Plains Indians.* Norman: University of Oklahoma Press, 1993.

Annie E. Casey Foundation. *Kids Count Data Book.* Baltimore, Md.: Annie E. Casey Foundation, 1993.

Athearn, Robert G. *The Coloradans.* Albuquerque: University of New Mexico Press, 1976.

Big Horn County Local Government Study Commission. *Final Report of Proposed Alternative Form of Government*. Hardin, Mont.: Oct. 4, 1976.

Bradley, Charles. *After the Buffalo Days*. Vol. 1. Crow Agency, Mont.: Crow Central Education Commission, 1972.

Brophy, William A., and Sophie D. Aberle. *The Indian: America's Unfinished Business.* Norman: University of Oklahoma Press, 1960.

Brown, Dee. *Bury My Heart at Wounded Knee.* New York: Holt, Rinehart & Winston, 1971.

Browning, Rufus P., Dale Rogers Marshall, and David H. Tabb. *Protest Is Not Enough: The Struggle of Blacks and Hispanics for Equality in Urban Politics.* Berkeley: University of California Press, 1984.

Bryant, Charles S., and Abel B. Murch. *A History of the Great Massacre by the Sioux Indians in Minnesota.* Cincinnati, Ohio: Rickey & Carroll, 1864.

Carlson, Paul H. *The Plains Indians.* College Station: Texas A & M. University Press, 1998.

Carrier, Jim. *West of the Divide.* Golden, Colo.: Fulcrum Publishers, 1992.

Chapin, Frederick H. *The Land of the Cliff-Dwellers.* Boston: Appalachian Mountain Club, 1982. First published 1892 by Appalachian Mountain Club.

Chaudhur, Joyotpaul. "American Indian Policy: An Overview." In Deloria, *American Indian Policy in the Twentieth Century,* 15–33.

City of Riverton and the Northern Arapaho and Eastern Shoshone Tribes. *Intergovernmental Agreement Between the City of Riverton, Northern Arapaho Tribe and Eastern Shoshone Tribe* [video]. Riverton, Wyo., April 29, 2008.

Collier, John. *The Indians of the Americas.* New York: W. W. Norton, 1947.

Confederation of American Indians. *Indian Reservations: A State and Federal Handbook.* Jefferson, N.C.: McFarland, 1986.

Crow Tribe Constitution of 1948. Crow Agency, Mont.

Crow Tribe of Indians. *Crow Tribal Housing Condition Survey, 1985.* Crow Agency, Mont., July 1, 1985.

Davidson, Chandler, and Bernard Grofman, eds. *Quiet Revolution in the South: The Impact of the Voting Rights Act 1965–1990.* Princeton, N.J.: Princeton University Press, 1994.

Delaney, Robert W. *The Ute Mountain Utes.* Albuquerque: University of New Mexico Press, 1989.

Deloria, Vine, Jr., ed. *American Indian Policy in the Twentieth Century.* Norman: University of Oklahoma Press, 1985.

Deloria, Vine, Jr., and Clifford M. Lytle. *American Indians, American Justice.* Austin: University of Texas Press, 1983.

Denig, Edwin Thompson. *Five Indian Tribes of the Upper Missouri.* Norman: University of Oklahoma Press, 1961.

Dixon, Joseph K. *The Vanishing Race: The Last Great Indian Council.* New York: Popular Library, 1972. First published 1913 by Doubleday, Page & Co.

Dyche, S. E., "English Achievement of Seventh Grade Crow Indian Students and Proposed Ways of Improving Their Language Skills in the Hardin Public School." M.Ed. thesis, Montana State University, 1963.

Equal Opportunity Commission. *Determinations, February 5 & 11, 1986.* Denver, Colo.

Fair Housing Assistance Program. *Final Report.* Helena, Mont.: Montana Human Rights Commission, 1989.

First American Education Project. *Native Vote 2004: A National Survey and Analysis of Efforts to Increase the Native Vote in 2004, and the Results Achieved.* Olympia, Wash.: First American Education Project, 2005.

Fletcher, Alice C. *Historical Sketch of the Omaha Tribe of Indians in Nebraska.* Washington, D.C.: Judd & Detweiler, 1885.

Fletcher, Alice C., and Francis La Flesche. *The Omaha Tribe.* New York: Johnson Reprint, 1970.

Fonner, Eric. *Reconstruction: America's Unfinished Revolution, 1863–1877.* New York: Harper and Row, 1988.

Foreman, Grant. *Indian Removal: The Emigration of the Five Civilized Tribes of Indians.* Norman: University of Oklahoma Press, 1938.

Fowler, Loretta. *The Columbia Guide to American Indians of the Great Plains.* New York: Columbia University Press, 2003.

Franklin, John Hope. *Reconstruction after the Civil War.* Chicago: University of Chicago Press, 1994.

Gibbon, Guy. *The Sioux: The Dakota and Lakota Nations.* Oxford, England: Blackwell, 2003.

Hamilton, Charles V. "Political Access, Minority Participation, and the New Normalcy." In *Minority Report: What Has Happened to Blacks, Hispanics, American Indians, and Other Minorities in the Eighties*, edited by Leslie W. Dunbar, 3–25. New York: Pantheon Books, 1984.

Heidenreich, Adrian. "The Persistence of Values among the Crow Indians of Montana." Paper presented at the American Anthropological Association annual meeting, Washington, D.C., November 1976.

Hodge, William. *The First Americans, Then and Now.* New York: Rinehart and Winston, 1981.

Hoebel, E. A. *The Cheyennes: Indians of the Great Plains.* New York: Holt, Rinehart and Winston, 1978.

Hoig, Stan. *The Sand Creek Massacre.* Norman: University of Oklahoma Press, 1961.

Horsman, Reginald. "Scientific Racism and the American Indian in the Mid-Nineteenth Century." *American Quarterly* 27, (1975): 152–168.

Houghton, N. D. "The Legal Status of Indian Suffrage in the United States." *California Law Review* 19 (1931): 507 –520.

Hoxie, Frederick E., ed. *Encyclopedia of North American Indians.* Boston: Houghton Mifflin, 1996.

Interchurch Ministries of Nebraska, Inc. *"The American Indian in Nebraska."* Report. 1971.

Kappler, Charles J., ed. *Indian Affairs: Laws and Treaties.* Washington, D.C.: Government Printing Office, 1903.

Keech, William R. *The Impact of Negro Voting: The Role of the Vote in the Quest for Equality.* Chicago: Rand McNally, 1968.

Kennedy, Lawrence M. "The Colorado Press and the Red Man." Master's thesis, Denver University, 1967.

Key, V. O., Jr. *Southern Politics in State and Nation.* Knoxville: University of Tennessee Press, 1984.

Kousser, J. Morgan. *The Shaping of Southern Politics: Suffrage Restriction and the Establishment of the One-Party South, 1880–1910.* New Haven, Conn.: Yale University Press, 1974.

Lazarus, Edward. *Black Hills: White Justice.* New York: HarperCollins, 1991.

Leitch, Barbara. *A Concise Dictionary of Indian Tribes of North America.* Algonac, Mich.: Reference Publications, 1979.

Lowie, Robert H. *The Crow Indians.* Lincoln: University of Nebraska Press, 1983. First published 1935 by Holt, Rinehart & Winston.

Lurie, Nancy O. "Winnebago." In *Handbook of North American Indians*, vol. 15. Washington, D.C.: Smithsonian Institution, 1978.

Madsen, Brigham D. *The Shoshone Frontier and the Bear River Massacre.* Salt Lake City: University of Utah Press, 1985.

Marriott, Alice, and Carol K. Rachlin. *American Indian Mythology.* New York: Thomas Y. Crowell, 1968.

McCool, Daniel. "Indian Voting." In *American Indian Policy in the Twentieth Century*, edited by Vine Deloria, Jr. Norman: University of Oklahoma Press, 1985.

McCool, Daniel, Susan M. Olson, and Jennifer L. Robinson. *Native Vote: American Indians, the Voting Rights Act, and the Right to Vote*. New York: Cambridge University Press, 2007.

McDonald, Laughlin. "The 1982 Extension of Section 5 of the Voting Rights Act: The Continued Need for Preclearance." *Tennessee Law Review* 51 (1983): 1–82.

———. "The Quiet Revolution in Minority Voting Rights." *Vanderbilt Law Review* 42 (1989): 1249–1297.

McDonell, Janet A. "Land Policy on the Omaha Reservation: Competency Commissions and Forced Fee Patents." *Nebraska History* 63 (Fall 1982): 399.

Meriam, Lewis, Ray A. Brown, Henry Roe Cloud, and Edward E. Dale. *The Problem of Indian Administration*. Baltimore: Johns Hopkins Press, 1928.

Milner, Clyde A., II. *With Good Intentions: Quaker Work among the Pawnees, Otos, and Omahas in the 1870s*. Lincoln: University of Nebraska Press, 1982.

Montana Historical Society. *Not in Precious Metals Alone: A Manuscript History of Montana*. Helena: Montana Historical Society Press.

Montezuma-Cortez School District No. RE-1 Parent Advisory Committee. *Recommendations and Responses*. February 9, 1994.

Morris, Milton D. "Black Electoral Participation and the Distribution of Public Benefits." In *The Right to Vote: A Rockefeller Foundation Conference*. New York: Rockefeller Foundation, 1981.

Nabokov, Peter. *Native American Testimony: A Chronicle of Indian–White Relations from Prophecy to the Present, 1492–2000*. New York: Penguin Books, 1999.

National Economic Research Associates. "Preliminary Estimate of Revenues Derived by Wyoming and Fremont County Residents and Businesses on the Wind River Reservation and Expenditures by Wyoming and Fremont County for Services to the Reservation." Report prepared June 3, 1988.

Northern Cheyenne Constitution of 1936. Lame Deer, Mont., Northern Cheyenne Tribal Headquarters.

Olson, James C. *Red Cloud and the Sioux Problem*. Lincoln: University of Nebraska Press, 1965.

Ostler, Jeffrey. *The Plains Sioux and U.S. Colonialism from Lewis and Clark to Wounded Knee*. Cambridge, England: Cambridge University Press, 2004.

Oswalt, Wendell. *This Land Was Theirs: A Study of North American Indians*. New York: Wiley, 1978.

Otis, D. S. *The Dawes Act and the Allotment of Indian Lands*. Norman: University of Oklahoma Press, 1973.

Parkhill, Forbes. *The Last of the Indian Wars*. New York: Collier Books, 1961.

Peterson, Helen L. "American Indian Political Participation." *Annals of the American Academy of Political and Social Science* 311 (May 1957): 116–126.

Pevar, Stephen L. *The Rights of Indians and Tribes*. Carbondale: Southern Illinois University Press, 1992.

Philip, Kenneth R. *Indian Termination Policy: American Indians on the Trail to Self-Determination, 1933–1953.* Lincoln: University of Nebraska Press, 1999.

Porter, Robert B. "The Demise of the Ongwehoweh and the Rise of the Native American: Redressing the Genocidal Act of Forcing American Citizenship upon Indigenous Peoples." *Harvard BlackLetter Law Journal* 15 (1999): 107–183.

Prucha, Francis P., ed. *Documents of United States Indian Policy.* 2nd ed. Lincoln: University of Nebraska Press, 1990.

———. *The Great Father: The United States Government and the American Indian.* Lincoln: University of Nebraska Press, 1984.

———. *The Indians in American Society.* Berkeley: University of California Press, 1985.

Ridington, Robin, and Dennis Hastings. *Blessing for a Long Time: The Sacred Pole of the Omaha Tribe.* Lincoln: University of Nebraska Press, 1997.

Riverton City Council. *City Council Meeting* [of April 29, 2008, and June 3, 2008]. DVD obtained from city of Riverton under a Freedom of Information request.

Royce, Charles. *Indian Land Cessions in the United States.* New York: Arno Press, 1971. First published 1889.

Russell, Don. "Indians and Soldiers of the American West." In *The Book of the American West* edited by Jay Monaghan, 193–260. New York: Julian Messner, 1963.

Smith, Duane A. *The Birth of Colorado.* Norman: University of Oklahoma Press, 1989.

———. *Song of the Hammer and Drill: The Colorado San Juans, 1860–1914.* Golden: Colorado School of Mines Press, 1982.

South Dakota Advisory Committee to the U.S. Commission on Civil Rights. *Native Americans in South Dakota: An Erosion of Confidence in the Justice System.* S.Dak., 2000.

———. *Native American Participation in South Dakota's Political System.* S. Dak.: 1981.

South Dakota Task Force on Indian–State Government Relations. *April Staff Report of the Task Force on Indian–State Government Relations.* S.Dak., 1974.

Spence, Clark C. *Montana: A Bicentennial History.* New York: W. W. Norton & Company, 1978.

Stamm, Henry E., IV. *People of the Wind River: The Eastern Shoshones 1825–1900.* Norman: University of Oklahoma Press, 1999.

State of Nebraska Equal Opportunity Commission. *Conciliation Agreement, June 1985.* Lincoln, Neb.

Svaldi, David. *Sand Creek and the Rhetoric of Extermination: A Case Study in Indian–White Relations.* Lanham, Md.: University Press of America, 1989.

Szasz, Margaret C. *Education and the American Indian—The Road to Self-Determination Since 1928.* Albuquerque: University of New Mexico Press, 1974.

Tyler, S. Lyman. *A History of Indian Policy.* Washington, D.C.: Government Printing Office, 1973.

Vandenbusche, Duane, and Duane Smith. *A Land Alone: Colorado's Western Slope.* Boulder, Colo.: Pruett, 1981.

Washburn, Wilcomb E. *The American Indian and the United States: A Documentary History.* Vol. 4. New York: Random House, 1973.

Welch, James. *Killing Custer.* With Paul Stekler. New York: Penguin Books, 1924.

Wind River Indian Reservation Land Owners' Council, Lander, Wyoming, to Congress of the U.S. and its Proper Committees, the Public Land Committees, and the Committees of Indian Affairs" (1941). National Archives, Rocky Mountain Region.

W.I.N.D.S. Project: *Wind River Indian Needs Determination Study.* Fort Washakie, Wyo.: Wind River Joint Business Council, August 1988.

Winnebago Tribe of Nebraska. Community Environmental Profile, http://www.mnisose.org/profiles/winnebag.htm.

———. "Resolution no. 74-35." In *Minutes of Meetings of the Tribal Council.* Winnebago, Neb., 1974.

———. "Resolution no. 85-31." In *Minutes of Meetings of the Tribal Council.* Winnebago, Neb.

Wolfley, Jeanette. "Jim Crow, Indian Style: The Disenfranchisement of Native Americans." *American Indian Law Review* 16 (1991): 167–202.

Woodward, C. Vann. *Origins of the New South, 1877–1913.* Baton Rouge: Louisiana State University Press, 1951.

Yatrakis, Kathryn B. "Delivering the Goods: Electoral Demands and Political Benefits, The Case of Newark 1970–1986." Paper presented at the American Political Science Association meetings, Chicago, September 3–6, 1987.

Index